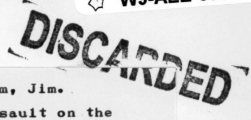

© THE BAKER & TAYLOR CO.

The Assault on the Sexes

JIM FORDHAM
With his indispensable wife Andrea

ARLINGTON HOUSE·PUBLISHERS
NEW ROCHELLE, NEW YORK

Manufactured in the United States of America

Library of Congress Cataloging in Publication Data

Fordham, James.
  The assault on the sexes.

   1. Feminism—United States—Anecdotes, facetiae, satire, etc. 2. Sex role—United States—Anecdotes, facetiae, satire, etc. I. Fordham, Andrea, joint author. II. Title.
HQ1426.F78   301.41'2'0973   77-2263
ISBN 0-87000-377-1

From all that I had read of history and government, of human life and manners, I had drawn this conclusion, that the manners of women were the most infallible barometer, to ascertain the degree of morality and virtue in a nation. . . . The Jews, the Greeks, the Romans, the Swiss, the Dutch, all lost their public spirit, their republican principles and habits, and their republican forms of government, when they lost the modesty and domestic virtues of their women.

JOHN ADAMS

If any human society—large or small, simple or complex, based on the most rudimentary hunting and fishing, or on the whole elaborate interchange of manufactured products—is to survive, it must have a pattern of social life that comes to terms with the differences between the sexes.

MARGARET MEAD
Male and Female

Intellect is . . . .a vital force in history, but it can also be a dissolvent and destructive power. Out of every hundred new ideas ninety-nine or more will probably be inferior to the traditional responses which they propose to replace. No one . . . can come in one lifetime to such fullness of understanding as to safely judge and dismiss the customs or institutions of his society, for these are the wisdom of generations after centuries of experiment in the laboratories of history. . . . It is good that new ideas should be heard, for the sake of the few that can be used; but it is also good that new ideas should be compelled to go through the mill of objection, opposition, and contumely; this is the vital heat which innovations must survive before being allowed to enter the human race.

WILL AND ARIEL DURANT
The Lessons of History

Contents

A Note from the Authors / 7

An Introduction / 11

The Unisex Assault / 31

Anything Goes? / 65

Radical at the Core / 97

Monitoring the Mass Media—The Sexes Get the Sack / 121

Will the Real American Woman Please Stand Up / 155

But Sex Differences Are Just Cultural, Aren't They? / 179

The Case for the Five-Foot-Two Cop / 207

Playing the Role of the "Person" / 243

E.R.A. or E.R.R.O.R.? / 287

Sexism—That New Word in *Webster's* / 337

Let's All Live at the Bazaar / 371

Repeat: They Do Know What Is Best for Me . . . They
    Do Know . . . / 411

In Conclusion: A Few Concerned Words from an Unseasonably
    Happy Housewife / 447

Selected Bibliography / 469

Index / 475

A Note from the Authors

People often want to know how we manage to write together as a team. Or as a woman once put it in a letter she wrote to us: "It's so interesting the way you two do it together." Actually, we find it hard to explain how we work, because our literary collaboration is mostly a matter of continually talking to one another in ways that eventually end up as words on paper. The truth is that since the day we met, we've been engaged in a sort of mutual cerebral activity that we still don't fully understand, but which we enjoy and have been able to turn into what seems to us at least to be a fairly constructive and rewarding critical process.

But if we *had* to describe how we work together, we could give you a rough idea by saying that Annie contributes primarily as an investigative reporter, social analyst, slave driver and all-weather pundit, while Jim serves as essayist, typist and editor-in-chief. You could put it another way: she makes the big decisions, like what to say and how to say it, and he makes the lesser ones, like exactly *which* words to use. Annie is fond of saying we're intellectual opposites ("I'm intellectual and he's opposite"), but actually we seem to think remarkably alike.

In any event, we want to acknowledge the encouragement and help of many friends and acquaintances, especially those who gave us their time, thoughts and insights through personal interviews and correspondence. Thanks to the *National Observer,* the *Washington Post, MORE, Girl Talk* and the *Washington Star* for permission to reuse brief passages from our articles in those publications. We are especially grateful to Deborah Klein and Howard Hayghe of the Bureau of Labor Statistics, Bob Warren of the Bureau of the Census, Vance Grant of the National Center for Education Statistics, and Dr. Harold J. Dupuy of the National Center for Health Statistics for their patient and generous assistance in getting all the numbers straight. We are also much obliged to our editor, Karl Pflock. And of course our fond appreciation to Al Laoang, whose sensitive and creative collaboration has been a rare pleasure and privilege for both of us.

We dedicate the book to the millions of people everywhere who are still well satisfied with being one sex or the other. Hope for posterity, we surmise, ultimately depends on their kind.

The Assault on the Sexes

An Introduction

Before my wife Annie and I consciously chose to begin our research for this book, we had slowly grown aware of unusual, even bizarre, phenomena emerging on the sexual front. We had read of course of the rise of the "new morality," which some said was identical to the old immorality, but this latest assault was not merely against the sensibilities of those who believe you can carry a good thing too far. The attack was against society's sexual orientation itself, the relations between men and women in everyday life, their ancient roles—in a word, against the *sexes*.

Women, we read—that is, a *few* women—had burned their brassieres like so many draft cards as a means of expressing their extreme lack of support for the Miss America Pageant. It must have been about 1969 when my wife pointed out to me a woman on the David Frost Show who, as I recall, was there from the National Organization for Women to announce that the next great humanitarian social crusade being planned for us was a new one to raise the womenfolk up from slavery. When Annie's laughter stopped, it was because she had suddenly realized that Ti-Grace Atkinson, the woman from NOW, wasn't joking.

"She actually wants to reduce women to the same condition as men," my wife said in horror.

When David Frost told Ti-Grace: "That will be the day when most women agree with *you*," Annie and I averred as how we had to go along with him on that.

As the 1970s rolled in, we learned of the proliferation of something called "consciousness-raising groups." "I

"She actually wants to reduce women to the same condition as men," my wife said in horror.

don't understand why they don't just call them con-
sciousness-*changing* groups," said my wife. And indeed it was hard to imagine what it was the minds of
the feminists were being raised higher *than*. I recall
observing their kin in elevators, air terminals, hotel lob-
bies, physicians' waiting rooms and on the shoulders of
highways—usually in jeans and straggly hair—peering
grimly through their granny glasses into copies of *Sexual Politics* or the *Women's Rights Almanac*.

Annie most often encountered them at parties hosted
by old friends from our college days, where some feminist was sure to ask her, "And what do you do?"

"I'm a housewife," she would say proudly.

"But what do you *do?*" the woman would persist.

"I make a home for my husband and myself."

"You mean you don't work?" would come the reply.

"Yes, I work," I would hear my wife explaining. "I
do plenty of work *at home*."

I have observed that very few of those who question
women about this subject see the slightest excuse for a
woman to waste her time at home when she obviously
could be bringing in a perfectly useful paycheck. One
couple whom my wife and I visited at their condomin-
ium pressed their viewpoint like an attack on the cita-
del. "What do you do?" came the question that by this
time had come to be dreaded.

"I am a housewife," Annie replied stubbornly,
steeled by now to the disapproval to follow.

"Oh, you shouldn't say you are *just* a housewife," the
husband objected.

"I didn't," Annie corrected. "You did. I said 'I'm a
housewife.'" He was so used to thinking that way that
he heard "just a housewife" even when no one had
said it.

"Why don't you get a job?" the wife asked next.

My wife tried to explain to them that she has lots to

13

do at home and that both of us like our life just the way it is presently arranged. She said that she keeps our apartment clean and cooks our meals (the old-fashioned way without instant foods and mixes). She told them how she manages through careful food selection and home cooking to provide us with well-balanced, economical, enjoyable meals despite inflation and the modern pace of life. She even confessed to them that we often arrange to consume breakfast, lunch and supper at home *together*. I seem to remember her reciting a long list of other essential tasks she performs— she handles most of our financial affairs and correspondence, sets up our appointments with doctors, dentists and the like, handles such matters as insurance arrangements and Blue Cross claims, plans our leisure activities, exercises each day, does volunteer projects occasionally, and more often than not has some special research effort of her own under way.

Our hosts thought practically nothing of her explanation. The husband quickly informed her that she was an obvious victim of Parkinson's Law, and had expanded what she had to do to fill the vast amount of spare time she was wasting.

"I'll bet you could get a good job with the government," the wife said.

They both seemed unshakably convinced beyond any reasonable doubt that my wife was cheating both of us by staying home squandering all of those precious woman-hours that with any luck might be directed toward earning a paycheck or building a magnificent career. Furthermore, their attitude implied that nobody can be fulfilled without a job. All women should work, said she. The government should pay for national day-care centers, said he. Etc., etc., etc.—they gave us the entire lib litany. Our visit that evening ended early, but not, my wife declared, early enough.

14

As the mid-1970s approached, we became more and more aware of the influence the feminists seemed to be exerting through newspapers and magazines and on people's attitudes. At any rate, some people's. Every day some new aspect of womanhood became the subject of grave analysis and commentary in the mass media. Dozens of new books appeared on the oppression and emancipation of women. Even the TV networks now took feminist ideas seriously, and the women's magazines heralded the newly discovered glories of the paid job, and began using words like "liberated," "oppression," and "sexist."

The next thing we knew, David Frost had disappeared and the feminists were hosting their *own* TV shows. And many of the TV personalities who used to seem like normal men and women suddenly turned into liberation-conscious *persons* as though they really had been secret bra-burners all along.

But it wasn't until Annie discovered that the feminists were actually persuading people to change laws,

"I'll bet you could get a good job with the government."

school books and TV programming to conform with their peculiar ideas, and burrowing their way into just about everything from the Girl Scouts to American foreign policy, that she really started taking the whole matter seriously.

"Do you know that they have nearly succeeded in changing the Constitution?" she said.

It was true. The federal "equal rights" amendment, which seemed to many to be largely a symbolic effort in the feminist campaign, was only a few states short of ratification, and most people did not even know what it was. In fact, we had both voted for the state ERA in Maryland in 1972 without knowing anything about it, simply because it had the beneficent-sounding label of "equal rights" attached to it.

I counseled a magnanimous point of view. "Look at it from the viewpoint of the working girl," I said. "After all, there are *some* disadvantages to being a woman." I reminded her that some women had experienced difficulty obtaining credit and landing certain kinds of jobs, getting equal education and pay. "I was just reading the other day where less than two percent of engineering students are female," I said.

But Annie, the dauntless researcher, wasn't persuaded, and by now she was lugging home armloads of library books on the subject of women's lib, and had commenced collecting articles, opinion surveys and what previously would have seemed like remarkably obscure newspaper clippings. Anything and everything she could locate on the cravings, claims and complaints of females found its way into our five-room apartment.

For instance, we both read historian Mary Beard's *Woman as Force in History*, which dealt a seriously damaging blow thirty years ago to the notion of the subjugation of women, an idea Beard called "one of the most fantastic myths ever created by the human mind."

16

She says that as civilization advanced through the centuries, women have been "members of all castes from the slave stratum at the bottom to the ruling families at the top, and even when restrictions were the tightest, took part in nearly everything that went on in the world. ... They have shared in the burdens and privileges of their respective classes, have joined in wars, have owned and managed vast estates, have insisted on dominance in disputes among ruling families, have displayed the lusts of men, have served the temples, and have been deified as gods. ... There was no great historical contest in politics in which they did not appear somewhere. There was no religious cult which they did not affect. There were no exercises in intellectualism which they did not practice."

If you read Mary Beard and other historians, you see that women have labored along with men in the fields and factories, performed arts and crafts, held property and ruled along with men. It appears that women have been about as well educated as men have since the Middle Ages, and some of them, we are told, have spoken with authority on ethics, philosophy, art, science and mathematics in every century.

"It was a woman," Mary Beard reminds us, "Queen Isabella of Spain, who was chiefly responsible for the underwriting that sent Columbus forth on the voyage of discovery destined to open a new epoch in the history of Europe. ... It was mainly by the salons of French women that ideas were patronized, tried out, and set in circulation. ... Women have been identified with the ideas and movements of social amelioration from the sixteenth century to the latest hour, as thinkers, experimenters, propagandists and administrators."

It does seem that women have usually shared with their husbands the burdens and advantages of their lot in life. Regardless of their sex, most people throughout

17

history seem not to have had much choice of careers or lifestyles. Most of them have been poor, ignorant, dirty and have served the ruling classes in one way or another. It is difficult to justify the contention of the feminists that women have been the subjects and men the rulers—neither men nor women have had much social or political freedom until very recently.

We read historian Page Smith's *Daughters of the Promised Land,* and found that in colonial America women ran their own manufacturing establishments and businesses, operated retail stores, produced textiles, and were tavern owners and innkeepers. In fact, regardless of the now famous complaints of Abigail Adams, colonial women appear to have been "liberated" to a considerable degree, for Professor Smith writes that women "in the absence of any theory about what jobs were appropriate were everything from blacksmiths to newspaper editors." Their right to own property after marriage was soon established, and women also had the legal capacity to make contracts and conduct their own businesses. After 1837, the doors of education opened rapidly to women, so that by the end of the nineteenth century more girls graduated from high school than did boys. Numerous women's colleges grew and other colleges opened their doors to give women the same educational opportunities as men.

Opportunities also opened up in industry and the professions during this period. According to Professor Smith: "Of one hundred and ninety-eight medical students in the Boston University School of Medicine in 1866, seventy-nine were women. In Chicago several women held chairs as professors of medicine and more than a hundred and fifty practiced in the city. . . . By 1890 there were between four and five hundred 'lady dentists' as well as thousands of 'assistant operators' for male dentists."

Professor Smith also mentions: "In the early 1890s there were some ninety women lawyers in the United States. . . . Over five thousand women in New York and Brooklyn . . . were working as stenographers. . . ."

Mary Beard examined the U.S. patent records for the years 1892 through 1895 and found that women were involved in devising or improving a surprising range of devices, tools and implements from sewing machines to motor vehicles. In the decade after 1910, she found that women had received patents on more than 5,000 inventions, everything from spark plugs to bobby pins.

Annie and I found that history supports our feeling that it's ludicrous to pretend that the 1970s represent the great coming out of women in the United States. World War I was the decisive turning point in the full emergence of women in our society, and educational and occupational opportunities had begun to expand greatly for women at least forty years before that.

It was, however, during the 1920s that the real revolution occurred in the relations of the sexes and in sexual morality. The Modern Girl, or the New Woman as she was often called, had taken over the men's jobs during World War I, and now she proved that she could be as free and easy as a man, and in many ways a lot more daring. She took off her corset along with many of the Victorian attitudes and strict moral values against which she rebelled. She wore lipstick, short hair, short skirts, trousers, and backless dresses. She used cigarettes, liquor—very often contraceptives—and she spoke as freely and enthusiastically of sex and equality as the most dedicated women's libber today.

The very topics that feminists today consider so stylish and fascinating are precisely those that their grandmothers discovered in the twenties and brought into fashion—sexual promiscuity and sexual openness outside of marriage, great interest in more equal relationships between the sexes, much discussion about the "new marriage," and relaxed attitudes toward sex roles, marital fidelity, abortion and divorce.

History professor John LuKacs of Chestnut Hill and La Salle Colleges recently wrote an article that appeared in the *New York Times Magazine* remarking the misconception that we are presently going through a social revolution: "Public thinkers keep saying that we live in an era of unprecedented change, in a revolutionary age to which the minds of people find it difficult to accustom themselves. In reality, there has been surprisingly little real change, all superficial impressions notwithstanding. . . . The radical froth of the sixties—wild pacifism, radicalism, sexual liberation—was, in reality, the same ideas of the twenties trotted out again in psychedelic garb. . . . Compared with the truly revolutionary changes in manners and modes after the First World War, the highly publicized changes during the last 30 years amounted to little or nothing."

Annie visited the Library of Congress, where she tracked down earlier historical research by Mary Beard which described the rapid rise of female professional workers early in this century, reaching the half-million mark during the twenties. There were some 11,000 women dentists and physicians. Thousands of women worked as lawyers, professors, missionaries and in other professional jobs. In Michigan, 45 percent of workers in automobile accessories and parts factories were female by 1927. Recently we read that in that same year the University of Southern California Dental School graduated more female dentists than in any year before or since.

By 1929 women received 40 percent of all master's degrees and 15 percent of Ph.D.s—about the same proportion they received in the 1970s. More than 27 percent of the academic staffs of universities were women at the end of the decade of the twenties.

20

Women had established their right to professional training in virtually every field and earned more doctoral degrees during the twenties in proportion to their numbers than women in the 1950s. The proportion of coeds was up to 43 percent, exactly the same as it has been in recent years.

At the Library of Congress, she also found records of millions of women who have been "liberated" all through this century—in the 1920s, she found real people like Mary Judge, who served as a Navy Yeomanette during World War I, then worked as a stenographer, and later established her own printing and advertising firm, which she ran for nearly 40 years. People like Geraldine Wilson, who was a secretary who longed to fly, so she took up exhibition parachute jumping as a means to pay for flying lessons. People like Magdaline Kump, who left West Virginia at age 18 with only a

"But Grandma—how come you were liberated fifty years ago?"

dime in her pocket, went to work in a millinery store in Washington, D.C., and eventually built her own real estate business. People like Delia Akeley, who conducted zoological expeditions to Africa. Or attorneys Annette Adams and Mabel Willebrandt who both became assistant attorney generals of the United States. Or Josephine Roche, a coal mine operator who became an executive of the United Mine Workers, and, later, the first woman to serve as assistant secretary of the Treasury. Or Mabel Orr, who ran her own oil-well-drilling rig . . . Amy Carter (that's right!), who welded aircraft . . . Frances Wieser, a paleontologic draftsman —Annie soon discovered that you could spend a lifetime compiling lists of the things ambitious and enterprising women were doing in the twenties, or, for that matter, in the thirties or forties, or any decade since.

In February 1929, the *Ladies' Home Journal* presented an article called "Jills of All Trades" by Ann Hark, which began like this:

A woman who goes to the bottom of the sea to bring up treasure from sunken ships; a girl who earns her daily bread by manufacturing glass eyes; a lady who climbs up flagpoles and balances on iron girders as she plies her trade as steeple jack; a young matron who is known round the world as champion broncobuster; a feminine telephone linesman who climbs poles, strings wires and splices cables on a line covering forty-six miles of rugged mountain country; a lady steamboat captain plying up and down the Mississippi; a woman who goes into a hospital operating room and sketches the living vital parts of the human body; a female bootblack; a woman hog caller—

Yes, the ladies are expressing themselves. And what's more, they're proud of it. "Why shouldn't we do the work we like to do?" they pertly ask. . . .

And so today we have our lady sheriffs and taxi drivers, our female pastors and pawnbrokers, our fair blacksmiths and jockeys, our gentle stevedores and lighthouse keepers, our lady foresters and station agents, our feminine veterinarians and trolley motormen—and so on down a long and lusty list. All over the country women are taking up odd and unusual jobs that once were considered taboo. If a lady has a desire to walk among the clouds, no longer does she suppress it; she simply becomes a parachute jumper or a mountain-peak guide. If an unfulfilled yearning for the bright lights obsesses her, she buys a uniform and takes a job as fireman. And if by any chance she has a top-sergeant complex, she becomes the warden of a penitentiary!

Nowadays no woman with a hidden longing—or the necessity to earn a living—need despair. She may not have the talent or the training to become an artist or a writer, a physician or a lawyer, but she can always be a cooper or a constable, an auctioneer or an undertaker, a professional packer or a teacher of jiujitsu, a stonemason or a plasterer, a longshoreman or a lifeguard, a railroad porter or a policeman. Other women are doing all these things, and many more besides; in fact, of the 572 gainful occupations listed by the United States Census Bureau in 1920, only thirty-five had not yet been invaded by the gentle sex. And that was eight years ago.

There were more well-known women who truly inspired American girls in the twenties than there are today. Eight of the ten bestselling books of 1925 were written by women. Nearly everyone has heard the names of the many popular female writers of the twenties, such as Dorothy Parker, Anita Loos, Edna St. Vincent Millay, Pearl Buck, Emily Post, Rebecca West, Mary Roberts Rinehart, Edith Wharton, Willa Cather, Edna Ferber and Kathleen Norris. There were even women sports writers, such as Margery Miller Welles, who wrote about boxing, among other things.

Women were influential through the theater, the mov-

23

ies, radio and the arts, and there were hundreds of popular female personalities, such as Clara Bow, Gloria Swanson, Ethel Barrymore, Helen Hayes, Mary Pickford, Mae West, Greta Garbo, Blanche Sweet, Mabel Normand, Lillian Gish, Jeanne Eagels, Theda Bara, Bessie Smith, to name just a few, and of course Adele Astaire, who was even more popular than her brother Fred.

There were important women in nearly every field you could name, and they served as inspiration and living proof to youngsters that females could go anywhere, do anything, and be anything they really wanted to be and had the talent to achieve. Gertrude Ederle swam the English Channel and received great acclaim. Amelia Earhart flew the Atlantic, and the Pacific, and was worshiped as she performed at air exhibitions from coast to coast. Hazel Wightman was known everywhere as "Queen Mother of American Tennis." Ruth St. Denis pioneered modern dance and Martha Graham debuted in 1920 as a member of the Doris Humphrey troupe. Georgia O'Keeffe held her first major art exhibition in 1923. In 1925, Congresswoman Mary Therese Norton, Democrat of New Jersey, was the first of her sex to head three committees of the House of Representatives, the first to serve as a state party chairman and the first also to head a national platform committee. Isadora Duncan thrilled audiences with her interpretative dancing. Gertrude Stein reigned over her Paris salon of artists and intellectuals. Irene Castle and her husband made ballroom dancing the rage. Helen Keller, deaf and blind, inspired millions as she traveled and lectured on behalf of the unsighted. Jane Addams won world acclaim for founding Hull House Settlement for poor orphans. Marie Curie, the codiscoverer of radium, was the center of attention when she visited the United States in 1921. Perle

24

Mesta was not only an industrialist of note, but managed her own cattle ranch. Harriet Chalmers Adams lectured on her explorations of Latin America. Anthropologist Margaret Mead published her classic *Coming of Age in Samoa* in 1928, and Ruth Benedict was beginning her influential work on the patterns of human culture.

Annie collected most of this information at the library and on her day-long excursion to the National Archives. It wasn't long before I realized that she was building a pretty good case for the contention that although women had been considerably less active in the world of affairs in our great-grandmothers' day, opportunities have expanded continuously for the past century until recent decades when historians noted that women were working in virtually every job category listed by the Bureau of the Census.

"And besides," Annie reminded, "has anyone noticed the jaded condition of the average man lately?"

"People are being hoodwinked about a lot of this stuff," she said at last. "I think we should do something . . . maybe write a book about it . . . sort of an exposé."

"Why must we write a book about it?" I objected.

"Oh, because . . . it is just ridiculous the way people accept this idea that women have been oppressed and enslaved by men. It's such a slander," she said. "And besides, you're getting fat." For a nonfeminist, my wife really knows how to intimidate a fellow.

As the days went by, both of us grew more and more aware of the insidiousness of the new trend. Here are some of the fully documented incidents that came to our attention:

The Manpower Administration began a process that eventually led to changing its name to the Employment and Training Administration and removed all gender references from its lists of job titles. (This was accomplished at enormous public expense, and of course was the result of feminist pressure.) Thus, "stewardess" becomes "flight attendant" and "fireman" becomes "fire fighter."

The Credit Union National Association advised its customers in its quarterly consumer advice booklet: "Toys should challenge children, but not frustrate them. Buying strictly male or female toys is also not advisable. Girls may want to play with tools, erector sets and microscopes. Or maybe your boy would like to play with a toy vacuum cleaner—or even a doll. . . ."

Jean-clad militant feminists stormed the stage during a beauty pageant, raising clinched fists and yelling antisexist slogans.

One of my students at Montgomery College told of having been kicked when he mistakenly tried to hold a door for a women's libber.

"We want equal opportunity . . . er, uh, I mean—STOP SEXISM NOW!"

Another student, a young woman of about 19, told the class in all seriousness that she believed that the only reason men are stronger and larger than women is because they get more exercise as kids.

Feminists launched a protest at the state capital because they thought the restrooms in public buildings were discriminatory. "Men do not have to pay to use the urinals," one of the demonstrators explained, "but women must pay in all circumstances."

It was in May 1975, however, that the die was ultimately cast with the publication of a report of the United States Commission on Civil Rights stating: "The President should issue an Executive order establishing a national policy declaring women as a group to be socially and economically disadvantaged" and therefore, the commission went on to say, eligible for subsidies to go into business just like blacks and American Indians.

"That's it!" my wife declared. "Limber up your typing finger." I began to limber.

At first, we spoke to friends and acquaintances to plumb their feelings about the new drive to push more women out into jobs, and especially about the headlong rush of some elements of society to promote unisex values. Many people, we found, were unaffected by these matters, while others seemed dismayed. Some appeared to be so demoralized by social events of recent years that they now just took it for granted that, welcome or not, radical social changes were inevitable.

One 59-year-old woman who had spent her life as a homemaker told me: "You have no idea how all of this women's lib business makes me feel. It makes me feel as though I'm nothing, as though all I've done has been for nothing. I feel as though I should have accomplished so much more than I have. Yet, before, I always felt as though I was doing so much good for my husband and children . . . it seemed important then." This woman is a fine cook, an accomplished seamstress, a priceless wife, and now a loving grandmother. She has spent the past thirty years inspiring her hard-working husband, motivating her successful children and donating her energies to work for the community and the church. Now she feels like "nothing."

"Women's liberation movement?" another woman replied to my casual query. "If you ask me, those people are just getting together to keep each other company in their misery. They ought to call it the women's *miseration* movement!"

For several years now, in the evenings I've taught an adult education class in communication at Montgomery College in Rockville, Maryland. In one class exercise I usually ask the students to discuss some topical issue, so a couple of years ago I began making the topic of discussion women's lib. These are middle-class, suburban adults who live in what is reputed to be one of the most sophisticated counties in the country. It is certainly one of the richest. But what I found, in general, was that these bright, affluent people—women and men—often accepted uncritically and without question the idea fostered in the mass media that women in the U.S. represent an oppressed minority group. We will take the opportunity later to consider some of the other viewpoints of the students.

Eventually, Annie and I extended our investigations to include interviews and correspondence with women from many walks of life across the country. Our researches convince us that the new sexual game plan which has gained such a foothold in some homes, offices, schoolrooms, in the pages of many publications and on our TV screens is not the pure and simple path to justice and equal rights it is represented to be. What is more, most men and women don't seem to want it. When the concerns of most Americans are looked at in depth, you don't find them longing for females "liberated" from the home, males emasculated of their breadwinner roles, children left to government day-care programs, federal domination of our schools and businesses, or encouragement of the "sexual preference" for promiscuity or homosexuality.

On the contrary, most of us want a return to the old virtues, to sensible moral standards, to family, to schools that teach, and to the return of the benefits of their enterprise to people as well as businesses. But before I dash ahead of myself, let me just declare at the outset a few things Annie and I are *for*: (1) Equal pay for equal work (but as we shall see, the issue isn't as simple as that). (2) We favor community property laws, and we strongly advocate careful planning by couples for the long-range security of both spouses. (3) We are not opposed to working wives—if there really is dire financial need, or if they really do enjoy it (and don't neglect the kids). (4) Contrary to malicious rumor, we do believe that men should dry an occasional dish—in fact, in an emergency I have even been known to vacuum a rug. (5) We are for according dignity and respect to all people who labor—whether at home, in the front seat of a Bluebird Taxi, or in the bowels of the Time-Life Building. (6) And we definitely are for separate restrooms for ladies and gentlemen, visible differences between the sexes, husbands who are proud breadwinners and lots of full-time wives and mothers to raise healthy, striving children in this nation. And it is of these time-honored values and their momentary decline that we doggedly opine.

The Unisex Assault

Any man reckless enough to venture into the frays of women's lib soon finds himself up to his apronstrings in discrepancies, contradictions and anomalies. The feminists, for instance, insist it is not their intention to drive the housewife from the hearth-fires. In the next breath they will tell you that their most urgent longings are for day-care centers, opportunities for women to do the same jobs as men, to earn the same money men do, and to achieve representation in the labor force equivalent to males.

I suppose this is no more incongruous than the fact that the most ardent defenders of the rewards of staying in the home are often jet-powered, professional panegyrists who spend most of their time lecturing, writing books and climbing on and off of the sets of TV talk shows.

I think we are all developing an increasing tolerance for ambiguity these days. In a land where pornographic movies and books are known as "adult entertainment"

31

and erotic massage parlors are called "health clubs," nobody should be disconcerted to learn that the unisex assault is currently traveling under the byname of "equal opportunity." This is not much of a secret. Feminists admit that merely guaranteeing fair consideration to females who take a mind to apply to West Point, law school, for a loan at the bank or a job at the local lumber yard is a totally inadequate approach. What we must have, they insist, is a sex-role revolution to ensure that the status of men and women is exactly the same. But what do they really mean by that?

"I think I mean something that involves a change of head as well as a structural change," says feminist leader Gloria Steinem, "so that not only are we talking about an almost total redistribution of wealth and services and goods and properties but in addition we are talking about a very deep attitudinal change. If we are talking about doing away with the sexual caste system and the racial caste system—which certainly are twins —then we're talking about doing away with the deepest ways we've been divided and the deepest sets of assumptions that have been given to us in order to keep us in those roles. That's very important."

According to Kate Millet, the feminist theorist, "Women's liberation and homosexual liberation are both struggling towards a common goal: A society free from defining and categorizing people by virtue of gender and/or sexual preference. 'Lesbian' is a label used as a psychic weapon to keep women locked into their male-defined 'feminine role.' The essence of that role is that a woman is defined in terms of her relationship to men."

Feminist writer Gabrielle Burton says that women's lib is seeking the most radical revolution of all, because "it is challenging the nuclear family structure, monogamy, sexual expressions, child-rearing practices, the economy, and our ways of thinking. . . ."

In our talks with people about this matter of unisex revolution, my wife and I find it is hard for the average person to take today's femlib revolutionaries very seriously. Maybe they don't really mean it, people suppose, or perhaps it's just a fad. Most people simply can't believe the radicals want to bring such extreme changes to our lives. The fact is that they do, as we shall see.

In 1975, writer Haynes Johnson reported in the *Washington Post* that a team of computer scientists at the Massachusetts Institute of Technology—known as the Systems Dynamics Group—is developing a computer model of the social and economic behavior of Americans. The purpose of this work being carried on under the direction of Professor Jay W. Forrester, according to Johnson, is to plan the shape of the future of our children and our children's children.

In Professor Forrester's view of this future, warns Johnson, "laws, attitudes, goals, expectations, traditions, religions, and government and corporate activities must all change—not might, or should, *must*."

Some of the changes these planners have in mind are rigid control of the size and composition of cities, banning of free migration by citizens within the U.S., and strict population control. And, oh yes, they want a reexamination of "the overly simplistic view of right and ethics" that they say has been fostered by the churches.

"They challenge virtually every assumption of the American experience," writes Johnson. "They are unsettling; relinquishing many of our basic liberties, rethinking our religious and humanitarian traditions, rejecting the belief that size and economic growth are a virtue, minimizing the choices available to individual citizens, facing up to the necessity for long-term planning over many aspects of our lives."

It is well known that for several years MIT has been quietly bringing together selected members of government, industry and the educational establishment for research projects, seminars, workshops and other meetings designed to promote, in the words of one of their workshop reports, "communication and cooperation which can ultimately result in a commitment to new programs and the creation of new and more adaptable institutional forms and practices. . . ." In plain words, MIT is one of many institutions of higher learning that have become centers for planning and engineering radical changes in the everyday lives of Americans.

"You won't find exactly a new religion along the banks of the Charles in Cambridge these days," declares Haynes Johnson, "but ideas are being generated here that deal with the shape and direction of a new American society."

And I am certain that in at least some of these get-togethers you *do* encounter the zeal of religious conversion—such as at the meetings of May 1973, when representatives of government, business and education came to MIT to figure out ways they could work together to persuade Americans to abandon their traditional ideas about sex roles and the ways of women in the world of work.

This was the beginning of the big push to unisex in our society. By 1973 there was already a significant trend toward acceptance of the feminist theory that sex roles are an arbitrary, discriminatory human condition that can and should be changed. Strong institutional forces—particularly in the federal government, mass media and educational institutions—adopted the fundamental feminist goal of destroying the sex-role system. The ostensible reason for this is that sex roles institutionalize prejudices that keep women from enjoying equal opportunity with men. But as one personnel officer told me: "You have to remember that whenever they say 'equal opportunity,' they really mean equality of results. Everybody is supposed to be the same now."

If you read the literature of feminism, the bottom line becomes clear. Only by totally destroying the normal patterns of sexual relationships and roles, the feminists believe, can they ever free women completely from responsibility for domestic life and begin to make men and women exactly alike in every possible way.

As I perused the report of this MIT workshop, it seemed that the biggest problem confounding the planners was figuring out how to persuade members of the diminutive sex not to think of their primary role as being in the home, how to motivate more of them to want to compete with men in the labor force. The planners were especially keen for women to do jobs that have traditionally been done by men, and for men to take the women's jobs. But the grand challenge facing crusaders after more options and opportunities for females is trying to arouse appreciable numbers of women to take advantage of the opportunities and options already available to them.

An executive from AT&T, John Kingsbury, described to the MIT planners "how the Bell System is struggling with the problem of finding more women for technical jobs on the professional level, and increasing the flow of women into skilled craft jobs, such as central office maintenance personnel, installers, repair workers, and other outside craft workers."

The words of John Kingsbury and many others at these meetings affirm that social planners are doing everything they can to move women out of their homes and into jobs. "We have been wrestling for some time with precisely the same problem that is the subject of the workshop," declared the AT&T executive, "how to increase the participation of women in scientific and technical jobs . . . [and] a corollary of the problem . . .

how to increase the participation of men in jobs formerly seen by them as 'female' jobs. . . ."

In essence, Kingsbury declared the allegiance of the Bell System to the primary beliefs and objectives of the feminist revolution. "The entire fabric of society tends to reinforce the tradition of sex roles, including television and motion pictures, guidance and career counseling, advertising, textbook pictures. . . . Speed of change is uncertain, and the degree to which youth is responding is slow. . . . And, though I do not see it as primarily our responsibility, we are committed to participate in and aid this process of change in as many ethical ways as we can."

Ma Bell seems to mean business. The organization has sought the advice of Dr. Leona Tyler, president of the American Psychological Association, and Dr. Valerie Kincade Oppenheimer, a research sociologist at UCLA, in developing a broad program to change attitudes and behavior of employees in the Bell System, and to encourage males and females across the country to accept jobs traditionally associated with the opposite sex.

"We have many plans that are designed to work on attitudinal factors that operate to inhibit youth from seeking nontraditional jobs," said Kingsbury of Bell's plans to manipulate the minds of the sexes. "We are working on a series of employment films portraying men and women actively performing our entry-level jobs. . . . We are developing an affirmative action brochure for use in schools that will show men and women performing nontraditional jobs. . . . We are planning model ads for use in high school newspapers and in daily papers, and a lecture demonstration for use in our speakers' bureaus around the country, all of which stress the theme of nontraditional jobs and motivating men and women to strike out for that which they have not considered in the past."

36

Bell has also changed its recruitment materials and advertising to show men and women in unisex roles. When my wife first noticed the Western Electric ads on TV she shook her head in wonder. "Who would have thought that the same Ma Bell who gave us the Princess telephone would one day use psychological engineering to give us male telephone operators and female linemen?" she said.

Bell has also set up goals, to use the polite term, for moving women into jobs that were previously filled mostly by men. Ma Bell has instituted "awareness training" to ensure that her employees know what attitudes toward sex roles are expected of them. The organization has also produced a new film, entitled *All Kinds of Jobs,* showing men and women performing nontraditional work roles. Besides showing this film all over the country, Ma Bell is also conducting her own "consciousness-raising type" workshops in cities across the U.S. to encourage Americans in all walks of life to support the new unisex program.

It all adds up to a massive assault on traditional sex roles packaged and sold under the label of "equal opportunity." Regardless of how you or I may feel about the changes this could bring, it is a new sociological phenomenon confronting us as citizens—a broad and concerted effort by multiple organizational forces, including the federal government, to engineer new social attitudes within the populace so that men, women and children everywhere will accept the feminist belief that as a matter of principle there should be no differences whatsoever in the responsibilities, roles and job participation of males and females.

"My own feeling," says Edith Ruina, director of MIT's Work in Technology and Science Project, "is that people are being asked to grow and to modify their attitudes and behavior in ways that they would want to anyway." This may be, but it is the understatement of the decade to suggest that the present overwhelming push toward a sex-role revolution is merely "asking" people to change. It is an unprecedented campaign of social persuasion which in many instances amounts to economic coercion, as we shall discover.

"Employers and educators now have the obligation and the opportunity to intervene in the cycle that restricts women's career choices," declares the MIT workshop report prepared by Director Ruina. "Programs devised separately or through cooperative efforts can increase women's incentive to prepare for and commit themselves to any career at all, and to careers in science and technology in particular. Increasingly, public policy expressed in legislation and executive action affirms the collective desire for equal opportunity for all individuals, but designs for implementation in varied institutional settings are necessary to effect the kind and quality of change that is called for." This, of course, is where the "goals" come in.

"To bring about the changes that will invite women to nontraditional careers," Director Ruina avows, "committees of employers, male and female employee groups, and resource people should be established to discuss and evaluate company programs. These committees could also design strategies for attracting and retaining women employees. Outside these committees, all employees should have occasions to discuss and monitor company-sponsored programs, such as job training, job assessment, and benefits, for conformity with company policy. . . ."

No doubt Director Ruina would have thought it frivolous had a less committed planner hazarded to ask when the company's work would ever get done with all of this meeting and monitoring, discussing and assessing going on. In fact, the MIT planners were cozily united in the conviction that with strong leadership

38

and innovation much would be done right in local communities to break down sex-role stereotypes, change school curricula, influence attitudes of teachers, parents and youngsters, and recruit girls into jobs previously filled by males. The planners, says the director, were "acutely aware of the marvelous complexities of schools and the myriad small steps necessary to change attitudes and behavior."

Furthermore, she declares, "much needs to be done at the state and national levels, and the formation of new groups will be necessary. Industry and occupational organizations, individual employers, and educa-

tional policy makers and school systems at all levels
need to maintain on-going interaction. To achieve this,
interinstitutional committees can be established, com-
posed of varying combinations of employer and educational organizations, occupational and professional organizations, women's caucuses and unions, media representatives, civic planning groups, etc."

As we digested Director Ruina's report, it occurred to
Annie and me that those who are undertaking to plan
the future of America are arrogating to The Committee
control of matters which, until now at least, have always been the primary responsibility of the family—
such things as motivating and advising one's children,

CENTRAL
INTERVENTION
AGENCY

guiding their ambitions, goals and values, focusing their allegiances.

The planners, moreover, envisioned all of this activity as eventually being brought under a "central agency" to coordinate efforts across the nation. Responsibilities of this central agency would include educating employers, teachers, parents and students as to proper sexual attitudes; providing technical assistance to schools and employers in motivating women to enter nontraditional occupations; monitoring textbooks, magazines, newspapers, broadcasting, job recruiting materials, et cetera, to make certain that the unisex point of view is consistently encouraged.

"An effective central agency of this type would require a regular staff and perhaps a new professional role," declares Director Ruina, "that of an education/work liaison consultant."

One of the most conspicuous opportunities created under the "equal opportunity" program for women seems to be that lots of new jobs are created for the professional class of feminists who try to make sure the unisex programs are enforced.

The MIT report concludes: "The workshop's suggestions can be summarized in large part by saying that institutional change calls for leadership commitment to it, better communication within institutions, between institutions, and greater sensitivity to the subtle ways in which females are guided by their parents, teachers, and employers."

"But since individuals and institutions procrastinate despite sincere intentions to promote equal opportunity," adds Director Ruina, "schemes and structures must be devised that hold people accountable for implementing and monitoring activities that will facilitate the removal of traditional sex role expectations."

Another MIT planner, Associate U.S. Commissioner

of Education Robert Worthington, told his fellow missionaries that the federal Office of Education in Washington, D.C., already is developing programs "that expose girls and boys to technology and work that contribute to new role definitions for women." He described federal programs which he said were aimed at "eliminating sex discrimination" and spoke of "new occupational attitudes we would like to elicit in our young children." At the Office of Education in Washington, he said, "to counteract sex-role stereotyping at the pre-school and early elementary levels, we have recently completed an experimental series of films to be shown on the CBS television show 'Captain Kangaroo.' "

Planner Helen Astin, director of research and education at the University Research Corporation in Washington, encouraged those at the workshop to "use research knowledge to design creative ways to reverse the negative effects of the socialization process on girls." (If I am not mistaken, by "socialization process" Director Astin means all of that careless unprogrammed learning that children pick up from associating with their parents and from other unprofessional sources such as neighbors, relatives, friends and acquaintances.) "If we examine the interests of young boys and girls," she told the planners, "we find that the choices made by them very early in life are along traditional lines. . . ." She spoke avidly of the need for educators to intervene to change this untidy state of affairs.

Planner Frank J. Toner, an employee-relations manager at the General Electric Company, supported her enthusiasm for intervention. "It will take a multi-sectored effort," he said. "The business and industrial community, the educational establishment, including primary and secondary schools, and the government all have to be enlisted in this effort. . . . GE and all of industry have a responsibility to include women in . . . training programs, and the educational institutions have a parallel responsibility either to train women for these kinds of jobs and/or to provide counseling and guidance that would motivate young women to seek out these opportunities."

I am sure that not all of the planners at the MIT workshop were fiery-eyed revolutionaries, nor were all of those at the thousands of other meetings and work sessions convened in the unisex cause in recent years. But something has persuaded organizations such as AT&T, GE, Xerox, General Motors, Polaroid, DuPont, IBM, the YWCA, the National Research Council, John Hancock Mutual Life, and scores of others, to seriously consider participating in a gigantic national campaign of social engineering to convince the sexes that their occupational and domestic ambitions and achievements should be identical.

No one familiar with the facts believes that women aspire to participate in the labor force to the same extent as men. Feminist theorists and social engineers alike are convinced that most women will never aspire to it without an intensive long-range drive to sexually disorient the society. So how did the official policy of nearly the entire national establishment come to support the unisex vision of feminism? How have the feminists come to advance their ideology so successfully even though most people in the country seem not to want a unisex world?

I don't think there is a simple answer. We will be taking up some important aspects later on, such as the colossal contributions made by the federal government and the media. But first let's consider the indispensable role in this process played by the shock troops of the unisex assault—those militant, radical feminists who in strident, fanatical bands have waged political

43

warfare on the government, business, education, religion, the family and just about every other American institution.

The National Organization for Women is undoubtedly the largest and best-known of the radical feminist groups. Who has not heard of its dauntless campaigns against "sexism"? NOW is not the Girl Scouts. For instance, NOW advertises that if women have complaints against their employers and will notify the organization, its members will harrass the employer and allow the employee to remain anonymous. NOW, of course, encourages and defends homosexuality, and its members have teamed up with members of the Gay Activist Alliance to picket and prod broadcast studios into projecting more favorable images of homosexuals on TV.

Perhaps I should say a few words about the long campaign to persuade the mass media to adopt feminist views on sex roles and homosexuality. This assault began in 1970, the year bands of radical women's groups invaded the offices of the *Ladies' Home Journal*, the *New York Times* and the *San Francisco Chronicle*, and disrupted the annual meeting of the stockholders of CBS.

In the raid on the *Journal* on March 18, 1970, the offices of the magazine's editor-in-chief, John Mack Carter, were occupied for eleven hours by about a hundred angry feminists demanding that the *Journal* adopt feminist standards in its editing and in its portrayal of American women. According to reports, at one point in the siege one of the feminists leapt onto Carter's desk and entreated her comrades to throw Carter out of his own office. "We can do it," she is said to have yelled. "He's small!"

It is my impression that by and large the mass media have responded cooperatively—to a great extent even enthusiastically and applaudingly—to the onslaught of feminism. The *Ladies' Home Journal* responded to its attackers by turning over an entire issue of the magazine to the feminists. The *Journal* has also allowed them to continue to participate in determining the publication's contents and policies in the years since then.

Annie and I have taken occasion to study the influence of lib upon the press, and we have observed that publications with tremendous national influence—such as the *New York Times*, the *Washington Post, Time, Newsweek, U.S. News & World Report* and the mass-circulation Sunday supplement *Parade*—have been regular boosters of feminist ideas and objectives.

In 1971 the *New York Times* and CBS News joined forces to produce a book, *Rebirth of Feminism*, which they called "an authoritative analysis of today's feminism." A thoughtful reading of this book reveals that

"Let's throw him out! We can do it. He's small!"

although it conveys an impression of objectively interpreting events and debates of the recent feminist revival, in actuality the volume is a subtle endorsement of the liberationist tide. While couched in judicious-sounding language, the treatment is so approving of the basic principles and concepts of feminism that the overall effect is to give the impression that the cause is not only just, but the wave of the future. The movement is so compelling, the authors suggest, that it "apparently touches a raw-nerve sensitivity in women regardless of their political orientation or lack of one." (I checked with my wife on that and she affirms that, yes, lib definitely gets on her nerves.)

This *New York Times*–CBS book, I should add, provides a wealth of factual information on the feminist fomentations of the early seventies. It describes, for example, one of lib's most ambitious antimedia projects: "The National Organization for Women employed the resources and membership of its nearly 100 chapters and launched a nationwide campaign monitoring the television networks and local stations. NOW members filled in lengthy survey forms rating stations on the basis of the image of women portrayed; the quantity and quality of the coverage of news events about women, e.g., Supreme Court decisions, Equal Rights Amendment progress; the orientation of women's programs, amount of time devoted to household hints and fashion, to day care and job opportunities. The survey form was reprinted in *Woman's Day* to encourage non-NOW members to participate in the monitoring effort. The end goal of the project was to collect data about the stations and to challenge the license of any station with a 'bad record' when it came up for renewal before the Federal Communications Commission. . . ."

NOW has used this same lever to force TV and radio stations around the country to sign contracts giving

NOW members the opportunity to help determine the content of programming and public service announcements and to assist in formulation of new hiring and personnel policies. Stations that have given in to this pressure and actually signed such agreements have opened doors to the libbers to put their people on the public affairs programs, to create feminist talk shows and choose the guests, to move feminists into job vacancies in the studios, to bring in feminist consultants, and to conduct lib orientation sessions among station employees.

Orientation sessions have also been conducted in the offices of newspapers and magazines. In December 1974, journalists from across the country gathered at the Watergate Hotel in Washington, D.C., to participate in seminars sponsored by the Washington Journalism Center. The reporters spent four days in briefings with such leading feminists as Betty Friedan, Karen De Crow, Ti-Grace Atkinson, Wilma Scott Heide, Nancy Polikoff, Pat Lindh and Jill Ruckelshaus. The reporters learned the ABCs of feminism from the libbers, whom they apparently regarded as the experts on the thoughts and aspirations of American women, as their leaders. Their movement, Ms Friedan assured the journalists, "was a necessary first stage of a very profound sex role change for both women and men to break through those polarized masculine and feminine roles that have locked us both in torment."

Nowhere have the effects of women's lib been more dramatic than in the field of journalism, where feminists have flocked in recent years to establish whole careers interpreting lib ideology, rhapsodizing over the fulfillments of glamorous occupations (such as their own), and belaboring the risks and rigors of marriage, homemaking and, *ugh,* raising children.

Lib's impact in the book world, according to author

and professor of anthropology Lionel Tiger, has been so profound as to produce a double standard of reviewing new books. Those about the sexes, he says, are judged according to their level of commitment to feminist ideals rather than on the basis of the quality of research and writing. "Both men and women seem to have succumbed to the temptation to judge books with formal numbness just so long as they are bristling with feminist energy and abet the cause of sociosexual change . . . ," wrote Professor Tiger in the *New York Times Book Review*.

To me, it is crystal clear that the multi-sectored effort heralded in 1973 by Frank Toner, the MIT planner from General Electric, has become an overwhelming reality.

"It takes longer to change minds than it does to change laws," declares a full-page advertisement I saw in *Esquire*, placed by the United Nations as part of its International Women's Year publicity. "Laws and our cultural background have allowed men to 'get there' first," continues the ad in the feminist mode. "But it's 1975. And we can't afford to waste woman-power any longer. Let's change our minds while we change our laws."

In January 1976, Jane O'Reilly, feminist writer-in-residence at the *Washington Star*, reported that Washington, D.C., is the center of a broad (no pun intended) network of feminists—government workers, journalists, lobbyists and political staff workers—who cooperate closely to promote lib objectives (and, I might add, to boost one another in the Washington scramble for influence and status).

The effects are far-reaching and surprising. The Department of Labor, for instance, was somehow persuaded to accept members of the Washington chapter of NOW as representatives of the nation's women in matters relating to federal labor policies. Following the initial meetings between the members and government officials, the NOW chapter announced that the success of this collaboration would "result in a more formalized regular meeting schedule with top Labor Department officials so that the women of this country may be assured of strong advocacy representation in the policy-making process." My wife is still trying to find out who elected the members of NOW to represent *her* interests.

NOW of course has been an aggressive advocate of ERA. The usual arguments of these feminists appearing on TV focus mainly on popular themes such as "equal pay for equal work," but the actual platform of NOW—bannered as "Revolution: Tomorrow is NOW"—emphasizes such issues as getting rid of school textbooks that portray women in the home, government-funded day-care centers for all children, free abortion on demand, free contraception and sterilization, proslesbian legislation, eliminating laws giving special preference in jobs and education to veterans and laws exempting women from combat and the draft. NOW also advocates a guaranteed annual income for everybody and laws that would require businesses to provide "parent leave" to both parents instead of only maternity leave for the mother. All of this so that both sexes will be treated exactly the same.

Examples abound of the effects of the feminist coalition on the course of government business. There was the time, I recall, when hundreds of Washington's lib lobbyists combed Capitol Hill for an entire week until they succeeded in influencing members of Congress to reject a notably sensible amendment that would have prevented forced integration of the sexes in physical education classes and campus honorary societies.

The federal feminist network has been supremely

successful at such chores as persuading President Ford to stack such public bodies as the National Commission on International Women's Year with such certified representatives of lib as Pat Carbine of *Ms.* magazine, TV actor Alan Alda, Barbara Walters, Senator Birch Bayh, then Congresswoman Bella Abzug, former Congresswoman Martha Griffiths, and the woman who was called the Gloria Steinem of the Republican Party, Jill Ruckelshaus. (The commission subsequently opened for business in offices of the Department of State with $275,000 in federal funds and with up to $5 million more authorized by the Congress.)

And then there was the packet of information that Annie received in the mail from Pat Lindh, special assistant to the president—under the White House letterhead—promoting the International Women's Year Conference recommendations, which state that "genuine reforms should be carried out in all educational systems starting with early childhood education so that girls and boys will consider each other as equals. . . . Training for teaching, counseling, and administration should be without sex bias or discriminatory attitudes and should heighten teachers' awareness of the full range of abilities in both sexes. . . . All teaching media and materials should be free of sex bias and should be directed toward changing discriminatory attitudes . . . identification of authentic skills and all human resources of the community, and full use of these skills and resources in the educational process, with particular emphasis upon the contribution of women . . . the establishment of training and promotion centers for women . . . continuing research and evaluation of education programs as they affect girls and women, and as they bring about changes in attitudes and roles for women and men."

This White House mailing also urges that "structures and strategies be evolved and implemented to these ends on a massive scale," and suggests that governmental and nongovernmental organizations cooperate in developing such a national program. The objectives envisioned by those at the International Women's Year Conference and promoted from within the White House in 1975 appear to be the same plans for creating a unisex society that were conceived two years before at the MIT sessions.

We have recently been seeing other ways feminists in the federal network are using their influence to promote the lib trend. In 1975 the Civil Service Commission announced that it had decided to make official the use of the *Ms* form of address for women who prefer it. But the fact is that Ms had already been in widespread use in government offices whether women preferred it or not. The *Washington Post*'s "Federal Diary" column reported that it "is a widespread practice in government agencies for those who want to promote the 'lib' perspective to apply the Ms. form to all women whenever an opportunity arises, regardless of the preferences of individuals." The government agencies, the report suggests, are "moving the nation toward the official use of the term Ms., which many feminists prefer to the traditional titles of Miss or Mrs." Even the White House is doing this. Whenever Annie has written there requesting information or documents—clearly signing herself *Mrs.*—the reply has always come back addressed to *Ms.*

Lib advocates are active in every federal agency, and they are trying to entrench feminist programs within the government and across the nation through such feminist-oriented bodies as the Federally Employed Women, HEW's Education Division, the Women's Bureau of the Department of Labor, the Citizens' Advisory Council on the Status of Women, and the International Women's Year Commission.

The federal Status of Women Council has acted as a

government-funded lobby for the Equal Rights Amendment and much of the rest of the sex-role revolutionary program. Beyond this federal council, moreover, scores of state and local "status of women" groups, appointed by governors and mayors, are now functioning in nearly every state with public support. Among the stated purposes of these groups are: to research aspects of sexism in education, employment and the law; speak out on day care, continuing education and divorce; monitor the media with respect to women's image as presented to the public; encourage the formation of more local status of women groups; and to further develop the network of cooperative organizations that support feminist legislation.

Numerous agencies of the federal government are involved in substantial educational activities intended to forward sociosexual changes in the society. Notable among these are HEW, the Women's Bureau, the Justice Department and the Equal Employment Opportunity Commission, all of which spend large sums of money paying officials to fly to conferences, to lead group discussions, and to teach courses—all relating to sex-role education or discrimination.

I talked for quite a while with a senior budget examiner at the President's Office of Management and Budget to try to get an idea of how much money the federal government is actually spending on the unisex push. "No one has actually put all of this together," the official told me, "but there is a substantial amount of educational effort going on. We are talking about tens of millions of dollars per year."

Federal involvement in applying the unisex ideas to schools really got rolling when in 1974 HEW issued its regulations implementing Title IX of the federal Education Amendments passed by Congress in 1972. Under the new regulations, fraternities and sororities on college campuses across the country quickly became subject to monitoring by the government, and physical education classes and programs were required to be sexually integrated. NOW tried to pressure HEW into using the Title IX regulations as a pretext for monitoring and regulating the contents of school textbooks, but the government hesitated to go that far.

In July 1975, the Women's Action Alliance, another feminist group, produced a document which contained ingredients collected from more than 80 different organizations from the Camp Fire Girls to the Lesbian Mothers National Defense Fund. This was presented to the Congress and the nation's governors and mayors under the rubric of the "U.S. National Women's Agenda."

The plan, billed as an expression of the "demands . . . of the women of the United States of America . . . on the Government and the private sector," calls for firm policies and programs aimed at accomplishing the unisex revolution, to wit:

(1) Elimination of sex-role, racial and cultural stereotyping at every level of the educational system, and in educational materials.

(2) Incorporation of women's issues into all areas of educational curricula.

(3) Development of programs that counter prevailing myths and stereotypes regarding women workers and that recognize the ability of women and men alike to set goals and to achieve success in work.

(4) Ending stereotyped portrayals of women and girls in all media and encouraging efforts to portray them in positive and realistic roles.

(5) Implementation of the legal right of women to control their own reproductive systems.

(6) Inclusion of realistic curricula on health and human sexuality throughout the educational process.

(7) Protection of the right to privacy of relationships between consenting adults.

(8) Extensions of all civil rights legislation to prohibit discrimination based on affectional or sexual preference.

Stripped of feminist jargon and code words, these eight items comprise the key objectives of the unisex agenda—abolition of sex roles, devaluation of the traditional marriage and family, legitimization of homosexuality, "free" universal day care of children, abortion on demand, and feminist indoctrination in the schools. These are the objectives clearly enunciated in *Ms.* magazine month after month, and which *Ms.* editor Gloria Steinem unquestionably had in mind when she announced to the press in October 1975 that she and other feminist Democrats had formed the Democratic Women's Alliance to attempt to force the "women's agenda" into the 1976 platform of the Democratic Party.

By the time the Democrats met for their convention in New York City, the U.S. House of Representatives had already approved the Vocational Education Act, and a Senate version sponsored by then Senator Walter Mondale of Minnesota was awaiting consideration. "The strongest feature in the Senate bill," wrote Nancy Hicks of the *New York Times,* "is the $100,000 earmarked for each state to set up an office for women in the state vocational education department. This office would be responsible for raising consciousness among high school students, many of whom identify strongly with traditional sex roles, and among vocational education instructors, who are among the most traditionally minded of teachers.

"The House bill would desegregate home economics courses, allow states to review for sex stereotyping all curriculum material it normally selects, and would provide special support for young women entering traditionally male occupations." This is just one of numerous bills brought before Congress in recent years to advance the drive to unisex.

We have glimpsed some of the interlinking activities of the government, mass media, educational institutions and myriad women's groups pursuing the unisex society. They are complex and ubiquitous, and we have only scratched the surface.

Efforts to achieve ratification of the Equal Rights Amendment by the states have forged a broad coalition of sometimes strange bedfellows, as diverse as the Playboy Foundation and the newly feminist League of Women Voters. The Rockefeller Foundation awarded the California Commission on the Status of Women $288,000 for a two-year program to promote the ERA and to determine what laws would need to be changed should it become the law of the land.

The feminists have gained a strong foothold in many different kinds of organizations, not the least of which has been organized religion. Protestant, Catholic, Unitarian and Jewish congregations have been besieged by groups of feminists urging support of lib ideology and goals. Besides insisting that males and females perform exactly the same social and ceremonial roles in churches and synagogues, the feminists are pressing for ordainment of females as priests, the purging of hymns, creeds, prayers, and the Bible of all "sexist" references, and mobilization of the considerable clout of numerous religious organizations behind the feminist crusade. One editor of a religious magazine referred to the upheaval as an effort to transform Christianity from "an ideology of oppressors" into "a gospel of liberation."

The Young Women's Christian Association, at its national convention in 1970, announced formation of a National Women's Resource Center through which the

YWCA intended to place its full power behind the movement "to revolutionize society's expectations of women and their own self-perception." The purpose of the center is to collect and disseminate films, books, articles, tapes, surveys and research information, and in general to serve as a clearinghouse for information about women's groups, books and TV programs with "good role models" of men and women. The center, according to its director, Helen F. Southard, tries to reach "young girls throughout the country and educate them about the options available to them besides marriage."

The YWCA, with a membership of more than 2.5 million women and girls in 7,800 local chapters, is more than 100 years old. Once prim and proper, now many of the YWCA's facilities are being used by women's liberation groups to promote feminism among females of all ages. One young woman said she had not expected much when she first visited the YWCA. "I was just amazed at the women I met there—wonderful, angry, dynamic young feminists who were a diverse mixture of class and color and who were determined to use the enormous resources of the YWCA more productively."

Among the more productive uses to which the YWCA has now been put has been the establishment of Women's Divorce Cooperatives, forums on sex and sexuality, a free abortion referral service, and a Lesbian Resource Center—where "lesbians can get together for coffee and a sharing of problems," according to a member of the YWCA's National Board.

In 1975, Annie received scores of letters from women across the country who had read her article in the *National Observer* pointing up current social problems that seemed linked to the feminist trend of recent years. "I've recently spent a year as a sorority housemother and two summers as resident advisor at a YWCA residence," wrote Kathryn Toomey of Golden,

Colorado, "and I have been surprised to learn how effective the Movement has been in capturing the minds of the young."

It is surprising—but not too difficult to understand—as Annie and I quickly found out when we recently revisited the college scene.

As recession arrived at campuses and a serious shortage of students ensued throughout higher education in the early seventies, the colleges, universities and adult education departments focused on the burgeoning trend of lib. The schools soon began riding the new feminist wave and the recruitment of women of all ages quickly became a major emphasis at academe. All across the land, there arose previously unknown courses with names such as "Options for Women," "Life Development for Females," "Emerging Women," "The New Woman," "Focusing Female," "New Horizons for Women," "Assertiveness Training for Women," "Women Dare Daily," "Female Breakthrough," "Workshop for Women," "Seminar for Women," etc., etc., etc.

Many of these courses have been advertised in newspapers and on the radio, with mildly goading spurs to the homebody, such as: "Stuck in a rut? Why don't you add a new dimension to your life? Come to the Community College's Course on Career Empowerment for the New Woman!"

If these courses are not exactly consciousness-raising groups, they *are* intended to change women's attitudes toward their social roles. Writer Jean O. Johnson investigated a number of the courses in the metropolitan area of Washington, D.C., for the *Washington Post*. She found the offerings mainly concerned with attuning women to "the values of society as interpreted by academia," she said, and with introducing women to new ways of living.

"But no matter what the specific focus," she reported, "in all of the classrooms the women seem engaged in varying degrees in changing their traditional mind-sets. 'This is not a women's lib group,' one instructor announced at the first class session. But personal liberation was certainly one of the messages—liberation from the dominance of society, family and husband."

Perhaps another indication of the purposes of these courses is the fact that university psychologists are now busy investigating the effectiveness of various approaches in "changing mind-sets." In 1975, a team of social scientists at the University of California at Los Angeles reported their study of undergraduate women who had taken women's studies courses. The study showed significant changes in the coeds' beliefs about the traditional roles of women and in their perception of problems they attributed to sex discrimination.

According to the researchers,

It appears that women's sex-role beliefs are comprised of certain definable areas and that some of these areas are more susceptible than others to the influence processes of women's studies courses. In particular, Traditional roles of women, Nonstereotypic beliefs, and Perception of sex discrimination were the variables most easily changed. . . .

One problem in fully understanding the findings is that it is difficult to determine what aspects of the women's studies courses were most effective in producing change. These courses provided information through lectures, small group discussions, female role models, and an environment supportive of less traditional attitudes. Each of these factors could be important singly or in interaction with other factors in producing attitude changes. Future research should attempt to control or systematically manipulate these variables. . . .

In summary, the data support the conclusion that

> consciousness can be raised and sex-role attitudes
> changed through participation in women's studies
> classes. . . .

The campaign to change the minds of Americans about the roles of men and women has been brought most strongly to bear on schools, boards of education and publishers of textbooks because the youth of today are regarded as the most important link to a unisex future. Not only have the feminists persuaded publishers to expunge material the liberationists consider "sexist" from new textbooks and readers, they have persuaded many school districts and state governments to devise "antisexist" educational programs. Local school systems all over the country are participating in these activities (some much more than others), which are being pursued nationally through the federal Title IX anti-discrimination rules for education.

During 1976, HEW required all school systems to evaluate themselves for compliance with the unisex regulations or risk losing federal funds. When the reports of several suburban counties surrounding Washington, D.C., were completed, a number of interesting plans for improving the circumstances of the sexes emerged: (1) launching a strenuous antisexist program to reduce role-stereotyping by teachers and in textbooks, (2) setting up coed classes in courses previously restricted to either boys or girls, (3) eliminating sexually lopsided enrollments in courses such as home economics, industrial arts, science and math, (4) sex integration of all physical education courses, (5) launching an affirmative action campaign to attract both sexes to traditionally male or female courses, (6) eliminating sexist language and masculine pronouns from all school regulations and course guides, (7) creating new courses in which students will be taught how to recognize and "deal with" sexism, and (8) eliminating sex discrimination in student restroom facilities (the problem here was that the girls' restrooms were found to have doors and dividers between the toilets that provided more privacy than those in the boys' rooms; thank heavens we will now be protected from the threat of girls growing up with more modesty than any other sex).

Similar efforts are being encouraged in every state. The Carnegie Corporation of New York in 1972 awarded a $300,000 grant to the Council on Interracial Books for Children to develop a "resource and publication center on racism and sexism in education." Each year the people at this center propose to rate children's books on how well they conform to their ideas. They intend to purge the materials of "racism and sexism and other distortions of human values." This center also develops and distributes its own lesson plans, teaching strategies and various other items designed to "eliminate racist and sexist stereotypes."

In her book *Unlearning the Lie*, Barbara Harrison sets forth the beliefs which advocates feel justify all of this purging and planning, and she describes how the feminists incorporated a "Sex-roles Committee" to pressure an entire school into "a new awareness of sex-roles stereotyping." These women were being paid to teach children, but it is hard to understand how they found much time, energy or motivation for teaching after spending so much of their energies on what they themselves describe as "revolutionary activity." This is what Ms Harrison says she and her colleagues were doing at school:

> When the Sex-roles Committee at Woodward began to make its influence felt at the school . . . our goals . . . were tangible if not easily achieved. But in the course of two years of consciousness-raising

and political activity, we realized that the question
that underlay all our talk and all our action was . . .
Whom—what—do we want to be? . . . We are left
with . . . profound questions, which trouble and exercise our minds even as they exhilarate us, because we have never dared ask them before. When
we talked and argued at Woodward about whether
we valued more highly those characteristics traditionally associated with men or those traditionally
associated with women, when we discussed
whether our fulfillment meant aping men, we were
not giving voice to bloodless abstractions: we were
asking ourselves what we really wanted to be, and
what we wanted our children to be. When we tried
to define *work,* when we tried to define *success,*
when we asked whether a person *is* what she *does,*
we were asking ourselves to discover the source of
our self-respect. We were also, as we sought to find
a work in the world that would bring us joy, asking
ourselves what we wanted the world to be. . . . We
were asking ourselves how we really wished to
behave, what our natures *really* demanded of us,
what our ideal of social intercourse was. . . . Our desire to change ourselves is indistinguishable from
our desire to change society, our desire to change
the world. . . . True revolutionaries are like God—
they create the world in their own image. . . .

Consciousness-raising activities have been encouraged by such groups in high schools all across America,
because the feminists are convinced that "it is in high
school that boys and girls are irrevocably 'tracked' into
traditional life-roles."

In New York City, a group called the High School
Women's Liberation Coalition distributed to high
school students a questionnaire entitled "What Every
Young Girl Should Ask." Among other things, the girls
were asked: "Can you play basketball, soccer, football?
Did you ever pretend to be dumb? Are your brothers

asked to help clean house? Did you discuss masturbation and lesbianism in your sex education class? Did you discuss intercourse? Orgasm? Abortion? How many famous women do you know about (not counting Presidents' wives or movie stars)? How are women portrayed in the books you read? How do your classes react to 'ugly' women teachers? In extracurricular coed organizations, do girls make decisions? Or do they take minutes? Are girls with boyfriends winners? What did they win? Do you ask boys out? If not, why not? Do you believe boys get sexually aroused faster, at a younger age, and more often than girls? Who told you *that*? Do you ever hug or kiss your girlfriend? Do you like your body? How much time and money do you spend on your makeup? Why? Do you think of unmarried women as 'bachelor girls' or 'old maids'? Is your mother an oppressed woman?"

When my wife first came across this handout for high school girls and showed it to me, I read it over and then I added a few questions of my own at the bottom of the list:

Why are you reading this material?

Why do you suppose people are distributing such strange lists of questions for you to look at?

What else do you suppose they want to do to your world?

Anything Goes?

A piquant cartoon in *Genesis* (the sex magazine for men) depicts a bosomy, voluptuous woman standing in her apartment doorway, her body exposed through a half-open, diaphanous robe to a young man taking a political poll in her building. "I'm a conservative," she is saying.

Well, perhaps in the wide-open, let-it-all-hang-out, different-strokes-for-different-folks, anything-goes society of recent years, she *is* a conservative. I admit I don't know anymore.

In the anything-goes society, nothing can really be considered wrong anymore, can it? Certainly not a little innocent public nudity. Look at streaking. Anyway, liberation has done away with *wrong*. Drug abusers are now members of "cults of the greater awareness." Homosexuals are advocates of "gay liberation." Those who formerly would have been known as adulterers and adulteresses now are participants in "open marriage." People used to suffer the terrible fragmentation of sexual identity—now they enjoy the new "bisexual lifestyle." What used to be the ignominy of merely shacking up has been raised to the status of "cohabitation" and even "trial marriage."

Instead of the Golden Rule, we have bumper stickers that say "Do Unto Others—Then Split." (The first time I saw this on a car, the thought flashed through my mind that it might be the motto of a national association of hit-and-run drivers.)

In his book *The Age of Sensation*, psychiatrist Herbert Hendin says the compulsion after sensation—"fulfillment" in the form of more and more kicks—is replacing the traditional, external moral and legal controls in today's society. He asserts, "What were once personal choices are now causes proselytized and offered as the wave of the future."

I think the essence of publicity for the anything-goes society was expressed by the writers of the advertisements for that epic Paramount Picture of the 1970s, *The Joys of a Woman:* "Let me be your guide in the art of love," they bade. "Let me, Emmanuelle, take you to a new world of pleasure. In my new movie I will show you how to enjoy the new morality. If everybody else is taking part in today's new sensual freedom, why should you be left out? You have every right to pleasure. This is my lifestyle. Make it yours. Believe as I do that nothing is wrong if it feels good."

I suppose Anything Goes really got started in 1959 when *Lady Chatterley's Lover* was first allowed to be circulated in the United States. In the next few years, there arrived the Playboy Philosophy, newsstand nudity, and the topless phase, soon followed by the revised standards known as the new morality. If the gamekeeper taught Lady Chatterley that personal fulfillment is more important than the social rules, the new morality taught that freewheeling fulfillment and personal pleasure are *everything*. So in recent years, the Anything that Goes has included promiscuity, homosexuality, illegitimacy, easy abortion, easy divorce and the drive to abandon sex roles.

I know many people today who, although they have never thought of themselves as prudes, look around in wonderment at their anything-goes world. Now we have "combat zones" of pornography and sex-for-hire. Homosexual musical groups are featured at the national Kennedy Center for the Performing Arts. School children read *The School-Stoppers Textbook—Handbook for School Disruption and Violence,* which describes 84 methods of disrupting schools. Adults read *Cosmopolitan's Living Together (married or not) Handbook. Newsweek* reports that male and female university students at some places are not only sharing dormitories and beds, but bathrooms as well. Large audiences watch motion pictures in which naked women appear to be ravished, and even hacked to death, on the screen. It is small wonder that some people are beginning to ask whether our explosion of freedom in recent years might not have loosed more than we expected.

Are we experiencing a general breakdown of all moral senses? In saying, all right, it's okay to play with yourself, and it's okay to play around with the other person's mate, nothing can be wrong if it feels good— could it be that we have inadvertently released ourselves from qualms about playing fast and loose in matters of honesty, allegiance and basic integrity? Might we even have unhinged some unstable people to the point of toying with the bizarre excitements of violence, cruelty, intrigue and terror? More and more voices are expressing concern that the fabric of society is being threatened.

There can be little doubt that many people have lost their commitment to rules, or to any kind of absolutes.

67

It seems to me that many more people are ignoring traffic lights and other rules of the road than in times past. And having lost their commitment to external controls, they seem less able to make any kind of real commitments to each other.

According to Dr. Naomi Heller, a psychiatrist at our local community psychiatric clinic, it is no longer assumed by people, as it once was, that if you are in love with someone and have a "meaningful relationship" you also have a commitment. "Now that's not the assumption anymore," she said. "One partner may say, 'We'll stay together as long as it feels good.' A sense of imbalance, mismatches, periods of instability result. There's no social assumption to back things up."

And this weakening of social expectations affects the stability of marriages, according to Dr. Heller. "It used to be," she said, "that if a woman found out, for instance, that her husband was having an affair, her assumption, society's assumption, was that it was wrong, he shouldn't be doing this. Now it's no longer what a woman can count on. He can just shrug and say, 'So what?' There is a lack of support systems in society for the way things are supposed to be."

Considerable disagreement exists, of course, as to the actual seriousness of the revolution in our society's moral structure. Although many people deplore the rise of moral relativism and the new morality, these do not tend to be the sophisticates of the intelligentsia who dominate the mass media and set the trend, and who agree with Paramount Pictures and Emmanuelle that nothing ever really can be wrong if it feels *good*. To them, anyone who views the latest fashion in morals, or rather amorals, with alarm is by definition a professional crepehanger.

And then there are the sex-role revolutionists who actively encourage disarray in the sexual mores because they believe that this prepares the way for the world to be rebuilt according to their own vision. For example, psychologist John Money of Johns Hopkins University often appears in the pages of popular magazines and on TV screens encouraging the new freedom. He says the recent changes in the "ethics of recreational sex and in the morality of sex-coded roles are the basis of the sexual revolution," which he sees as the welcome, inevitable result of modern contraception, a longer life span and problems of population expansion.

"The need for a new ethic of recreational sex is not a luxury or an option," he says. "It is an imperative from which there is no escape. Our old ethic is, like Venice, sinking imperceptibly into the sea. We have succeeded neither in shoring up the old customs and morality of sexual relationships nor in restructuring them to meet the new tide of history."

On the other hand, there are those such as Professor Duncan Williams, author of *Trousered Apes*, who sees these changes not as a positive "new ethic," but as a disastrous shift from traditional Judeo-Christian ethics to the chaos of popular belief in godlessness, situational ethics and uncontrolled sexual lunacy. He wrote:

> Basically, I have no quarrel with such views which uphold the substitution of individual (i.e., internal) standards for the old-fashioned, legalistic and external ones. There is, however, a very real danger in the *popularization* of such ideas. Self-fulfillment demands a certain measure of restraint, of self-control. This is an adult concept, as I think even its exponents would agree, and in between these two plateaux, the old morality and the new self-fulfillment (or "self-actualization"), there exists a chasm into which, while attempting to cross, the majority falls. This chasm is self-indulgence, a descent to mere animal gratification, which pres-

ents the greatest danger to the immature who, vaguely aware of the demise of the old sanctions, delight in the permissiveness which increasingly pervades our society . . . instant gratification of all appetites with no bill to pay. . . .

Whether you regard the liberationist tide as "an imperative from which there is no escape" or as the dangerous "permissiveness which . . . pervades our society," you should be aware that it is being strongly promoted through the schools and colleges.

Robert Rimmer, author of *The Harrad Experiment,* in a 1973 interview with *Playboy* magazine said: "One of the things that absolutely fascinates me is the extent to which premarital cohabitation is being studied in the colleges. There's even a cohabitation-research newsletter. And they've had plenty to study. Last year at the University of Michigan, a student group called *Xanadu* set up a pattern of living with members of the opposite sex. Roommates were selected by pulling names out of a hat. This was very shocking to some parents and administrators. Yet I think it's a very valid idea; it lets you have the learning experience of being thrown in with another human being. You learn to see a man or a woman as a whole person."

When *Reader's Digest* editor Lester Velie reported the results of his extensive study of the "War on the American Family," in 1973, he noted that "the key battleground is the college campus." Velie found that "publishers are knocking themselves out to print books that predict marriage is finished and offer 'alternatives to marriage and the family.' "

Velie mentioned two books in particular—*The Family in Search of a Future: Alternate Models for Moderns,* and *The Family in Transition: Rethinking Marriage*—which discuss such alternatives to traditional marriage as mate-swapping, group marriage, homo-sexual marriage, communal families and polygamy.

"Checking with publishers," reported Velie, "I found that *The Family in Search of a Future* is re-quired reading on 150 campuses from Maine to Califor-nia. Another 100-odd campuses require students to read *The Family in Transition.*"

Professors admitted to Velie that even though the incidence of such practices are actually rare in society, they were teaching these alternatives to conventional marriage, not just as deviant forms of behavior, but as "workable and possibly even desirable alternatives."

"We hope," one professor said, "that our students will begin to question the values that they always have taken for granted [i.e., the values of monogamous mar-riage and a family] and at least consider the alterna-tives."

Public school courses have been influenced for the past 20 years by the work of the National Science Foun-dation, which recently has been criticized for its efforts to shift child development from the values of the local communities to those of the new intelligentsia. It turns out that millions of public dollars have been invested in development of school curricula, such as one that has come under fire called "Man, A Course of Study" (MACOS).

MACOS is a course for elementary school children that one of its developers, Peter B. Dow, says questions "some values that might be regarded as characteristi-cally American" and "the notion that there are 'eternal truths' that must be passed down from one generation to the next."

Republican U.S. Representative John B. Conlan, who has opposed the curriculum, puts his criticism bluntly: "Embedded in the MACOS material is an 'anything goes' philosophy which subtly unteaches morality, pa-

71

triotism, American values, Judeo-Christian ethics and beliefs, so that children will be more accepting of a 'world view' rather than an American view."

In reply to such attacks by citizens' groups who see such courses as encouragements to children to abandon the value systems they are taught at home, Peter Dow says, "Our object is not to break down American values but to generate sensitivity to other values. We are trying to break down the view that because your culture is good for you, it is necessarily good for someone else."

One mother of three who has worked to get rid of the MACOS program told me, "Well, we are trying to break down the view that it is any of the National Science Foundation's or the school's business to be dabbling in our children's social or political values."

Another mother said, "While the schools are doing all this, they are not teaching our children the basic skills."

These curricula do have a certain Orwellian quality about them. For instance, a teacher's guide to one program for high school students, called "Exploring Human Nature," states: "As the population crunch becomes more severe and as more is learned about the genetic basis of particular human traits, it is likely that there will be increasing advocacy of various sorts of eugenic measures. . . ."

"Such policies could be enforced," the guide says, "with the aid of various types of coercion, ranging from propaganda and tax incentives to government licensing of the right to reproduce."

For class discussion, the guide suggests the students consider: "How could we, as a society, decide which genes to favor and which to select against? Who would make these decisions, and how would they obtain the authority to do so? What values do we value most in human beings?"

In another section on adolescence, students are asked to read diaries in which other youngsters tell about sexual experimentation and premarital intercourse, and in a related course the students are asked to write their own sex diaries.

These curricula are just a few of hundreds across the country that are being challenged in recent years in the national conflict over what social, moral, political and personal values should be taught to children and who should be responsible for teaching them. One evening last year, I asked the students in my adult education class at Montgomery College to discuss the situation:

"Well, I just can't believe all that is going on in the schools today," one mother responded. "The children are not disciplined, and they aren't even supposed to be taught anything like patriotism, or even what is right and wrong."

"I think the kids get the idea that their parents' values haven't worked, and eventually they just give up and wonder why they should have any values at all," said a father in the class.

"There is so much anger and violence in the teenagers today," said a woman. "Especially the boys."

After the class, a woman came up and spoke to me, confiding that she was divorced and felt at a loss to exercise any control at all over her children. "You just can't tell them anything about how to behave or to treat people. They just laugh and say that that's all old-fashioned. All they understand is just what their friends think—do your own thing, and whatever you feel like doing is all right. They don't have any respect for me or for anyone else."

It is almost as though many parents and teachers today have given up and expect the young people to invent their own values without reference to those of their families, or to any religious or cultural heritage. It is as though we believe that the knowledge of the young might really be more valuable than the social learning that has delivered us through the ages as a culture. There is likewise a trend away from requiring any special standards of conduct in the private lives of teachers, as though high moral character is no longer considered a relevant qualification for leading the young.

Midge Decter, author of *Liberal Parents, Radical Children,* has written a great deal about the postwar generation who are now young adults and about the difficulties many of them seem to have had taking their places in the world. She also speaks widely on problems of youth and on the sex-role revolution. Not long ago, I heard her speak at the National Town Meeting in Washington, D.C.

"I think that the sexual revolution has created a kind of chaos in the manners and mores and sexual lives of young women that they do not know how to deal with," she said. "It is one thing to say, 'Okay, here's the Pill, here's your freedom. No one's bothering you. Premarital sex is no longer considered immoral.' It's quite another for a young woman who suffers, let's say, as adolescent girls suffer, from all kinds of questionings and uncertainties about herself to know what to do with this freedom. And none of us is able to give her guidance anymore. I think that young women particularly are suffering from the chaos of feeling there is no way to trace a consequence from any action."

We live in a society that, rather than guiding its young, has come to look to its children to set the trend. And, yet, we also know that children need guidance, because whether they feel it is so or not, there *are* consequences to their actions, and eventually they have to deal with them. This, after all, is the great advantage to human beings of their arts, customs, traditions and the other forms of social knowledge that accu-

74

mulate over the generations. We don't have to keep starting over, relearning it all from scratch.

But the anything-goes society, it seems, despises the authority of knowledge from the past. The past gave us War, and Prejudice, and Sexual Repression. Why, everybody knows Sexual Repression is an awful thing to have. When it comes to sex, if we don't let it all hang out—so to speak—well, it can make us sick!

On the other hand, the advocacy of complete sexual freedom, some say *license,* would seem to make more sense if modern birth control were effectively protecting society from unwanted children and if the Pill were not linked to increased risks of liver tumor, gallbladder disease, kidney trouble, cerebral thrombosis, breast cancer and heart disease. Hypertension—high blood pressure—is a destructive, life-shortening result in 25 percent of women who use the Pill. Use of birth control pills is fatal to numerous women each year, and while this risk is said not to be great, for those who die it is 100 percent.

Researchers at the University of California at Berkeley suggest the possibility that female sex hormones contained in birth control pills may even inhibit normal brain development in women who take them over a long period of time. Another risk that has become known recently is to the babies of women who unwittingly take birth control pills early in pregnancy, before they know they are pregnant. The chances are nearly tripled that these children will be born with malformed hearts, and there is increased risk of other defects as well. And other recent reports suggest that the Pill may be responsible for physiological changes in the genital tract that make women more susceptible to venereal diseases and other infections.

Indeed, the social advantages of trying to temper sexual activity outside of marriage may make more sense when you realize that we have a teenage pregnancy epidemic and sexually transmitted diseases are pandemic—wildly out of control throughout the world today.

Government authorities estimate that the incidence of gonorrhea in the United States is between 2.5 and 3 million new cases a year, and the number of syphilis cases has increased to 100,000 annually. At a recent conference in New York City, Dr. Leonard L. Heimoff of Cornell University Medical College reported that of the 80,000 cases of syphilis discovered in 1974, about 30,000 were in primary and secondary infectious stages. Perhaps four or five times as many cases are never reported, the epidemiologist said.

Each year thousands of people are being infected with venereal diseases that have only recently been discovered. "The sexually transmitted diseases are no longer confined to syphilis, gonorrhea, chancroid, lymphopathia venereum and granuloma inguinale," Dr. Heimoff told his learned colleagues. He said the newly discovered diseases now include conditions caused by "viruses, chlamydia, myoplasmas, tricho-monas and *as yet unidentified agents.*"

Over 3 million Americans are known to contract these diseases every year. Moreover, not all of them are curable, and they can lead to a long list of complications, which include sterility, arthritis, Reiter's disease, prostatitis, pelvic infection, urinary tract infections, meningitis, birth defects and heart problems. A leading medical insurance organization recently circulated pamphlets to its customers, warning: "Among un-treated cases of syphilis: 1 in 200 will become blind, 1 in 50 will become insane, 1 in 25 will become crippled or incapacitated, 1 in 15 will become a syphilitic heart victim. And nearly 4,000 people die each year in the United States as a result of the damage done to their bodies by the ravages of syphilis."

Half of VD cases are among teenagers and young adults, and authorities have calculated that teenagers contract some form of VD at a rate of about one every two minutes. Perhaps the saddest complications are those passed along to the offspring of infected women and girls, as in congenital syphilis and what is known as neonatal infection by the herpes simplex virus. Both of these common venereal diseases produce deformed and diseased children. And there is *no known cure* for herpes simplex, a rampaging sexual disease that afflicts victims with extremely painful sores, and that often leaves an infected mother's offspring with serious disorders of the eyes and nervous system. (Some babies escape infection—if the disease is detected in the mother in time—through Caesarean delivery, but physicians say that unfortunately this is not always effective in avoiding contamination.) There is presently an epidemic of herpes in this country, as in most other countries of the world.

Mounting scientific evidence now indicates that herpes infection is directly involved in the development of cervical cancer in women. This tumor, frequently fatal, is far more common in promiscuous women than others, and scientists now believe that the potential for this cancer is often passed from males to females in the form of herpes infection during sexual intercourse.

And the situation is getting worse, not better. Research shows that syphilis can live and continue to progress in the nervous system, or eyes, even though the patient receives generous doses of penicillin. Medical experts are now worried about the possible emergence of entirely new strains of bacteria that may be completely untreatable. Scientists at the U.S. Center for Disease Control are on the verge of panic over the recent appearance of gonorrhea-producing bacteria totally resistant to even massive doses of penicillin. This penicillin-resistant gonorrhea is spreading rapidly around the world and has already popped up in many parts of the U.S. The next line of defense against these organisms is spectinomycin, an antibiotic that costs seven times as much as penicillin. This agent has been used successfully to cure most cases of this strain so far, but now spectinomycin-resistant cases have been reported, and public health authorities say they don't know what they will do if such cases become widespread. The ability of medical science to combat these new strains of "superclap" grows increasingly in doubt.

Dr. Ralph H. Henderson, director of the center's VD control division, told interviewers not long ago that the U.S. gonorrhea epidemic of the mid-1970s is "frightening."

"With any other infectious disease," Dr. Henderson declared, "people would be running around taking very extreme measures to see it didn't spread any further."

A rather perverse aspect of VD is that people often experience no immediate symptoms, and so they go around infecting others without even knowing it. Another serious side is the cost. The text of the Health Information and Health Promotion Act passed by Congress in 1976 states that "it is conservatively estimated that the public cost of care for persons suffering the complications of venereal disease exceeds $80,000,000 annually."

We worry about the pollution of our rivers and air, but somehow we don't hear very much about this pollution with devastating disease that the sexual revolution is inflicting on our own bodies. There is no doubt about it, with epidemics of such grave, complicated and costly diseases threatening the public health, there are solid grounds for regarding promiscuous sexual behavior as a *serious antisocial activity.*

Why don't we hear much about this direct link between rampant sex and ravaging disease? The answer by and large is simply that our conventional wisdom in the 1970s is that nothing could be as bad as the dread Sexual Repression. In the absence of any rules of right and wrong, it is just plain *unfashionable* to suggest that anyone ought to restrain his sexual impulses.

Ann Landers advises mothers who discover that their daughters are fooling around to fix them up with birth control provisions. "And please," she says, "don't any of you out there write and clobber me for not advising the mother to give her daughter a lecture on morals. It's too late for that."

Dear Abby advises parents who discover their daughter is a lesbian to "accept her as she is and let her know it."

I recall hearing Dr. Joyce Brothers recommend adultery as a possible cure for troubled marriages. She said so many women had told her how helpful an affair can be for a stale marriage that she came to favor the idea. But when she was asked if there is any way to tell ahead of time if such an adventure would be helpful or harmful to a particular marriage, she replied, "No, there is no way to tell."

In *Today's Health,* sociologists William A. Simon and John Y. Gagnon tell us that sex no longer exemplifies "health and illness, good and evil, excess and restraint, the essence of the masculine and feminine—if it lies not only in the domain of personal morality, but in the domain of personal choice, then sex can no longer stand for significant social or personal oppositions." Sex is now just a form of "play," they conclude.

> If sex is merely a form of play, then our concerns with who does it, how old they are, what their marital status is (unless we are concerned with disease or pregnancy) is misplaced.

When sex is fun, it is subject to the morality of fun. It is entered into by choice and anyone may do whatever good manners dictate; the rules are made up by the partners. We may wish to restrict elders with children, but what objection do we have to older people teaching younger people about games or sport? Since play is nonconsequential, it is done with low emotional input except by professionals whose livelihood depends on the activity. There is an interest in skill, but only to improve the content of the game itself.

These writers also speak of sex as a private matter, *not a public concern,* and declare that this is "an increasingly important value in the society."
They also assert:

It is apparent that the psychosocial changes necessary to alter the process will not affect all sectors of the population at the same time or penetrate them at the same rate.

The major pattern of change will be the softening of gender identity lines. It will take most of its force early in life by more strongly curbing aggression among males, an increased dressing alike among children, and patterns of child rearing in which the occupational dimension of male life is nearly totally removed from the life of the child.

These lib planners go on to tell us:

It is our expectation that young people in the future will be more sexually active than their parents or even any generations over thirty in 1970. These changes will be relatively slow in occurrence, and increases in the proportions of the sexually active will be smooth and not eruptive in character. Toward the end of this 25-year period, there will begin to be a steady increase in sexual activity among young people under 16, and general increases in erotic behavior during early adolescence.

Recent years have brought a flood of such writings in books and articles encouraging unbridled sex, cohabitation, swinging, open marriage, you name it. The authors of one book, *Hot & Cool Sex*, advocating open marriage as a means of adding dimension to humdrum marital existence, prefer to speak of the practice as developing "satellite relationships." This I gather is intended to update the connubial state for the space age. Benjamin DeMott in the *Atlantic Monthly* had this to say about the recent deluge of writings on the sexual scene: "What lies ahead, apparently, is a struggle between the parties of Intensity and Cool—trust and commitment versus variety and surprise—that could change the minds of millions. And perhaps the single sure thing about the prospect is that if, in choosing sides, people are guided by purely technical sexological considerations (and vocabulary), nobody on earth will win."

The vocabulary of the Sexperts, as writer George Gilder has called them, is that of sexual liberation. The word *restraint* is not a part of it. And yet, if we are rational we see that every lesson of life supports the knowledge that when we are under siege, whether by human enemies or bacteria, survival as a species demands that we not respond as children playing a game, but that we resist with the discipline and prudence of adults. But these are not congenial qualities to the disseminators of the anything-goes perspective. The Sexpert "sociologists" Simon and Gagnon give their game away with their demur, "unless we are concerned with disease or pregnancy." How can we *not* be concerned unless we abandon social responsibility al-

81

together? But that, it seems, is exactly what many people have done rather than risk the appearance of prudery in the face of a rising sexual revolution.

I once heard Erica Jong, a popular writer for the anything-goes audience, say, "I firmly believe that given complete promiscuity in adolescence, most healthy people choose not to be promiscuous later on. I firmly believe that even people who are given sexual freedom wind up monogamous eventually, because monogamy is really a better way to live, but it's not forced on them by guilt—it is, rather, freely chosen after a period of painful experimentation."

Erica Jong *recommends* promiscuity as a sort of training ground for monogamy. Like so many other liberationist theories, however, this one seems feasible only in a make-believe world. What if during your recruit training for monogamy you contract a disease that can't be cured, infect a dozen or so fellow recruits, later fall in love with a person who, it turns out, prizes chastity, and as an encore eventually pass along your little ailment to your subsequently retarded child? Unfortunately, it happens every day. Personally, I'll take a mild dose of Sexual Repression any day over a case of herpes simplex or a new strain of gonorrhea that nobody knows how to cure. I have even known of people surviving total abstinence.

Another condition you don't hear much about these days is chastity. But one epidemiologist, Dr. Charles Millard of the Rhode Island State Health Department, criticized his colleagues in the medical profession not long ago for what he called the "paucity of information and agencies advocating and supporting premarital chastity among young girls."

Writing in *Resident & Staff Physician*, a journal for M.D.s, the doctor points out that studies throughout this century have consistently reported that half of the women born since 1900 have had sexual relations before marriage, and that this incidence of premarital relations is exactly the same today. What has changed, he says, is the pressures on girls. In past years, the pressures of public opinion worked to reinforce the value of chastity.

"Today," declares Dr. Millard, "the girl who doesn't want to 'go all the way' before marriage is considered ridiculously puritanical not only by her peers, *but also by her professors*. From every side she gets pressure to experiment, to 'free' herself of her 'inhibitions'. . . ."

The doctor blames all of this on the overall social atmosphere that recklessly encourages runaway irresponsibility. "The inundation of the public—via newspapers, magazines, radio and TV—with stories and articles with marked emphasis on sex, sexual freedom and the advocacy of new sexual mores is apparent to even the casual observer," he says. "All of these factors, plus peer pressure, are subjecting these young people to an unfair and unjust psychological assault. . . ."

"I don't care, Norbert. My doctor says chastity is still the safest method!"

Dr. Millard encourages physicians to offer supportive counseling to young women who choose premarital chastity by pointing out that this approach to sexual liberation offers some valuable freedoms, such as freedom from the possibility of the various disorders, infections and tragedies that can accompany sexually transmitted diseases, freedom from the possible risks associated with the Pill, freedom from unwanted pregnancy, freedom from the trauma and complications of abortion, and freedom from the family unhappiness and stunted prospects often imposed by unwanted pregnancy, and the disadvantages of a single-parent home.

"There is hardly a doctor who cannot discuss VD and the advantages and disadvantages of various kinds of contraception," declares Dr. Millard. "But when a girl comes in and asks why she shouldn't participate in sexual activity before marriage, the doctor is often at a loss to come up with arguments that are acceptable to her and will make sense when she relays them back to her peers."

Dr. Natalie Shainess, a New York psychoanalyst, made similar observations. "The prevailing attitude is that virginity is something a girl must 'get rid of,' " she says. She thinks this is destructive to young women. "The first sexual experience for a young woman involves some physical pain. There should be a feeling of eagerness and a loving orientation to overcome this discomfort. What is happening, however, is that girls are giving themselves to anyone, willy-nilly, just to shed their virginity. What should be an important experience as the beginning of sexual maturation for a young woman instead teaches her nothing positive about sex that can lead her into a more enjoyable sexual experience as time goes on. It's very damaging for the girl emotionally."

Despite widespread speculation by advocates of the

new morality that increased sexual activity will lead to better selection of mates and more gratifying and lasting marriages, it may not be true.

"There are no reliable studies," says Dr. Millard, " . . . which support the thesis that premarital sex will result in a happier or more satisfactory marriage— either sexual or otherwise. . . ."

It is the same with sex education for children. Not long ago, I noticed a diagram in a popular magazine intended to demonstrate through analogy that the need for sex education by children is similar to their need for good nutrition.

The funny thing about the article was that the authors demolished their own argument by admitting that they could find no proof either that children suffer from not having sex education or that they grow up to be any different from those who do get it.

Lack of adequate nutrition, on the other hand, produces demonstrable consequences. So does overeating, underexercising, undersleeping, overdrinking and smoking. The point is that that article on sex education got me to thinking—I wonder if a better analogy in our anything-goes society might not be between overeating and oversexing. They're both personal indulgences that have serious effects on the health and vigor of the nation. The thing about overeating of course is that the effects are more conspicuous than those of oversexing (not *always,* but generally speaking). You get fat, and everyone can see it.

Obesity is a serious disease that greatly increases a person's chances of suffering from high blood pressure, heart disease, gallbladder and liver disorders, angina pectoris and diabetes. Yet millions of people willingly jeopardize their health every day by stuffing themselves with hundreds of extra, harmful calories, while the nation foots a staggering medical bill ($133 billion in a recent year) to try to salvage the bodies people often don't care enough about to protect in the first place.

Obesity is just one example. The major killers of Americans—heart disease, cancer and stroke—are also among the many disorders frequently associated with the personal habits of their victims. Government authorities now say that six of the ten leading causes of death in the U.S. are diet-linked. In 1976, a spokesman for the Public Health Service, Dr. Marvin Schneiderman, told a National Cancer Society seminar for science writers that 30 to 40 percent of the deaths from cancer every year could be prevented if Americans would change bad habits of eating, drinking and smoking. Nearly 100,000 lives a year could be saved from cancer alone if people would take better care of their health.

Let's face it. The physical fitness of Americans, young and old, has steadily *worsened* in recent years largely because of the anything-goes attitudes that permeate the habits of the nation. Whether we are talking about our health, sexual behavior, or any other aspect of our lives, the anything-goes way of life is directly opposed to the self-discipline and prudent concern for the consequences of our behavior essential for effective and mature living. Somewhat the way we have come to blame "society" for our personal failings, obese persons often blame their condition on faulty "metabolism." Yet physicians say that only about one percent of obesity cases actually result from endocrine gland disorders. Perhaps we should look carefully at our national character for a clue to the sources of our current sloppy societal condition.

Let's take a look at ourselves. During the period between 1950 and 1973—while the proportion of mothers (with husbands) who marched out to jobs doubled

—the suicide rate among teenagers almost tripled, soaring from 2.7 per 100,000 in 1950 to a shocking 7 per 100,000 in 1973.

In the 1970s, the proportion of mothers (with husbands present) who go out to work has grown to an all-time high of 40 percent—at the same time that assaults on teachers in the schools have increased 77.4 percent, robberies of students and teachers have increased 36.7 percent, rapes and attempted rapes by youngsters have risen 40.1 percent, and juvenile homicide has increased 18.1 percent.

In the years since 1963—which just happen to be the same years of the drive to get wives and mothers out of the home—the performance of school children in reading, writing, mathematics and other tasks of critical thinking have taken a nose dive unequaled in the history of American education. Despite unparalleled expenditures of money for education, tests of youngsters in elementary and secondary schools and in higher education in every part of the country show a steady deterioration of basic skills. In these years of rising divorce, broken homes and faltering family life, educators have become alarmed at the mounting evidence that the coming generation knows less about nearly every academic subject than previous generations, and that their written work has degenerated into "primitive sentence structure and vocabulary."

The federal National Assessment of Educational Progress program reported late in 1975 that "American teenagers are losing their ability to communicate through written English." The report said, moreover, that an unprecedented proportion of the kids lack skills essential for functioning in modern society. Not only are they unable to read well, they can't even relate what they read to the everyday tasks of life.

Dr. Terrel H. Bell, U.S. commissioner of education,

admitted that he was shocked with the results of the NAEP report, and declared: "The results of this study call for a major rethinking of education on several levels."

In 1976, the National Cancer Society noted that smoking among teenage girls had risen 5 percent since 1969 and was still rising. The girls also smoke more cigarettes per person, according to the society, which attributed the trend to changing values and increasing permissiveness in the society. Oh yes, the girls have really come a long way, baby, and a quarter of the cigarette smokers also smoke marijuana regularly, too.

A national survey of 13,000 young people in 1975 by the National Institute on Alcohol Abuse and Alcoholism showed that 28 percent of the nation's teenagers are problem drinkers. The study revealed that more than 80 percent of 17-year-olds have done at least some drinking, even though drinking is not legal until age 18, and about one-fourth of 13-year-olds are regular drinkers.

Women have been advancing in the FBI's Crime Index too. While the number of female offenders is still much lower than males, the number of women arrested for serious crimes increased more than 275 percent since the 1960s, as compared to an increase of 87.9 percent by males. More than 7,000 women were arrested on weapons charges in 1973, for instance, compared to just over 1,700 in 1960.

"It's fashionable for women to act aggressive and carry guns now," explained a young woman serving a life sentence for homicide. "It's part of being liberated."

Runaway wives and mothers became another statistic of liberation in the 1970s. Tracers Company of America, Inc., a firm in New York that investigates missing persons, reports that runaway wives have outnumbered missing husbands by two to one in recent years, compared to a ratio of 300 husbands to one wife who ran away in 1960. One investigator said, "Women's lib is constantly in the news. Wives are told by women's groups that they should be tired of being confined at home, of being sex objects."

One wife and mother who deserted her family expressed her inability to commit herself to the demands of marriage in these words: "I think that marriage as it is presently constituted, within the law and the church, is such a raw deal for women. It really is. When the law says that a man's job in a marriage is to provide support —not emotional support, not love, not anything, just support—and a woman's job is to provide household duties and sexual consortium, then it stinks! It really does, until they have marriage laws, for example, that say—all right, there are two people in this marriage who have agreed to be mutually supporting in every possible way."

Then she paused, and, thinking better of even this kind of commitment, declared, "But then, on the other hand, how can you promise that you are going to feel a certain way for X amount of time. I mean, that doesn't make a lot of sense to me."

Perhaps as many as a million children in the United States each year are now thought to be victims of abuse or neglect, according to the National Center on Child Abuse and Neglect, and some 2,000 victims are said to die each year. "If this were a communicable disease that affected so many children," declared the center's director, Douglas Basharov, "we'd call it an epidemic."

This problem like all the others I have mentioned has grown as women have moved out of the home more and more in recent years. "There are a lot more children that don't have supervision because both parents are working—that seems to be an increasing trend," said another official at the National Center.

The country's leading authority on this subject, Dr.

89

Norman A. Polansky, prepared the official government report on child abuse published in 1975, which said:

> Some experts have the impression that there is now more neglect in middle class families from the affluent suburbs than heretofore. Children are left alone at relatively young ages while their parents go out of town; many are left unsupervised for long periods; others turn up at school unkempt or inappropriately dressed for the weather. Often, such instances are associated with parental alcoholism, but sometimes they reflect a more pervasive trend to abdicate parental responsibility in favor of personal gratification.

A pediatrician told me, "There has been an alarming increase in child abuse during the past ten years, and if anything, it's getting worse."

No one can doubt that these distressing facts result from an array of complex factors operating in society in recent years. And no one can actually prove exact cause and effect relationships between these complicated webs of behavior. But there are bountiful grounds for the suspicion that the reason so many of this nation's children are out of hand and desperate, and its schools in chaos, is that the guidance and discipline of family life have been eroded by the fashionable expectation that other institutions can take its place.

The chief of police in the county where we live, Kenneth W. Watkins, retired a short time ago. Before he retired, however, he was interviewed about the problems of juvenile crime in our area.

"Women's liberation," Chief Watkins said, "with mothers competing outside the home, often leads to neglect in the family. I think a young elementary or junior high student looks at his parents being home as a real resource for him. Youngsters who don't have this kind of thing to hang on to go to a peer or something else that is going to fulfill that need, be it right or wrong. Youngsters need something. They have to know 'mom's going to be there when I get home.' When they know she's not going to be there, I think there's a certain amount of trauma."

This distress due to parental neglect, Chief Watkins said, can lead to dependence on drugs or membership in a gang as youngsters grope around for something to fill the void experienced from being left to their own resources and interests too early in life.

The feminists in our county shrieked when Chief Watkins spoke his mind, but there are, in fact, many voices these days raising questions about the value and wisdom of the sex-role revolution.

An attorney who taught at the Georgetown University Law School for many years, Al. Philip Kane, recently wrote a letter to the editor of the *Washington Star,* in which he said: "As individual rights come to be considered more important than familial rights, the 'domestic' marriage deteriorates into an 'atomistic' form of family where the so-called individual rights run riot and the family virtually ceases to exist as a unit. . . ."

Mr. Kane related the fall of the civilizations of both Greece and Rome to the decline of the "domestic" marriage, which "became 'atomistic' and unable to support the civilization in which it existed."

"If anyone thinks that 'women's lib' and 'zero population growth' are new and previously untried movements, they should but read the histories of Rome and Greece," wrote Mr. Kane.

"The force of public opinion is tremendous on the side of increasing individual rights as against those of the family," he continued. "But what the 'rights' exponents do not realize is that for every right there is a correlative duty. . . . A woman has the right to determine whether she shall marry. Marriage (absent birth control and abortion) normally results in having children. Having exercised her rights and having had children, is there not a duty imposed upon her to care for them (and for her husband) which may impose on her the correlative duty of not making her principal life outside the home?"

If the feminists shrieked at Chief Watkins, I can just imagine the reaction to Mr. Kane's remarks. The belief of the sex-role reformers, of course, is that the wife has no more responsibility to stay at home than the husband does, and the husband in turn has no special responsibility to support the wife and kids.

Perhaps the most cogent assault upon the conventional perception of these ideas as a "liberating" force for women has been George Gilder's *Sexual Suicide*. Gilder describes women's lib as just one of the destructive forces combining today to undermine the value of the family, to divorce sex from procreation, to reduce women to the condition of men, and to encourage promiscuity. When this basically male social orientation prevails, says Gilder, males dominate everything in the culture, and society begins to disintegrate. He goes on to observe,

> The women's movement, the *Playboy* chauvinists, the gay liberationists, the sexologists, and the pornographers all tend to indulge and promote such a disintegration. They all present alternatives to loving sexuality. The man and woman who are attempting to fulfill their sexual natures in an affirmative way are bombarded with contrary ideologies. The pornographer persistently and pervasively advertises the potential joys of promiscuity—of unknown but shapely bodies—continuously stimulates primitive male impulses, and subverts the at-

tempt to maintain monogamous ties. The sex manuals present utopian images of the bliss that comes with an abandonment of "inhibitions" and "stereotypes" that may be important to affirmative sexuality. The women's movement offers visions of a spurious sexual equality, in which women are to be considered erotically the same as men. The homosexuals romanticize a pattern in which ultimate sexual fulfillment is impossible and in which the temporary gratification is paramount. These forces together create an undertow that threatens to sweep into a chaos of male rhythms the enduring structure of civilized sexuality.

In short, Gilder thinks that civilized society depends upon the complementary sexual natures of males and females—that we are not infinitely malleable. It is the nature of female sexuality that encourages long-range economic and social considerations, because the requirements of female sexual fulfillment extend beyond the exertions of the chase and the sex act to the prolonged activities of feeding, nurturing and raising the young. When these aspects of female sexuality are diminished in significance in favor of the male sexual rhythms of tension and release, with their emphasis on temporary gratification, the human patterns of continuity with nature and society break down. Writes Gilder,

Under these conditions, males find it increasingly difficult to observe long-term erotic horizons. Their sex lives become increasingly oriented toward the next conquest of a tempting body. And because their social and work motivations are so profoundly intertwined with their sexuality, they find their commitment to their jobs and communities also eroding. The emergence of impulsive male sexual patterns leads to short-circuit pursuits of crime and drugs. Other men may immerse themselves in the vicarious male rituals of T.V. football and violence, bombard their minds with the macho rhythms and incantations of high-volume rock or fuel their vanities with alcohol, immediate sex, and pornography. The commitment to work and community dissolves as the commitment to female sexual horizons declines.

Columnist William Raspberry once wrote of a man he had watched on TV who declared that what we need to do to remedy the recent crisis of discipline and learning in the schools is to "get back to structured learning . . . to get prayer back into the classroom, and the Star-Spangled Banner, and military science and moderate dress."

All of this reminded Mr. Raspberry of the child who wished he had a bushy tail so he could crack nuts with his teeth. "I'm not sure there's any more of a causal relationship between singing the national anthem and behaving in class (though those things used to happen simultaneously) than there is between the bushy tail at one end of a squirrel and the nutcracking ability at the other end."

I am not sure that there is such a causal relation either, but neither can I be sure that there is not. I do know that in science when different things occur in association with one another, when scientists suspect that they *could be* linked together in some causative relationship—such as cancers and environmental agents —they begin to take a serious look. What they do *not* do is encourage people to continue to indulge their taste for the suspicious agent, until it is shown absolutely not to cause disease.

"How I envy the Gibbon," said Malcolm Muggeridge, "who, looking back across the centuries at our decline and fall, will remark on how, as we systematically destroyed the values and restraints of our inherited way of life, we remained convinced that each innovation, each new assault on marital fidelity, on the home and parenthood, was bound to be conducive to our well-being and enlightenment."

Radical at the Core

If you ask a group of people what comes to mind when they hear the words feminism or women's lib, you are likely to get a variety of answers. A short time ago, I asked some of my students to jot down their answers to this query, and here is what some of them said:

"A lot of fanatical women."

"Equal opportunity for women."

"Gloria Steinem and Betty Friedan."

"A strident crusade."

"Equal pay for equal work."

"Lack of femininity, bra-burning."

And one woman replied simply, "Complete bewilderment." I think this last response expresses what my wife felt when she first began to look into the lib phenomenon. Most people, I find, don't know what to think of this movement, because feminists are working on various levels in their push for the sex-role revolution. On the one hand, they court public acceptance by striving to create an appropriately mainstream image through the mass media, emphasizing short-term goals such as equal pay, jobs and education. On the other hand, less diplomatic factions plug away openly at the whole sex-role revolution, of the nature of which most Americans remain perilously ignorant. You hear a great deal in the press from time to time about the feminists' "image problem." This is their dilemma of trying to figure out how to conduct a radical revolution without the general public finding out about it. For the most part, they have been very successful, but occasionally they fail at this, as we shall see.

From the beginning, the thing that has bothered Annie and me about the whole business is that most people just are not aware of the deep-down radical nature of this movement. This is true despite the fact that feminists are quite candid about the revolutionary nature of their intentions in their literature, in private discussions, and occasionally even in the press. For instance, *Ms.* magazine editor Gloria Steinem assures us that the women's movement is engaged in "a very major, deep revolution."

Most people pay only scant attention to such remarks, and despite the fact that the sex-role revolution is almost a decade old by now, it still hasn't occurred to most folks that the libbers may actually mean what they say. But if you *listen* to what they say, as we're about to do here, you are left with little doubt that the whole

98

recent campaign to change our consciousness of the nature and roles of women has found its base in a radical fermentation.

This is what New Left sociologist Marlene Dixon, for example, wrote in *Ramparts* magazine in 1969 about the variety of feminist organizations she had found that had sprung up "from the nationally based middle-class National Organization of Women (NOW) to local radical and radical feminist groups in every major city in North America. The new movement includes caucuses within nearly every New Left group and within most professional associations in the social sciences. Ranging in politics from reform to revolution, it has produced critiques of almost every segment of American society and constructed an ideology that rejects every hallowed cultural assumption about the nature and role of women."

Ms Dixon was exhilarated by what she described as an underground movement with its own literature, mostly unknown outside of feminist circles. "Groups are growing up everywhere," she reported, "with women eager to hear a hard line, to articulate and express their own rage and bitterness. . . . The extent to which groups have become politically radical is astounding. A year ago the movement stressed male chauvinism and psychological oppression; now the emphasis is on understanding the economic and social roots of women's oppression, and the analyses range from social democracy to Marxism."

Since those days the literature of lib has become much less esoteric as it has found its way into books and anthologies on library shelves that describe the program and history of feminism for anyone to see. Some of these books have also been used in university courses in history and women's studies. Not long ago,

99

Annie and I decided to visit the book exchange at the University of Maryland to see what kinds of feminist literature were being used there.

We found a number of books on feminism being used in courses at Maryland, and two were of special interest. One was *Rebirth of Feminism*, the *New York Times*–CBS report mentioned earlier, and the other was Jo Freeman's *The Politics of Women's Liberation*. Both of these were required reading in a course called the History of Women in the U.S. since 1865.

I learned that this course was taught by Assistant Professor of History Hilda Smith, and I phoned Professor Smith to ask if she considered the volumes to be reliable references on the history of feminism. She told me that she did.

"Can you tell me if they are very widely used in university courses around the country?" I asked her next.

"Both of them are very widely used," she said.

These works serve as significant evidence of both the radical nature of the feminist revolution and of the fact that the unisex assault is—despite its diverse aspects— a coherent and unified movement to alter our system of sex roles, our traditional educational values and the fundamental direction of society. Both books were created with the help of numerous "moderate" feminists who hold important jobs within the Washington establishment, such as Catherine East, the executive secretary of the Citizens' Advisory Council on the Status of Women, and Mary Eastwood, an attorney in the Department of Justice. These works are intended to be, and indeed are recognized to be, authoritative references on the nature of the sex-role revolution. Let's see what they have to say.

The *Times*-CBS report states: "Each major branch of the women's movement—women's rights and women's liberation—from its own perspective is working toward the elimination of the sex-role system: By external reform of social institutions and internal raising of consciousness. . . . Thus, any action from lobbying for the equal rights amendment to establishing small groups to talk . . . about the nature of women's oppression is deemed appropriate if it challenges sex-role stereotyping. Not only are all such actions 'appropriate,' but for the women's movement to progress toward its stated goal both external and internal approaches on each issue are essential. . . ."

The *Times*-CBS report goes on to say, "It is upon their perception of sexism as the underlying ideology of society, molding both social institutions, social relationships, and individual psyches, that feminists base their analysis, define their goals, and undertake activities to effectuate those goals. Whatever the tactics employed and language used, the goal for feminists is a sexual revolution, not simply in the traditional usage of that phrase—an easing of moral strictures on sexual relations—but rather a revolution to eliminate sexism in all its manifestations."

Specifically, we go on to learn that the key objectives of the revolution are abolishment of all sex roles, lessening of the importance of marriage and family, legitimization of homosexuality, free universal day care, abortion on demand, and feminist indoctrination in day-care centers and schools.

"Whereas moderate feminists describe marriage as an unequal partnership," the report states, "radicals define it as oppressive. In consequence, the moderates want to restructure the institution, the radicals to abandon it. . . ."

"Like so much of the current feminist activity," the report says, "the child care issue involves short-term and long-term goals. The short-term goals are simply to

101

get child care facilities from whatever source possible to serve whoever might need them. The long-range goal is, not surprisingly, the implementation of radically different theories of child rearing and preschool education. . . ." As Ti-Grace Atkinson, a founder of NOW, has said, "Any real change in the status of women would be a fundamental assault on marriage and the family. People would be tied together by love, not legal contraptions. Children would be raised communally; it's just not honest to talk about freedom for women unless you get the child-rearing off their backs."

In *The Politics of Women's Liberation*, feminist Jo Freeman declares, after years of direct personal involvement in the movement,

> There is clearly a symbiotic relationship between feminists within our governmental institutions, feminists operating in the private sphere, and even feminists who are openly opposed to and/or alienated from the American political system. . . .
> While there are disagreements over strategy and priorities, such differences are usually viewed as mutually complementary or irrelevant rather than contradictory to one another. . . .
> New ideas or activities are widely shared through both the feminist and commercial media. This keeps different segments from becoming totally isolated from one another. . . . There are interlocking informal communications networks throughout most of the movement through which information, ideas, contacts, and some resources are shared.

Jo Freeman's book describes, for example, how the Women's Bureau of the Department of Labor functions as a referral service for women who write asking how they can take part in feminist activities. Using lists provided by NOW and the Women's Equity Action League, federal employees at the Women's Bureau refer the women to women's liberation chapters in their vicinity.

An illuminating example of the way the Women's Bureau and the Status of Women Council cooperate with radical feminists to further their common cause is Jo Freeman's tale about the radical feminist "alienated from the American political system" whose directory of feminist groups, called *The Mushroom Effect*, ended up being used to answer government inquiries—including some received by the White House.

"Copies of this directory had been taken by its compiler to a small Minneapolis women's liberation conference in September 1970. Among the people there to whom it was given was a Midwest feminist who was also in occasional contact with Catherine East. As East's office was across the hall from the Women's Bureau, she was aware of their need and acquired a copy of *The Mushroom Effect* for them. Thus the work of a politically alienated feminist on the other side of the country was used to answer the White House's mail. . . ."

Jo Freeman makes it clear that without the radical feminists, there would be no push for the sex-role revolution, and without the less strident variety working within the establishment, the push would have no political effect:

> Because the movement was raising some issues and making some demands that were within the American value structure, it created a climate of expectations that something would be done. Issues such as the abolition of marriage or the use of

103

women as sex objects were not immediately transformable into valid public concerns, but those on educational and employment equality were. . . .

By making women's rights a public issue and expanding the area of conflict, the movement created a constituency for those "woodwork" feminists already within government. Many had been concerned with women's issues for years, but had been unable to impress those in positions of power with the priority of such issues. A public, politically active women's movement enabled them to say there was a popular demand for solution of such problems and thus strengthen their claims. As relationships between government officials and feminists developed, the former could also provide

"It's from the government. It says the president has referred my letter to the Women's Bureau of the Department of Labor, and they suggest I contact the Lesbian Center of the YWCA."

inside information to the latter about upcoming issues in which public pressure would be of mutual benefit. . . .

There are hardcore feminists, and among these there are the kind who dissimulate (my wife has dubbed these the "dissimulibbers")—they systematically deny for public consumption many of their radical purposes, pretending that they are just for equal pay, liberty and justice for all. Many dissimulibbers, for instance, have promoted the Equal Rights Amendment by insisting ERA has nothing to do with feminist issues. Then there are the lip-service libbers, who believe in a kind of pop feminism, of whom we'll have more to say in a later chapter.

From the beginning of our research, when we first started reading the feminist literature, Annie and I have been impressed with how different feminism is from the popular version presented in the media. For instance, it's almost amusing to see lib publicists on TV in recent years denying they ever meant to put down housewives, because the truth is that the feminist movement of this decade was begun with a book, *The Feminine Mystique,* which did just that.

In this book, Betty Friedan says that the *feminine mystique* is an awful affliction that "makes the housewife-mothers, who never had a chance to be anything else, the model for all women: it pre-supposes that history has reached a final and glorious end in the here and now, as far as women are concerned. Beneath the sophisticated trappings, it simply makes certain concrete, finite, domestic aspects of feminine existence— as it was lived by women whose lives were confined, by necessity, to cooking, cleaning, washing, bearing children—into a religion, a pattern by which all women must now live or deny their femininity."

The way she told it, you would never guess that in those days fathers were the biggest boobs in TV comedies or that it had been asserted in a White House Conference on Children and Youth (1960): "In the suburb the parental roles undergo considerable alteration. The mother becomes the authority figure of the family, since the father is away for such extended periods of the day." Perhaps she was an oppressed figure of authority. In fact, you would almost forget that the reason daddy is away so much is that he is working for those concrete, finite dollars that make all those trappings of domestic existence possible. No, it took an imagination of considerably devious resources to malign the American housewife the way Betty Friedan did in her writings of 1963.

She saw boring, wasted lives wherever she looked among the kitchens of America, even when the denizens professed to be perfectly happy!

In her book, she draws a portrait of a busy, happy homemaker, one who enjoys her home, family and friends, and performs her work with efficiency and satisfaction. Now you might think that Betty Friedan gave this woman the respect she deserved (especially if you had been reading the author's speeches of a decade later); you might think Ms Friedan saw this woman as a striving, constructive individual who had succeeded in building a satisfying and valid life for herself. In fact, you *would* think that, if you had been talking to Ms Friedan recently. But the truth is she didn't. Instead, what she actually wrote was: "Staring uneasily at this image, I wonder if a few problems are not somehow better than this smiling empty passivity. If they are happy, these young women who live the feminine mystique, then is this the end of the road?"

It was not long, of course, before Ms Friedan and others of her interloping persuasion wiped the smiles off of those feminine faces by presenting them with problems most of them had never thought of before.

Gabrielle Burton was one such convert. In the luxury and boredom of her upper-middle-class home, she wrote her own book (which Annie discovered at our local library) describing her flight from the life of a suburban housewife and mother of five into women's lib. (Ms Burton gave Betty Friedan the credit for turning her on to the pleasures of unhappiness.) Ms Burton writes in *I'm Running Away from Home, But I'm Not Allowed To Cross the Street:*

> My friends all considered me a great success—the most relaxed mother on the block. Few people knew of my discontent. It was not something I could articulate well, and I was ashamed that I felt it. I had no consistent culprits to accuse, no constructive alternatives to propose. There was only the recurring thought, "There's got to be more than this."
>
> I finally sought out the Women's Liberation Movement because of my constant guilt over daytime sleeping. Every afternoon, I would think, "I am going to wake up and discover that I am old and have never done anything with my life except sleep away time." Then I would lie down and take my nap.
>
> I went there with nothing to lose. It was a last ditch attempt with no high expectations. Perhaps I might be able to save my daughters. I knew that my life was irrevocably beyond my control.
>
> They told me I still had a chance. All around me there were women who had experienced the same things I had felt so guilty about. It wasn't me. It was something outside of me, and we were going to change it. . . .

A few pages later in Ms Burton's amazing confession she declares that "all of the women I have met through the Movement are stimulating, bright, creative, interesting human beings." Maybe so, but it is irresistible to pose the question: If women are driven to feminism for such reasons as hers—because of discontents beyond their control that lead to days of guilt-ridden sleep—isn't it just possible they could have used some of that brightness and creativeness to lead useful and satisfying lives within the context of everyday society? It's something to think about.

Gabrielle Burton tells us, "In my town, there is a collective of twelve lesbians. They are making their sexual commitments to women but they still wished to experience the pleasures of child-rearing. They took an infant to raise, each adult assuming one-twelfth parenthood. Anyone seeing the child at eighteen months cannot doubt her present happiness. She is a smiling, joyful creature, going readily to one and all."

Gabrielle Burton describes how the consciousness-changing groups help women confront the problems of life: "In the group we use a specialized way to talk to one another, called raising consciousness. This technique increases our sensitivity to the various forms of oppression in our lives. In order to adjust successfully to our conditions, most of us have had to develop elaborate blinders. Raising consciousness helps us recognize our blinders and let out our angers and frustrations so that we can take hold of our lives and rechannel ourselves. Ideally one raises consciousness to the point where one can and must change her life."

As we read on, we find there is more to it: "However," declares Ms Burton, "one quickly realizes that there are no personal 'solutions' possible. This is because it is not a personal 'problem.' Initially, most women join a group because of their personal unhappiness without realizing the ramifications of that unhappiness. A group can help individuals find partial alternatives, but eventually it must function as a collective action to change basic social structures. . . ."

And here we have the basic truth about women's liberation—it's not actually meant to be liberation for the individual women who take part in it; *the liberation is for the collective.* At bottom, what is meant is *liberation from the traditional laws, customs and beliefs bearing on the sex roles in Western society.*

"Remember above everything else," declares feminist Claudia Dreifus in *Woman's Fate,* her book of instructions on how to run a consciousness-changing group, "the primary goal of consciousness-raising is political. Always frame one's personal experiences within a political context."

Ms Dreifus makes it clear that the whole idea of

"The function of consciousness raising is to make you aware of how you are oppressed, so you can help your husband change."

consciousness-changing is to become aware of the radical feminist ideology. "Some feminist leaders think CR groups should be homogeneous, consisting only of members of the same ethnic, age, social, or marital group. They suggest sameness of background helps women reach feminist conclusions at a faster pace. . . . Most husbands are in some way culpable for the oppression of their wives. CR's function is to make you aware of how you are oppressed so you can help him change." Now what husband wouldn't want his wife to get into something like *that?*

"At our weekly discussions," says Ms Burton, "we piece together these common parts of our experiences to recognize prevailing conditions that stifle us all. We carefully look at society so we can see what it's done to us and what we can do about it."

All right, you are ready to become a real feminist. What do you suppose you will discuss at your weekly meetings? Here are a few "Rap Group Topics" from the "Do-It-Yourself Guide to Consciousness Raising" by Claudia Dreifus:

> Discuss attitudes of parents, brothers, and sisters toward girls. Talk about early sexual experiences. Was your brother given privileges you were not? . . . Tell about sexual experiences during puberty, early dating, menstruation, being pushed into sex roles. Were you attacked by a dirty old man? . . . What was your first sexual experience like? How do you relate sexually to men? Can you be aggressive? Do you need love to have sex? Do you believe in monogamy? Is the vaginal orgasm a myth? What is the relationship between love and sex? Is love a trap for women? . . . How are the sex roles divided in your household? Why did you marry in the first place? Is there another way for two people to love each other and live to-

110

gether? . . . Have you had close relationships with women? Were they satisfying? Are men the enemy? . . . Are you afraid of homosexuality? . . . What is the role of religion in oppressing women? . . .

According to Maren Carden, a feminist sociologist, "The idea of the consciousness-raising group probably derived from the New Left's discussions of Chinese Communists' group criticisms and from the young radicals' encouragement of open, democratic, and non-hypocritical expression of feelings. The groups are given many different names including 'cells,' 'affinity groups,' 'rap groups,' 'collectives,' 'support groups,' 'small groups,' or simply 'my Women's Liberation group.' . . . In the movement's early years they followed no specific guidelines but more recently participants have adopted suggestions about first, organizing, and second, running the groups from the movement literature."

When you actually read what the feminists have written, and listen to what they are saying, you get a clear impression of where they are heading.

Maren Carden says: "From its support of lesbians to its emphasis on sisterhood to its questioning of what are the biologically based sex differences, the new feminism presupposes social change. In order to better serve women's needs changes must be made in people's attitudes, in laws, institutions, and, ultimately, the whole social structure of American society. . . ."

In the epilogue of the tenth anniversary edition of *The Feminine Mystique*, Betty Friedan writes: "The changes necessary to bring about that equality were, and still are, very revolutionary indeed. They involve a sex-role revolution for men and women which will restructure all our institutions: child rearing, education,

111

marriage, the family, the architecture of the home, the practice of medicine, work, politics, the economy, religion, psychological theory, human sexuality, morality, and the very evolution of the race."

Another feminist writer, Jane O'Reilly, has said, "A feminist is someone trying to get more than just their [sic] slice of the Establishment pie. Feminists want a total change of attitude, not an enlarged, existing, competitive, aggressive, role-differentiated mess. A feminist is radical per se, against the deepest arrangements of the power structure."

"How will the family unit be destroyed?" asks Roxanne Dunbar in *Sisterhood Is Powerful*. "After all, women must take care of the children, and there will continue to be children. Our demand for full-time child care in the public schools will be met to some degree all over, and perhaps fully in places. The alleviation of the duty of full-time child care in private situations will free many women to make decisions they could not before. But more than that, the demand alone will throw the whole ideology of the family into question, so that women can begin establishing a community of work with each other and we can fight collectively. Women will feel freer to leave their husbands and become economically independent, either through a job or welfare. . . ."

Feminist Kate Millet wrote in *Sexual Politics:*

> In America one may expect the new women's movement to ally itself on an equal basis with blacks and students in a growing radical coalition. It is also possible that women now represent a very crucial element capable of swinging the national mood, poised at this moment between the alternatives of progress or political repression, toward meaningful change. As the largest alienated ele-

112

ment in our society, and because of their numbers, passion, and length of oppression, its largest revolutionary base, women might come to play a leadership part in social revolution, quite unknown before in history. The changes in fundamental values such a coalition of expropriated groups—blacks, youth, women, the poor—would seek are especially pertinent to realizing not only sexual revolution but a gathering impetus toward freedom from rank or prescriptive role, sexual or otherwise.

Anyone who doubts the radical intentions of women's lib has only to read what they say in their own literature. It's all plainly stated in books such as *The Second Sex* by Simone de Beauvoir, a very influential feminist author, and in magazines such as *Ms.* Here are some recent remarks of Simone de Beauvoir that reveal the sorts of things she has in mind for us:

> No woman should be authorized to stay at home to raise her children. Women should not have that choice, precisely because if there is such a choice, too many women will make that one.... Encouraging women to stay at home will not change society.... In my opinion, as long as the family and the myth of the family and the myth of maternity and the maternal instinct are not destroyed, women will still be oppressed.... We are trying to change society so that women, who do happen to be the people who give birth, can be full people in society. A whole new approach to child-rearing needs to be created—not just mother, but mother, father, society as a whole, the communal situation, if you wish, and the child care center and so on....

Listen to Betty Friedan, *nouveau* theologian, speaking on educational TV: "The women's movement is converging on the ecumenical movement with profound revolutionary implications for theology. It is that crisis out of which will come a humanist theology, and either the institutions of the church, of organized religion, are going to come to these new theological terms of the personhood of women, and in effect, of the new sexual morality or I would think that they are going to, as institutions, die."

Radical feminist Jill Johnston says in *Lesbian Nation* that women should reject men altogether, because they have oppressed women and become their natural enemies. Therefore, "it follows," she says,

> that the continued collusion of any woman with any man is an event that retards the progress of woman supremacy. The continued economic dependence of women upon men, both individually and through the social institutions, is perhaps the central concrete factor holding back the liberation of woman. . . . The totally woman committed woman, or lesbian, who shares this consciousness with other women, is the political nucleus of a woman's or lesbian state—a state that women cannot achieve by demand from the male bastion but only from within from exclusive woman strength building its own institutions of self-support and identity. . . . The male remains the biological aggressor and as such especially predisposed to take cultural-political advantage of the woman. It is against this advantage that feminism deploys itself.

Marlene Dixon writes in *Ramparts:* "The institution of marriage is the chief vehicle for the perpetuation of the oppression of women; it is through the role of wife that the subjugation of women is maintained. . . ."

Lib leader Germaine Greer declares in *The Female Eunuch:* "If women are to effect a significant ameliora-

114

tion in their condition it seems obvious that they must refuse to marry. . . . Women must also reject their role as principal consumers in the capitalist state. Although it would be a retrogressive step to refuse to buy household appliances in that women's work would be increased and become more confining than it need be, it would be a serious blow to the industries involved if women shared, say, one washing machine between three families, and did not regard the possession of the latest model as the necessary index of prestige and success. They could form household cooperatives, sharing their work about, and liberating each other for days on end."

According to feminist Martha Shelley in *Sisterhood Is Powerful:* "Lesbianism is one road to freedom—freedom from oppression by men. . . . Lesbianism involves love between women. Isn't love between equals healthier than sucking up to an oppressor?"

Not all feminists have appreciated the significance of lesbianism to the cause, but by the time of the 1975 meetings of the National Women's Political Caucus (an organization of feminists in the mainstream of American politics) this seemed to be changing. One of the members in Boston declared: "The movement in the past has resisted having lesbians up front and, say, on the media or as an open presence, because they were so afraid that women would be afraid to come into the movement or that everybody would be labeled a lesbian, and I think that this has very much changed now. There is a very supportive atmosphere and a real sharing together. We're beginning to understand the issues, and how lesbianism really affects all women and all people really."

If you investigate the literature of lib, you'll find writings by well-known figures such as *Ladies' Home Journal* columnist Letty Pogrebin, whose piece "Born

Free: A Feminist Fable" in *Woman: The Year 2000* glorifies collectivism, lib radicalism and homosexuality, and disparages free enterprise, marriage and the family.

You'll find, perhaps, Shirley MacLaine declaring as she did in the *Ladies' Home Journal* that she wants to "help make socialism respectable, because that's where we've got to go now. We're seeing that capitalism hasn't worked," she informs us, so now we "should be workin' to *change* the values.... We should be bandin' together to socialize oil and steel and medicine and education...." (In May 1976, on NBC News, John Lofton made an interesting comment on the character of Ms MacLaine's socialism: "I heard actress Shirley MacLaine denouncing capitalism, calling it a 'poisonous' and an 'exploitative' system. She said it is impossible to be both a feminist and a capitalist. Later this same day I opened the *New York Times* and there was a full-page ad promoting MacLaine's one-woman show at the Palace Theater in New York. The ad said that her performance had been the largest grossing show in the theater's history, bringing in $329,000 from April 19 through May 1, a sizable hunk of which, presumably, went into Miss MacLaine's bank account....")

Maybe you'll come across the strongly Marxist-Leninist writings of the Students for a Democratic Society, which have been disseminated on campuses across the country, declaring that "the struggle for equality of women is a revolutionary task—that is, one which cannot be completed under the present system of private property and the exploitation of the majority of people by a social class which is defined by its ownership of the means of producing wealth.... The fight for women's liberation is a concretization of the struggle for the liberation of all people from oppression. It doesn't stand apart from the fight against capitalism in our society, but rather is an integral part of that fight."

What all of this boils down to is that while there are undoubtedly some women who think they're just working for "equal pay" and "equal opportunity" when they promote the ERA or some other aspect of the feminist program, the movement is actually a unified thrust that gets its force from the radicals.

The trick of revolutionary fermentation is that it creates an unstable environment in which unexpected political shifts can happen before people know what is going on. Many a club woman who just believes in justice, equality and niceness is serving as the unsuspecting foot soldier of the feminist forces. Jo Freeman describes how it works:

> The existence of a diverse movement spanning a wide spectrum of feminist attitudes pushed the leaders of the more respectable women's organizations to more strongly feminist positions. Leaders of the Business and Professional Women's Clubs, who in 1966 had disdained activity that might be labeled "feminist," found themselves lobbying actively for all the women's legislation of the Ninety-second Congress and urging their large membership to apply pressure in their home districts. . . . The support of women from such established and responsible organizations added an aura of respectability to feminism. . . . Their acceptability was increased by those groups labeled radical or revolutionary and ridiculed by the media. The latter groups provided a "radical flank" against which other feminist organizations and individuals could appear respectable. . . .

Women's lib diplomats on TV may pretend, as I once heard Billie Jean King suggest, that feminism is just

117

about "equal pay for equal work," but if you read the literature of lib you will never again accept that idea. "Most feminists," says Jo Freeman, ". . . share a set of common ideas and symbols which provide for a basic unity. What ideological conflicts have emerged have been entirely within the younger branch of the movement and are not shared by all of it (e.g., whether one has to be a lesbian in order to be a feminist). . . . Unlike many sectarian leftist groups, different activities are seen more as a division of labor than as a means of divisiveness."

Sociologist Maren Carden says that "whether they accept the less radical or the more radical interpretation of the ideology, Women's Liberation participants become committed to that ideology in the same way. They exchange accounts of personal experiences, identify shared problems, and interpret these problems in terms of the movement's ideology. Having examined all aspects of their lives from this new perspective, they eventually reconceptualize their thinking and accept that perspective as the correct way to interpret women's experience."

Most people are for equal pay and equal opportunity. But a feminist, it seems, is something else. Whether she admits it or prefers to hide the fact, a feminist is someone who is encouraging a restructuring of society through obliteration of the sex roles. And in the end, perhaps the truth is just that you can't be a little bit feminist any more than you can be a little bit pregnant. All who work to deny and defeat the value of sex roles, however faint or fierce their contribution, are supporting the same revolutionary scheme.

Monitoring the Mass Media – The Sexes Get the Sack

My wife can't stand the press anymore, which is strange for a girl who married a budding journalist. Well, perhaps "can't stand" is too strong. Let's just say that our studies of the mass media's assault on the sexes have been disturbingly enlightening to both of us. Fortunately, there is also a certain amusement in the pastime of observing the pageantry of how clever writers, editors and social-scientific charlatans etch their chimeras about the complex doings of women and men.

The preeminent chimera among those defining the sexual situation of the nation in recent years should perhaps be considered Betty Friedan's *Feminine Mystique*. After studying the matter, Annie and I came to the conclusion that the book, widely credited with launching the recent feminist trend, presents a drastically distorted version of reality. Let's take a look at where this whole business began.

Ms Friedan says in her book that at one point in her

early career as a writer, she sat for many days in the New York Public Library, poring over past volumes of women's magazines. On one occasion, she says, she noticed that there seemed to be a great transformation in the image of women reflected in the pages of the old magazines. She detected a distinct shift of emphasis from the spirited career girls of the thirties and forties to the image of the happy, housewife-mother that prevailed through the fifties. (This is the image she came eventually to call the *feminine mystique*.) Betty was perplexed. Why was it, she wondered, that just as the proportion of American women working outside the home was increasing, the housewife-mother image of woman was spreading in the pages of the women's magazines? Eventually, she says, she discovered the answer: "I found a clue one morning, sitting in the office of a women's magazine editor—a woman who, older than I, remembers the days when the old image was being created, and who had watched it being displaced. The old image of the spirited career girl was largely created by writers and editors who were women, she told me. The new image of woman as housewife-mother has been largely created by writers and editors who are men."

She describes in her book how the portrayal of women in the mass media, especially in women's magazines, shifts periodically according to trends of the times and the whims of editors. But the answer of her editor friend as to the reason for the shift away from strong emphasis upon "the spirited career girl" seems to me a bit too facile, especially when, in the next breath, Betty Friedan tells us that *she helped create* the feminine mystique image of the fifties, which she says "makes the housewife-mothers, who never had a chance to be anything else, the model for all women. . . ."

Annie and I decided to retrace Betty's steps, so to speak, by spending some days of our own, not at the New York Public Library, but at the Library of Congress, going over the old magazines for ourselves.

What we discovered was that if you look through the women's magazines of the past fifty years or more, you find a variety of editorial mixes dealing with the same general ingredients—the basic subject matter of successful magazines aimed specifically at American women over all these years has to do with marriage, homemaking, family, child care, fashion, food, health, beauty, jobs, love, money, education, entertainment, civic affairs, travel and men. While the relative emphases on these subjects vary according to the era and the particular publication (*Mademoiselle, Cosmopolitan* and *McCall's,* for instance, have completely different emphases), the basic ingredients remain the same. These ingredients did not change during the 1950s, the era of "togetherness," but the *focus* was very much on the family. These styles come and go as the writers and editors get bored and the expectations of readers are gradually shifted to new focuses of interest.

Just to show you how consistent have been the broad themes in successful women's magazines, let's try a little test. Look over the following six lists of titles of articles from women's magazines from 1920 through the 1970s, and try to guess which list of articles appeared in which decade. Go ahead, try it:

(1) The Joys of Being Married / Cross-stitch Rose Place Mats / Children Who Need Care / How Husbands Really Feel About Working Wives / Blouses on the Soft Side / Mothering / Women in Engineering / Salads That Bear Fruit / The Candidates and Their Wives / Bathrooms Can Be Beautiful / The Power of a Woman / Swing at the Gym.

(2) Wife-ing It / Needlework Designs Older Than

123

King Tut / Your Child's Emotions / The Fifty-fifty Husband / Chic For Street or Travel Wear / The High Cost of Babies / Women in Wall Street / Fresh Fruit Desserts —Icy Cold / The Crime Wave in Art / Divorce / Baked Potatoes Can Be Delicious / Women in Athletics and Competitive Games.

(3) Making Good as a Parent / This Nice Kitchen Works / Why Children Stutter / I Support My Husband / Foot Fashions For Fall / Leaves from a New Amazon's Notebook / I Decided To Reduce / The Republicans Start Looking Around / Have a New Face for Summer / Don't Be a Sissy—Do Something Active Outdoors—And Get Clothes That Will Help You Do It.

(4) Bringing Up Parents / Make It. Trim It. Adore It / Don't Divorce Your Child / Men Make Wonderful Mothers / Four Ways To Look This Spring / We Don't Want a Baby Now / What Are Career Girls Made Of? / First Aid and the Home Medicine Cabinet / Our Unstable Foreign Policy / Do Men or Women Lead The Harder Life? / Which Is the Weaker Sex? / Would You Marry Your Husband Again?

(5) We Can't Let the Children Down / Cross-stitch Quilts / What Are Fathers Made Of? / Learning To Care for Skin and Hair / The Plight of the Young Mother / When a Woman Runs the Town / Meat at Its Savory Best / 14 Points for Beginners in Politics / Is My Marriage a Mistake? / News about Bathrooms / Never Underestimate the Power of a Woman / It's Time Women Took Direct Action.

(6) How To Be a Good Wife / Look Who's Sewing / The Sins of the Parents / The Social Life of Married Couples: Its Pleasures and Problems / Collections by Chanel / When the Wife Wears the Pants / The New Outdoor Women / The Bride Makes a Deep-dish Fruit Pie / How To Tell a Democrat from a Republican / Summer —And Basic Thinking: Lingerie / Never Underestimate the Brainpower of a Woman.

I think you get some impression of how, despite shifting attitudes and interests, the basic concerns of women's magazines have remained remarkably the same when you look back at such articles over the decades. List one is from the 1970s. List two is from the twenties, three is from the thirties, four from the forties, and so on in consecutive order.

If it's not completely clear as yet how this awareness led my wife and me to develop a certain skepticism toward Ms Friedan's research and the conclusions she and her cronies drew concerning the nature of women and their magazines, it will be soon.

In her book, the inventor of the feminine mystique presents an analysis to buttress her case, which she says is a description of the complete editorial contents of a typical issue of *McCall's* in 1960. Then she writes: "The image of woman that emerges from this big, pretty magazine is young and frivolous, almost childlike; fluffy and feminine; passive, gaily content in a world of bedroom and kitchen, sex, babies, and home. The magazine surely does not leave out sex; the only passion, the only pursuit, the only goal a woman is permitted is the pursuit of man. It is crammed full of food, clothing, cosmetics, furniture, and the physical bodies of young women, but where is the world of thought and ideas, the life of the mind and spirit? In the magazine image, women do no work except housework and work to keep their bodies beautiful and to get and keep a man."

"I just don't recall the magazines of 1960 being quite that way," Annie said upon reading this passage aloud to me one day. "I'm going to check that issue of *McCall's* next time I go to the library."

We checked it together, and we made a very interesting discovery—*The Feminine Mystique*, the book that has been taken so seriously, isn't nonfiction at all! It is nearly as contrived as a Barbara Cartland novel. Betty

Friedan had written: "In the early 1960s *McCall's* has been the fastest growing of the women's magazines. Its contents are a fairly accurate representation of the image of the American woman presented, and in part created, by the large-circulation magazines. *Here are the complete editorial contents of a typical issue of McCall's (July 1960). . . ."* (Emphasis added.)

She then listed 17 items from the issue, with little one-line descriptions, such as: "A lead article on 'increasing baldness in women,' caused by too much brushing and dyeing" and "A short story about how a teenager who doesn't go to college gets a man away from a bright college girl."

All 17 of the items appear to the reader to support Betty's contention that "the world of thought and ideas, the life of the mind and spirit" were nowhere to be found in the women's magazines of 1960, indeed of the

The items that would have disputed the argument of her bestseller did not make the list.

whole prior decade. That is, her list seems to support her contention until you actually go to the library and track down the July 1960 issue of *McCall's*. If you do, you will discover, as we did, a very significant fact: the *reason* the world of thought, ideas, mind, et cetera, was nowhere to be found on Betty's list of the "complete editorial contents" of the issue is simply because she *left it out of her list!* It is the truth. Every item in the July 1960 issue that would have served to dispute her argument was simply ignored in her account of the magazine's contents. Here is *our* list of the items from the world of thought, ideas, spirit, et cetera, that were present in the July issue, but absent from Betty's list:

(1) A full length feature by Clare Booth Luce on the influence of television upon political attitudes and results of political campaigns.

(2) A memoir of Eleanor Roosevelt's participation at political conventions through 44 years of her life.

(3) A two-part commentary in the feature "My World at Large," in which Dave Garroway discusses the social problems of latter-day McCarthyism and alcoholism.

(4) Letters to the editor discussing a Senate Joint Resolution aimed at reducing the national debt.

(5) Six poems appeared in the issue.

(6) A lengthy feature called "Sight and Sound: Notes and Comments on What To Read, See, and Hear, Today and Tomorrow." This feature, which takes up ten full columns of print in the magazine, reports on five movies, including *The Adventures of Huckleberry Finn* and *Song Without End* (a screen biography of pianist-composer Franz Liszt). Twelve books are discussed, including a biography of the Soviet leader of the day, titled *Khrushchev*, Plato's *Republic*, *Jane Eyre*, *Moby Dick*, *Madame Bovary*, works of the poets Keats, Shelley, Whitman and Blake, a biography of author

Thomas Wolfe, and a novel by Wright Morris called *Ceremony in Lone Tree*. Recordings are discussed, among which are *Music for Strings, Percussion and Celesta; Hungarian Sketches; Rachmaninoff's Piano Concerto No. 3; Violin Concerto in G Minor* by Bruch; Gilbert and Sullivan's *H.M.S. Pinafore; Folk Songs of Russia;* and *Ragtime Classics.* "Sight and Sound" also contains a long commentary on the coverage of political conventions by the TV networks.

After discovering how much had been left out of Betty's representation of a "typical issue of *McCall's,*" Annie and I decided to take a good look at all twelve issues of the magazine for that year. They revealed further evidence that the charge that *McCall's* showed women only as fluffy, feminine and passive, to use Betty's words, was fictitious. Here are some of the other items we found in 1960 issues of the magazine:

(1) An article explaining the mysteries of stereophonic sound equipment (using terms such as woofers, tweeters, satellite speakers, amplifiers, and dual-channel pre-amps) and telling women how they can learn to build their own stereo equipment.

(2) "If You Ask Me," a regular feature in which Eleanor Roosevelt discusses subjects such as politics, education, social issues, economics, government, ethics, careers and international affairs.

(3) A two-part series on the Suez crisis, excerpted from the memoirs of former British Prime Minister Sir Anthony Eden.

(4) An article titled "Go, Josephine, in Your Flying Machine!" about a woman's adventures in flying.

(5) An inspiring article about how a brave and intelligent woman helped her adolescent daughter cope with diabetes.

(6) "Without Portfolio," monthly commentaries by Clare Booth Luce discussing politics, history, literature and social problems.

(7) A feature presenting 36 examples of interesting courses women might like to take at a sampling of large universities across the country. The courses include: Landscaping, Real Estate Fundamentals, Skin and Scuba Diving, Enjoyment of Theater, Furniture Refinishing, Great Cities of Europe, Planning Today's House, Law for Women, Basic Publicity, and Family Financial Management.

(8) An article on the problems and complexities of dealing with foreign currency when traveling abroad.

(9) In the Christmas issue, a lovely series of prints of paintings by Morton Roberts illustrating Christmas customs over the past 400 years.

(10) An article, "A Pox on Your Husband's Ego," which applauds self-fulfillment for women and women with jobs, and pooh-poohs the idea of coddling the male ego.

(11) An article on the complexities of purchasing life insurance.

(12) An article describing the accomplishments and careers of nine women to whom *McCall's* presented awards. These women were executives, broadcasters and educators.

(13) A regular feature, "Booklets You Can Use," offering literature such as: "Careers for Women in the Physical Sciences," "Careers for Women in Retailing," "Future Jobs for High School Girls," "Your 1960 Social Security Benefits," "Motor Travel Directory," and "Choose a Career in Mental Health."

(14) A feature titled "Careers for Young People in Merchandising."

Betty Friedan's notion that *McCall's* only sang women one kind of tune just isn't credible. Next we looked at the July 1960 issues of several other women's magazines to see what alternatives they offered, and here is just a sampling of what we found:

In *Mademoiselle:*

129

(1) An article by a female author about the job of being a writer.

(2) An article about female archeologists digging at an excavation in Colorado.

(3) A photo feature showing a woman exploring the mysteries of Brazil, even the slums of Rio, all by her lonesome.

In the *Ladies' Home Journal:*

(1) A story about a family that climbs a mountain each year—females climb along with the males.

(2) An article about two women touring native villages in the jungles of Africa.

(3) A photo-story about people in Georgia, showing women tossing horseshoes and paddling a boat along with the men.

Perhaps the silliest thing about the Friedan argument is the assumption that women's magazines have such an overwhelming influence on women's lives, and that these are the only sorts of publications women read. Even if her analysis of the contents of the women's magazines had been accurate, such magazines are only a small part of the reading matter available to women. There were scores of other periodicals read by women in the 1960s, not to mention their exposure to books, the theater, TV, radio and motion pictures. The whole idea that the reach of female minds is limited by the fact that there is a market for homemaking magazines is ludicrous.

The women's magazines, such as *McCall's,* are aimed at that segment of the female audience most interested in fashions, sewing, cooking, men, marriage, family, and so on. To see what else women might be reading in popular mass-circulation magazines, we looked at the July 1960 issues of three others—*Life, Look* and the *Saturday Evening Post*—and we found articles about women in politics, in careers, women with social problems, young women graduates aiming for big jobs, women writers, athletes and professionals. In the advertisements, we saw women sailing, bowling, horseback riding, playing baseball, on the tennis court, working in business and laboring beside men as electronic technicians.

Considering all of this, Annie and I had to totally discount Betty's analysis of the July issue of *McCall's*, in which she observed that

> this magazine, published for over 5,000,000 American women, almost all of whom have been through high school and nearly half to college, contained almost no mention of the world beyond the home. In the second half of the twentieth century in America, woman's world was confined to her own body and beauty, the charming of man, the bearing of babies, and the physical care and serving of husband, children, and home. And this was no anomaly of a single issue of a single women's magazine.

It wasn't even that. It was, when you took the trouble to investigate, simply a fabrication.

The opinions of Betty Friedan and the criticisms of other feminists who object to the contents of women's magazines reveal childishly unrealistic notions about our system of free enterprise. The feminists appear to imagine that these magazines are operated as eleemosynary institutions rather than as commercial media supported by advertisers with particular products to sell.

Not only have successful women's magazines depended for their popularity on the same basic ingredients throughout this century, they have depended for their survival on their success in reaching buyers of women's clothes, food, soap, cosmetics, beauty and cleaning aids, sanitary napkins, home appliances, home furnishings, and kitchen and dinner ware.

The basic ingredients of women's magazines are not determined by "male chauvinistic" editors, but by the commercial necessity for publishers to produce periodicals that large numbers of women will buy. If you want to print feminist-oriented magazines of interest to only a small segment of women, such as *Ms.* or *New Woman*, then you have to look for your support primarily among advertisers of automobiles, cigarettes and liquor, as do such men's magazines as *Playboy* and *Penthouse*.

But Betty Friedan was in the business of fabricating media images about women out of one part reality and one part whole cloth. She claims to have helped create the "togetherness" trend, and when she and other writers and editors got tired of it, she helped destroy it for the more dramatic images of women's lib. In *The Feminine Mystique,* she wrote: "American women no longer know who they are. They are sorely in need of a new image to help them find their identity." Publication of her book virtually created a new career for her,

in which she has ever since undertaken to create that new identity in her *own* image.

Such image-making by practitioners in the mass media, as we've already seen, consists primarily of selective reporting. This is the simple process of leaving out what doesn't fit the desired effect and putting in what does. In the words of a popular song of the 1940s —"You gotta accentuate the positive, eliminate the negative, latch on to the affirmative, and don't mess with Mr. In-between." In the 1970s, the editorial emphasis in the mass media shifted the gears of its selective reporting machinery to pursue the rising women's liberation trend. Almost overnight, the freedoms that women had been enjoying for most of this century were rediscovered and dressed up to seem brand new. Publications of all descriptions, from the women's magazines to leading national newspapers, began running regular items promoting the themes that women have been discriminated against and are now gaining new freedoms to work in men's jobs, to participate in sex outside of marriage without stigma, and to compete equally with males in every kind of activity from pool-shooting to auto racing.

By November 1975, even *American Home*, a magazine which in years past had been devoted to "articles on home subjects, to appeal to both young men and women" and "home improvement articles on remodeling, redecorating, landscaping, etc.," had shifted its editorial emphasis toward the "working homemaker," because, it told potential advertisers, "we serve the lifestyle of a new breed of woman. A woman with a professional attitude toward her job and her home. A woman in balance, proud of herself and what she can do. One of the things she can do is help your sales grow. We invite you to reach her in the new *American Home*."

A new feature was introduced in the November issue

of this magazine, called "The Emerging Woman." It serves as a sort of showcase to applaud women who successfully combine jobs and home life. One "Emerging Woman" feature, for instance, is titled "The Worst Thing in the World Is To Be Bored." It begins with a blurb that says, "And what do you do? Any woman who would answer self-pityingly, 'I'm only a housewife' had better hide. Women like Beverly Ellsley—a vital new breed—are tearing that one apart. Their redefinition of A Woman's Place involves rapid scene shifts that would have frazzled an earlier generation."

"Can you tell our readers the secret of your success as a liberated mother?"

It turns out that Beverly Ellsley—the dynamo from whom mere housewives must hide—is a mother of two young children who is supported in style in Westport, Connecticut, by an affluent husband, and who has established her own business as an interior designer. Readers are assured that it all just works out wonderfully for everyone, especially Beverly, who says she is "working to feed my soul."

Such items glorifying the woman with a paid job and denigrating the housewife have become regular fare in every sort of popular newspaper and magazine in the seventies. An article in *Newsweek* of November 24, 1975, declares, "There are now more than 20 million working married women, and many of them are committing their ambitions and energies to full-time careers. For these working couples, the problems—and pleasures—of coping with their households and two separate careers are creating a whole new life-style for which there are few traditional rules. . . ."

This kind of story is contrived on two counts, because first of all there is nothing new about working wives—they were writing these same stories in the 1920s—and secondly, the kinds of people described are hardly typical working folk. The kind that *Newsweek* presented were people like Carla Hills, the secretary of housing and urban development, and her husband, the chairman of the Securities and Exchange Commission. Then there was U.S. Congresswoman Patricia Schroeder and her husband, an attorney, and Charlotte Curtis, associate editor of the *New York Times,* and her hubby, who is a neurosurgeon. Other two-career spouses mentioned were a Superior Court commissioner in Los Angeles and a Columbia Pictures executive, a director of publications at the University of California and an artist, a public relations executive and a lawyer, a research assistant and an architect, an advertising executive and a vice-president of a public relations firm, a newspaper columnist and a plastics designer ... just your average couples! These are the kinds of people who have *always* found it convenient to pursue dual careers if they wished, members of the affluent professional class. Such people usually have far more options than the average, because they have more education, skills, money, household help, professional contacts and experience.

Another sort of "women working" story that is sheer contrivance is the kind we found in *U.S. News & World Report* on November 17, 1975, featuring 13 photographs of women performing jobs that are most often done by men. The pictures showed women in such jobs as truck driver, train engineer, garbage collector, highway safety patrol, mounted policeman, control-room operator in an electric power plant, blacksmith, baseball umpire, geologist, security officer, tile-setter, zoo-keeper and clown.

The lead-in to the story declares: "The photos on this and following pages provide ample evidence: women in growing numbers are widening their work horizons, taking jobs once considered exclusively for men." Yet when Annie and I visited the photo collections of the National Archives a short time later, we found hundreds of photographs of women doing similar jobs all through this century. We found "evidence" almost identical to that published in *U.S. News & World Report* that might have been published in the same kind of photo-story 50 years ago.

As a matter of fact, such stories have been routine in newspapers and magazines all through this century. If you visit the National Archives, you'll find photographs distributed by news services in every decade celebrating female truck drivers, aviators, scientists, laboratory technicians, police officers, and so on. For example, we saw a picture of a woman welding—in 1927—and the story says: "The Fair Sex Invades a New Field—Another new business for women has captured the fancy of Miss Florence Schell, who designs, makes, and trims beautiful wrought iron lamps, gates, novelties and what not. She received a great deal of training at the Carnegie Technical Institute in Pittsburgh and came to Chicago as a designer of lighted signs."

A 1929 photo-story from California says: "In these days of modern careers for women, who go in for interior decorating, bridge building, aviation and taxi driving, there is one ultra-modern girl in San Francisco who has made a success of an old, old trade. She is Miss Blanche Spillman, a petite Belgian Miss, who has succeeded with a vengeance—at horse trading! She is shown here at work in her stable, which she operates, shining up a saddle."

Another 1929 photo-story reads: "Conductorettes Man St. Louis Street Cars—When in St. Louis, do not be surprised when a woman collects the fare as you board a street car, as the use of women conductors has been going on in the Mound City for the past 12 years. Eleven women are on the payroll of the Public Service Company who [sic] handles the street transportation in St. Louis."

Another photo-story from St. Louis from 1930 says: "A New Line for the Weaker Sex"—Pretty Loretta Rabbitt, 18, of St. Louis, Mo., who is probably the youngest of her sex to own and operate a gasoline station in the U.S. Since her father's death six years ago, she has been operating her station in the Mound City and is kept so busy by her work that she 'can't seem to find enough time to go out with her boy friends.' She is shown here filling a customer's gasoline tank."

A photo-story from 1939 pictured Mrs. E. O. Rainville in the driver's seat of her transport truck after

137

having covered more than 315,000 miles during her seven-year career of hauling automobiles from factories to distributors.

We found similar news stories about women learning carpentry, electronics, auto mechanics and welding. Such stories were news in the twenties and thirties, but by the war years of the forties, women were practically running everything on the home front, and "women moving into new jobs" actually stopped being real news during those years.

If the folks down at *U.S. News & World Report* are so inclined, they can put together the same photo-story they ran on women working in 1975 with material they'll find at the National Archives from the 1950s, the years Betty Friedan suggests women were practically chained to the kitchen stove. We found dozens of photos they could use, such as those of: Miss Marilyn Jorgenson, an engineer with the Division of Highways of California, shown inspecting drainage and construction on the San Diego Freeway; Helen Devlin, Barbara Canvana and Dorothy Bates—just three of 36 women cab drivers that a Detroit cab company hired in 1950; Miss Marion Harvey, an atomic scientist who during the fifties helped install nuclear reactors and trained personnel in the theory and operation of reactors; Mrs. Clara Ortiz Clothiaux, pictured in front of the nuclear reactor that it was her job to operate; Mrs. Everett Card, Miss Irene Ingison and Mrs. Ray Whitehouse, all of whom were "switchmen" on the railroad.

No, "women going into new jobs" is not news in the 1970s, and these stories that have become so prevalent are not really meant to inform or to entertain, as were such stories in the past. Something else is happening. The mass media have turned on to the sex-role revolution and are helping bring it about. Month after month, they hammer away at the themes of the sexual assault

138

—sex roles are disappearing; women are catching up to men; sexual behavior is just a matter of personal preference; macho, the villain, is dead. They promote these themes by devising story after story based on unusual or exceptional people, or on bizarre behaviors which they characterize as a rising trend. They search out every psychologist or "expert" willing to say that these oddities are destined to be the normal patterns of tomorrow, and showcase these ideas.

The *Washington Post*, for example, printed a long feature story on November 23, 1975, which began with a question: "Is conjugal equality a 70s myth or reality? Put another way, in a liberated marriage where both partners have careers, is the wife's of equal importance?" Several paragraphs follow asserting that the feminist movement has changed the current generation's attitudes "to what once were male-dominated conventional problems," and that now people less restricted by sex-role stereotyping "are swapping domestic tasks when children are involved, commuting long distances between two residences, relocating at the expense of the husband's career or compromising in a turn-taking approach."

Next, the reader is given three case studies that are supposed to exemplify this burgeoning trend. As usual, the subjects of the piece turn out to be people far removed from what can be considered ordinary circumstances. Two of the situations concern married couples who have decided not to have any children. (This places them in a very exotic category, since the polls indicate that only about 4 percent of all couples say they intend to remain childless.)

As we read on in the *Post* article, we learn that in couple number one, the husband is an analyst with the Central Intelligence Agency who has decided to leave the agency (which at the time was being racked by scandal and organizational turmoil) so his wife can accept a position as a member of a cancer research team at Boston University. (Now if that's not your average couple changing jobs, I never heard of one!)

Childless couple number two, we learn, have decided to live in two separate cities, she in Greenwich, Connecticut, where she works as an IBM new products manager, and he in Bethesda, Maryland, where he works as a research biologist. This "average" couple, both of whom were then in their late thirties, spent weekends together.

The third run-of-the-mill couple that the *Post*'s writer managed to turn up consisted of a black female television reporter, making $20,000 in Washington, D.C., and her husband, who quit his job in Little Rock, Arkansas, to come with her to the big city. What fascinated me about this pair, as an example of the turning sex-role tide, is that the husband said he was sorry he had ever decided to make the move *at all,* and the wife said she would like to give up her job right then and *raise a lot of babies!*

An eminent scholar of the workings of the press, Professor Bernard Roshko, says: "A fundamental concern of the sociology of news is why particular individuals, institutions, and events—rather than others—are routinely observed by the press while the rest are usually overlooked."

It seems to me that there are two primary factors involved in this process (after you eliminate the out-and-out ideologues). First, not the press nor anyone else can ever tell it all, so there are the twin limitations of selective perception and selective reporting—the personal limitations that cause reporters to notice and report some things but not others. The other factor I see operating in the reporting process is the tendency of reporters to work not as independent agents out for an original report, a scoop, a fresh point of view, but as scavengers in a herd, following whatever trend comes along.

In the mid-1970s, the trend calls for stories about women with careers, house-husbands, couples living together outside of marriage and single parent families. So the editors and writers set their minds on finding these stories, no matter how small a slice of reality they represent. It doesn't matter that most people still get married, that most marriages continue without divorce, that the house-husbands usually turn out to be writers or artists or some other type of eccentric—the trend, once in motion, must be satisfied.

We discovered during 1975, for example, that *Parade*, the mass-circulation Sunday supplement, had made women's lib part of its weekly formula. Scarcely a week went by that the editors didn't find some gimmick to justify a headline such as "Women Are Stronger," "Girls Do as Well," "Female Dentists," and "Male Midwives." They presented articles encouraging the new trend, with titles such as "Baseball Diamonds Are a Girl's Best Friend," applauding mixing girls and boys in the Little League, "The Young Call It Cohabitation," encouraging parents and college officials to accept the trend toward young men and women living together outside of marriage, and "Women Discuss Their Changing Role," a panel discussion suggesting that this "entire generation of women has broken decisively with the tradition that cast them exclusively in the role of homemakers."

A favorite formula employed by publications of all sorts is to select their own panels of opinion leaders which to no one's amazement come up with opinions supporting the latest trend. In an article in *Today's Health* entitled "What Happens to a Marriage When the Wife Goes to Work," the writer reports:

My own informal survey of husbands and marriage counselors has confirmed that most husbands
... whose wives have returned to work, are
pleased with their new arrangement.

For one thing, they like the extra money. Most of
them also speak with delight of a new liveliness
and expanded dimension that brighten their wives'
personalities. They seem to enjoy hearing about
her day at the office. They sound proud of their
women and admit to little resistance against taking
over some of the shopping or vacuum cleaning.
The anticipated resentment of husbands against
"home-abandoning" wives doesn't appear to have
materialized.

This, of course, is one of the marvelous advantages of
informal surveys—they have a wonderful way of ending up as idealized and inspiring as the writer wants,
because unwelcome points of view somehow just don't
"materialize."

The big difference between the editorial proselytiz-
ing of today (that urges women out of faithful marriage
and home life) and that of the "togetherness" era
(which urged men and women in the opposite direction) is the stridency of today's campaign. It is aggressive, abrasive, insistent.

A *Woman's Day* article declares: "Despite their reservations and mixed feelings, most of today's husbands
would not want to be married to Alice-sit-by-the-fire.
They like the idea of a wife who can be self-reliant,
who broadens her interests and skills, who shares
family responsibilities, who is better able to understand what *men* must cope with on the job...."

Mademoiselle's Karen Durbin, writing of the traditional breadwinner and homemaker roles, tells her readers: "I find the risks inherent in this kind of marriage
singularly unappealing. But, then, so do a lot of other

142

people, apparently. The number of women who opt for marriage and child rearing as a full-time occupation has been steadily dwindling for the last 20 years, and, if the most recent trends continue at their current pace, toward families of two children or less and toward women working at jobs that bring in more than just a supplemental income, then the old-fashioned, role-divided marriage may eventually become a rarity."

An example of the murky thinking that permeates such publications as the new magazine *Working Woman* appears in an article on "How to Make Your Kids More Self-reliant" by Carol Saline. "We were in the yard when the telephone rang," she writes. "I, working fertilizer into the rose bushes, and my then four-year-old daughter, digging in her sand box. Since my hands were coated with mud, I told her to run in the house and answer the phone. She didn't budge, involved as much in her play as I was in my gardening. I started to get angry. 'Sharon, go answer that phone,' I repeated. And she, looking thoroughly annoyed, said, 'This is supposed to be a free country. Why do I always have to do what you tell me?' " By this time, writes Ms Saline, the phone had stopped ringing. "And though I read her my standard because-you-are-the-child-and-I-am-the-mother lecture, I was secretly delighted. I knew I had a daughter who was already on her way to self-reliance."

Contemplating this article and many others like it, I find it disquieting to say the least to think that American mothers today are reduced to receiving guidance and advice from magazine writers who can't distinguish signs of healthy self-reliance in a child from expressions of patent impudence.

New Woman is another new magazine (despite the fact that its title is from the nineteenth century) that is dedicated throughout to promotion of the idea of identical jobs and roles for the sexes. Its cartoons have women saying such things as "Of course I've given birth—to the Acme Corporation and its eleven branch offices," and "My husband and I have a marvelous relationship. He's married to his work, and I'm married to mine." In another one, a teenage girl is saying to her father, "Are you afraid of bright, funny women, Dad? I notice you never watch 'Maude.'" In another, a little girl meets her working mother at the door, and asks, "Mom, what's a housewife?" *New Woman* offers items on men who work at home like women, and on women who wear men's suits to work. There are articles on becoming more assertive and on how to become a "New Woman." One such article declares, "Obviously, the lifestyle most conducive to ownership trips is the coercive monopoly marriage [this, apparently, is what most of us think of as a normal, traditional marriage] since it is based on ownership in the first place. But, setting aside the issue of marriage itself for now, the lifestyle question for *New Women* is: to live with or apart from your lover." A cutesy item in one issue was a "Who's

News" story about a woman who operates a tune-up garage for women. In the accompanying photograph, she is shown looking under the hood of a car with her hand resting casually on her male mechanic's bottom.

The involvement of the news media in restructuring of attitudes toward women's roles is apparent both in the kinds of women who receive attention and in the way they are described. The sort of woman most likely to get wide coverage is one like Janet Guthrie, who was hailed for *weeks* when the press thought she was going to make it into the Indianapolis 500 auto race. A headline in the *National Observer*, which, like most newspapers, wrote her up repeatedly, blared: "Go, Janet, Go!" This same approval hasn't been evidenced toward the occupation referred to by the *Washington Star*'s Anne Crutcher, who wrote about another woman prominent in the news: "Margaret Thatcher, the British Conservative party's first woman leader, doesn't like being presented as 'a phenomenon' any more than she likes being introduced as a housewife. . . . The word that is to women almost what 'nigger' is to blacks actually crossed the lips of the President of the National Press Club when he was introducing her as Friday's luncheon speaker. . . ."

When Supreme Court Justice William O. Douglas resigned from the bench, there was a flurry of speculation, and even enthusiasm in the press, over the prospect that a woman would be nominated to take his place. While this could in some measure be justified on the grounds that it was a common speculation, this expectation might reasonably have died when nomination of U.S. Circuit Court Judge John Paul Stevens was announced by the president on November 28, 1975. Even *then*, however, some reporters were bemoaning the fact that a woman had not been chosen. For instance, Tom Petit, of NBC-TV's evening news (who

145

supposedly was not delivering an editorial), reported that an "obscure midwestern judge" had been chosen to fill the Supreme Court vacancy. "The President will expect quick confirmation," he said, "and that may be why Stevens was picked. . . . We do know he will make the Supreme Court more conservative than it was when Justice Douglas served, and *we know that it will be a long time before a woman serves on the Supreme Court of the United States.*" This last remark can in no way be classified as news, nor as anything but advocacy of the lib ideological view. (This variety of editorializing on TV news is now routine, and I imagine generally regarded as undeserving of comment.)

Consider the *Time* magazine article of May 26, 1975, on the status of American women, headlined "Women: Still Number Two But Trying Harder." This piece concluded that "feminism is not a fad, as men—and many women—once believed, but a strong and enduring social force. Still, the progress of women has been severely hampered by tokenism, chauvinism and women's own reluctance to abandon their submissive roles. . . ."

Time promoted the feminist ideas from beginning to end, and left the impression that women's lib was catching on with almost everyone. "Many husbands are now assuming their share of domestic duties," we were told, "greatly easing the burden for 34.5 million women who choose to remain in the home." (Actually, sociological surveys at the time both in the U.S. and abroad were indicating somewhat the opposite of this utopian assertion.)

The piece was jam-packed with figures that seemed to show women making upward strides by leaps and bounds. "Today," *Time* proclaimed, "the Labor Department says that, while the overall ratio of women to men in the work force has not changed significantly in the

146

past few years (38% are women v. 32% in 1972), many more women have moved into professional and technical job categories. Nearly 32% of the nation's 36 million working women are now employed in these higher rated areas, up from 14.5% in 1972."

I'll bet those figures really seemed impressive to a lot of readers. The only trouble is that when Annie checked them out with the Department of Labor, she found the statistics were untrue. The overall proportion of women in the labor force was not 32 percent in 1972, according to the Labor Department, it was 38 percent, the same as in 1975. And the *Time* report that the proportion of women in professional and technical jobs had risen from 14.5 percent to 32 percent, Annie discovered, was not only inaccurate, it was preposterous. If such a surge *had* occurred, it would mean that more than 7 million women had suddenly moved into professional and technical jobs, more than doubling their numbers in less than three years. This did not happen. What did happen, apparently, was that the women who prepared the femlib article at *Time* got a little carried away in their zeal. The issue also carried a letter from the publisher proclaiming that "women, still sharply discriminated against, are making strong gains in fields once dominated by men," and pointing out that the article just mentioned was produced by no less than six of *Time*'s women staffers.

"Maybe if they had assigned *seven* of them to do the piece, they would have gotten it straight," said Annie, with what I thought was perhaps a little too much satisfaction.

On the other hand, it's difficult to blame her for feeling that way. In the course of our research, we've encountered a virtual mountain of distortion, misrepresentation and outright fraud directed toward the greater glorification of "liberated woman."

147

The lib mentality has been programmed into media at every level. For example, on a local TV broadcast, I recall hearing a newscaster describe feminists who booed and hissed a high official of our state of Maryland as "highly aware women"—the official, it seems, had made the mistake of referring to the women as "girls."

Even advertising agencies have picked up the liberation theme. An institutional ad for Mobil Oil Corporation declares: "YOU FOUGHT FOR YOUR VOICE. NOW USE IT! You're getting close. To equal rights under the law. To a fair crack at the good jobs, at the same pay as men. . . ." The ad promotes the standard line that women do not have equal rights, ignoring as usual the flood of federal legislation that says they do. A Coca-Cola commercial shows us a beautiful blonde young woman working as a garage mechanic. Pepsi has male and female construction workers playing football together after lunch. General Motors shows us a shapely female foreman bossing men around one of its plants. Alberto VO5 gives us a gorgeous pants-suited architect in her hardhat discussing some blueprints with the foreman at a construction site. A little girl in the Shakey's commercial hits a home run over the fence while playing on a boy's baseball team. Breast of Tuna shows a young woman winning a foot race against men. J. C. Penney's used a unisex theme to sell its "super-denims" (the girls' are just as tough as the boys'). In a Joy ad, the wife has taken a job and has just brought home her first paycheck, when a dinner guest says, "You set such a pretty table, both of you!" Hubby is so proud to take credit, he just beams. A Clairol ad proclaims: "DO IT. Now you can do anything. Without worrying about it. Touch football. Or coloring your hair. . . ." (As though women have not been able to "do anything" for decades.) The idea that women are experiencing "liberation" in the seventies is even promoted by Kotex with an ad campaign launching "New Freedom Mini Pads"! And in a commercial for Fantastik Spray Cleaner, a woman chides: "Don't call me a housewife—I'm not married to a house!"

Many newspapers and magazines have responded to the pressures of feminists by accepting faddish usages such as "Ms" and "chairperson," by accepting the ideological bent implicit in the casual use of words like "oppression," "liberated," "sexist," and "male chauvinist," and by treating women exactly like men by eliminating courtesy titles after the first reference and just calling females *Jones* or *Smith,* as the case may be.

Reacting to these sorts of incursions, one reader wrote to the *New York Times:*

> I used to believe that one's name is his own but that titles are conferred on one by society. Now I learn that B. J. is to be addressed as Ms. King *because she prefers it.* I should prefer to be addressed as,
>
>
>
> HIS EXCELLENCY
> Thomas J. Wertenbaker, Jr.
> Princeton, N.J.
>

We'll be looking at TV's part in the unisex push in the pages ahead, but for now I would say that the most spectacular television show dedicated to promoting lib was the three-hour, prime-time network presentation "Of Women and Men." This production, which was aired on January 9, 1975, by NBC, was expensively advertised across the country as a "documentary." It was actually three tedious hours of advertising for the sex-role revolution and the new morality—which "coanchor persons" Barbara Walters and Tom Snyder suggested just might be "the most important revolution since 1776." George Gilder commented in a review:

> The most revolutionary aspect of the evening . . .
> turned out to be the willingness of a major network

"I should prefer to be addressed as His Excellency Thomas J. Wertenbaker, Jr."

to exhibit three hours of slickly produced but in-
eptly researched propaganda for a sexual revolution that has yet to take place, and in all likelihood
never will. . . . Even the distorted and sensational-
ized evidence presented by NBC itself indicated
that the sexual revolution is chiefly a media event:
a kaleidoscope of rotating styles and fashions designed to sell books and magazines, movies and TV
shows—to keep the turnstiles spinning and the revolution on stage, but lacking any traction in our
inner lives. . . . The program failed to exhibit a single happy or stable marriage and . . . artfully conveyed the impression that young people are promiscuous revelers. . . .

The exultant culmination of the show was when Walters and Snyder told those viewers who doggedly
watched to the end what the experts predict for the
world of the year 2000. It will be, we were assured, a
world in which marriage can no longer be permanent,
but will be "serial" and "contractual," on an "equality
basis rather than on a sexual basis."

WALTERS: I think also there will be a difference
in the openness between two people and that there
will be an easier sexuality, a franker relationship,
again, men and women as people. We see this especially with the young people. They don't have the
fears. They don't have the hangups. And there is
the honesty in all aspects of their relationship.
SNYDER: And there's going to be some change in
the way men and women live together. Do you not
think that we aren't simply going to have, for better
or for worse, till death do us part, from this day
forward, that sort of thing, where a marriage was
for a lifetime and you are my one-and-only and it's
going to continue for a long time? We've all heard
about these contract marriages, serial marriages—is
that not the term? Where there's a series of relation-

151

ships, of a man and a woman for a time and then going on to something else? But I think there'll still be marriage, and I think that men and women will grow old together, and I think that they will have children and watch their children have other children, and it's going to be a little bit different and, hopefully, everybody will be ready for it. . . .

WALTERS: Well, it may be that women are playing the parts of husbands. They may be earning more of the income. They may be on the executive level. And it won't just be the man up there on the executive level with the female drone beneath him. Isaac Asimov, the science writer, wrote, and I'm quoting here: "For the first time in history, we will be tapping the brain power of the other half of the human race. We will double our mental capacity without doubling our numbers."

It seems that there's going to be some fear on the part of the men. It will mean that there will be further competition in the economic market, but on the other hand, we will be tapping people we never have used before.

SYNDER: And, when he says, without doubling our numbers, there aren't going to be as many children born. We've achieved Zero Population Growth in this country. The birth rate, we can expect, will continue going down. So the outlook is going to be for fewer children for couples, or, possibly, no children at all.

WALTERS: We took an NBC poll to find out how you felt out there. And we asked whether you believe that a woman can be fulfilled without having children. You know what the answer was? The answer was: Overwhelmingly yes. From both men and women. Women don't have to be mothers to be fulfilled. And the younger the person answering, the greater the number who believed that.

SNYDER: And, if you think this is just Walters and Snyder quoting all this stuff, the people who know about the future, at least know about it in terms of their own research of the past, support all that has been said on this program.

152

One reason the press has come to support feminist notions so enthusiastically may be that its practitioners are convinced that feminists represent women, that they know what is best for women, that men and women are essentially interchangeable for nearly all valid commercial purposes, and that sex roles are passé. We'll explore the realities behind these assumptions in the pages ahead.

Will the Real American Woman Please Stand Up

Trying to determine who represents American women is a lot like trying to figure out who represents the best interests of mankind—all sorts of folks will suggest that *they* do, all with similar degrees of sincerity, confidence and enthusiasm. The press, too, often cues us as to who is wearing the white hats this week, sometimes subtly, sometimes not so subtly.

On June 27, 1975, for instance, ABC reporter Betsy Aaron declared to TV viewers across the nation: "These women walking through Boston know they represent 53 percent of the population in this country, and they want a representative slice of the political action." (Our contact at the Bureau of the Census states that females are actually 52.6 percent of the *adult* population, and 51.3 percent of the total population of the United States.) Of course, the members of the National Women's Political Caucus we saw on the TV screen didn't really *represent* the female population of the country at all, but we're used to hearing the press talk

155

like that. These days most people don't even notice. Most of us have almost forgotten that the differences among citizens that merit representation in the political system are supposed to be philosophical ones. They have never been biological differences of sex.

We frequently read headlines that say "The Women Win" or "The Women Lose" or "The Women Gain," but the fact is that women have never actually represented any sort of cohesive or homogeneous political bloc. In the 1974 Virginia Slims American Women's Opinion Poll, the Roper Organization states: "The views of women and men show more similarities than differences. In fact, gender appears to be among the weakest influences on attitudes and opinions. Far more significant are: social class (education and income), age, and race; followed by marital status, size of community, and geographic region. In fact, *gender is the least significant.*" (Emphasis added.)

The major activity of nearly half of the women in the United States is homemaking. Of the 47 percent who go out to work or say they are looking for jobs, a quarter are part-time workers and less than half work year round. Homemaking is also a major concern of most of these women. Nearly two-thirds of the women who work are engaged in clerical, sales, service jobs, or farm labor. Only about 10 percent of the women in America are in any sense professional or career women. And among these, only a small fraction seem intent on an aggressively independent feminist-style existence. Moreover, the work life of women in the labor force is much shorter than men's, on the average—the sole exception being women who remain single and childless. The years in the labor force of the working married woman with two children are only half the number served by males.

In view of these facts, it is understandable that many

156

people see the feminist assault predominantly as one by an elitist force of upper-middle-class professional women able to influence public opinion and policy out of all proportion to their numbers through inordinate access to education, government aid and the mass media. In fact, the comparative success women's lib has enjoyed is due to the presence of feminists in droves at the universities, in government agencies and women's clubs and on the staffs of publishers and broadcasters—and to their ability to coordinate their efforts through a network of social pressure.

"There's no doubt that the women's movement has had a real effect on the college generation's thinking," declared a typical promotional item in the May 1973 issue of *Glamour*. "But what's more important, despite the slowness of economic change for women, and the temporary setbacks, is that it has changed everybody's thinking—men's thinking about women, women's thinking about themselves, and society's thinking about the relationship of the sexes. A new idea has been implanted in our collective consciousness, an idea that's persistent, and spreading and turning more and more into reality every year. And once that has happened, there is no turning back."

By 1975, the year of what *Time* magazine called "the U.N.'s much ballyhooed, much-disputed International Women's Year," this millennial component had so infected NOW that its annual convention passed a resolution making promotion of lesbianism a top priority, and plans were undertaken to stage a national sitdown strike by women across the nation.

Alice Doesn't Day, as the proposed strike was called, was supposed to be the history-making day when American women would rise up *en masse* to "pull the plug on the system that abuses them." The plan, the feminists announced, was that on October 29, a Wednesday, all the women in America—each "Alice"—would refuse to work, spend money, cook supper, care for children or have sex with their husbands. Well, Alice Doesn't Day came and all but a few smatterings of Alices *did* (go to work, spend money, cook, et cetera), with those few true believers who *didn't* gathering for straggly demonstrations, which mostly occurred on university campuses and on the streets of a few large cities. As Annie and I had easily predicted (based on the kinds of data we'll consider subsequently), all Alice Doesn't Day ended up demonstrating was the perfectly obvious fact that most American women don't have the slightest emotional, intellectual or political commitment to the ideas or ambitions of feminism. The nonstrike of the nation's women on October 29, 1975, stands in effect as a historical referendum on the *lack* of interest of our female citizenry in fomenting a sex-role revolution.

I can understand how the feminists managed to make such a colossal mistake. First of all, they believed their own fiery rhetoric about the impending female upris-

"Okay, troops, this is our chance to show that there is overwhelming support for the movement!"

ing, and, secondly, they had what seemed like verification of this belief from the pollsters. For example, in 1974, Roper was reporting: "For the first time since Virginia Slims has conducted its study, a majority of American women—57%—have come out in favor of most efforts to improve women's status in society. In 1972, 48% expressed such support, and in 1970 only 40% were in favor." (Roper was actually exaggerating a bit in using the word "most" in this analysis, since the question the pollsters asked didn't mention "most efforts," but simply whether or not the women favored *efforts* to strengthen or change women's status in society. A small point, but typical of the way even pollsters' reports are subtly slanted to convey more than they actually mean.)

In this case, the illusion was disastrous for the feminists, who failed to realize how utterly shallow were the pollsters' results. Polls in recent years have consistently shown that "most women support efforts to improve women's status." But this revelation is very misleading if you don't know that most people habitually will say they're in favor of anything that sounds like freedom or rights. To use such questions is like asking people if they believe in life, liberty and the pursuit of happiness. You have to look at much more subtle poll results from a variety of sources to get a reasonable notion of women's attitudes toward the purposes of women's lib.

In 1975, the planners of Alice Doesn't Day had every reason to believe their push toward a sex role revolution was working. At least, they thought they did. They'd obviously succeeded in making a lot of women discontented. The Gallup Opinion Poll of April 1975 showed that for the first time more women said they thought men had a better life than women did. The Gallup report states: "The growing dissatisfaction

159

among women would appear to reflect growing expectations, their notable gains in many fields, including politics, notwithstanding." The feminists, although they had *not* convinced most women of the importance of feminist ideas, had influenced legislation and created political and commercial opportunities (which were mainly of benefit to upper-middle-class professional women). In the process, they had also stirred up a psychology of rising expectations—and accompanying frustration—among millions of women whose exaggerated hopes could not be fulfilled. In addition, there was considerable backlash among women, like Annie, who resented feminist efforts to undermine homemakers' feelings about their lives and the way women, in general, feel about themselves, their men and children. This says something, I believe, about the powers of observation and analysis of the planners of Alice Doesn't Day—they simply did not realize that most Alices were *not* fellow feminists.

Annie and I have attempted to get a firmer fix on the attitudes and ambitions of the female population. We've learned to look with considerable skepticism, for instance, upon claims of organizations such as the National Women's Political Caucus that they represent all women in America. When the Caucus drafted its National Women's Agenda, its leaders publicized the plan as being backed by 30 million women who are the members of 80 organizations, ranging from the Camp Fire Girls to the Gay Task Force to the Women's Division of the United Methodist Church.

But when we looked into the matter we found that it wasn't the *memberships* of these organizations that generated the agenda—which calls for "rights to sexual preference" (for lesbians) and "expansion of opportunities for women in the arts, on newspapers and magazines and in radio and television" and "an end to

160

stereotyped portrayals of women by the information industry, and education of the industry to the fact that all news is 'women's news.' " Most of the millions of people who are members of all of those organizations *don't have the slightest interest in such things and never voted on these issues.* The National Women's Agenda, it turns out, was the agenda of the professional organization women and publicists who have moved into control of so many organizations in recent years. The feminists have taken charge, and for the foreseeable future the official agenda of women in our society seems to be theirs to arrange.

It is interesting to learn that even the resolutions of NOW represent less than 4 percent of its membership, because NOW doesn't use a delegate system and the only members who have a voice are the 2,000 or so who are able to attend its conventions. So it's difficult to attribute much significance to NOW's membership figures as indices of female opinion. Many people listed as members of organizations don't actually participate in meetings or register their opinions or cast votes. And how much less do these organizations speak for the millions of women who don't even belong to them? Some researchers say that the majority of Americans have never been members of *any* organization whatsoever. But the ones who *do* join tend to belong to a lot of them.

Harvard social psychologist Tom Pettigrew, commenting on the nature of these organization types, has said: "A highly isolated minority of activists makes up all those clubs and associations. There is a tremendous amount of overlapping." One thing that is abundantly clear is that, compared to the memberships of organizations that are even remotely feminist in their purposes and views, the number of women in the U.S. who belong to groups that are absolutely *not* feminist is vast.

In 1972, the National Secretaries Association took strong exception to the ideas feminists were beginning to spread about the role of women in the office. "NSA does not presume to speak for 'women's liberation' organizations, yet some of them have taken it upon themselves to speak negatively about the role that secretaries play in government, business, industry, education and the professions," the Board of Directors of the organization said in an official statement.

That same year, NSA launched a survey of the attitudes of secretaries in 50 states to ascertain their feelings about their work and the charges put forth by the libbers. "The survey reveals a striking blow against the women's liberation movement," announced a report of the survey results in the NSA's monthly journal, *The Secretary*. "A large majority of NSA member and non-member secretaries support neither the women's lib group nor its ideals. Only one percent of the members and three percent of nonmembers belong to a women's lib organization."

, The report declared that just at the time "when the more vocal liberation spokeswomen are crying for equal rights and opportunities for women, *The Secretary* survey reveals those claims of unfair and demeaning treatment are unfounded." The report said the large majority of secretaries disputed the feminist claim that their function is menial or subservient, and that 78 percent denied the feminist charge that secretaries are not fairly compensated for the work they perform. Only about 5 percent said they objected to doing errands or going for coffee and serving it to executives. More than 85 percent of the secretaries said they do *not* believe that their company has any responsibility to provide a day-care center for employee's children. And 88 percent of the secretaries agreed that a company should have the right to establish dress codes or standards.

"In the name-calling category, only 15 percent among members and 18 percent among nonmembers prefer the use of Ms. rather than Miss or Mrs.," concluded the report. "Gloria Steinem may be speaking for a lot of Ms.'s, but she's not carrying the banner for most secretaries, 54 percent of whom are Mrs.'s. . . . The secretary is neither aligned with women's lib, nor does she side with the radical left."

Despite claims of the feminists, the evidence does not seem to show that a large proportion of women are unhappy with their way of life. In its June 1975 issue, *Good Housekeeping* reported results of a poll of its readers on their attitudes toward working at an outside job versus working at home. "Their answers," the magazine states, "indicate that, to a surprising extent, women are content with the roles they are currently filling. Many of the respondents take a long view of their lives. They expect to alternate periods of working outside the home with periods when they stay home, depending on the ages of their children and the pressure for additional income. Thus, most women tend to see themselves with a foot in both worlds."

Good Housekeeping reported, furthermore, that its readers who worked at home "expressed an overwhelming preference for their role. Eighty-five percent said they favored staying at home. Only 12 percent would rather go to work." Among those readers who worked at a job, "a solid 66 percent preferred the job life, while 28 percent would rather stay home." When these readers were asked if they envy women in the other group, "one in four working wives admitted jealousy, while only one in 12 at-home women confessed to that feeling."

In its April 1976 issue, *McCall's* published the results of a random poll of its subscribers. Of 2,000 respondents, 87 percent of the women said they were satisfied with their lives, and 71 percent said it was their children that brought the most satisfaction. Sixty-seven percent said it was their marriages. The majority of these women said they had not been discriminated against because of their sex, and one out of three of the *McCall's* readers said she was angry with the women's movement, primarily because of its "effects on family life, morals or religious teachings," and for "downgrading the roles of housewife and mother."

These findings seem to support the feelings expressed by many women we have interviewed around the country, such as Mrs. Carol Rutte, a homemaker in Veneta, Oregon, who told us: "I would rather have the kind of life I have now. I taught school for almost ten years before I married. Teaching is interesting and challenging, but it is also a drag at times. There is more independence, creativity and meaning in what I am doing now."

Mrs. Rutte described what many women seem to feel —that their best talents are needed more in the home than in the working world, and that the social roles of men and women should *not* be the same. "I think," she said, "that women have definite feminine gifts of sympathy, understanding, warmth, softness and love that they contribute. Men are physically more powerful and more aggressive achievers. Women should be equal in rights, pay and opportunities, but they are now taking on the masculine roles and qualities instead of bringing the feminine qualities to the same work and this is a loss to the world of the unique gifts of women." This theme was often expressed in our conversations with women.

Another indication that large numbers of women reject the so-called liberated approach to life is the gigantic audience that has emerged in recent years for courses and books such as *Fascinating Womanhood* by

164

Helen B. Andelin, and *Total Woman* by Marabel Morgan. These approaches to womanhood—which are anathema to libbers—encourage women *not* to compete with men, but instead to work at complementing the masculine role with a feminine personality that is accepting, admiring, adapting and appreciative of the male. More than a half-million women have taken these courses to become, they hope, better and happier wives. By mid-1975, *Fascinating Womanhood* had sold nearly a million copies at $7.95, and Bantam Books reported that the paperback version was selling at a rate of 1,500 copies a day. *Total Woman* topped the nonfiction bestseller list in 1974, selling over 575,000 copies at $5.95 each despite derisive reviews by critics in the press too "sophisticated" for a book with a religious point of view that encourages wives to devote themselves to caring for their husbands and children. Pocket Books paid $675,000 for the privilege of printing a paperback edition. In spite of the opinions of many newspaper and magazine writers, and the explanations of the psychology experts they summon to tell why such notions are not up to liberationist standards, these books provide insight and direction to great numbers of women who don't relate to feminism.

Much commotion has been made in the press in recent years over *Ms.* magazine, which in 1972 introduced the ideas of feminism to the drugstore newsstand and the supermarket. TV commentators and editorial writers have hailed *Ms.* as a "phenomenal" success, and its monthly presence on magazine racks across the nation has caused many to suppose that feminism is of central concern to a great many women.

But if you take a look at the circulation figures of popular magazines for women, as published in the bible of the advertising industry, *Standard Rate and Data,* and discover that in terms of paying readers, *Ms.*

is not very influential at all among American women. In fact, its circulation of 453,952 readers is only a fraction of one percent of the readers of popular women's magazines, and its circulation is only about 5 percent as great as any one of the most popular traditional publications, such as *Family Circle* (8,479,519 readers), *Woman's Day* (8,164,817), and *Better Homes and Gardens* (8,093,646). These leaders of the field of magazines for women may pay occasional lip service to feminist ideas or drop an occasional plug for equality, but their overall perspective is worlds away from the ideological slant of *Ms.* or *New Woman* (331,443).

"Equality. It's with this one word," declares a writer in *Better Homes and Gardens*, "[that] misunderstandings begin. We've discovered that many people think equality would somehow require that men and women be just alike; think alike, act alike, even dress alike. Perhaps there are a few radical feminists who would like to see a world of unisexual anonymity, but this patently absurd notion is held only by a minority of women. . . ." Furthermore, the writer declares, "*BH&G*'s family life survey revealed that 79 percent of our readers felt that 'the dominent role of the husband in the American family is declining in importance.' And 71 percent of our readers felt that decline to be bad."

If true, this report means that over 5.5 million readers of *BH&G* feel the husband should be the dominant marriage partner—*14 times as many women* as read *Ms.*, and two and a half times as many as read *Cosmopolitan* (2,214,655), the leading lib-laced, cosmetics-selling medium for working girls. *Glamour* (1,855,835) and *Mademoiselle* (873,686) offer similar smatterings of liberationist-chic articles, but their overall thrust, like *Cosmopolitan*'s, seems more to be aimed at liberating young, single women from traditional morals, from se-

166

rious thought, and from their money (for clothes and cosmetics) than from the "sexist oppressions" that plague the readers of *Ms.*

The prevailing emphasis in most successful women's magazines is upon matters reflecting the conventional preoccupations of American women and traditional sex-role orientations, both in the magazines for single, working girls and in the journals for married women, such as *Redbook* (4,574,495), *McCall's* (6,511,891), and *Ladies' Home Journal* (6,080,058).

We examined the contents of the 18 leading magazines for women (with combined circulations of over 61 million readers), and found that 57 percent of this readership chooses thoroughly traditional magazines. These were publications such as *Family Circle*, *Woman's Day, Good Housekeeping*, and *Better Homes and Gardens*.

The entry for *Family Circle* in *Standard Rate and Data* states: "*Family Circle* is edited for women. About 90% of the editorial content is devoted to service features dealing with home management, family care and self-improvement. Articles offer ideas and practical advice which provide bases for reader-action. Areas of coverage: food, home decorating, equipment, fashions and needlework, beauty and grooming, health and medical science, child care, travel and leisure-time activities, creative crafts, gardening and flowers. Regular departments include Here's News in Medicine, Creative Women's World, News to Use, Buyers Guide, Shopping Circle—a mail order section."

By contrast, the entry for *Ms.* states: "A magazine by and for women. A forum for women and men to share honest information about their changing roles. In-depth articles on child-rearing, politics, medicine, psychology, economics, films, books, music, art and education. Both male and female writers emphasize the

167

'how-to' as well as the theoretical aspects of change."

Why is *Family Circle* (or any one of the top women's magazines) 20 times more popular than *Ms.* or *New Woman*? I think it must have to do with the kinds of things most women are interested in. For example, in the spring of 1976, Billie Jean King, the tennis champion and originator of *WomenSports,* clashed with the new editor of the publication, who wanted to put more emphasis on fashion and activities of male/female couples in an effort to attract a wider audience. The strident feminist approach that the magazine had assumed when it was first issued stifled readership and brought complaints from readers.

Despite great interest by people in the mass media, the reason only a small proportion of American women are interested in feminist concerns, it seems to me, is because their values are elsewhere and they prefer to focus their time and energies on less abstract matters with meaning in their everyday lives. Considerable evidence suggests they are far more absorbed with problems of attracting and keeping husbands, and creating comfortable homes. The most successful women's magazines, now as in the past, are those whose contents emphasize home, fashion, cooking, beauty and love.

In September 1974 a major article in *Scientific American,* "The Changing Status of Women in Developed Countries," gave a historical and demographic survey of the roles of women in industrialized countries in the twentieth century. The author, Dr. Judith Blake, a professor of demography in the Graduate School of Public Policy of the University of California at Berkeley, reported that the evidence does not support the notion that women are any more anxious than they were thirty years ago to work outside the home.

Two important tendencies are apparent, however, according to Dr. Blake: ". . . no matter whether one looks

168

at the proportion of married women working, the pattern of women's participation in the labor force with respect to age, the types of occupation in which women are engaged, the relative earnings of women or feminine attitudes toward the primacy of work, one finds that women typically participate in economic activity only as a secondary supplement to their primary status inside the home."

This study makes it clear that even at their highest levels of activity in the labor force, women work outside the home at rates much lower than do men. Not only do they drop out of the work force to rear children, but their work rates are much lower at every stage of their life cycle. They also tend to work part-time much more frequently than do men. In 1973, for example, one-fourth of the female work force in the U.S. worked less than 35 hours per week.

We hear much in the media about the increasing numbers of women going out to work in recent years. The fact is that this large increase has been due to the rising demand for workers in sales, clerical, and teaching jobs, and in the expanding service sector of our economy—hardly the glamorous careers promised in *Cosmopolitan* or *Glamour*.

"In the light of the typically modest occupational status of women in highly developed countries," declares Dr. Blake, "it is to be expected that they earn less than men even when the comparison is confined to full-time, year-round employment. Studies suggest that the complex causes for the differences are related less to wage discrimination per se than to the concentration of women in low-paying occupations and to the secondary role of work in their lives; men normally have greater continuity of employment, work longer hours and get more job training."

Dr. Blake states that more women now feel free to

work, or need to work, because their families are smaller, more women are divorced, and inflation puts more pressure on them to maintain their standard of living. Some are drawn to jobs because they have been educated and feel that they should be doing something besides working in the home. But, says Dr. Blake, there are also strenuous reasons why many women don't wish to leave home for a job: "Perhaps the most important is the overall assumption by both men and women that the primary obligation of a woman is to her home and family."

Dr. Blake points to the National Fertility Study of 1970 in which 6,740 women under 45 years of age were questioned on sex roles. Almost 80 percent of the women agreed: "It is much better for everyone involved if the man is the achiever outside the home and the woman takes care of the home and family." On the other hand, less than half of these women agreed that "a working mother can establish just as warm and secure a relationship with her children as a mother who does not work." Over two-thirds of the women agreed with this statement: "A preschool child is likely to suffer if his mother works."

Dr. Blake declares, moreover: "Studies in most of the highly developed countries show that significant proportions of women who work do not want to; also, among those women who are not working, typically half or more either do not want to be employed or want only part-time jobs. In fact, the strongest preference among women appears to be a part-time job: in effect a work situation that does not interfere with their primary status." Overall, Dr. Blake's findings are a devastating denial of the feminist proposition that women are longing to be freed of their domestic role and responsibilities. She reports that she could find no evidence of widespread discontent among women in the course of her studies of women in the developed countries of the world. "When they are asked," she says, "they typically seem to be as satisfied with life as men."

These findings are reflected in virtually all objective studies of the attitudes and ambitions of women. In 1972, a national sample of American women conducted by Louis Harris and Associates showed that more than 60 percent of women surveyed said that motherhood is just as challenging an occupation as you will find in an outside job, and this was true of both younger and older women questioned. Just a little over 20 percent of these women indicated they frequently hoped that their daughters would have more interesting careers outside the home than *they* had experienced. Most women reported that they hardly ever had such a feeling.

In the 1974 Virginia Slims American Women's Opinion Poll, the Roper Organization reported that 92 percent of women said they think "it takes as much intelligence and drive for a woman to bring up children properly as it takes to hold a good position in business or government."

According to Roper, "Two in 3 (64%) express strong views that 'having a loving husband who is able to take care of me is much more important than making it on my own.' " Eighty-three percent of the women expressed some agreement with this statement, and only 13 percent actually disagreed.

A majority of women (56 percent) believes that neither sex has more advantages in life, according to Roper. Only 31 percent of women say they feel that there are more advantages to being a man, and this is true even after several years of intensive propaganda in the mass media asserting the notion that women are oppressed. Among those who do think there are more

171

advantages for men, only 12 percent say it is because "women are still discriminated against, not treated as equals," and less than half (47 percent) think it is because men have "more, better job opportunities." The majority of men either do not perceive any special advantages in being male or have no opinion on the subject.

Less than half of the women polled by Roper (46 percent) feel that it is the woman who gives up more freedom in marriage. Thirty-five percent feel that both sexes give up the same amount of freedom, and 15 percent say that men give up the most. The majority of men who were polled said that it is equal or that men give up the most liberty.

Three out of four women reject the idea that "being a woman has prevented me from doing some of the things I wanted to in life." And nearly two-thirds (63 percent) say they do *not* feel "if I had been born a man, I would have gotten a lot further in this world." And only 14 percent say they strongly feel that they would have gotten further as men.

"Four out of 5 women," Roper reports, "deny that their educations are wasted." On the contrary, they believe that child-rearing and homemaking require as much knowledge, creativity and intelligence as an outside job. In fact, Roper says, "Strong majorities—nearly 3 out of 5—of both women and men say they are 'very satisfied' with their lives today."

Contrary to the contentions of women's lib, the 1974 Roper poll shows that "women claim a consistently high degree of personal satisfaction with their lives. And in spite of the American youth culture, most women appear to be happier over 30." Furthermore, twice as many married women say they are "very satisfied" with their lives as divorced or separated women. When you compare these statistics of 1974 with the replies of women to these same questions in the 1972 Harris survey, it is apparent that women have become slightly less satisfied in those years—as might be expected considering the intensive feminist pressure exerted through the media in recent years.

"When asked what women want for their daughters," Roper states, "according to 3 out of 4 women (76%) a happy marriage is the primary choice. Only 1 in 6 women would choose an interesting career for her daughter over a happy marriage and only 3% rank financial success as the chief goal." This is true of the young women as well as the older ones. "A majority of women also want a happy marriage for their sons, but a career and financial success are much closer competitors."

Marriage is the preferred way of life for 96 percent of women and 92 percent of men, according to Roper. Half of all women, in fact, say they believe the most satisfying and interesting way of life is "a traditional marriage with the husband assuming the responsibility for providing for the family and the wife running the house and taking care of the children." Forty-six percent say it would be a "marriage where husband and wife share responsibilities more—both work, both share homemaking and child responsibilities." Despite the broad attention focused on alternative lifestyles by the mass media, the desire of people to participate in nonmarriage styles of living is very limited. Roper says: "The prevailing popularity of marriage today is underlined by the small numbers of both sexes who want to stay single and alone (1%), live in a commune (1%), live with someone of the opposite sex without marrying (1% women, 3% men), live with someone of the same sex (less than 1%)."

Only 2 percent of women are so interested in having a career that they say they would forego marriage and children to have it. Another 4 percent think the most satisfying and interesting life would be to have a career and marriage but no children. Thirty-eight percent of women say they think the most interesting and satisfying life would be to marry and have children, but not to be employed outside. Fifty-two percent think some combination of marriage, family and a job would be most satisfying and interesting.

"But," Roper emphasizes, "it should be remembered that two-thirds of women feel strongly that 'having a loving husband who is able to take care of me is much more important than making it on my own.'"

Roper found that the majority of American women are not in favor of the so-called new morality, and do not believe that it will lead to better choices of marital partners or more successful marriages: "Two out of 3 (64%) believe it will weaken the institution of marriage, and over half (56%) say that the country's morals will break down." Only one in ten (10%) regards sexual freedom before marriage as a change for the better. This attitude, moreover, seems linked to the college experience, because college women are twice as likely as high school graduates to believe that sexual freedom before marriage is a good thing for society. In 1974, Roper reported that 53 percent of American women still said they believed premarital sex to be immoral. Only 11 percent said they would want their daughter to live with someone outside of marriage; only 8 percent said they would find it acceptable for their daughter to have a child outside of marriage; and one percent thought it would be acceptable for their daughter to have a homosexual relationship.

Nobody knows for sure exactly where the 70 million or so adult females in the U.S. stand on every issue raised by women's lib. There is wide divergence of opinion in many areas, and women don't hold to one coherent body of thought. Nevertheless, based on the

174

kinds of demographic data presented above, Annie and I have constructed a rough profile of the stance of American women on women's lib that we think is closer to reality than the vague impressions created by the media's emphasis on radical and bizarre points of view. Our best "guestimate" looks like this:

Radical, hardcore lib true believers:	4%
Committed, but less radical, true believers:	9%
Lip-service libbers:	30%
Traditional-minded women:	57%

Among the 4 percent of hardcore radicals, we would place all of those who belong to such distinctly feminist organizations as NOW, the Lesbian Feminist Liberation, the National Women's Political Caucus, and so on, as well as certain individuals who work to radical-

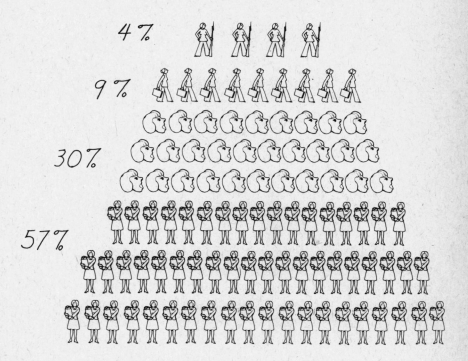

ize groups such as the YWCA, the League of Women Voters, and many other organizations that are not fundamentally feminist. This is the hardcore of revolutionaries who generate and distribute the literature of lib, provide the impetus, or say in their writings and utterances that they are dedicated to the subversion of sex roles, free enterprise, marriage and the family.

The 9 percent of committed, but less radical, true believers seem to be by and large those club women, teachers, university professors, journalists and certain other types of career women who believe strongly in the basic tenets of feminism, but whose objectives and expectations are less cataclysmic than the hardcore revolutionaries. These people carry the faith and are dedicated, but they think they can salvage the best of both worlds. They believe sex roles can be abolished without destroying our present social system. They're not as likely to be lesbians as their more radical sisters, but they still would prefer to be linked to lesbians than to be identified with housewifery.

We estimate that about 30 percent of American women fall into the category of being lip-service libbers. They have no real commitment to the tenets of women's lib and actually understand very little of it. They may speak of being "liberated," or call someone a "male chauvinist pig," or try to remember to say "he or she" instead of just "he" when they are around certain people because they think it is chic—but they are not really interested in the history, literature or issues of feminism. In general, "liberation" for them means repeating the faddish litany of lib they pick up from pop feminists in the mass media. They are ambitious working girls ready to accept whatever benefits the lib carousel may bring them, dissatisfied wives anxious for anything that relieves the monotony of their lives, and millions of the bored, frustrated or insecure people

176

who characteristically go along with anything that promises to focus some attention on them or make them seem "with it." As one lip-service libber put it: "Of course I support the Women's Liberation Movement. Who wouldn't be for equality, liberty and husbands doing the dishes?"

We believe that a full 57 percent of American women are thoroughly traditional in their attitudes toward work, marriage, politics and the complementary roles of the sexes. These women pay little attention to subjects of women's lib, except to wonder why so many other females have taken leave of their senses, and to worry about the decline of traditional values in the society. Nearly all of this group believe in equal opportunity in education, employment and credit, and in equal justice under law. They are by no means, however, supporters of the 13 percent of women in the U.S. who consider themselves political feminists, and they don't believe they are oppressed or deprived. "I'm not inferior to men and I'm not superior to men," one of them told me once, "but I sure am different from men, and I don't want anyone to forget it."

But Sex Differences Are Just Cultural, Aren't They?

One evening, Annie showed me an article in a magazine she was reading. "Somewhere between the cradle and first grade, children pick up the popular conviction that boys are stronger than girls and that women are weaker than men," the *McCall's* writer declared. "As in most myths," the piece continued, "there's some truth to this one."

"Why drag in the word 'myth' if they're talking about something that is usually *true*?" said Annie. "They're just trying to muddle the differences between the sexes. It's the same old thing."

The *McCall's* writer went on to say that although "boys do develop into generally stronger, heavier physical types than their female counterparts, the difference is less than is thought." The rest of the article suggests that the differences in strength between males and females is mostly due to social conditioning, and that women can minimize these effects by lifting weights and encouraging their daughters to take up skiing, tennis, baseball, basketball and the like.

Such items have been regular features in many publications in the past few years. We frequently find little reminders in *Parade*, such as: "Women are slowly and inexorably surpassing the world sports records established by men." The basis for this bold statement turns out to be the fact that in 1972, female swimmer Shane Gould clocked a better time in the Olympic Games than the best male time in the Olympics of 1956. The piece continues: "In track and field events, the women still have a long way to go." And the writer concludes, "At their current pace they will need another 20–30 years to match the records set by males. . . . But eventually they will do it. They are becoming better athletes all the time." The unfortunate part about this line of reasoning, of course, is that the performance of men is improving too, so women remain far behind them in almost every arena.

A more sensational sort of intellectual parry tries to avoid all recognition that there are real sex differences by promoting the kind of millennial component suggested in this ad for *Forum* magazine:

> Women movie-goers are profoundly aroused by what they see in the movies. But *only*, says FORUM magazine in its September issue, if it involves the total man-woman relationship.
>
> It seems, FORUM says, women are much less moved by watching narrow-focus sexual contact— the core of hard-core.
>
> But as women become more willing to trust their own responses to visual stimulation, then things will change and hard-core will turn them on in greater numbers.
>
> This and other articles of vital interest to men and women in the September FORUM. . . .

It always seems to us that these little items in the press are like Doublemint Twins or Chiquita Banana ads—just little reminder advertisements to keep alive the notion that there aren't clear and significant differences between the sexes, to subtly inculcate the feeling that it's okay for males and females to be treated exactly the same in every way. While this idea has been widely and uncritically accepted, it didn't seem to us to be grounded in reality, and so we set out to explore just what the differences between the sexes really are.

The "popular conviction" we pick up that men are larger and stronger than women in most cases is firmly rooted, not in myth, but in fact. Among infants, boys double their birth weight significantly earlier than girls, because of the growth of more bone and muscle. By adulthood, the average man weighs about 35 pounds more than the average woman, and is nearly a half-foot taller. Moreover, if you have the impression that females are also fattier and less muscular than males, it's not social conditioning that makes you think that; it's really true. Compared to boys, girls have narrower shoulders, knees that turn inward, elbows that turn outward, a lower center of gravity, a broader pelvis that gives a certain angle to the legs that affects the way they walk and run, and significantly less cardiovascular capacity. Women have shorter vocal chords (you almost never mistake a man's voice for a woman's).

In his book *Sport: A Philosophic Inquiry*, Professor Paul Weiss of Yale University says that "Women have comparatively less muscular strength and lighter arms, do not use their muscles as rapidly, have a longer reaction time, faster heart rates, and achieve a smaller arm strength in relation to their weight than men do. Their bones ossify sooner, they have a narrower and more flexible shoulder girdle, smaller chest girth, and smaller bones and thighs. They also have wider and more stable knee joints, a heavier and more tilted pelvis, longer index fingers, and a greater finger dexterity.

181

They have shorter thumbs, legs, feet, and arm length, a smaller thoracic cavity, smaller lungs, smaller hearts, lower stroke volumes, a smaller average height, lower blood pressure, fatigue more readily, and are more prone to injury. Their bodies are less dense and contain more fat; they have less bone mass, and throw differently."

Feminists have often tried to convince us that the differences between the sexes are no more than the differences between blacks and whites, but this isn't so. Whereas blacks and whites are known by scientists to be variants of the same genetic body, with no essential difference between body cells, examination of the smallest cell from the human body will reveal whether the donor was a male or a female.

Some other differences we discovered in our researches verify the impression most people have that men and women are quite different creatures when you take a careful look. Women (believe it or not) are far more subject to cyclic hormonal fluctuations than men, are prone to the exigencies of menstruation, pregnancy and childbirth, and suffer a variety of gynecological disorders unknown to males. They're three times as likely to have rheumatoid arthritis, and four times as likely to suffer spinal osteoporosis (they have two and a half times as many hip fractures as men). Females suffer *50 to 100 times* more urinary tract infections than males, because the female urethra averages little more than an inch in length and empties into an area easily contaminated by bacteria.

On the other hand, men are known to suffer in much greater numbers from coronary disease, arteriosclerosis, alcoholism, ulcers, diabetes, kidney stones and a long list of other disorders. Prostatitis, for instance, is a chronic condition that bears heavily on many older men, but does not affect women. It seems that in the practice of medicine, at least, there are important reasons why the M.D. must pay attention to the differences between the sexes when he goes to fix them up —they're two very different physiological models.

Physicians who've studied the effects of premenstrual tension know that the majority of women experience unusual hormonal effects during the final week or so of their cycle. Dr. Katherina Dalton of the University of London has studied these effects extensively, and she estimates that about 40 percent of women suffer a variety of distressing symptoms, which may include abdominal bloating, headache, breast tenderness, irritability, mental depression, increased weight and swelling of the legs with fluid. In her book *The Menstrual Cycle*, Dr. Dalton writes: "The premenstrual syndrome has been described as the world's most common disease. . . . The menstrual influence on mental ability . . . occurs throughout a woman's menstrual life. . . . One has only to watch typists in a large pool and notice how on one day some typists are filling their wastepaper baskets with spoiled work, and on other days it is a quite different group of typists doing the same thing. . . . The menstrual influence affects women in all grades and all skills of employment, from the top executives who make hasty decisions, errors of judgment or are temporarily deprived of drive and initiative, to the office assistant who slops the coffee on the saucers with such regularity. . . . Similarly the effects of menstruation are apparent in all phases of women's employment."

Dr. Dalton describes studies of hospital admissions that have shown that half of women admitted to mental wards for acute psychiatric illnesses were menstruating or were about to begin. She says that 53 percent of these women who had attempted suicide were either having their period or were about ready to begin.

Later in life, of course, about three-quarters of women experience another hormonal disruption in their lives known as the "menopausal syndrome." This syndrome, which often affects women for several years during their forties or fifties, in many cases leads to severe emotional disturbances, including severe depression and loss of interest in normal activities.

Although most of us have observed these differences between the sexes sufficiently in life to know that they are real, feminists have tried to pretend that somehow they are not actually differences at all. For example, they say that menopause is not an exclusively female thing, because men have something called a "climacteric," and so really we're all practically the same. But if you look into this idea in an authoritative medical reference, you find that the "climacteric" of the male is not a comparable phenomenon at all. The *Textbook of Medicine,* for instance, reveals that unlike symptoms of menopause in the female, which can usually be anticipated, in the male "spontaneous testicular deficiency of sufficient degree to produce symptoms is an exceedingly rare occurrence."

Perhaps the most extensive collection of evidence on the differences between the sexes ever compiled is that of two Stanford University psychologists, Eleanor Emmons Maccoby and Carol Nagy Jacklin, who wrote *The Psychology of Sex Differences.* The authors admit in their introduction to having a feminist bias, and declare: "Although we have tried to be objective about the value-laden topics discussed in this book, we know that we cannot have succeeded entirely. . . ."

Yet they must have overcome their feminist tilt to a remarkable degree through dedication to scientific truth, because their conclusions support the belief that men and women are far from equally equipped to compete in the hard, real world. According to Maccoby and

184

Jacklin, there are fundamental differences between the human sexes that would seem to give men decisive advantages in economic and occupational competitions. Boys, they tell us, from adolescence on are better at visual-spatial tasks, and they think this may be due to a sex-linked gene. They also say boys after adolescence show greater mathematical ability than girls, while the girls do better in verbal skills. Boys, furthermore, are "more aggressive both physically and verbally" than girls from the age of two years. This is so, they say, *despite efforts of the society to restrain the boys, whose aggressiveness is recognized to be more dangerous than that of the girls.* (This, of course, is the reason

boys have traditionally been taught *not* to be physically aggressive toward girls. It's interesting that feminists, who seem most anxious to have boys assaulting girls on the athletic field, are the most vehement railers against society's inefficacy at disciplining wife-beaters. For all of their confidence in the influence of social conditioning, feminists seem to want to abandon the fairly effective learning that is mainly responsible for such protection against male aggressiveness as females now enjoy.)

But anyone who thinks boys are boys and girls are girls *just* because they were brought up that way should hear what scientists at Cornell University discovered in the Dominican Republic. Over the past few years a team of doctors has been studying children born in an isolated village about 150 miles from Santo Domingo who are of very special interest to the physicians. These youngsters were born and raised as little girls, and that is what the people of Salinas—including the parents of the kids—believed them to be until they reached the age of puberty. Then to everyone's astonishment, these "girls" began developing muscles and deep voices, the genitals of boys began to protrude, and like other males their age, they began taking an interest in girls.

This is a true story documented by scientific evidence and reported in the distinguished journal *Science*. As fantastic as it seems, the problem results from a rare hereditary disorder in which masculinization of the male fetus is incomplete due to inadequate enzyme action during development in the womb. In these unusual cases, the brain and sex organs are programmed to be male, but the genitals do not fully develop, and when the child is born it seems to be female.

When these children first appeared three generations ago, they were raised as though they were normal fe-

186

males, and everybody was dismayed when, with the heightened production of male hormone at puberty, the children became unmistakably male. Not only did their bodies change, but their sexual interest was masculine in every way, and eventually they married and enjoyed normal sex lives as men.

Dr. Imperato-McGinley, one of the scientists from Cornell University Medical College who went to the Dominican Republic to study these cases, said these children are of considerable scientific interest since at least 18 of the children were known to have been raised as girls. "It appears that despite the sex of rearing, the affected were able to change gender identity at the time of puberty," she said. "They consider themselves as males and have a libido directed toward the opposite sex." This kind of research gives us some idea of the vast importance of the male hormone in establishing male sexual behavior.

There is a great deal about these matters the experts don't know. Dr. Julian M. Davidson, a physiologist at Stanford University, wrote in the journal *Hospital Practice* not long ago that "despite the extensive experimental information that is available on the endocrine as well as neural factors involved, we know very little of the physiologic basis of sexual behavior in humans, no doubt largely because of the taboos historically associated with such behavior. One result of this has been the development of widely divergent views on the relative importance of physiologic and psychologic factors in the control of human sexual behavior. . . ."

The children of Salinas are not unique in the medical literature. Dr. Robert J. Stoller, professor of psychiatry at the University of California at Los Angeles, in his book *Sex and Gender* describes another case in which parents of a child they believed was a girl were surprised. Dr. Stoller says: "To the bitter dismay of her

187

feminine mother, the child from birth on acted as though she were convinced she should be a boy. All the effects of learning of gender, so crucial in almost all instances, left this child untouched. Then, at puberty, physical examination revealed she was a male with a penis the size of a clitoris, bifid scrotum and cryptorchid [all of which had given her at birth the appearance of a normal female]. The child had been right all along; his gender identity had been male in the face of all of society's pressures to act like a female. . . ."

A large body of modern biological research supports the belief that male sexuality and behavior are inherently distinct from those of the female. Biologists have discovered the process known as endogenous androgen masculinization of the male brain, which probably accounts not only for these purely male characteristics, but also for the tendency of males to dominate throughout nature.

Masculinization of the brain comes about like this: When a child is conceived, the tendency of nature is to produce a female, and this is what happens unless the egg receives a Y chromosome from the father to make a male. This will activate the formation of male testes in the embryo. When these are formed, they're triggered to produce the male hormone, androgen, which stimulates formation of the external genitals, and another substance, which prevents development of the female organs. The male hormone also circulates to the central nervous system, and, in some way that is not thoroughly understood as yet, actually programs parts of the brain (known to the experts as "hypothalamic pathways") so that the child will behave characteristically as a male, and not as a female. (This is why the children of Salinas exhibited thoroughly masculine sexual behavior in adolescence even though they had been raised as girls prior to that time.)

Researchers at Stanford University have demonstrated the role of the male hormone in stimulating aggressive behavior. "In women, unlike females of other species, the influence of hormones on sexual behavior is not established and is probably of minor importance," states Dr. Davidson. "This 'evolutionary discontinuity' does not, however, apply to the human male, in whom hormonal control of sexual behavior appears similar to that in other animals. . . ."

In experiments on primates, for example, both males and females who are given extra androgen show much more aggressive behavior. Experiments on many species have demonstrated that the male hormone is directly related to male sexual behavior as well as to other responses of the male reproductive system.

Even John Money, a professor of medical psychology at Johns Hopkins University who has been one of the most active crusaders for abolishment of sex roles, says in his book *Sexual Signatures* that his view of recent research "points to the conclusion that the prenatal sex hormones triggered the development in you—whether you are male or female—of the potential for strenuous physical activity, dominance behavior, and parental behavior. If you had the higher percentage of androgen in that prenatal mix that males normally have, the potential for strenuous physical activity and dominance behavior was later apt to be more sensitive, would respond to weaker stimuli, than if you had less androgen."

Investigators like Dr. Money are careful to interpret the new findings on prenatal programming of the male brain in ways that best serve their hopes of engineering a unisexual world. It is interesting that this phenomenon, which is accepted in the scientific world even by those who are crusaders for unisex, such as Dr. Money, hasn't penetrated the mass media and is virtually un-

189

known by most people. Such is the selective reporting of those who write for the popular media. (To the best of my knowledge, neither *Parade, New Woman* nor *U.S. News & World Report* has rushed to break the news.)

We are just on the brink of learning the profound effects that sex hormones have on our lives. Before puberty, boys show higher levels of androgen in their systems than girls, but at adolescence the levels in males soar to amounts perhaps ten times those in most females, and these levels are maintained throughout their lifetimes. Only recently have bioscientists begun to penetrate the possible role of the male hormone in raising the risk of heart disease in men.

Even though prenatal masculinization of the male brain has virtually been kept secret from most people, it is a basic fact of life that will doubtless ensure that no matter what we do (barring massive chemical or surgical intervention into people's bodies), most little boys and girls will continue to grow up to be two quite different kinds of people.

Much evidence tells us that males are naturally more venturesome, curious and risk-taking than the smaller sex. Not only do men find their way into situations where they get maimed and killed much more frequently, but they are four times as likely to succeed if they try to commit suicide. Data from the National Center for Health Statistics show that males are murdered more than three and a half times as often as females. Men suffer a much higher rate of accidental injury and death by violence.

When it comes to adventures such as climbing utility poles, vastly more boys are electrocuted each year than girls. When the National Safety Council completed its five-year, nationwide "Survey of Non-Employee Overhead Electrical Contacts," it reported 865 deaths and 3,652 nonfatal injuries to people who didn't work for the utility company, but nonetheless felt compelled to climb its power poles. Ninety-three percent of these unauthorized mishaps happened to males, a great proportion of which turned out to be boys between the ages of 9 and 18 years old.

Regardless of the highly publicized incidents of female violence in recent years, the evidence still shows that men are far more prone to violence than women. Without question men are just naturally more aggressive and dangerous creatures. In his book *Violence,* psychiatrist and criminologist Dr. John Gunn writes,

> There is good evidence that in most mammals the male is more aggressive and hence more violent than the female. Females can be very aggressive at times, it is true, and in some species (e.g., the gibbon) there is not much to choose between male and female aggressiveness. The male hamster, in fact, is less agressive than the female. This does not detract from the general point, however, and there are few mammalian species in which the female initiates attacks more frequently than the male, and is generally dominant to the male.
>
> You do not have to be an ethologist to recognize the general truth of these statements. Among domestic mammals—the dog, the horse, cattle, sheep, the pig, etc.—the difference in aggressiveness can easily be seen. Farmers do not keep herds of adult bulls together because of the severe fighting that would occur if they did, but they successfully keep large herds of cows.
>
> Equally one does not need to be a physiological zoologist to guess that this sexual difference in aggressiveness is related, fairly directly in mammals, to the sexual hormones. . . .

In the competition of adult life, males outstrip and dominate females in ways that can't be attributed to their purely muscular advantage. Not only has this always been true among human beings, but it is also the characteristic situation among nearly all of our fellow mammals in the animal kingdom. Primates—however much the fact may offend the sensibilities of unisex planners—are organized into social structures based on dominance, sex attraction and mother-child relationships.

Dominance hierarchies are established on the basis of strength, agility and personality. Such groupings are characteristic not only of human and nonhuman primates, but of most mammals. The order, structure, and harmony of the group are maintained through conflict —or more often the threat of conflict—and through mutual bonds of affection, admiration and appeasement.

Social hierarchies, far from being the evil contrivances some people seem to imagine, are natural systems that result in more or less permanent social organizations in which each individual comes to recognize his relative position to others. As we know, we all learn eventually whom we can dominate and who can dominate us. (If we don't learn this, then we don't adjust to a social order.) The typical pattern in nature is an order in which males occupy the most dominant positions over *lesser males and females alike.*

The social life of wolves, for instance, seems similar in many ways to human society. Wolves live in highly organized groups, or packs, and are very concerned with establishing and maintaining a hierarchy in which each wolf has a definite status and knows his rank within the pack. Within such a system—which is not unlike the usual human condition—the wolves live mostly in harmony and order, usually monogamously, and with strong affectional ties to one another. By many human standards, wolves are admirable creatures who nurture their young devotedly, work together effectively, control their population and conserve their food supply. Of course males are dominant in the social hierarchy of the wolf pack, and, as with humans, the status of the female is often determined by the status of the male she manages to attract.

Many other species show similar patterns of domination and leadership by the largest male animals. Wild ungulates, such as horses, elks and zebras, follow a lead stallion. At mating time, the dominant male fights to establish his possession of the females. The male ostrich has a bellowing voice with which to signal danger. He is also larger than the female and unquestionably the protector of the family. Domination over harems of females by dominant males is characteristic of many mammals, as varied as ostriches, elks, walruses, seals, gazelles, bats and lions. Zoologists and anthropol-

The typical pattern is an order in which males occupy the most dominant positions over lesser males and females alike.

ogists alike have observed that threat behaviors, such as those necessary to maintain the dominance hierarchies of social cohesion, are among the most familiar activities of mammals, human or otherwise. Whether it be our own punitive frown, the wolf's bared teeth, or the hisses, growls, glares or posturing of other animals —all serve to weld an order that is second nature to man and beast alike.

The animals most similar to man, of course, are the other primates, such as chimpanzees and baboons. Scientists have spent a great deal of time studying these animals, which behave like us in so many ways. When Jane Goodall observed primates in Tanzania, East Africa, she found that aggressive patterns of behavior are much more characteristic of male animals than of females, even among the very young. Adolescence is an especially aggressive and turbulent period among male monkeys—just as it is with humans—partly because they are beginning to enter the dominance hierarchy that absorbs adult males, and partly because of the effects of the male hormone.

According to Dr. David A. Hamburg of the Stanford University School of Medicine, another prominent primate researcher, "Chimpanzee males (and also gorillas) make elaborate aggressive displays in adult life, and the young males, even in infancy, show more interest in such behavior than do females. Young males are keen observers of older males in such matters."

Baboons are the largest monkeys. A male baboon weighs about 75 pounds, a female about 30 pounds. They often live on the ground in an environment similar to the one from which early man emerged, and their social behavior is remarkably like ours. They form sexual bonds at mating time and generally maintain these monogamous relations. The males, who are much more able to defend the troop, take up defensive positions when predators such as leopards, lions or cheetahs approach. They also fight over females, over preferred sleeping sites, and over food, and although both sexes are generally affectionate and companionable, the males dominate almost everything.

In the *Washington Star* of August 24, 1975, we found a cutesy item headlined, "I'm in Charge Here, You Baboon." The reporter seems to have written one fem-lib story too many. "In the female hierarchy of baboons, guess who wears the pants?" he wrote. He goes on to say that "an assistant professor of psychology at the University of Virginia has come up with fresh word that Mama Baboon wears the pants. Figuratively speaking, of course." As we read further along in this flighty account, it becomes clear that the assistant professor's report was not really as revolutionary as the reporter's slant might lead us to believe. Let's face it—with males that weigh twice as much as females, which baboons do *you* think wear the pants?

Actually, although baboon life does center around the females and their young, experts tell us that the males always predominate in a hierarchy determined by age, size, strength, aggressiveness, and the condition of their massive canine teeth. The male's canines are several times the size of the female's and represent an important part of his arsenal for protecting the troop. Baboon males are distinctly the men of the family, exploring strange and dangerous places, defending the troop, choosing partners and settling disputes.

The deep gut feeling of being a man is perhaps the thing that automatically convinces most adult males that the differences between the sexes are obvious and unalterable. This is probably why most men still consider women's lib to be harmless, if not a joke. Men know there is a special feeling to being a male, and that it's this feeling, not any conspiracy, that bonds them in their awareness of being a definite sex.

I've heard feminists complain bitterly about the whistles and catcalls often endured by women who pass by men working at a construction site. Why, they wonder, can men not relate to us sedately as "persons" instead of undressing us with their eyes as though we are merely sex objects? Gabrielle Burton, the feminist writer mentioned earlier, laments that "boys grab at you, men in subways rub up against you, grown men meet your breasts before they meet your eyes."

I think it's perhaps unreasonable to ask a man to be just a "person." That makes it seem like male and female persons have the same feelings and responses, and who can believe this is so? Women don't really know what it feels like *inside* to be a man. A woman can't fully comprehend the hormonal effects a man feels when he watches a voluptuous woman walk by, the instant, deep physical reaction. These responses are automatic, persistent, all-pervading realities of male sexual awareness.

Both our everyday experience and much scientific research seem to prove that males and females respond differently to visual images, and that the male is far more erotically aroused by visual stimuli and attracted by the sight of the opposite sex at a distance. Some neuroscientists believe that the curves of the female rump and breasts act almost like a visual magnet to the eye of the male.

I once had the opportunity to chat about this with Dr. Paul D. MacLean, chief of the Laboratory of Brain Evolution and Behavior of the National Institute of Mental Health. Dr. MacLean is a leading brain scientist who has spent a long career experimenting on the workings of the human brain and speculating on its effects upon behavior. Dr. MacLean told me he thinks man's attraction to the body of the female may be built into the material of what he calls the "old brain," the lower brain stem which he says may contain ancestral learning that was programmed millions of years ago.

"On the basis of behavioral observation," Dr. Mac-Lean said, "we might infer that the old reptilian brain programs certain stereotyped behaviors on the basis of some kind of ancestral learning or memories." He thinks this program built into the genetic structure of this part of the brain plays a primary role in numerous human activities, such as mating, breeding, hunting, finding shelter, establishing territory, forming social hierarchies and selecting leaders.

A lot of people these days assume that nurture more than nature directs our behavior, that social conditioning is the only thing that determines what we are, but biologists insist that life always involves a *combination* and no one really knows for sure how much of our behavior is learned after birth and how much may be built into our genetic material. We do know, however, that the appeal of shapely hips and legs or bulging busts and bottoms was not invented by Madison Avenue. Archeologists have found pictures drawn on the sides of caves where men lived 25,000 years ago depicting voluptuous females, sometimes involved in sex acts, with emphasis on large breasts, buttocks and sex organs—not at all different in essence from the pictures reproduced in magazines for men today.

A state appeals court in Los Angeles not long ago ruled that a law requiring women, but not men, to clothe their breasts was *not* unconstitutional. "Nature, not the legislative body, created the distinction between that portion of a woman's body and that of a man's torso," the court said in upholding the city's laws against nudity. "The classification requiring female breasts to be clothed is reasonable, not arbitrary, and rests upon a ground of difference having a fair and substantial relation to the object of the legislation, so that all persons similarly circumstanced are treated alike."

No matter how much some feminists try to be like

197

men in every way—gazing at magazines with pictures of nude males or indulging in the novelty of visiting bars with male go-go dancers—only rarely are women found who are actually aroused in the same way as men by such visual displays. Not long ago, the editors of *Viva* found out the hard way that the novelty of seeing pictures of nude males wears off quickly for female

"What first attracted you to me?"

readers. As its sales dived, *Viva* was embarrassed to discover that male homosexuals had become a significant portion of the audience for what was supposed to be a women's magazine. The *Viva* editors soon cut out the male nudes after surveying women across the country and learning that they really didn't care for the soft-core pornography at all. They found it boring.

The average, normal man has a different reaction. The male looks at a picture of an attractive, naked female and immediately visualizes her as his sexual partner. Men are universally excited by the sheer visual display of female sexual parts with no need to know who they belong to or what she is like as a person. They respond to the pure *hunk* of her as a female.

Women seem to become aroused when they are able to project themselves into the image of the woman in a scene, when they can imagine that the man is a romantic figure with whom they are involved on various levels of feeling, not just sexually. To most women, the personality and character of the man who arouses them are far more significant than his physical features or the fact that his genitals are hanging out. This is perhaps why romantic novels for women still outsell all other categories of fiction, including those that feature raw sex.

We are told that these have been the normal responses of men and women through the ages, and it's not difficult to see that they are reflected in their differing roles. Man was the seeker, the fighter, the hunter, the provider, who looked out over the land to see what must be done to survive. While he was looking around, if his kind was to be perpetuated, he had to be irresistibly drawn to the charms of the female, enough to be persuaded to stay with her, to provide for her and their infants, and to protect them. (Even then, it was a jungle out there.)

This process served to weed out the representatives

of both sexes who were least valuable or desirable as mates—physically, mentally and sexually. Men were apparently selected according to size, strength, and courage, because of the female's need for protection and nurturing of her young. Competition between the males acted as a selection process favoring these same qualities of survival.

The females selected by men through the ages tended to have attractive hair, smooth skin, full breasts and buttocks, and helpful, nurturing dispositions. Such attributes increased a woman's chances of finding and keeping a mate, of living to reproduce, and of joining with a man who was also better endowed. The characteristics of successful, intelligent women were those capable of providing an environment in which a family could survive and grow, and these qualities complemented the attributes of men capable of sheltering and protecting women and children. These seem to have been the kinds of forces that have operated over millions of years to form the real differences we notice presently between the sexes.

This difference in the nature of males and females is frequently observed both in daily life and by scientists, who repeatedly report differences in the responses of boys and girls to lights and sounds applied in psychological experiments. Males respond more readily to visual stimulation and females are more affected by sound. If the typical male is likely to favor magazines with pictures of the most physically alluring women, the typical female is more interested in hearing her heartthrob's voice on a recording or reading about his personality in the women's magazines. This difference was expressed by an Elvis Presley fan of many years: "When Elvis sings, I feel as though he's singing to me. His songs are tender and romantic. He sounds very masculine though, kind of warm and protective. He looks big and rough, and his face is kind of pushed in, but his personality is the important thing. That's what turns girls on. I just think he's very sexy."

Among the many women with whom Annie corresponded during our researches was Dr. Rhoda L. Lorand, who has been a practicing psychotherapist in New York City for more than twenty years. In recent years, Dr. Lorand has also been an outspoken opponent of the drive of women's lib to teach school children that there aren't innate differences between the sexes and that sex roles are detrimental to women. To the contrary, contends Dr. Lorand, the push to undermine traditional sex roles in favor of unisex is damaging to both sexes and a source of serious confusion and unhappiness.

In one of her letters, Dr. Lorand referred Annie to her book *Love, Sex and the Teenager*, which when we finally tracked it down we found to contain a wealth of insights and information on the attributes and relations of the sexes.

"The psychological differences between the sexes are as great as the anatomical dissimilarities would lead one to expect," says Dr. Lorand. Male psychology, she says, can be characterized as "aggressive, uncomplicated directness, a pride in accomplishment. . . ." Girls, on the other hand, tend to suppress their sexual feelings, she says. "The indirect expression of sensuality which is characteristic of girls seems to lead to the development of other typically feminine qualities. She is more self-centered, more concerned with what is going on within her mind and body. Her stronger fantasy life, her more personal approach to situations and people, seem to enable her to identify herself more easily with others. Women seem to understand their own feelings better than do men, as a result of which they seem to be better able to understand the feelings of others. . . ."

Marabel Morgan, the author of *Total Woman*, says,

201

"Women need to be loved; men need to be admired. We women would do well to remember this one important difference between us and the other half."

Once a magazine writer asked Shirley MacLaine why she thought it was that her brother Warren Beatty was more of a sex symbol than she was. She replied, "Well . . . I think Warren really enjoys sex, but I enjoy other things more. I like sex, but it wouldn't bother me if I went for long periods of time without it. It would bother me if I didn't have privacy, or silence, or time to think and read and express myself. . . . There are many things I really essentially need, and sex isn't one of them. I think it is with Warren. What appeals to me sexually is always someone's mind, someone's imagination, someone's sense of humor. That is all very sexy stuff to me. Whereas with Warren, evidently, the act itself is what is sexy. So the different ways we project on film are consistent with our characters." Shirley MacLaine probably didn't realize it, but she was giving a perfect description of the essential differences in male and female sexuality.

According to a report presented to the 1975 Conference of the Midwestern Psychological Association, men may actually be five times as interested in sex as women are. Paul Cameron, an associate professor of human development at Maryland's St. Mary's College, and his associate Pat Fleming, collected in three American cities what they regard as representative samples of people's attitudes toward 22 daily activities. A total of 818 people in all were asked to rank numerous activities, such as travel, music, smoking, watching television, eating, family activity, church work, et cetera, according to how important they were to them personally. In each of the three states—California, Kentucky and Maryland—results were the same: sex ranked number one with the males for about half of their lives, but it never ranked above fifth with women!

In his book *Sexual Suicide,* writer George Gilder discusses the ways male sexuality is different from that of women. Gilder writes:

> Most young men are subject to nearly unremitting sexual drives, involving their very identities as males. Unless they have an enduring relationship with a woman—a relationship that affords them sexual confidence—men will accept almost any convenient sexual offer. This drive arises early in their lives, and if it is not appeased by women, it is slaked by masturbation and pornography. It is not a drive induced chiefly by culture. Rural boys, conditioned to avoid sexual stimuli, avidly seek pornography when they scarcely know what it is—and when it is outlawed. The existence of a semi-illegal, multi-billion dollar pornography market, almost entirely male oriented, bespeaks the difference in sexual character between men and women. One can be sure that if women passionately wanted pornography, it would be provided.

A major fallacy of some feminists has been the mistake of thinking that sex for the male is just a culturally induced lusting after pleasure. Another strong critic of women's lib, Midge Decter, has also emphasized the distinct differences between male and female sexuality. She writes in *The New Chastity and Other Arguments Against Women's Liberation:*

> For a man, sex is an attainment like the other attainments of his life; it is indeed often felt by him to be paradigmatic of them: each incidence of potency in bed providing some intestinal reassurance of his adequacy to deal with the world outside it. For a woman, coitus is a happenstance, roused and dispensed with on the same occasion, being only itself and touching nothing else. . . . The truth is, of course, that the pursuit of orgasm for a woman is an

entirely irrelevant undertaking. Not that she has no "need" of sex; nor is she indifferent to the "quality" of her sexual encounters. But what that need really is, and what the qualities really are which for her become the true determinants of pleasure, cannot be understood by an analogy with these terms in the experience of men. . . . Her need for sex is diffuse, not focused on its consummation but on a hundred different small reminders of the nature that is by daily circumstances mostly hidden from her.

Most women learn that their bodies exert a powerful influence over men just by being near them, and that a woman can succeed at sex in a significant way just by presenting herself and accepting the exertions of the man. She can merely relax and yet her performance will be satisfying to him. As George Gilder says, whatever problems she may have otherwise, her identity as a woman is not at stake in intercourse in the same way as is the man's. "The man," says Gilder ". . . has only one sex act and is exposed to conspicuous failure in it. His erection is a mysterious endowment that he can never fully understand or control. If it goes, he often will not know exactly why, and there will be little he or his partner can do to retrieve it. His humiliation is inconsolable. Even if he succeeds in erection he still can fail to evoke orgasm—he can lose out to other men who can. And if he is impotent, it will subvert all the other aspects of his relationship and will undermine his entire personality. . . . In general, therefore, the man is less secure than the woman because his sexuality is dependent on action, and he can act sexually only through a precarious process difficult to control."

If the sexual identity of the male is so closely linked to his ability to perform—not just with the female, but in the world—and if the needs of male and female in this area are truly different, then surely the imperatives of male sexuality hold implications for the unisex trend that are as yet unrealized. Conventional wisdom currently asserts that not only are sex differences unimportant, but gender should not affect our thinking in matters of social organization and performance on the playing field and on the job. Ask not if the person is male or female, we are told, only the individual performance counts. Let us now turn momentarily to the arenas of the unisex principle in action.

The Case for the Five-Foot-Two Cop

The idea of sexual equality has an understandable, a natural, appeal to Americans. After all, we believe in fair play. We're all for the underdog. We have subjected ourselves to decades of upheaval in the attempt to assure equal opportunities to minority groups. What could be more reasonable now than to undertake a similar endeavor on behalf of women? All that's necessary to start us on the path is to accept as gospel the idea that all of the generations before us have been foolishly socialized, that is to say hoodwinked, into believing that females are intrinsically unable to compete with males. How exhilarating to suddenly realize that for the first time in the history of "personkind," there need be no barriers to free and open competition between the sexes, that women are the equals of men in every way —and don't need protecting, thank you!

How exhilarating, too, for the new believer each time the press reports another breakthrough for the emerging sex—unless, of course, the believer is a closet skeptic and starts asking too many questions, for then there can be disappointments. I'm reminded of the many articles in recent years showing women invading the bastions of men. Of one, for example, in the *Washington Post* of March 7, 1976, on the new women recruits at the Marine Corps Recruit Depot at Parris Island, South Carolina. There was a picture with this front-page story captioned "A recruit strains to hold chinning for a full 60 seconds." And sure enough, there was a short-haired gal in tennis shoes and exercise clothes grimacing determinedly at the bar. I am sure that a lot of people who saw that picture believed that the Marines were training some really tough women down there in South Carolina—women who can do chin-ups right along with the men. So Annie and I routinely verified with the public affairs officer at Parris Island that, indeed, the recruit was *not* "chinning," but performing the "flexed-arm hang."

This was just research as usual for us at that time, because we had recently been in touch with officials at Annapolis and West Point concerning their preparations to receive the first female candidates ever to attend the service academies. One of the first things we learned when we inquired whether women would have to pass the same aptitude tests as male candidates was that they would not be required to do chin-ups (or *pull-ups* as they are called).

I asked Dr. Robert W. Stauffer of the Office of Physical Education of the U.S. Military Academy at West Point about this differential treatment. "If women are equal to men, why don't they do pull-ups?" I wondered.

"Because men and women are *not* equal," Dr. Stauffer told me. "Women can't do pull-ups at all," he said. "Ninety-two percent of all women can't do even one pull-up."

So they're required to do the flexed-arm hang. Annie and I were amused when we received materials from the U.S. Naval Academy describing the pull-ups men are required to do and then the flexed-arm hang for women. Test One for the men read:

> Candidates should grasp bar with both hands, palms facing forward (away from candidate), and assume a fully extended position with feet clear of ground. When candidate is in correct starting position, examiner gives signal to begin. Candidate pulls with both arms until chin is *over* the bar, then lowers to fully extended position and repeats until unable to continue. . . .

The Naval Academy had printed a special addendum for female candidates indicating that instead of pull-ups, Test One for them would be performed like this:

> Candidate should stand on a chair or stool positioned beneath the bar. She should grasp bar with both hands, palms facing forward/away from her. . . . *Assistant should then grasp candidate's legs just above the ankles and lift her into starting position* (arms fully flexed and chin leveled above bar). . . . As soon as the candidate is in the starting position, the command "go" is given, the assistant's hold is released. . . . The candidate holds starting position as long as she can. . . . (Emphasis added.)

Well, *that* is the flexed-arm hang. A candidate has to be able to hold herself in that position for three seconds to be a midshipman.

Another popular bastion that the press is fond of reporting women invading is the arena of long-distance running. Annie happens to be a long-distance runner, so this is an area where we have some special experience and interest. Many articles have appeared in recent years suggesting that somehow women are actually better marathon runners than men, even though their times are considerably worse. The theory is that women are lighter and can use their fat more efficiently over the long haul.

Last year, Annie was listening to the noontime news,

Assistant should grasp candidate's legs and lift her into position . . .

and heard the reporter on a feature called "Today's Woman" announce that "Nina Kuscsik won the Boston Marathon in 1972, the first year women were allowed to enter the race officially. She now holds more than 20 national and state records." What the reporter failed to say was that Nina only won the Boston Marathon against other women—she was *not* the winner of the marathon. Likewise, the records she holds are in *women's competition*, not in general competition with men. It's funny how these little technicalities have a way of getting lost by enthusiastic writers and broadcasters.

The fastest time for a woman marathoner is a half-hour behind the fastest time for a man, and in the Boston Marathon in 1976, the first woman finished behind 164 men. Not that there aren't some darn good women runners, but they're *not* better than the top men, although you might think so to read and hear about them in the media.

Then there was "The Challenge of the Sexes" TV show in which they pitted the women against the men. The only catch was that in order to make it a competition, the odds had to be stacked against the fellows. On the obstacle course, for instance, they had the men scaling ten-foot walls while the gals trotted up little six-foot ramps. When Ilie Nastase went up against Evonne Goolagong on the tennis court, he only got one serve against her two and had to defend a doubles court while she defended just the singles. And, at that, he made her look pretty bad until his wind began giving out from running all over that big court.

Following the threats by the Women's Tennis Association to "girlcott" Wimbledon in 1977, Stephen Banker wrote an article in the *Washington Post* objecting to the women's idea that they should have parity with men in the number of players and the size of the purse. He detailed the vast differences in the comparative capabilities of the top men and women tennis players, which he attributed to the notably different construction of males and females, and declared: "The stunning result as far as I and a Library of Congress staff researcher (female) can see is that there has never been a woman who could play any sport on a championship level with men." He noted that the only exceptions he was able to find were in activities where equipment was of prime importance, such as in contests with guns, cars or horses.

"I have talked with numerous tennis professionals about this," Banker wrote. "All of them said they were better than the world's top women by the time they were 14. . . ."

In general, women cannot compete with men in any fair athletic competition. The reason seems to be that after puberty males are stronger and have quicker reflexes, greater speed and coordination of the kinds of gross body movements used in actions such as running, jumping, climbing, throwing, catching, and so on. Men have a crucial ability to bring their muscles into play faster, with more power and accuracy than women are generally capable of. According to the textbook *Physiology of Exercise,* "Untrained women are about two-thirds as strong as untrained men. Women are less responsive to training and require more work and time to increase their strength. Their maximal strength capacity is about one-half that of men."

The greater amount of fatty tissue in female breasts and legs makes them float better in the water and allows women to be more efficient swimmers than men. Researchers at the State University of New York at Buffalo have found that women are about a third more efficient at swimming than men because they don't have to use as much energy to propel themselves through the water. Even with this advantage, however, females perform about 7 percent below men in swimming competition.

When you also consider the fact that men have been found to outperform women in tasks involving space perception, as in judging distances and estimating the size and speeds of moving objects, it's easy to see why women must be given special advantages when they go up against men in athletic competition. Women have also been found to be at a disadvantage in sports due to the fact that their body thermostats are set a little higher than men's, making it more difficult for them to get rid of body heat and to perform at optimal efficiency in hot, humid situations.

Occasionally it's suggested that women might in reality be more "manly" than the men, because they're sometimes said to be able to withstand more pain. But according to recent objective tests of actual tolerance to pain of more than 40,000 people by the U.S. Public Health Service, men in every age group could withstand more pain than the women. The report states: "Pain tolerance decreased with increasing age for both sexes . . . but even the oldest men had a higher average pain tolerance than the youngest women." This could be the answer to why nearly three times as many men donate blood as do women, according to another recent report by the Public Health Service, which states that "this sex difference exists regardless of age."

One of the prime objectives of the Equal Rights Amendment has already gone into effect in Pennsylvania, where a court decreed that boys and girls have the "right" to compete against one another on school sports teams. That seems like a dubious privilege indeed for females when you consider what a team of medical doctors reported in the September 1974 issue of the *Journal of the American Medical Association* about the effects of sex differences in athletics. They declared that

it is in the long-range interest of both male and female athletes that they have their own programs. During preadolescence there is no essential difference between the work capacity of boys and girls, except that girls reach their maximum work capacity sooner than boys. However, following puberty, most boys uniformly surpass girls in all athletic performance characteristics except flexibility, mainly because of a higher ratio of lean body weight to adipose tissue. Thus, only the exceptional girl will have the necessary ability to make and compete on a boys' team. . . . Since girls are at a distinct disadvantage (in vigorous contact sports) because of their lesser muscle-mass per unit of body weight and bone density, it is advisable on medical grounds that they not participate in such programs. The differential between the weight of boys and girls opposing each other would be substantial. Even if competitors are matched according to weight, girls are still exposed to potentially greater injury, since the ratio of adipose tissue to lean-body weight varies considerably between the two sexes, to the disadvantage of girls.

People involved professionally in athletics or physical education know this is true. The physical performance levels of boys and girls in school after the age of puberty are so different that there are always distinct standards for each sex. To earn the President's Physical Fitness Award, for example, a 17-year-old boy is required to run nearly 30 percent faster than a girl, to broad jump 34 percent farther, and to do 37 percent more sit-ups.

It's not difficult to understand why this is so. A man's body is about 40 percent muscle, as compared to about

214

30 percent in a woman. "An average man will have nearly 60 pounds of muscle and an average woman will have nearly 35 pounds of muscle," says Isaac Asimov in his book *The Human Body*. He adds, moreover, that "this disparity in muscle weight is explanation enough for the fact that men are more powerful than women. . . ."

Considerable controversy arose during 1976 over the question of whether Dr. Renee Richards, the ophthalmologist who underwent surgery and hormone treatments to change from a man into a woman, should be allowed to compete professionally against female tennis players. "Although Dr. Richards may be psychologically and surgically a female," wrote Dr. Ira M. Dushoff, a surgeon in Jacksonville, Florida, to *Medical World News*, "she has two anatomic characteristics that give her an unfair advantage in competition with genetic females. These seem to have been overlooked in the controversy. In the first place, she has a male or android pelvis, which gives her a mechanical advantage over genetic females in any sport involving running. In the second place, the male carrying angle of her arm gives her an advantage in any sport involving throwing, or swinging a tennis racket. All other contentions pale into insignificance compared with these two anatomic advantages."

According to Dr. Dushoff, moreover, "If we could create a mixed sex pair of 'identical twins' with the same athletic prowess, the male would always beat his female 'identical' counterpart in any sport dependent on running or throwing. Basic anatomy accounts for the difference between male and female sports records."

Researchers at the Biomechanics Research Center at Wayne State University in Michigan have investigated the relative numbers of injuries to men and women in automobile collisions. They found that women are far

215

more prone to injury than men. Professor L. M. Patrick of the Wayne State College of Engineering told me that the reason appears to be the differences in skeletal and muscular development between men and women. This is particularly significant in the area of the neck, he said, where the head weight of a female is quite large compared to the size of the neck and the strength of the muscles supporting it. Whether on the highway, on the athletic field or in combative situations, there is hard evidence that women are generally far more vulnerable than men.

Even feminist militants such as Kathrine Switzer, who in 1967 instigated publicity that resulted in opening the Boston Marathon to women, admit they cannot really give male athletes a run for their money. "There are plenty of men I can beat in a race," Ms Switzer told a reporter for *Medical World News,* "because I may have trained harder or may have more physical talent. But on the very tip-top level of performance, the best man is always going to beat the best woman."

In the sedate game of golf, women would be completely washed out of competition against men if they weren't permitted to tee off about 20 yards closer to the green. Even in the game of pool, where speed and brute strength don't seem to be a factor, there's a big difference. "There's no comparison in pool between the men and the women," U.S. women's pool champion Jean Balukas told an interviewer in 1975. Steve Mizerak, four-time U.S. men's champion readily agreed. "She's the best female player I've ever seen," he said, "but I don't think Jean could ever really compete with the top men. Women just don't have something that men do. You can't pinpoint it." In horseshoe pitching, the distance for men is 40 feet, while women and children compete at 30 feet. Even in marbles tournaments, males and females are separated for championship competition.

You would think that if there is any sport where women would excel, it would be horse racing. A jockey has to be small and light and sensitive to animals. Yet only about 3 percent of jockeys in the U.S. are female, and none of them are really top jocks. *Turf and Sport Digest* ran a special issue devoted to women in October 1975. In regard to female jockeys, the editors stated: "Any woman who can take the bad with the good, who works hard, has the talent and the desire to learn and the desire to succeed can make it. And the first woman who really makes it big, will be a national heroine."

Turf reporter Jane Goldstein, attempting to find out why women jocks are *not* more successful than they are, interviewed various professionals at several different race courses. "I've seen trainers ride a girl on a particular horse a few times without success, then put a man on the same horse, and there's such a difference in how he runs," said Dan Smith, publicity director of Del Mar race track in southern California. "It could be coincidence but I don't think so. . . . I'd love to see a girl come along who could really compete."

"One of the problems with women jocks generally," said Lou Cunningham, publicity director of Atlantic City Race Course, "is that a lot of the gals ride and are terribly interested at first, but then find out how rough a sport this is and get discouraged by the brutal work load. A lot of them disappear from the scene."

According to Cunningham's observations, "Women can compete in *a* race with male riders, maybe even a couple of races a day, but not day in and day out, seven or eight races a day, six days a week. Most females aren't built to handle that kind of physical strain. A work load like that would be the turning point."

Women show themselves to be at a distinct disadvantage on the basketball court, lacking the height, strength or power of men. A coed at the University of

Maryland, admitting her team would be no match against the men, said, "Girls' hands are smaller and all their skills have to be viewed from that point of reference. No girl can hold the ball in one hand, and consequently, her ball handling is not going to look as skilled as a man's, even though she may be able to pass just as effectively. On the backboards, girls will position themselves differently because they are shorter. As the ball rebounds, a man can take it off the backboard, but if a girl is too close, it will go over her reach."

Dorothy McKnight, former coordinator of the women's intercollegiate program at the University of Maryland has fought against the recent trend to make women's college athletics as competitive as men's. In an interview not long ago, she said, "There is no way, after the age of 12, women are going to have the same strength, size, and muscle mass as men. Even in diving there is a strength factor." Miss McKnight strongly disagrees with feminists who think women can compete on an equal basis with men. "Women were screaming for so many years," she said. "They were vehement that separate but equal was demeaning to them. But from everything I've heard, most people are now really beginning to see the picture."

"Women and men should not compete against one another," another women's coach said, because "women can never catch up with men. The physiology will just tell you the differences straight away."

A lot of people thought it was smart when girls were given their "equality" to play on Little League baseball teams with boys. But when boys began to take over the girls' softball competition, many people began to have second thoughts. In 1976, when Westport's all-star softball team (on which 10 out of 14 players were boys) won the *girls'* Connecticut state championship, the president of the losing all-girl team threatened to withdraw from the national Little League unless rules were changed. "They're so much bigger physically," said Nancy Devaux, the shortstop on the all-girl team from Durham. "They're stronger. Next year there'll be all boys in the league. There's no point to it." Cheryl McCall, the catcher on the losing team, commented, "The boys are going to wreck it for us."

The feminist theory that women might equal men in athletic performance if females trained harder from an early age has already been disproved scientifically in Communist countries, especially in East Germany, whose athletes dominated the women's track and swimming competitions at the 1976 Olympics. For decades these Communist athletes have been selected and trained in Olympic sports using the most advanced technology, but even with such intensive, expert training, girls do not grow up able to compete against top male athletes.

Yet many feminists continue to believe that somehow the physiological differences between the sexes can be overcome, and that if women lift enough weights and hit enough tennis balls, they will catch up to men. Gabrielle Burton (the feminist who wanted to run away, but was afraid to cross the street) took karate, but she gave it up after the introductory course, because, she said, "I'm committed to pacifism and nonviolence and that's a little tricky to reconcile with the aggressive essence of karate." Perhaps the depth of her feminist commitment was revealed in these words about her experience among the male combatants: "Occasionally I was accorded a little preferential treatment, and when I expressed conflict over deference because of gender, Roger [her husband] would point out that we were existing in a death-prone setting and I was a simpleton if I made the odds any greater. I must admit to being very happy when Sir [the karate

219

instructor] was walking around slugging people with a rubber bat and he merely tapped me on the fanny. People were lying on the ground like flies and for once I didn't say 'Equal treatment, please.'"

Another karate class buff was Susan Brownmiller, author of the widely heralded *Against Our Will: Men, Women and Rape.* She had her collarbone broken in her training sessions for manhood.

Even so, in the final lines of her book, Ms Brownmiller, no chicken like Gabrielle Burton, announces that her answer to the age-old problem of rape is: "Fighting back. On a multiplicity of levels, that is the activity we must engage in, together, if we—women— are to redress the imbalance and rid ourselves and men of the ideology of rape."

Ms Brownmiller's notion of "the ideology of rape," she tells her readers, was an idea she found in a book by "the half-crazed genius Wilhelm Reich." The half-crazed genius just left the phrase hanging there in his opening chapter, she says, "begging for further interpretation." Not one to let such a phrase go begging, Ms Brownmiller interprets the ideology of rape like this: "Man's discovery that his genitalia could serve as a weapon to generate fear must rank as one of the most important discoveries of prehistoric times, along with the use of fire and the first crude stone axe. From prehistoric times to the present, I believe, rape has played a critical function. It is nothing more or less than a conscious process of intimidation by which *all* men keep *all* women in a state of fear."

I won't take time here to criticize all of Ms Brownmiller's zany ideas, such as that somehow I am responsible for the vile acts of all of the rapists running around town just because I am a man, or that if I wheedle my wife into sex when she really would rather not (not that I would ever do that, of course) I am also committing rape. I won't even mention how ridiculous

220

is the whole business of criticizing our cultural heritage with all of its quirks and horrors, just because it grew from primitive life rather than flying full-blown from the head of a feminist sociologist.

What I do want to point out about Ms Brownmiller's book is that she has the simplest physiological facts about the sexes all twisted around. She keeps saying that it is because a man has a *penis* that he has power over women, that the *penis* is the dangerous weapon against which "there could be no retaliation in kind— a rape for a rape," that the *penis* is the object of fear. Anyone who has ever seen a penis knows that this is just plain silly. It is the force of the *man* that is dangerous. The dense muscles are the weapon. And this weapon and force do not confine their aggressions to the poking of a penis in rape, but penetrate into nearly every corner of human life, compelling men as well as women. As important as the subject of rape has been to the literary fortunes of Ms Brownmiller, it is only a tiny nick, so to speak, compared to the overall impression the sheer physical differences between the sexes have upon the courses of our lives.

When you go a step further and look beyond the realm of the purely physical differences, beyond the fact that men are stronger, faster, bigger creatures, capable on the whole of greater heart and lung activity and of feats of sheer brute endurance—there is reason to wonder if the prenatal conditioning of the brain by male hormone might not also account for differences in the mental performances of men and women. According to Dr. Lorand, the clinical psychologist mentioned earlier:

> The great geniuses of the world have been men. All the child prodigies—the lightning calculators and musical geniuses—have been boys. Does that mean that men are superior to women? Brilliant

221

women have made important contributions in many fields, but it is irrefutably clear that the most highly endowed men are significantly superior in creative intellectual power and artistic creativity to the most highly endowed women.

It has been proposed that the reason great intellectual and artistic creativity and genius, and outstanding capacity for abstract thinking have appeared in men only is that women have never been given a chance to develop their intellectual powers to the fullest. While it is true that in Europe women were restricted in certain activities, they were nevertheless encouraged to study music; but how many sonatas did they compose? Modern American women have not been restricted. Russia gives every intellectually gifted youngster the finest education possible. Israeli girls and women are encouraged to develop their intellectual potential to the fullest extent. Still, all the evidence points to the fact that the most outstandingly gifted men are indeed superior to the most outstandingly gifted women. . . .

Let's consider the world of chess. It seems to be an uncommonly accessible land where we all may enter. While there is virtually no discrimination on the basis of sex, the game itself discriminates on the basis of the vigor and acumen of the players. Chess is to the mental powers what sports are to the physique. Championship chess demands the strength of the athlete, the shrewdness of the trader, and the creative and analytical genius of the scientist and artist. Top play requires the same kinds of tenacious mentality, energy and will to win that distinguish the best creative minds in industry, the professions and the arts. As has been said of yacht racing, if you relax or deviate from the end result, then you will lose.

In view of the nature of this game, which tests

the combination of physical, emotional and mental strengths, it is striking to learn that although women have had complete access to the competition and distinctions of the chess world, they have scarcely made a mark. Women have played chess in America since colonial days, yet none has ever risen to compete in top play with men. The first American Women's Chess Congress was held in New York City in 1906, but the small proportion of chess players who are female has hardly changed since those days, despite the fact that throughout this century the chess establishment has worked to encourage development of women chess players.

In Russia chess is an immensely popular sport played by millions. The government promotes the game as a means of building character and mentality in the Soviet people. A few Russian women have even achieved championship status, but for the most part they lag far behind the men, and Soviet officials have been known to complain of the unsatisfactory performance of women in chess.

Female play is so inferior to top male performance that the World Chess Federation has to offer special contests for women's championships at a much lower standard than for men. If this were not done, no one would ever hear of a woman distinguishing herself as a chess player—but for the rarest exceptions, women would be totally invisible in the world of chess. When the United States Chess Federation published its recent list of Chess Masters and top players, no women appeared among the 191 names—and none ever have. Yet for decades males and females of all ages from every part of the country have played in open competition for these titles.

The same situation exists in the world of bridge. There are few outstanding female players. As one woman player said, "I don't think anybody really knows why it is. Most people say that women can't concentrate for long periods—don't concentrate their energies the way men do. Whatever it is, women are not winners at bridge."

It's just possible that audacious shrewdness, driving energy and individual powers of analysis, imagination and synthesis are more important requisites for success in such highly competitive activities than all of the laws and government-sponsored opportunities we can provide. So before we put more money and effort into experimental schemes to equalize the sexes—such as integrating sports teams, training female combat troops, or establishing sex quotas for jobs, government contracts and loans—perhaps we should just keep an eye on the world of chess for a while. We could have a President's Council on Chess to encourage people everywhere to take up the game—then keep a close eye on how well the women's liberation ideology advances the girls up that tough road toward National Champion, International Champion and, ultimately, Grand Master.

At the least, this would be cheaper, safer and more fun than the direction we have been going in recent years. Consider what happened, for example, when AT&T launched its drive to persuade women to become phone installers and line workers. Half of the 2,000 or so women who signed up had dropped out by the end of the first week. Within six months, 75 percent of the trainees had departed. And at the end of a year, according to James Sheridan, project chairman of AT&T's Human Resources Laboratory, "We couldn't find anybody we had started with." When Sheridan's staff investigated to find out why the gals weren't sticking with the program, the interviewers discovered that: (1) injury rates for women were three times higher than for men, (2) the women had difficulty handling the very heavy ladders used on these jobs, and (3) most of the women said they were just plain afraid to climb telephone poles!

We have all read how the FBI, the military service academies, and the police and fire departments across the country have been forced to lower their height and strength requirements to make it possible for women to qualify. Reports repeatedly indicate that the women are helped through training by sympathetic males or programs dedicated to making "equal opportunity" a success. For instance, this is how an FBI woman described her training with a class full of men at Quantico, Virginia, not long ago: "It was heartbreaking at first. I was quite ready to leave by the second day." But then, she recalls, "the fellows adopted me. . . . When I had trouble running, two guys grabbed my hands and dragged me along." It's small wonder that many FBI agents consider it a dubious high honor to be sent on dangerous or difficult assignments with such women, who sometimes stand no higher than five-foot-two.

The same feeling exists among officers and their wives in other paramilitary organizations, such as the San Francisco Police Department, where requirements were lowered and quotas instituted because females couldn't meet the standards for male officers. Whereas the old height requirement was five-foot-seven, the average height of the women hired after the standard was dropped was five-foot-three. Standards on the written test were also lowered, and it's been reported that whereas only about 30 percent of applicants qualified under the old test, under the new one as many as 80 percent pass.

Carol Landrum of the Prince Georges County, Maryland, police force has been a policewoman for several years. She says that although she feels she has proved she can do the work, many women are not equipped for it. She tells of the response of one such policewoman who encountered an accident situation in which a child had been hit by a car.

"She sat down on the curb and cried, and then she got up and made her report," Officer Landrum said. "That kind of thing shouldn't happen in this business. You've got to suppress your emotions. You have to be in control of the situation at all times. That's the major part of being a police officer."

When you talk to people who have been intimately involved with the results of these changes, you realize that we have not even begun to face up to the conflict between notions about equal opportunity and the fact of unequal abilities. In jobs such as police work, women have long been known to be capable of handling most of the routine duties (although very few have ever cared to do so), but there is serious question as to the ability of most policewomen to perform at the level of men in violent situations where lives are endangered.

One police officer told me, "When it comes to the crunch, where physical strength is required, the men believe a female officer just can't hold up her end."

And the wife of an officer said, "My husband has been assigned to ride with a patrolwoman. I have plenty of objections to that. But my biggest objection is that I don't think women are physically capable of handling many kinds of violent situations that happen on patrol. This is dangerous for the public they are protecting, and it's dangerous, especially, for the male officers."

Even the policewomen themselves usually admit that they're not the same as the men. "We're not equal in every way and interchangeable," said one. "There's quite a difference."

Another woman commented, "A lot of jobs require force, and I might not have enough force."

The Los Angeles Police Department, which is considered the finest in the United States, decided to make its force *truly* equal for male and female officers. They would draw the same assignments as long as they met all of the same physical requirements and passed the same tests usually required of policemen. When this system went into effect, it soon became apparent that under these rules there wouldn't be many patrolwomen on the job. Whereas more than 97 percent of the male applicants passed all of the tests, only about 5 percent of the female aspirants were able to do so. (In 1976, the Los Angeles City Council refused to accept a $3.5 million grant from the federal Law Enforcement Assistance Administration, because the feds were trying to pressure the Los Angeles Police Department into lowering its standards and accept minority hiring quotas.)

This approach to equal opportunity seemed destined for a strenuous challenge across the country when in

June 1976 a three-judge federal panel in Alabama ruled that minimum height and weight requirements for police are discriminatory against women. These judges indicated they were convinced that the size of police personnel was unrelated to the effective performance of police work, and this ruling may have far-reaching implications for law enforcement organizations everywhere in the United States. As a result of the decision, the two female plaintiffs—one who was five-foot-six, 135 pounds, and the other five-foot-two, 110 pounds—were judged eligible to be considered for law enforcement jobs in Alabama. Officers in that state previously were required to be at least five-foot-nine and to weigh 160 pounds or more.

Another reality that must be faced is that emotional equations arise when males and females are mixed, equations that just aren't present in all-male forces. According to Dr. Harvey Schlossberg, psychologist for the New York Police Department, "In a car, partners share what we call 'intimate space.' This evolves into an 'us against them' relationship, which becomes a deep emotional relationship. Sexual tension has to be there between a man and a woman under those circumstances. If it's not there, I'd wonder why not."

This was a topic of concerned discussion when the police chiefs of major U.S. cities gathered at the FBI training academy in September 1976 for a seminar.

"One of the most destructive things in police work is male-female partners, as far as breakups of families go," declared Ed Tully, an FBI agent.

The Dallas chief of police, Dan Byrd, said that if you put two women together in a squad car, they fight. "If you put male and female together," he said, "they fornicate."

Seattle's chief, Bob Hanson, said he wouldn't be surprised if the wives of police officers soon organize into a determined lobby. "These women were married to police officers and they knew their husbands' roles were dangerous," he said. "But at no time did anyone explain that their husband would be working in a prowl car with a woman from 8 P.M. to 4 A.M. Do we have a moral obligation to that family? You bet your bippy. My legal adviser says that we will be sued and we will lose—it's called 'alienation of affection.'"

Chief Hanson also spoke of the relationship that necessarily grows between officers who work together under the intensive stress of patrol. "You learn to depend on your partner. You're there eight hours a night side-by-side. You have to get to know your partner."

"You translate that to male-female," added another officer, "and you get sex."

In fact, sexual complications of various sorts arise spontaneously in these kinds of situations. The Washington, D.C., police force, which in recent years has been recruiting policewomen in much greater numbers than previously, has been racked by repeated reports of sexual harassment and other complaints arising from tension between the sexes. An investigation was launched in 1975 after several policewomen complained that female officers are perpetually bombarded with pressure from the men to submit sexually.

One woman described a situation in which her partner on patrol pulled their cruiser into a wooded area and tried to persuade her to have sex with him. When she resisted he warned her not to say anything about the incident. "If he had put his hands on me I would have shot him," she told a reporter later, after these problems came out in the press. One woman charged her sergeant with raping her while they were on duty together. In another case, 17 policemen were alleged to have had intercourse with the same policewoman. One female officer, who said she had been on

229

the force just a year, commented matter-of-factly, "It's like Peyton Place."

As though the police force in Washington didn't have enough problems since it began assigning men and women to patrol duty together, at one point the president of the Metropolitan Police Wives Association, Goldie Johnson, held a press conference to expose the coed locker room situation. Male and female officers, it seems, were being assigned indiscriminately to lockers at police headquarters in a locker room with a men's toilet area that stood in open view at one end. "We all know we're not in Europe," Goldie Johnson declared passionately to the reporters, "and American people just don't do these things."

In Los Angeles, policemen were reported to have become sexually involved with teenage girls who belonged to the Law Enforcement Explorer Girls (LEEGS), an Explorer Scouts program for girls aged 14 to 18, who were supposed to be helping the police fight crime.

Just about the time a lot of people were beginning to think that a reasonable defense against the exploding anything-goes chaos of the schools might be to return to sexual segregation in the classroom, the U.S. Congress decided to admit women to the armed forces academies. From press reports, you might think that locker rooms and toilets were about all that had to be changed at those once male bastions. In reality, the very atmosphere and spirit of the academies was altered from the time the women disembarked there, unable, in many cases, to manage their own luggage. Annie and I watched the TV news reports in rapt amazement in July 1976 as the first female plebes arrived at Annapolis. When they moved off in their first formation, one of the women literally dragged her metal trunk across the concrete behind her by a strap, as another repeatedly dropped her luggage and scrambled to pick it up as the mostly male squad marched off stiffly without her.

The squad leader, a Midshipman Smith, the *Washington Post* reported later, finally was forced to say: "Look, we're going to be getting a lot of stuff to carry. And some of you guys are big dudes. You know what I mean? We're in this together. Everybody helps everybody else here, and I don't want to see anybody falling behind." I'm sure everyone knew what Midshipman Smith meant, but I couldn't help but think that I never heard anybody say anything like that when I was in the Navy (in fact, I thought it was the law of the sea or something that every sailor has to carry his own sea-bag), and I'll bet no plebes ever heard the likes of it before either.

Much of the traditional hazing at the academies was eliminated for the ladies, and although officials continue to insist they're going to require women to go through the same rigors as men, the men can see things won't be the same. When the first females at West Point went for hand grenade practice, one candid young woman, Priscilla Walker of Detroit, reportedly remarked, "I couldn't throw it as far as the guys. You

We watched in rapt amazement . . .

know, we're supposed to get it out into an area to explode. And we throw them and they land about two feet from where we're standing. We'll just have to practice. We don't have the upper arm strength that the guys have or the technique that the guys have throwing hand grenades. We wouldn't kill anybody but ourselves."

Another young woman, who dropped out of West Point after the first two months of training, admitted she had trouble functioning under so much stress. "I didn't do too well. I cried a lot," she said. "So that was my big breaking point. That was a big problem with a lot of the women at first." And Dr. Nora Scott Kinzer, an anthropologist who directed the integration of women into West Point, admitted that even though the women who did not drop out of the academy were pushing themselves to the limits of their endurance to try to keep up with the men, they were physiologically unable to do so.

The women at West Point were given a special protected status new to the Point when Superintendent of the Academy Lieutenant General Sidney B. Berry announced, "If I hear of anyone purposely mistreating or hazing a woman cadet because of bias, they'll [sic] be out of here very fast." On the other hand, the academy is providing the women with birth control counseling and devices, so a male cadet would have to be a very backward boy not to know upon which side his bread is buttered where the gals are concerned.

Just as we were writing this chapter, the New York Times sent a reporter to Jack's Valley, Colorado, to see how the 15 young women recruits of Invaders' Squadron were standing up to basic training at the Air Force Academy.

"One was on crutches," the Times correspondent reported, "several others were in sneakers instead of black boots. Among the first differences between men and women that showed up at the Academy was the relative inability of female feet to take a constant pounding in Air Force boots. Dozens of women had developed shin splints, many got stress fractures and at least half were suffering from blisters."

Some of the female cadets cried when their hair was cut to regulation length. (Symbolic of their "equal treatment," perhaps, instead of having their heads shaved like the men, the gals were given their *choice* of four short hairdos.)

The woman from the *Times* followed the women cadets over the obstacle course, and reported that "women are at a serious disadvantage in some physical activities." They had problems keeping up with the men on ropes, hurdles and parallel bars, but as usual they were accommodated. "I was just scared to death of that assault course," said one young woman, "but as we started yelling, I was determined to do my best. I wasn't going to let it get me psyched. And at the end, when all those guys were helping us, and yelling 'Invaders,' it really made me feel good."

One of the male cadets, an upperclassman, said he was supposed to boss the women, but he admitted: "When I see a pretty girl, my first impulse is to smile."

Another said, "Here, all of a sudden, I have to be tough, or at least firm. Sometimes they wink at you!"

The reporter described the training the recruits were getting with weapons, such as attacking targets with the barrels of M-1 rifles (the bayonets had been removed after one of the women stabbed herself in the head during a drill). Of the pugil stick fights, the reporter said it was there that the males were separated from the females (in more ways than one): "The men, tired as they were, seemed immeasurably more adept and dangerous as they whacked at each other to the cries of encouragement from squadron members on the sidelines."

The woman reporter didn't care much for the fighting, and she didn't think the female recruits did either. "I was appalled—almost nauseated," she said, "by the sight of two young women trying to bash each other's brains out. Aggression and self-defense surely are as much a part of women's makeup as men's, but I'm convinced women don't *enjoy* a fight as some men do."

The woman from the *Times* had other criticisms of the rigors of life at the Air Force Academy. She thought the lecture on the ethics of warfare was "simplistic." She thought the regulation against sexual fraternization was "contrary to human nature." And in general, she declared, "I found the gung-ho *macho* atmosphere in Jack's Valley repugnant and much of the authoritarianism arbitrary. I was told that this sort of training was necessary to mold a corps of professional soldiers who would defend me and my country against future enemies, but maybe a friend of mine is right in predicting that feminine presence could eventually lead the service academies to tone down this strident militarism."

Maybe so. Her report says that already the young men and women at the Air Force Academy are dancing together in the recreation rooms, and although some upperclassmen still decry the lowering of standards, the academy's General Allen says that in accepting women "our goal was that we'd work for an equal level of effort in the physical activities rather than an equal level of performance." (Behold the wonders of our new equality.)

As one coed soldier at an Army Reserve Officer Training Corps camp summed up her experience in the unisex military, "We are really breezing through. All the girls are. I mean I'm always screwing up, and this drill sergeant keeps saying what a sharp little cookie I am."

One of her superiors explained, "We want these women and this program to succeed. After all, it's the right thing to do."

The trend elsewhere in the military services was outlined in a report of May 11, 1976, from the comptroller general of the United States to the U.S. Congress. "With the advent of the All-Volunteer Force and the anticipated passage of the Equal Rights Amendment," the report began, "the Department of Defense intensified efforts to recruit women and to increase their use in a wider range of occupational specialties, including some previously restricted to men. [The General Accounting Office] initiated a review to determine how effective the services' efforts have been to recruit, train, and utilize women."

The report states that during 1972, the policy throughout the military services became to open as many job categories as possible to women, and to "tell women about the jobs for which they qualify and encourage them to select those previously restricted to men." In general, the initiative was intended to drastically increase the number of women in the service and to move women as quickly as possible into nearly all noncombat jobs. The report declares, "Our objectives were to determine the extent to which the Army, Air Force, Navy, and Marine Corps have increased the opportunities for women, to determine the extent to which women have accepted these opportunities, and to obtain information about women's performance in specialties which have traditionally been considered primarily or solely available to men. We obtained information on the (1) entry requirements for men and women, (2) procedures for establishing goals and quotas for women, (3) procedures for recruiting and assigning women to specialties, and (4) distribution of women in the specialties. We also interviewed headquarters officials and commanding officers, supervisors, instructors, and women at several training centers and military installations."

The GAO report states that while some progress had been made in moving women into nontraditional jobs, most women still prefer to go into the traditional administrative and medical occupations. In some cases, quotas were established for jobs such as mechanical and electrical specialties, and female applicants "were forced to accept these specialties if they wanted to enlist at that time." In the Air Force, for instance, "plans for fiscal year 1974 provided for assigning 3,662 (50 percent) of 7,280 women to 86 newly opened specialties, including 3,241 to newly opened mechanical and electronic specialties."

As with the MIT planners, the military commenced its own program for liberating women from on high, pushing them into men's jobs whether they wanted them or not. The rationale offered for this was that "fewer men were expected to join the services and partly because of potential Equal Rights Amendment requirements." (I gather from reading his report that the comptroller general did not find it at all presumptuous for the federal government to have begun implementing a constitutional amendment that the American people had not yet ratified.)

The report states that the Office of the Surgeon General of the Air Force had determined that "an average woman has only 60 percent of the strength of an average man and that it is doubtful that all occupational specialties should be filled with an equal distribution of women." One chapter of the report, in fact, listed dozens of jobs in the military services that women could not perform effectively. "Some have not been required to meet the same training and performance requirements as men," states the comptroller general.

"We determined that some women were not performing certain duties required by the job. In most cases both the males and females interviewed indicated that strength was a significant factor where females were not fulfilling the job requirements."

Among the many people interviewed in the preparation of the report, the commanding general of an Air Force wing made these observations:

> Some women do receive unfair treatment because many men assume that they cannot perform a job. However, there is also resentment by many men who are ordered to treat women as equals, yet find themselves working longer hours because a woman has not done a job correctly.
>
> We have created a management problem by placing women in jobs where they cannot perform their share of the work, particularly aircraft maintenance and repair. We must find a way to correct the problem.
>
> Some women are being assigned to jobs they cannot physically handle. Women adapt well to the administrative side of law enforcement, but some situations are difficult for a man, not to mention a 110-pound woman. Women are not assigned to late patrols for safety reasons. As a result, work schedules must be developed around their availability. A military policeman should be able to handle all phases of law enforcement.

Supervisors of women assigned to the aircraft maintenance specialty said that most of the women are physically unable to perform many of the required tasks, such as removing and installing components like control surfaces, wheels and brakes, handling engine cowlings, removing screws, torquing bolts and moving ground equipment. Many of the women in these jobs agreed that they either could not perform the work adequately or had problems performing the strenuous tasks. Instructors at the aircraft maintenance school noted that women often have trouble carrying the tool boxes used in this occupation.

A supervisor of women in the specialty of airframe repair said that they could not perform more than 50 percent of the work required by the job. He said that they were unable to operate some drills and to open the doors of some aircraft, and he too mentioned that the women had problems handling their tool boxes. He said that sometimes two women working as a team cannot perform the work.

Reports from the Marine Corps were much the same. A commanding officer of a Marine training school told interviewers that women were being trained to climb

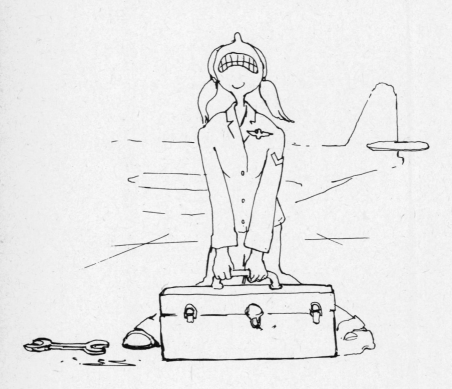

telephone poles, but that most of them were unable to carry 50 pounds of equipment up the pole with them. He said that most women just cannot "carry their own weight" when physical effort is required.

Army officials said they had tried to use women as ammunition storage specialists, but the women were physically unable to do the work. The interviewers located six women working as ammunition storage specialists at Army installations. The report states, "One of these specialists was hospitalized and the other five were performing clerical or administrative duties. Three had received enlistment bonuses."

In the Army's medical specialty, five women ambulance drivers were interviewed. "One was performing clerical work and one had not participated in field exercises," commented the interviewer. "The other three said that they have problems loading and unloading patients; one said that during field exercises, three women are assigned to lift patients normally lifted by two men. One also said that she cannot perform vehicle maintenance, including mechanics and changing tires and oil. She said that men drivers perform all the vehicle maintenance." One Army official commented that the women "have problems loading and unloading patients, braking and steering ambulances, and changing wheels and tires."

In the Navy, supervisors of women who have been trained as boatswain's mates said that "women physically cannot do much of the work," which includes "commanding tugboats, barges, and other small craft; handling and storing cargo, mooring lines, and anchor gear; cleaning, painting, and maintaining craft and equipment; and preparing rigging." As a result, the Navy spokesmen said, "men must perform a disproportionate share of the work." All of the women inter-

239

viewed agreed that they were unable to perform the heavy work associated with the specialty of boatswain's mate.

The same story emerged in occupation after occupation cited in the GAO report. In the final chapter, the comptroller general concluded, "We were told that because of the small number of women assigned to specialties with physical and operational restrictions, these factors apparently have not significantly affected the performance of the services. However, interviews with commanding officers, supervisors, and women indicated that assigning women to specialties in which their performance is restricted does result in inequitable workloads for men and could prevent mission accomplishment by affected units. . . ."

The report goes on to explain how this might be avoided if standards are developed so that persons of either sex are not assigned to jobs that they're not capable of performing effectively. We also learn that women are now being given defensive weapons training, and that one aspect of the research for the GAO report was to identify "legislation against assigning women to combat service."

The objective evidence is that women cannot perform in many areas on a par with men. (Even the Russians have quit training women cosmonauts because it is too demanding and dangerous.) But despite this reality, and despite the fact that most people in our society do not support the unisex ideal, we seem to be moving very rapidly toward the day when women will be assigned to combat roles. The trend is in that direction. Bills have been placed before Congress intended to achieve that goal, and the press is already suggesting, in a thousand little ways, that it's just a matter of time.

According to Morley Safer on the TV show "60 Minutes," for instance, "Women are not allowed to serve in combat or on warships, but that clearly is going to change." And he said, "The trouble is that if war between the sexes comes—as some say it will—the enemy is being trained right under our noses."

The trouble *is*, we all may be in for more troubles than Morley Safer knows.

Playing the Role of the "Person"

In his book, *How To Divorce Your Wife*, Forden Athearn included a section called "How To Take Advantage of Women's Lib," wherein he wrote:

> Paradoxically, the Women's Liberation Movement has gone a long way in liberating men. Demand for equal work and equal pay has made alimony less popular, not only with the public, but with the courts and legislatures. Naturally, this has made divorce less of a financial burden on men.
>
> Since the Women's Movement is fighting for social equality and the right to let women "do their own thing," men are feeling less guilty about leaving their wives and seeking a divorce. Women have given men a psychological lift. Now, when chastised by others for leaving your wife, you can say that equality, as well as freedom, works both ways. You want to do your own thing too!

I don't know whether it's really very psychologically uplifting, but, without a doubt, conflict between the

243

sexes has escalated in the 1970s. There are fewer people getting married and more couples getting divorced. And there are other signs that all is not entirely rosy in the lives of liberationists, male and female.

An article in the *New York Times* not long ago reported that "large numbers of the men and women who grew up in the 60s are now experiencing a generational malaise of haunting frustrations, anxiety and depression." The problem is reflected, according to the article, in growing numbers of young adults requiring psychiatric help, in more suicides and alcoholics among this age group and in the recent popularity of various charismatic religious movements and other cults that suggest a desperate searching after contentment by members of a troubled generation.

The *Times* quoted a number of psychiatrists who suggested reasons for these problems, which reportedly range "from disillusionment following the Watergate scandals, to disorientation caused by new sexual freedom, to the failure of life to fulfill the expectations established . . . during the idealistic 60s."

Dr. William Ackerly, a staff psychiatrist at Metropolitan State Hospital in Waltham, Massachusetts, said, "The values that worked for their parents are not holding today, so they don't have the same values to hold them on their journey; they feel alone."

Many of these young adults told counselors that they already felt "burned out" and "empty." Young women said they felt depressed because they had not been able to fulfill the hopes raised by the feminist movement.

"The women's movement has caused a lot of anxiety among both males and females," commented Dr. Felix Ocko, a psychiatrist in Berkeley, California. "Many men don't know how to handle the more aggressive women. And although women are more aggressive, many don't know what they want, what their role should be, how they should fit in, how much femininity they'll lose by pursuing a professional career."

"There's a tremendous amount of sexual freedom," remarked Dr. Fred E. Davis, director of Tulane University's counseling center, "but there has not been a parallel increase in wisdom on how to handle the new freedom."

"It's puzzling," Karol Marshall, a psychologist in Seattle said of the young adults, "as if no one taught them how to shape their future, how to make the future responsive to their wishes. They seem to have been taught: 'You can expect to get what you want out of life and it will come your way.' Now they're finding that this philosophy doesn't necessarily work. They can't get the job they want. They have a sense of helplessness, directionlessness, and this deteriorates into depression."

Dr. Calvin J. Frederick, chief of the mental health disaster assistance and emergency mental health section at the National Institute of Mental Health was interviewed in July 1976 by *Medical World News*. He commented on the fact that the most dramatic increase in suicides over the past 20 years—250 percent—has been among young males 15 to 24 years old:

> Many young men are Vietnam war veterans, and we are all familiar with their disappointments and problems: heroin addiction, unemployment, not feeling appreciated by society, etc. Another factor has been the souring of the economy—of the job market in particular. A lot of young people fresh out of high school or college can't find work suitable to their training, and their bright hopes for starting a career are cruelly crushed.
>
> But the most important reason, in my view, is the tendency among young people these days to "do

245

their own thing," to cut themselves off from their parents and society. While this exhibits a certain amount of healthy rebellion and independence, it calls for more strength and wisdom than most young persons possess. Once they cut loose, they suddenly find themselves completely alone, unable to manage their new-found freedom because they have no sense of structure or belonging. They become frustrated, tense, lonely, and anxious. They decide they can't cope, and their solution is suicide. The old stability and structure of the family unit is missing, with nothing to take its place.

Psychiatrist Herbert Hendin in his book *The Age of Sensation* views young men and women today as withdrawing from one another in defense against personal conflicts and demands they see as unnecessarily complicating problems they already feel helpless to control. He sees the unisex trend not as a sign that the sexes are becoming more alike, but as a desperate attempt in the popular culture to deny that there are two different sexes which are primarily engrossed in dealing with distinctly separate social and psychological problems. Dr. Hendin describes the generation that grew to adulthood in the 1960s as lagging behind in the usual growth into social maturity. He says:

> Commitments to work or to someone loved are often viewed as confining and restricting the subsequent variety of experiences available, as reducing one's options. The delay of such commitments once seen as the natural wish of many and a problem for only a few is turning out to be a widespread cultural change. The affluence of the sixties made careers and work seem less urgent; the economic anxiety of today makes them seem more cru-

cial. But an increasingly high percentage of young adults even in challenging professions regard work as merely the means to money for leisure. Comparably, most go on to acquire greater adeptness in relations with the opposite sex with little change in affective tone. This is not simply a matter of young people prolonging the time they take before making commitments. Instead increasing numbers are trying to work out life-styles in which there are only tentative commitments, all options remain open, and nothing in the way of sensation or experience is sacrificed.

The anxiety, frustration and depression that appear to be bothering many of the generation which should normally be stepping forth to assume its responsibilities as examples to the young, and as the leadership of tomorrow, also reflect a growing sense of disorientation and confusion by people of all ages, which results in part from the move to abandon traditional roles in our society.

Writers and opinion-makers throughout the media have picked up themes of the sex-role revolution, and scarcely a day goes by that it isn't drummed into our awareness that the new sexual game plan is to do away with all roles—we're just supposed to be ourselves, to do our own thing. That is the theory.

It has been intellectually chic in recent years among the hordes of bored, trendy writers of all sorts to play up the idea of the impending disintegration of family roles. For instance, the writers at the Institute of Life Insurance put out something they call the Trend Analysis Program Report as advisory bulletins to those in the life and health insurance business. In their Trend Report No. 8, for example, these institute writers tell their clients in the insurance business of possible changes in American lifestyles in the years ahead. They are perfectly ready, they indicate, to write off the family along with the concept of adulthood and legal marriage, if things seem to be leaning that way.

"It is the opinion of many authors reviewed in TAP that the head of the household, as a concept, will disappear in the not-too-distant future," they say. "One likely impact would be a blurring of the differences in the life cycles now operating for men and women. . . ."

Next they survey "alternative family arrangements," commenting as follows:

> The idea of a permanent man-woman relationship (marriage) will always be one alternative, but its popularity will decline. . . . Impermanence will be incorporated into many marriages of the future via two practices: ease and frequency of divorce, and marital contracts which bind two partners for limited spans of time (and which can be renewed or discontinued). . . . Unmarried cohabitation is often projected as one of the most popular future alternatives to traditional family formation. . . . Relationships which involve much the same responsibilities and interrelationships as the two-partner marriage may be extended to three, four and more parties within the same household. These might be legally binding or informal. Extended "families," such as communes, will be formed by different groups of people for a variety of reasons. . . . The pervasive concept underlying the thinking of most authors is that these options, and others, will be interchangeable over the course of the life cycle. Any one person can move in and out of a variety of relationships during life, as needs or environment dictate [sic]. Needless to say, the effects this will have on the traditional life cycle model are profound, as will be the effects on some basic institutions in society. Even religious principles are re-

laxing in order to accommodate the growing popularity of alternatives to traditional family stability
and child-rearing patterns.

The institute trend advisers say, "There is even talk
among social forecasters that parenthood in the future
will eventually involve intensive training, and perhaps
licensing, thus removing it from the normal chain of
events in the traditional life cycle." They also assert:
"Many authors who visualize increasing egalitarianism
between adult members of the household also predict
increased sharing of activities, tasks and interests
among all household members. They feel that the basic
orientation of the family will expand from economic
security to psychological fulfillment, with increasing
tolerance of differences between the individuals in the
household, including children. They believe that parents and children will defer to and learn from each
other."

One of the most revealing advisories offered by the
writers is quoted from a report by a team of Rutgers
University sociologists whose studies had been funded
by the Institute of Life Insurance. These investigators
reported: "It appears that much of the rush toward
adulthood which characterized young people in the
1950s and early 1960s is over." (I gather that what they
mean by "the rush toward adulthood" is what people usually regard as normal, mature acceptance of the personal and social responsibilities associated with adult
behavior.) "It is now becoming apparent that society is
recognizing another stage in the process of becoming
grownup. This can best be called transadulthood,
which extends from entrance to college, or the end of
adolescence to an indefinite point in the late twenties
or early thirties. It is a period of experimenting with

249

different life styles, of searching for career orientation, and for testing educational goals. It is often a time in which responsibilities are minimized and personal freedom is maximized. The desire to keep options open, to be constantly flexible and prepared for change, is characteristic of the transadult."

These writers say of the "transadults": "These young people see themselves neither as adults nor as adolescents. They are in a stage of transition, a period of change. Adulthood, or being a grownup, along with the permanent commitments it entails, is often perceived as unattractive, threatening, meaningless, and perhaps worst of all, downright boring."

Although Trend Report No. 8 did not say whether the institute's writers or grantee sociologists were themselves recruited from the transadult population, the Rutgers sociologists did admit to a certain confusion over the unexpected finding that "much of the restlessness and value disorientation associated with the transadult phase" is now appearing among people who are really too old to belong even to this new period of superextended adolescence. (I'm confident, however, that the Institute's sociology buffs will not be daunted by this. There is no reason why they can't just make up another new label and extend the period of adult irresponsibility right into old age.)

In case you're wondering, Trend Report No. 8 wasn't just an exercise in pop sociology for these writers— they went on in the final pages of the report to suggest ways insurance companies might be able to respond to these new trends. "It is within our collective power," they declare, "and to some extent our individual powers, to mold many of the trends we monitor into forces for a better future, or for that matter, a worse future." (Oh well, what's the difference, just as long as our creative writers are kept entertained!)

Another example is a pseudoscientific item in *Today's Health* which tells us: "Children are formed by the attitudes of parents and teachers, by the rewards that certain behavior brings to a boy or a girl, and by the disapproval that comes with other behavior. They are affected, too, by the set of expectations symbolized by the pink blanket in which we wrap a daughter and the blue one in which we swaddle a son. . . . To a great extent, children socialize themselves by imitating the role models they see. They learn a great deal of what's expected of them as boys or girls from watching other children of the same sex, from studying the grown-up sex models around them, from the constant bombardment of images received from television, books, and advertisements."

Next, the article quotes Dr. Lee Salk, director of the Division of Pediatric Psychology at the New York Hospital Cornell Medical Center. "There is a tendency to pass down, from generation to generation, certain social differences," the doctor says. "This can only be interrupted by some kind of cultural revolution, like the women's movement." Dr. Salk, we're told, "is an outspoken advocate of the elimination of sexism in child-rearing and education."

The *Today's Health* writer then goes on to tell us how "today's parents may be pioneers in the rearing of a new and braver generation" without traditional sex roles, and concludes by quoting Dr. Aaron Esman, chief psychiatrist of the Jewish Board of Guardians, who declares: "To the extent that the gender revolution allows for greater diversity, to the extent that it frees a child to develop in an individual way without feeling unloved or depreciated, it's a most desirable thing."

In an article in *Redbook* (later condensed in *Reader's Digest*) called "How To Make a Man Feel Loved,"

251

Avery Corman suggests giving him roses. "Or take your husband out to dinner. (Really take him—the wife figures out the bill and the tip, and pays them.)"

Writing in *True* magazine, Betty Friedan points to less loving expressions of the sex-role revolution:

> You've heard, of course, that women's lib wants to destroy the family unit and take the pants off men. There is a lot of bitterness and rage explod-

ing in women today. This rage, indeed, may temporarily turn a woman against the very husband, children, marriage and home women were supposed to live for; and because she wants nothing to do with men, may even temporarily turn her off of [sic] sex. The women's movement is not the cause of this exploding rage, but it may be the only hope for its cure. All this hostility is the *symptom* that something is terribly wrong with the way marriage, family and home are structured right now—built around separate sexist poles, the obsolete and unequal roles women and men have been trying to play. . . . When we break out of the roles that have kept us from being ourselves and know each other for who and what we really are—woman and man— then, and only then, will come real sexual liberation, and the end of both our loneliness. Then, and only then, will men and women be able to make love, not war.

Here is the crux of the feminist belief—the central ingredient that ties together all major feminist initiatives; it is the total faith that if somehow we could do away with the male and female social roles, then, and only then, would we have human equality, sharing, caring and universal happiness among persons all over the world. Whatever their short-term objectives or pragmatic rhetoric of the moment, the one essential of the hardcore feminists who propel the women's liberation movement is the absolute necessity of doing away with sex roles.

Let's give a few moments' thought to the real nature of social roles. Women's libbers, it seems, regard them as dispensable social contrivances that people over the ages—probably men—invented to keep people in their places and, in general, from having fun. It doesn't occur to them, I gather, that the fiery women's liberationist is herself performing a role which is in many ways more closely defined and inflexible than those against

253

which she rails. To whatever extent the role of "feminist" takes on social meaning and relevance, it is defined by the literature, slogans and catchwords of the women's lib movement. Now with these as support, people who are regarded as perfectly normal today can say things that a few years ago would have qualified them for the looney bin.

It's amusing to read or to hear about the cases in which parents actually try to put the feminist theories into practice. Annie and I know a couple who have tried valiantly to rear their son and three daughters free from the noxious sex-stereotyped roles. These children have come up watching daddy help with the cooking, housework and grocery shopping, and mommy tread off to a job. They've received the same unstereotyped toys to play with regardless of their sex, and they were introduced early to the new children's books expurgated of all sex-role models. The parents were at a loss when they discovered that despite all efforts, the girls still chose to play with dolls, the boy became aggressive and dominant, as little boys will, and all the children, by the ages of seven or eight, had learned that boys are bigger, stronger, and faster than girls.

In another family, a mother tells of having bought her young daughter a doctor's kit in the hope of encouraging the girl's liberation. Later, she looked in on the little girl, playing with a neighbor boy. The mother said she was brought to tears as she realized that her daughter was pretending to be a nurse preparing the patient for surgery, which the doctor, the little boy, was about to perform.

Feminists, recounting such stories in articles in the press, usually blame the overwhelming failure of their efforts to indoctrinate youth on the influences of other children, teachers, and, especially, the effects of television, "where sex-stereotyping shows the male providing the money and the female taking care of the ring-around-the-collar."

Aileen Jacobson, writing in the *Washington Post,* said, "To deviate from the traditional child-rearing norm does not just create guilt, as any psychiatrist might predict. It is also almost impossible. Parents who are trying now to prepare their daughters and sons for a fine new world of sex-role equality and shared responsibility are struggling in a transitional period, living in the gap between theory and the reality of their own emotions."

Ms Jacobson tells about the experience of the well-known feminist endocrinologist at Georgetown University, Dr. Estelle Ramey. It seems her four-year-old grandson was raised by "liberated" parents who tried to protect him from sexual stereotypes, which he managed to pick up anyway. Speaking of his aunt, who is a lawyer, the tyke told Dr. Ramey: "But she's not a lawyer. She's a she."

"My grandson!" exclaimed the horrified feminist professor. "The fight is over. This kid is going to grow up saying the right things intellectually, but inside he's going to say: She's not a lawyer. She's someone who went to law school with ovaries."

"And women," concludes Ms Jacobson, "will have the same problems inside. It may, in fact, take only 50 years to change the textbooks and the toys and the television programs. But that doesn't say how long it will take to change reality."

Perhaps the most spectacular example to date of the failure of the feminist ambition to eliminate sex roles is in Israel, where the *kibbutzim* were planned with equality of the sexes as a fundamental ideal. In these celebrated agricultural communes, things were arranged so that parents lived separated from the children with complete day- and night-care facilities.

255

Parents merely visited with their children rather than living with them in a family.

Yet despite these arrangements, which gave women and men equal opportunity to pursue careers in the world of work, reports have been that few women went after high-powered careers when they were free to do so, but still gravitated to such jobs as nursing, teaching and clerical tasks. In contrast, men in Israel hold most of the strenuous blue-collar jobs and those requiring executive ability. Seventy percent of Israeli women, according to recent reports, are housewives, and women compose only 8 percent of the Knesset, Israel's parliament. I understand there are practically no women in local government there. The women in the kibbutzim, it is said, instead of pushing for equality are now calling for more clothes and beauty parlors, and to have the children back to be cared for in the same living quarters as their parents.

The study of neither nature nor man seems to lend much support to the idea that social roles can be changed around at will or arbitrarily abandoned. On the contrary, what I've been able to learn about sex roles seems to me to support the understanding that they are ancient, essential and supremely serviceable social knowledge. A role has been defined by sociologist Peter L. Berger in *Invitation to Sociology* as "a typified response to a typified expectation." He says society calls the shots by predefining such behavior. "To use the language of the theater," states Professor Berger, "from which the concept of role is derived, we can say that society provides the script for all the *dramatis personae*. The individual actors, therefore, need but slip into the roles already assigned to them before the curtain goes up. As long as they play their roles as provided for in this script, the social play can proceed as planned."

There aren't usually *actual* scripts, of course, just general expectations about how people will behave. These are what we usually call "stereotypes." There is no such thing as having a society *without* them, because social life would then lose its mutual meaning for us and things would quickly deteriorate into chaos. It's true that society tends to place more or less strong pressures on people to observe the stereotypes and to be consistent in their social roles—in a word, to try to be "normal." But far from being the unnecessary "oppressions" imagined by feminists, there's good reason to believe that our social roles make it possible for us to plan and survive as an intelligent society.

I think it's important to recognize that people in our society, regardless of their sex or anything else, have much more liberty to deviate from ascribed roles—regardless of the normal pressures to conform—than most of us will ever require. The fact is that if a girl wants to have a career, or to fly a plane, or to put on a tie and act like a man—she is free to do it! As we've seen, women have done all of these things all through this century, but they continue to be exceptional. Most people like their ascribed social roles, because these are the means through which social groups give meaning to accomplishment, and through which we gain satisfactions from our associations with people. Acceptance is the normal response to the universal fact that human societies ascribe such roles. This positive reaction is the rule, and deviance from expected roles in any society is the exception. Few people anywhere tend to reflect much about such matters or entertain any serious notions about changing their roles. Most people just accept the social expectations placed upon them and strive to get what satisfactions they can out of life within these confines. In fact, it is exactly because most people are willing to fulfill their expected roles—such

257

as father, mother, employer, laborer or public servant—that there exists a base of social stability which allows citizens of a free country who want to change their usual roles to do so. But to expect to do it without paying any price is like expecting Texans suddenly to start bragging about Rhode Island. It just doesn't work that way.

Annie and I were discussing the feminist ideas about sex roles one day, and she showed me an item she had found in *Seventeen*, a magazine for young women. "Now, this is what they're teaching young people to believe," she said. The item announced:

> Both girls and boys have been manipulated and controlled by their assigned sex roles—which were supposed to guide them to happiness and fulfillment. But some young men have the mistaken idea that women's liberation means that females want to be more like males. They fear that women's achievements in sports, education and business will take opportunities from them.
>
> The real purpose of liberation for both women and men is not for them to become more like each other but to become more human—each a unique person rather than a stereotype. And it allows both sexes more choices so that they can choose to be competitive or passive, independent or dependent, cool or emotional.
>
> Liberation means to be aware of the kind of person you truly are, to trust your own experience of you and to be free to choose to become yourself. So that when you come up against a stereotype you can say, "Hey, wait a minute! That's not me. I'm a real man (or woman) and it's like this. . . ."

It struck me that this quote expresses in a nutshell the fundamental miscomprehension of the real nature of sex roles that characterizes the naive, albeit sincere,

258

attitudes to which it is the feminists' misfortune to cling.

To begin with, the purpose of sex roles is *not* to guide all people to "happiness and fulfillment." Sex roles are important to the organization of civilized society regardless of whether or not every individual is happy. But most people do find satisfaction within the constraints of conventional sex roles. In fact, the idea that a viable society can continue to exist without any social imperatives beyond the pleasure of individuals is the result of the teachings of trendy psychologists of recent years who have led the current generation to believe that the only necessities are sensitivity, self-fulfillment, self-gratification and the anything-goes philosophy (nothing can be bad if it feels good). The ultimate, unfortunate consequence of this trend is large

"Hey, wait a minute! That's not me. I'm a real man—and it's like this!"

numbers of people without significant interests, aims, ambition or social allegiances. They are people without discipline, initiative or purpose, because they have rejected the social framework in which meaningful, vigorous endeavor is possible.

The idea that we can approach life fresh each moment without stereotypes—that is, without any expectations about how people will behave—is ridiculous. The human mind functions on stereotypes. They are its basic conceptualizing ingredients. Without a mental store of incalculable numbers of expectations about people, places and things of all sorts, we wouldn't be capable of rational thought. We would actually be insane or mental vegetables.

What the unisex proselytizers are asking isn't that we give up stereotypes, but that we deny all of the evidence that makes it reasonable to expect different things of women than we do of men. But it's not rational to fail to take cognizance of the considerable differences between the sexes, and from a social perspective, there are imperative reasons why we must do so. It's a basic social necessity to reinforce social roles that serve to civilize the stronger, more aggressive male and to protect the weaker female who is the child-bearer.

Dr. Rhoda Lorand, the clinical psychologist who has written widely in opposition to the unisex assault, wrote a long opinion at the request of members of the Minnesota Committee for Positive Education as to the likely effects of a feminist program proposed for the schools of Minnesota. She declared that if the program were to be implemented, it would result in "the promotion of lesbianism, the downgrading of the institution of marriage, of motherhood, childbearing, the nuclear family, the advocacy of single parenthood and communal living, as well as contempt for all occupations and qualities traditionally recognized as feminine."

260

Referring to such feminist programs in the schools as "brainwashing," Dr. Lorand described the harm she sees in these efforts to mold the young:

Putting pressure on boys and girls to behave like the opposite sex is placing them under a great strain because these pressures are at odds with biological endowment. Therapists have begun to note the confusion and unhappiness resulting from the blurring of gender-identity. Conflicting pressures between environmental and instinctual drives hinder the development of a firm sense of identity as a male or female (an intended goal of Women's Lib), lacking which the individual cannot acquire stability, self-esteem, or clear-cut goals. Moreover, it is taking all the joy and excitement out of life. Girls are made to feel ashamed of their longings to be courted and cherished, to be sexually attractive, to look forward to marriage, motherhood, and home-making. Boys are made to feel ashamed of their chivalrous impulses. Feelings of protectiveness toward a girl and of manliness cause them to feel guilty and foolish, resulting in a retreat into passivity, while the girls end up unhappily trying to be sexual buddies of the boys. This unisex drive had its beginnings in the hippie movement and has been greatly intensified by all the publicity given by the communications media to the demands and accusations of the feminists (who really should be called masculinists, since they despise everything feminine).

The belief of the current fulfillment-oriented, pleasure-prone generation that any pressure from society upon them to get them to do *anything* is an intolerable encroachment on their freedom is not only insufferably arrogant, but supremely naive. There can be no stable or enduring society without distinct values which are either subtly or stringently, sometimes brutally, reinforced. Sex roles are ancient and natural values which, regardless of the current trend, are constantly re-inforced—in fact, so subtly and inevitably that at least some of the more astute feminists must be aware that it would take a miracle to erase them.

Confusion over these things seems linked to the direction the study of social science has taken in recent decades. Students learn in sociology or anthropology classes that diverse social patterns exist in different cultures of the world. They discover that their own society doesn't represent the only way things have ever been done. Soon they decide that maybe we should start changing around everything in our society. Unfortunately, their professors are receiving part of their support from the government to help the bureaucrats figure out how to do just that. There's scarcely anyone around to tell the students that sociology is supposed to be a value-free discipline, rather than a political erector set. Perhaps both professors and students should be reminded that the job of the true sociologist is to report as accurately as possible about the real nature of the social landscape.

"Sociology is not a practice, but an *attempt to understand*," says Professor Berger. He suggests that a good sociologist is like a good spy. "The good spy reports what is there. Others decide what should be done as a result of his information. The sociologist is a spy in very much the same way. His job is to report as accurately as he can about a certain social terrain."

The assault on the sexes, in contrast, is an intensive effort by pseudoscientists and feminist true believers to restructure our social landscape.

Let's look at some of what we know about what is there. As far as anthropologists have been able to find out, men and women in every time and place have exercised different social roles. The anthropological evidence indicates that there is not now and has never been a society anywhere in which women have held publicly recognized power surpassing that of men. Before human beings came to live in family groups, males undoubtedly dominated females and children alike, with little or no concern for their welfare or safety. The stability of the family appears to be responsible for the affectional ties that endure through long periods of time among male and female, and that provide the mechanism for both their protection and their advancement, as knowledge is passed from generation to generation. The family not only provided safety in which the female could survive, but it appears to have been the foundation upon which developed all of the achievements of civilization—language, technology, agriculture, ethics, art and science—that raised both male and female up from the desperation of survival in the wild.

Archeological and anthropological evidence points to the conclusion that sex roles evolved through the hunting and food gathering activities of hominids over millions of years. With civilization, man seems to have shifted from the episodic, aggressive activities of male hunting groups to the more regular and stable life of the family. The competition and aggressive activity that bond men together in hunting, fighting or achieving groups are tempered and made a secondary aspect of their lives as men are enticed to place more importance on home and family life. In the long run, this is achieved not by liberated females but by domesticated women who continually convince their men that they want and need their dedication and their protection.

Taking a long view of what civilization means, sex roles—particularly the male role as provider—appear to be essential if we are to achieve the social imperative of transforming aggressive young males, capable of broad social destructiveness, into constructive, respon-

263

sible citizens. Although feminists envision a society with complete sexual equality, this may just be a utopian dream. There have been many societies in which women have attained great social recognition, freedom and power, but anthropologists have not found societies in which females hold authority over males. In fact, the burden of evidence is that all but the most debilitated societies are dominated to some degree by men.

You get a sense of the ancient character and meaning of sex roles from these words of Dr. Bernard Campbell, professor of anthropology at the University of California, in his book *Human Evolution*:

> With the development of cooperative hunting in the Middle Pleistocene we can suppose that females became finally and fully dependent on males for part of their food supply; this dependence would have become critical during winter months in the north temperate regions. In turn, males would have become more dependent on the food-gathering activities of women. But the children would have been dependent on both for their survival. This interdependence we may suppose also coincided more or less with the evolution of a longer life-span and a more helpless human infant, unable to cling to the hair of its mother's body. In the course of time, any mature female would have had to support two or three dependent young as well as another whose birth was imminent. With the development of social hunting, therefore, we can see the one-male group bonded more closely, with division of labor and economic dependence.
>
> The human family is the simplest social unit with a complete division of labor between adult individuals. It is to the fact that the roles of man and woman are fully complementary that the family owes its continuance and stability. *Any interchange of roles, such as we see today in Western society, could threaten that stability. . . .*"
> (Emphasis added.)

264

Professor Campbell is an eminent scholar with degrees in zoology, botany, chemistry, anthropology and primate taxonomy. His work shows that the division of labor and complementary roles of the sexes are not recent innovations imposed by the patriarchal Victorian society and sustained by some sinister male conspiracy, but rather they are fundamental, life-sustaining, adaptations that evolved in nature over millions of years, and have been intimately involved in our survival as a species.

Moreover, there is little to be found among the volumes written on the relations of the sexes that persuades me that the sexes are essentially interchangeable. George Gilder has already dealt eloquently in his *Sexual Suicide* with the open-marriage philosophy which fantasizes that wives can march out of the home to millions of meaningful, creative, growth-inducing jobs and attain a marvelous equality. This, says Gilder, "interpreted in reciprocal, symmetrical terms, means defining one's success in relation to one's partner." And he adds: "Such insidious rivalry will usually erode the foundations of love and subvert all the other values of honesty, spontaneity, and trust. . . ."

Even if there were enough jobs, and even if the children and the emotional needs of the other members of the family could withstand the strain, Gilder's analysis of the anthropological evidence convincingly supports his conclusion: "Males always require a special arena of glorified achievement from which women are excluded. Their concern with sexual differentiation is obsessive. Men can be passive without grave psychological damage only if the women are passive also. Aggressive and competitive women, unconcerned with motherhood, produce more ruthless men—and a society so competitive that it disintegrates. . . ."

If George Gilder is right, then despite all of the pornography on the corner newsstand today, the magazine

265

called *New Woman* might actually be the sickest, most perverse periodical to be launched in recent years. It seems to be aimed at would-be *macho* women. It's packed with cartoons based principally on the idea of male-female role reversal, denigration of marriage and love, and glorification of executive careers for women. The articles encourage women first to get a job, and then to behave like the less mature males they will meet in the arena of work. This magazine is against the housewife, the family, children and every vestige of sex roles. Here's a typical sample:

> Women must make their own lives; we must not expect a man to make our life for us. Work is the constant, not another person. The "housewife" appears to have what the rest of us claim is obsolete —security in another person.
>
> The need to achieve isn't new to women: only the accessible routes to achievement are new. A country's worth of opportunity has just opened to women—the jobs are there, the responsibility, possibility, authority, power, engagement, money, excitement.

But the supreme irony of the whole feminist upheaval is that *there are not enough jobs!* If it were not such a disheartening situation for so many people, it would be laughable to realize that the feminists have arisen to spread discontent among housewives and to encourage a massive migration of women out of the home and into colleges and jobs just at a moment in our economic history when the nation has entered what promises to be a long period of chronic underemployment of skilled and well-educated workers. The same climbing educational level that has made feminists believe that women are too smart to stay at home has at the same time flooded the labor market with workers overeducated for the actual work that needs to be done. The Bureau of Labor Statistics projects a surplus of college graduates that will reach 140,000 people *annually* by 1980.

In these circumstances, it's difficult for me to understand why we should encourage any woman whose husband is already employed to go out and compete with breadwinners. And yet, in recent years the Women's Bureau of the Department of Labor has been holding conferences in major cities around the country, encouraging representatives of industry, unions and educational institutions to move more women into jobs traditionally filled mainly by men as rapidly as possible.

If it's true that most men will not settle for marriages in which the wife is the major earner (and it's certainly true that many more marriages have been breaking up since this trend began), then the whole idea of encouraging careers and education of the sexes on a fifty-fifty basis would seem to be a blueprint for societal disaster in the economic climate of today.

The truth is that the feminist idea of employing equal numbers of males and females in all areas of employment makes no sense at any time. If we didn't already have a sexual division of labor, the smartest thing we could do to get the world's work done, to advance civilization and to promote healthy, satisfying human life, would be to invent it.

In the first place, from the standpoint of using sheer muscle power in a responsible and efficient way, it would be folly to place equal numbers of men and women in the heavy jobs now performed by strong laboring men. I once calculated that if we were to require that our population of blue-collar workers be 50 percent female (it's currently about 85 percent male), we would sacrifice more than 300 million pounds of

267

muscle power. This energy would be lost to the work of the country, because we would be failing to take advantage of the muscular advantages strong men can offer that women can't.

But perhaps even more significant than the waste of this tremendous natural source of energy would be the foolish mistake we would be making in not allowing these men to take pride in their masculine strength which is often the central attribute that allows them to feel they're making an important contribution to society. For an inescapable lesson of life seems to be that when such men are not provided legitimate means of taking pride in their masculinity, they easily find illegitimate ways of gaining this recognition, ways that are usually harmful to society.

It's sobering to speculate that the idealistic people who today are so intent on "liberating" women into the labor force may be inflicting the same disease onto American society at large as warped the communities of American Negroes thirty years ago. In *Daughters of the Promised Land,* historian Page Smith describes what happened:

> Industrial capitalism, with the closing off of immigration, discovered an enormous, docile, highly productive native labor force, and after absorbing women by the tens and then by the hundreds of thousands, began, in the 1940s, to absorb them by the millions. This integration of enormous numbers of skilled and efficient women into the labor force received its greatest impetus from World War II. It is an additional irony that this supply of inexpensive and readily trained labor undoubtedly delayed by a number of decades the integration of American Negroes into the skilled jobs created by mid-twentieth-century capitalism. The great Negro migration to the industrial centers of the country

began at the same time as the influx of women into industry. If women had not been available, the Negroes, as the largest pool of inadequately utilized labor in the country, would almost certainly have been drafted into the industrial army. As it was, there were other recruits.

And as unpopular as it may be to point it out, those "other recruits" are coming forth in record numbers today to compete for jobs with male breadwinners, *black and white.* At the same time, it's a commonplace

As it was, there were other recruits . . .

to observe that much of American society and many of its families grow more and more to resemble the life of the tragic and chaotic black ghettos. (Even in times of slavery, blacks had more sense of family and less promiscuity than in these days of federal intervention, when abortions and illegitimacy are more frequent in Washington, D.C., the preëminent black city of the nation—our capital—than live births and legitimate offspring.)

It is the great accomplishment of civilization that strong, lusty, impulsive men can be tamed through the virtues of faithful, supportive, domestic women and motivated to bend themselves to the tedium and back-breaking labor of a regular job. It's a serious mistake to take this accomplishment of the civilizing process for granted, and to assume that strong men will stay civilized no matter what women do.

The damage from the assault on the sexes reaches deep into nearly every aspect of our social lives. This war on the sex roles is causing both sexes to be distrustful, leading each to refuse to commit itself to the other. It's driving men and women away from their previous devotion to the family, and causing both parents to renege on their traditional responsibilities to their children. Children are growing up without any vigorous sense of purpose, discipline or social structure.

Despite the feminist assertion that children are better raised through the institutional arrangements of the state, as in socialist countries, evidence from the real world doesn't suggest that this is true (even if it were the will of the American people, which it is not). There is no reason to believe good alternatives exist to the traditional American family, complete with a dedicated breadwinner, a devoted mother and well-supervised children. There simply is no other known system which allows whole societies of people to live with relative autonomy in clean dwellings with prosperity and the opportunity to pursue freely whatever dream of happiness and satisfaction for themselves and their children they choose.

Regardless of "alternative lifestyles," a true marriage remains the only way that a person can have the safety, security, love, and satisfaction of life over many years in the warmth of a sexual relationship with another who cares enough to accept a total commitment to the welfare, not only of the couple, but of offspring.

The reason a good marriage gives people a tremendous advantage is because of the principle of "synergy," which somehow works to give a combination of personal forces dedicated to the same goals far more strength and creative power than either of the partners possesses alone. Annie and I experience this every day, and I often think how misguided are those grim feminists who preach that it's "too risky" for a woman to invest herself in a marriage when she could be out building a career. One of the most basic principles of modern management is that *people work together far more effectively when they feel they are part of a team*. And the results of this kind of synergistic effect can be quadrupled in a good marriage. (It is exactly the aspiration toward this invaluable team-effect that women's lib has tried to destroy in women through its consciousness-changing techniques.) People who put all of their energies into a career get little in return unless they have somebody with whom to share the recognition and rewards when and if they come. For most workers, jobs are not "careers," but merely onerous labors that they're expected to show up to do every day for money. But even the most boring, repetitious job has importance and meaning in the life of a man when he goes to work feeling that he is contributing to the survival of a loving relationship with a wife who means more to him than anything else in the world. And when there are also healthy, aspiring children in a home where people love each other, everyone's life takes on significance that isn't found in a career, no matter how grand the achievement.

Amaury de Riencourt has said: "If man's intellect so often seems to be much more closely connected with his fundamental creative function than is the case with woman, if he has so often displayed mental inspiration amounting to the utmost creativity of a genius, it is essentially because woman's creativity is of an entirely different order and lies on a different plane which is not accessible to the masculine rational faculty."

For if man has been the creator, he declares, "it is she who provides the vital feelings and emotions that underlie every one of man's cultural achievements. She inspires, and he, pregnant with the idea, gives birth to the masterpiece. . . . It now becomes easier to see that, even if woman alone rarely proves to be intellectually or artistically creative, man cannot create without her; hence, her part in the cultural process, however indirect, is vital. The most appropriate symbol of the mutual interdependence that binds the two sexes together is to compare male and female to the two poles of an elliptic field of magnetic forces. The *correlation* between the two poles provides the creative power; no one pole, male or female, can achieve anything without the contribution of the other."

It is frequently supposed that a man and a woman who apply for a job are comparable only on the basis of their training, skills and experience. But consider some of the special advantages of a man who has a full-time, full-service wife at home:

(1) He's free of the time-consuming, worrisome details of domestic activity, such as caring for clothes, arranging appointments with doctors and dentists, deal-

ing with insurance adjusters, planning vacations and excursions, cooking, cleaning and looking after routine needs and problems of children.

(2) He's free of sexual frustration, agitation or preoccupation.

(3) He has his own private psychiatrist, advisor, and cheerleader.

(4) He has ready-made inspiration, purpose, and motivation.

(5) He has definite and conspicuous personal, social and legal responsibilities (all of which conspire marvelously to focus the mind).

Why should an employer fail to recognize the tremendous advantage in hiring a man who is equipped with such valuable resources? He will usually be far ahead in time, energy, motivation and mental application. Such assets can often be quite enough to justify greater confidence in an employee and higher pay.

Despite massive propaganda in the mass media today telling women that traditional sex roles are no longer valid, there are compelling reasons for believing they still make plenty of sense for men, women and children. It's a sign of a weakening society when more and more women are encouraged to work, and especially when that work includes moving into heavy labor, into the rigors of commerce, the military and police. How can it strengthen a society for the values of the nurturant woman at home to be shrugged off and the values of male performance, struggle and commerce to prevail in everyone's life 24 hours a day? Don't we need the gentler influences of comforting homelife to balance our lives? Such changes don't seem to me to spell liberation, of either women or men. They bespeak a hardening of our culture accompanying economic troubles, moral decay, decline of the arts—and a growing mood of social desperation. In a healthy society, large numbers of women are not driven from their homes to jobs under the illusion that they will be better off performing as independent agents and in the roles of men.

A healthy society protects its women for the simple reasons that women are the bearers of children, and that both women and children are normally more vulnerable than men. Regardless of fictions circulated through such popular media as the song of recent years that says "I am woman; I am invincible," the actuality is that women are absolutely dependent upon the protection of civilized men who have been raised to carry out the protective role. In circumstances where the protections of civilization do not prevail, women are weaker than men and they are their sexual prey.

There are other reasons why finding a marriage partner is of more critical concern to women, overall, than it is to men. The sexuality of men and women is different, as we've noted, and the male has a natural inclination toward depersonalized sex. It's satisfactory to men, therefore, to join into male-bond relationships in which sexual exploitation of women becomes a primary status value. Men don't necessarily have to recognize the children they sire, and it's far more likely that fathers will contribute to the upbringing of their children in a state of marriage than in any other kind of arrangement.

Women, on the other hand, are rarely interested in a life of sexual exploration just for the sake of lust and status. They can't effectively deny maternity of their children, and when they become pregnant, they're stuck with the child or with the trauma of getting rid of it. A woman on her own, furthermore, is at a cumulative disadvantage because of her comparative size and strength, her fluctuating hormonal status, her lack of a deep synergistic human relationship, and her exposure to sexual and economic exploitation.

274

One reason feminism is a mistake is that it tries to deny the essential vulnerability of women. It's totally irresponsible to reject the role of men as protectors, while at the same time insisting that society should somehow make it safe for a woman to walk through the streets in a mini-skirt at 2 o'clock in the morning (as I once heard a feminist say). Women *do* need protection, and it's the feeling of compassion, awe, respect and protectiveness toward women that inspires most men to treat women well rather than exploiting them. The ultimate absurdity is when Susan Brownmiller asserts that the reason women are oppressed is *because* they have to have men protecting them from rape. This is like saying the reason we're not all rich is because they make loans at the bank. It is the *reductio ad absurdum* of feminist logic. The truth is that women require protection from *vicious* men, and it's a basic civilizing aspect of normal male upbringing that they are taught not to attack girls, but to protect them. Should this inculcation of the role of the civilized male ever stop, females will be far more vulnerable than they are today.

It's all very well for feminists to sing songs about being invincible, and to act aggressively, and to demand quotas on police forces, and to enter the service academies under *present* circumstances in which most men have been taught not to compete seriously against females and not to attack them. But no one who has a realistic comprehension of the relative capabilities and propensities of the sexes could seriously believe that either women or civilization will survive happily if men become openly competitive against females. When this happens the weak men and almost all women will be the victims of whatever thugs eventually take over.

The role of protected wife has special benefits that are too easily overlooked by those who would push all women out of the home. In the first place, I consider it a tremendous benefit when a woman achieves a wifely status that allows her the privilege of *not* having to go out to work. There is a lot of baloney these days about how fulfilling and ennobling it is to have a "career," but my experience over nearly a quarter of a century in the work force is that *having* to go out to work every day isn't all that gratifying. In fact, it can be hectic, frustrating, grueling and a lot of other unpleasant adjectives that I'd as soon not think about. (Of course, I have to admit that the way *some* women do it, being on the job is more like a sorority soiree than labor, but I'm willing to assume that this type of liberated woman is the exception, gentleman that I still am.)

And let's consider that old canard about the housewife not having any income. Magazine writers and people on TV talk shows are forever discussing the latest figures worked out by experts who want to determine the market value of a housewife. You know—they figure out how much a maid would earn, and how much a seamstress would earn, how much a laundry worker would earn . . . and a chauffeur, a hostess, a nursery school teacher, a call girl, etc., and then put it all together and decide that a housewife is worth $14,000, or whatever. And the upshot is that they tsk, tsk at her lowly condition, because, according to their logic, she is unpaid labor, who doesn't earn a dime.

That's the kind of sociology department slander that drives my wife Annie right up the wall. And it ought to make *any* housewife mad, because it's nonsense. The truth is that housewives *do* have income, unless they simply allow themselves to be kept in servitude, but they are not paid salaries like chauffeurs, laundry workers or nursery school teachers. Wives are paid like surgeons, lawyers, architects and great artists—bluntly, the value of a wife is what she has been able to command in the market for husbandly patronage. It's ridiculous to pretend that a woman who lives in a $200,000 house, who drives a Mercedes-Benz to the supermarket, and who spends an annual allowance of, say, $25,000 on clothes, furnishings, beauty care, tennis lessons and sundry other frills, has no income. She has a substantial personal income due to the fact that she has been able to marry and keep a very successful man. The fact that her income doesn't come to her each week in a manila envelope with Social Security and income taxes deleted doesn't mean it isn't just as valuable to her as a paycheck is to the editor of *Mademoiselle*. (Economists, I believe, call this "in kind" pay.)

Quite frankly, most of the wives that Annie and I know *don't* live in $200,000 houses and *don't* drive Mercedes. But they still enjoy approximately the same level of income as their husbands do, because while the husband may bring home a check with his name on it, the money is used by both of them for their family life together. A wife may live in a $25,000 house and drive a six-year-old Chevy to the supermarket, but the chances are that if she does, she's living at the same economic level as her spouse, and if she's smart, and has made prudent arrangements, she has as much security. (Just as with surgeons, lawyers, architects and artists, it is possible for people in the wiving game to fail to exact everything they're worth from their patrons or to fail to prepare sensibly for their own futures, but some reckless people appear in nearly every avenue of life.)

It has been due to the wisdom of society, not to oppression, that women have been subject to protections not thought necessary, or considered prohibitively costly, for men. Although today we may be inclined to believe that because we are faced with overpopulation we needn't be concerned with safeguarding our reproductive potential, it is *never* safe to abandon our natural inclination to protect the human vessels necessary to the production of each new member of our species. A normal man has the biological capacity throughout most of his life to impregnate virtually hundreds of females annually. So while it takes some 3 million healthy women still in their reproductive years to reproduce enough children each year to maintain our current level of population, it's possible biologically for the male contribution to this reproduction to be per-

A man could conceivably, and quite happily, sire virtually thousands of offspring over a long lifetime . . .

formed by a few thousand virile men. To put the matter another way, while it would be asking a great deal of a woman to produce as many as ten children during her lifetime, a man could conceivably, and quite happily, sire virtually thousands of offspring over a long lifetime. Eventually, it would be biological suicide not to protect the sex whose bodies must carry and nourish the young.

If civilized societies have always realized the folly of wasting their women in wars, we are gaining new knowledge which seems to support the idea—which feminists reject—that there are good reasons for society to encourage special standards of health, conduct and protectiveness for women, from which men may be more or less exempt. A double standard seems irrational only to those who fail to recognize that there are two *different* sexes.

The Virginia Slims ads splash their congratulations across the magazine pages—"You've come a long way, baby"—encouraging women to take pride in the fact that more and more of them are smoking and drinking and behaving, in general, just like men. Yet scientific research has now disclosed that smoking, drinking and numerous pollutants encountered in industrial plants can cause damage to babies carried by pregnant women. Recent research has even shown that too much stress on a pregnant woman may result in retarded growth, brain injury or death to the fetus. And reports also suggest a mother might be inviting birth defects if she resorts to tranquilizers such as Valium or Librium during the first three months of pregnancy.

Research also reinforces the wisdom of the past that tells mothers that they are crucial to their children's early development. Nursing of babies gives them important immunological protection that they don't get through bottles, and it seems to provide them with special protection against developing a lifetime obesity problem. It's likely that there are also important psychological and emotional benefits that accrue to the child who has been nursed by his mother.

But motherhood today is under siege. Whereas social pressures once supported the impulse of a woman to stay at home and raise her children, the expectation today is that she will work until the time of delivery, take a few weeks off, and then return to her job at the earliest possible moment. The theory that the mother is no longer needed at home is being pressed, amazingly, at the very time that writers and social observers are noting the rising phenomenon of our youth's disconnectedness from people and society—the condition sociologists refer to as *alienation.* In an article in *Scientific American* in 1974 titled "The Origins of Alienation," Cornell psychologist Urie Bronfenbrenner said, "The crux of the problem lies in the failure of the young person to be integrated into his society. He feels uninterested, disconnected and perhaps even hostile to the people and activities in his environment. He wants 'to do his own thing' but often is not sure what it is or with whom to do it. Even when he thinks he has found it— and them—the experience often proves unsuccessful and interest wanes."

Among the many factors contributing to the alienation of today's youth noted by Dr. Bronfenbrenner, he points repeatedly to the fact that more and more mothers are working and that the care of children is being routinely delegated to specialists: "The demands of a job that claims mealtimes, evenings and weekends as well as days; the trips and moves necessary to get ahead or simply to hold one's own; the increasing time spent commuting, entertaining, going out, meeting social and community obligations—all of these produce a situation in which a child often spends more time with a passive baby-sitter than with a participating parent."

Dr. Bronfenbrenner asks: "What is the ultimate source of these problems? Where do the roots of alienation lie?" And then he answers:

Studies of human behavior have yielded few generalizations that are firmly grounded in research and broadly accepted by specialists, but there are two answers to the foregoing questions that do meet these exacting criteria.

1. Over the past three decades literally thousands of investigations have been conducted to identify the developmental antecedents of behavior disorders and social pathology. The results point to an almost omnipresent overriding factor: family disorganization.

2. Much of the same research also shows that the forces of disorganization arise primarily not from within the family but from the circumstances in which the family finds itself and from the way of life that is imposed on it by those circumstances.

Specifically, when those circumstances and the way of life they generate undermine relationships of trust and emotional security between family members, when they make it difficult for parents to care for, educate and enjoy their children, when there is no support or recognition from the outside world for one's role as a parent and when time spent with one's family means frustration of career, personal fulfillment and peace of mind, then the development of the child is adversely affected. The first symptoms are emotional and motivational: disaffection, indifference, irresponsibility and inability to follow through in activities requiring application and persistence. In less favorable family circumstances the reaction takes the form of antisocial acts injurious to the child and society. Finally, for children who come from environments in which the capacity of the family to function has been most severely traumatized by such destruc-

281

tive forces as poverty, ill health and discrimination, the consequences for the child are seen not only in the spheres of emotional and social maladjustment but also in the impairment of the most distinctive of human capacities: the ability to think, to deal with concepts and numbers at even the most elementary level.

Speaking some months after his article appeared, Dr. Bronfenbrenner described our society as one in which children are no longer being adequately socialized, no longer learn responsibility and consideration through shared activity with mature adults.

"If present trends continue," he told an interviewer, "I think children are going to grow up more confused about their roles—male, female; what it means to be a father or a mother, or what it means to take and hold a job."

Psychiatrist Charles W. Socarides, writing about the recent assault on sex-role identity in his book *Beyond Sexual Freedom,* says, "It is a social era which bears a strong resemblance to the stage of individual human life found in early childhood. Every child traverses a developmental period in his earliest years in which all sexual objects and aims are entertained and engaged in, instinctively and without restraint. This is a time of confused but emerging sexual-role identity, part of normal development, a period referred to as the phase of *polymorphous perverse sexuality.*"

Dr. Socarides says that there are striking similarities between the behavior of children in this early period and that of grown people caught up in the anything-goes attitudes of today.

"Those caught up in the pseudoliberation of the Polymorphous Perverse," he declares, behave astonishingly like the victims of another sexual era—that of the pre-Freudian sexual suppression. Both groups are characterized by denial: neither channels nor properly uses the sexual instinct. This is negation of sex which in our time takes a most curious form—it wears the mask of the wholesale release of all sexual expression (in direct contrast to the former suppression). But the end result is the same: lack of appreciation and understanding of the sexual instinct in its healthy manifestations. Psychoanalysis, on the other hand, rather than taking a position of either rigid suppression *or* wild abandon with regard to sexual questions, seeks to discover what is good for the human organism and what is bad for it, what makes for growth and enrichment of the personality and

self, and what makes for its destruction and impoverishment. In short, it says that sex should make the world a better place for men and women, as individuals *and* as a society.

But it is not enough, according to Dr. Socarides, that we merely recognize that we are going through a childish period in our social life. The important thing is that somehow we accept the dangers of following our impulsive quest after pleasures and recognize the necessity of bounds and controls in both our inner and social lives—because, he says, "not all cultures survive; the majority have not, and anthropologists tell us that serious flaws in sexual codes have undoubtedly played a significant role in their demise. When masses of people act similarly in changing their mind about previous sexual customs, their collective behavior will, in the last analysis, have a profound impact on the whole of society. This contradicts the contentions of so-called sex-liberationists who maintain that sexual behavior is merely a question of personal taste. A break with tradition has already happened, and the changes we are now being subjected to will determine the fate of our society."

We can't escape change. But we should try to approach our fate, whatever it will be, with our eyes open:

> Behold the role of the "person,"
> In the society of tomorrow,
> Which guarantees pleasure and ease,
> And eliminates all sorrow.

And of course with a grain of salt.

E.R.A. or E.R.R.O.R.?

When at last the definitive history of the course of the "equal rights" amendment to the U.S. Constitution is written, I hope that below the names of such illustrious adversaries as Alice Paul, Martha Griffiths, Sam Ervin and Phyllis Schlafly, there will somewhere be a footnote, perhaps, that says:

> New concern over the importance of "debate" of the issues of ERA was sparked in the mid-1970s when Jim and Andrea Fordham, a team of freelance writers, somehow persuaded the *Washington Post* to print an article skeptical of ERA in its editorial section. This unlikely event stunned ERA advocates and foes alike, and the reverberations lasted for years.

Our interest in the proposed Twenty-seventh Amendment began shortly after Annie and I moved to the state of Maryland. We went to vote one day in 1972 and found the state ERA on the ballot. We didn't know anything at all about the amendment at that time, but we voted for ERA simply because the words *equal rights* were attached to it.

Later Annie became curious about the amendment. I guess she wanted to see if we had done the right thing. She began reading up on ERA and discovered that it's not really just the "matter of simple justice" advocates often claim. Her first inkling of the seriousness of the feminist assault came when she realized that nobody really knows for sure how ERA will affect virtually thousands of laws across the land bearing on marriage, family, property, sexual offenses and public accommodations.

The wording of ERA is routinely quoted by proponents to demonstrate how uncomplicated it is— "Equality of rights under the law shall not be denied or abridged by the United States or by any state on account of sex." The problem, as we soon discovered, is that this wording is so vague that it's impossible to predict how judges will rule in the many cases that are sure to come before the courts. This isn't just an idle criticism raised by curmudgeons, but a realistic appraisal supported by numerous legal scholars. History shows that the Supreme Court doesn't necessarily interpret the law the way legislators expect. The court has inferred vast federal powers from the Constitution that could not have been anticipated by its drafters. Any lawyer knows that the more brief, simple and vague a law, the more room there is for confusion and misinterpretation. Who could have guessed, for instance, when the Fourteenth Amendment was ratified in 1868 for the purpose of protecting the Negro from discrimination that 18 years later the Supreme Court would decree that a corporation is also a person and apply the Equal Protection Clause to businesses?

Questions of the effects ERA is likely to have upon state laws such as those relating to marriage are fundamental to rational consideration of the amendment. Another legal implication that is seldom talked about is the prospect that Section 2 of ERA (giving the U.S. Congress authority to enforce Section 1) would pass authority in numerous matters (such as marriage and divorce) from state control to that of Congress and the federal courts. State laws protecting wives, mothers, widows and working women will undoubtedly be affected. The likelihood that ERA would require women to fight beside men in combat, or share public toilet facilities with men, has also been among those matters of serious legal speculation raised by distinguished constitutional scholars, lawyers and legislators.

The point is that no one knows for sure how ERA will affect existing laws. Proponents often pretend they know exactly how it will all work out. Opponents usually describe the dire effects they anticipate with an air of great certainty. But if anything is certain about the consequences of ERA, it is that many new court tests under the amendment will occur, that some will reach the Supreme Court, and that *nobody* can predict how the Supreme Court justices will rule.

No one familiar with the federal laws already on the books can take it for granted that ERA will add anything to the rights of women. Discrimination in employment on the basis of race, color, religion, national origin or sex is already prohibited by the Civil Rights Act of 1964, Executive Order 11246 and the Equal Employment Opportunity Act of 1972; equal pay for equal work is already guaranteed to every employee by the Equal Pay Act of 1963; discrimination on the basis of sex in education is prohibited by the Education Amendments of 1972; and the Depository Institutions Amendments Act of 1974 states: "It shall be unlawful for any creditor to discriminate against any applicant on the basis of sex or marital status with respect to any aspect of a credit transaction." And women, of course, are persons every bit as much as corporations under the Fourteenth Amendment to the U.S. Constitution, which guarantees "equal protection of the laws" to every "person."

Annie first became alarmed over the feminist assault when she realized that the libbers had almost succeeded in changing the Constitution virtually without real public debate or understanding of the issues involved in what she was coming to see was a blockbuster of an amendment.

What was just as disturbing, she became aware that our morning newspaper, the *Washington Post,* appeared to be subtly promoting feminism and ERA both in its editorial pages and in its reporting. She began to clip examples of this biased coverage from the pages of the *Post,* and before long, she had an impressive file. It was at about that stage that Annie's annoyance with the libbers and my interest in journalism connected, and we began to do some serious media research.

Eventually, our studies of the *Post* led us to the point of making a detailed appeal to the *Post*'s ombudsman, Charles Seib. We exchanged a series of communications with Mr. Seib, during which we offered numerous observations on the feminist bias of the *Post,* from pointing out its publisher Katherine Graham's connection with *Ms.* magazine to criticizing in detail a lengthy news story on ERA written by one of the *Post*'s top political reporters. In general, we told Mr. Seib we were chagrined to observe in our morning paper that (1) the thrust and tone of articles on subjects relating to feminism is enthusiastic, encouraging and applauding, but never critical; (2) balanced articles on such subjects which reveal in depth the intentions of feminist organizations, or which present the opinions, desires or ambitions of the majority of American women, are absent; (3) columns in the editorial pages on such subjects are feminist-oriented, but other points of view do not appear; and (4) letters to the editor supporting lib ideas and ERA appear regularly, but alternative opinions do not.

On February 21, 1975, Charles Seib wrote us a letter which, to our surprise, said in effect that he was in considerable agreement with our criticisms, and it was on the basis of this response (which persuaded us that the ombudsman experiment at the *Post* was working) that we decided to write our article on coverage of ERA by the press. Basically, we presented the information about ERA that I have already mentioned above, and we said that those whose profession is to report the news and comment on events of the day should be alert to the possibility raised by legal scholars that the terse language of ERA may be deceptive in its simplicity. "The serious issues of the ERA debate," we stated in the piece which the *Post* printed on March 31, 1975, "arise from the fact that amending the Constitution is a crucial legal act with legal implications and objectives. Debate in the Congress and state legislatures has centered upon implications for the state laws. Yet serious discussion of these issues has been conspicuously absent not only in the printed media but on television as well. . . ."

The article took up 35 column inches of space on the op-ed page. Adversaries on both sides of the ERA debate were dumbfounded that the *Post* had printed a piece expressing skepticism of the amendment. We learned later that feminists immediately organized a letter-writing campaign to pressure the *Post* into making up for its indiscretion. The editors soon acceded to this campaign by allotting 82 column inches of space for feminist rebuttal. This included an angry letter from Senator Birch Bayh, the prime sponsor of ERA in the U.S. Senate, and an article of 40 column inches by feminist law professor Ruth Bader Ginsburg.

Along with this show of force, a new show of concern over the matter of public debate surfaced among ERA advocates. In fact, the need for public debate was practically their theme song from the day our article appeared. Senator Bayh's long letter to the editor declared:

> The one point made by the Fordham article with which I concur is the need to make the public more aware of the issues at stake with the ratification of the ERA. Once the general public is informed fully of the implications of the ERA based upon the legislative history of the amendment, we will see a new upsurge in ratification by those few states remaining that have not done so. The public must be informed concerning what Congress intended the Equal Rights Amendment to mean and not be intimidated by the scare tactics and misrepresentation of those who want to deny the majority of Americans, who happen to be women, equal protection and equal opportunity under our laws.

Senator Bayh's remarks begged the questions our article had raised in the first place, but, more significantly, the senator's letter established a very curious definition of "public debate"—from then on, whenever ERA proponents spoke of the importance of "debate" or "discussion" of the amendment (as they began to do frequently) they were talking about the need to present *their own point of view*. To their minds, "public debate" did not include the opinions or insights of anyone who opposed the amendment or who was even skeptical of it.

292

Annie and I were surprised at the vehemence of Senator Bayh's reaction to our piece, which we had thought to be a model of judicious comment. If the senator surprised us, we were absolutely amazed four days later when we read in the *Washington Star* that President Ford had made a statement declaring his wholehearted endorsement of the amendment, and deploring that "the debate over ERA has too often degenerated into frivolous non-issues." The president said that amending the Constitution "calls for serious evaluation of the impact and meaning of the proposed change," but that ERA debate "should be a vehicle to inform legislators and the public of the many complex legal problems women still encounter." He further asserted: "Myths about the protected status of women can be dispelled through serious discussion. The way can be opened for the review of areas that will not be affected by ERA."

Annie could hardly believe it. "Do you really think the feminists at the White House got the president of the United States to say all that to counter our little article?" she said. The notion boggled our minds, but the wording and especially the timing of the president's whack at the very issue we had so recently raised led almost irresistibly to that conclusion.

A few weeks later ERA publicist Jill Ruckelshaus brought up the point again on ABC's "Issues and Answers," saying she thought debate was very healthy as long as it's relevant to the issues. Then Alan Alda, another promoter of ERA, said: "I agree with Jill that it is very important that we have a great national debate on the question of the Equal Rights Amendment." Then, a few moments later, he declared that ERA is a basic requirement. "My goodness," he said, "let's get this first basic thing done with. *It's incredible to me that we have to have a great national pondering over this.*"

Well, so much for the great national debate and the

marketplace of ideas. The thrust of the "Issues and Answers" interview—just like all the others where the ERA advocates are featured unopposed—was that there are no issues and nothing to debate about. For every TV appearance by ERA opponents, such as Phyllis Schlafly, we saw dozens of news reports and TV and radio appearances featuring glamorous ERA publicists

"It's very important to have a great national debate—but do we have to have a great national pondering, too?"

—few of whom ever had to submit to debate. In contrast, when Mrs. Schlafly appeared she was usually confronted by an aggressive interviewer, often accompanied by one or more feminists. When such prestigious advocates as Jill Ruckelshaus, Alan Alda, Jean Stapleton, Kathy Douglas, Gloria Steinem and Betty Ford publicized ERA, it always seemed to be with a sympathetic interviewer, and the overwhelming message sent to ordinary Americans was that no valid ERA issues exist and that no debate is necessary.

One interview (March 28, 1976), for instance, featured ERAmerica's Jane Wells explaining the proponents' new campaign to NBC's Claire Crawford. The conversation went like this:

JANE WELLS: I think clearly what has happened is that the proponents of the amendment have allowed the opposition to build and build and build. We've never had a national campaign *for* ratification. Individual national organizations and state organizations have quietly gone about working on it and each time it would come up they'd get themselves together a little bit. We've never had a national campaign so we haven't peaked. We never have been in the ball game in terms of having the organization that the opposition put together.

CLAIRE CRAWFORD: Well, what happened? Why not?

JANE WELLS: Nobody thought that it would be necessary. We naively thought that surely with the experience we had with other issues in the last 15. or 20 years, like the civil rights legislation, we wouldn't have to do it. The first 22 states just rolled in—it seemed like an idea whose time had come. How much simpler could it be to have women in the Constitution? . . .

CLAIRE CRAWFORD: You mentioned that the opponents have captured the media. I mean there's a woman who's running for president on an anti-abortion platform and so on, and the unisex bathrooms, and all that sort of stuff, and they've got fantastic sensational things. Is it possible to conduct a lady-like campaign and win?

During this cozy interview, the reporter nodded compliantly to every word the ERA publicist said, including the assertion, which became the standard line following the 1975 defeat of the New York and New Jersey amendments, that there is no connection between ERA and feminism.

Should a conscientious reporter let such distortions pass unchallenged? ERA was conceived and written in the early 1920s by radical feminists, introduced into Congress by feminists, and every feminist organization eagerly supports it. Informed reporters should recognize that ERA is an outgrowth of the feminist ideology and that feminists are intent on overhauling our society. As the *New York Times*–CBS report states, "Each major branch of the women's movement— women's rights and women's liberation—from its own perspective is working toward the elimination of the sex-role system: By external reform of social institutions and internal raising of consciousness. . . . Thus, any action from lobbying for the equal rights amendment to establishing small groups to talk . . . about the nature of women's oppression is deemed appropriate if it challenges sex-role stereotyping. Not only are all such actions 'appropriate,' but for the women's movement to progress toward its stated goal both external and internal approaches on each issue are essential. . . ."

A major distortion of coverage of ERA that we had found was the widespread tendency to equate the measure with "equal rights," as though the terms *Equal Rights Amendment* and *equal rights* were synonymous.

In *U.S. News & World Report,* for instance, we read: "Backers of equal rights for women now see 1975 as the year in which a 27th Amendment will be added to the U.S. Constitution. . . ." And Walter Cronkite declared: "What happened to the momentum of 1973 is that antiequal rights forces have been able to organize increasingly effective opposition to the amendment. Equal rights advocates acknowledge that the opposition has successfully changed the character of the debate, turning it from a consideration of sexual equality before the law to a host of highly emotional arguments concerning everything from lifestyles to religious principles. . . ." With these few words, Cronkite seemed to convey to listeners his judgments that opponents of ERA are against equal rights, that the issues they raise are irrational, and that the amendment is really a very simple matter after all. (Annie and I were intrigued at a National Press Club seminar in 1976 when Eileen Shanahan of the *New York Times* responded to this information by saying that bias is often just in the eye and ear of the beholder. "As it happens," she declared, "Walter Cronkite is an old friend of mine of something like 27 years standing, and I happen to know of my own personal knowledge and occasional screaming arguments that he has the profoundest reservations about the ERA." So . . . Walter Cronkite is skeptical of the ERA. And here we had been told it was just unsophisticated, fearful housewives who felt that way . . . my, the interesting things you learn at seminars!)

Although promotion of the amendment in most of the press continued as before, Annie and I were surprised to find ourselves the center of considerable attention following the appearance of our article in the *Post.* Reporters called to ask our opinions. We were invited to appear on several TV and radio programs to discuss ERA. Annie was interviewed by *Mademoiselle.* I was invited to speak about our media research at the ERA seminar of the National Press Club, and later to write an article on press coverage of ERA for *MORE*, the national media magazine. We continued our research and wrote further articles pointing out the abuses of profeminist publicists and the press, and by mid-1976 these critiques had appeared in numerous newspapers and magazines across the country.

On one occasion, we had an opportunity to study the reader response to a somewhat testy article, in which Annie cast certain doubts on ERA and the tenets of feminism, that appeared in the *National Observer*. Annie obtained all of the letters received by the *Observer* in response to her piece. Of the 84 letters, only 34— about 40 percent—disagreed with the views she expressed. The overwhelming majority of people who wrote were either skeptical or hostile toward feminism. Yet of the full page of letters the *National Observer* selected to publish, five times as much space went to comments from outraged feminists than to those of readers who were critical of feminism.

At the same time we were reporting these abuses, ERA publicists, as a counter-measure, had begun routinely accusing the press of being *anti*-ERA. As usual, they weren't obliged to debate these assertions, and they offered no evidence of the claims, but operated on the principle that the best defense was a good offense.

There was one occasion when Jill Ruckelshaus, the chairman of the Commission on International Women's Year, spread the story that a study had been conducted by the Journalism School of the University of South Carolina that revealed an overwhelming bias in the press *against* ERA. This story was printed in a variety of newspapers, and undoubtedly circulated throughout the U.S. At that time, Annie and I were preparing my presentation for the National Press Club appearance, and so we were very anxious to obtain a copy of such a relevant study. But when we contacted officials at the University of South Carolina, they had never even heard of it. After a good deal of confusion and querying of instructors of the Journalism School, they determined that the "study" actually consisted of *a brief term paper written by a graduate student!*

The most incontrovertible proof of the bias of the press, at least of the women's magazines, in favor of ERA came in July 1976, when more than thirty major magazines aimed at women joined in an unprecedented drive to urge acceptance of the amendment on their 70 million readers. Annie and I scanned these magazines all through the month of July as they appeared at our local newsstand and found that they were slanted overwhelmingly in favor of ERA. As a matter of fact, there was only one magazine—out of the nearly three dozen—that presented a completely balanced view of ERA in its July blitz issue. That was *Girl Talk*, which gave precisely equal space to an article by Annie, entitled "Why I Don't Trust the ERA," and to a piece by attorney Gloria R. Allred, entitled "Why the ERA Should Be Passed." The July blitz in the women's magazines of America stands as a historical demonstration of the unequal treatment dished out by the most persistent applauders of "equal opportunity" in recent years. Once again, so much for the marketplace of ideas.

Another example of the sort of research Annie and I did to expose the vacuousness of the claims of ERA promoters that they knew exactly how things would work out under the measure was our Great Potty Caper. The suggestion of ERA opponents that men and women might be required legally to use the same public restrooms under the amendment had been almost universally ridiculed and discounted by ERA advocates as well as by much of the press. For instance, *Modern Romances* told its readers: "Lots of things have been said about the ERA. Some of them are silly, some are serious. It's been said that ERA would mean women and men would have to share the same public bathrooms, and that the ERA would make homosexual marriages legal. These statements are in the silly category. They're not true."

We planned the Great Potty Caper...

Both of these questions are actually legal unknowns that will eventually be resolved by the courts under ERA. The people at *Modern Romances* weren't being quite honest when they pretended that these are not valid issues. Neither were the folks at *McCall's,* who told their readers: "As to unisex toilets, the right to privacy that is guaranteed by the Constitution, and reinforced by the Supreme Court, rules out the possibility that public restrooms could be forced to integrate."

Bess Myerson of *Redbook* answered the editorial question, "Will men and women be forced to use the same restrooms under ERA?" with this reply: "No. The Constitutional right to privacy guarantees the separation of the sexes in restrooms, sleeping quarters and all other public areas where bodily privacy is a concern."

Better Homes and Gardens told its readers: "Those who worry that the ERA will require men and women to share the same toilet facilities can put their fears to rest. The amendment does not affect laws governing privacy."

An item in *Parade,* later reprinted in *Reader's Digest,* assured Americans that because of their inherent right of privacy "separation of the sexes in public restrooms, prisons and military barracks will be preserved." The *Christian Science Monitor* told its readers that "ERA would not eliminate such facilities reasonably separated by sex as restrooms or sleeping quarters in public institutions. In other words, the concept of equal rights is harmonious with the rights of individual privacy."

And Dear Abby declared: "In 1965, the Supreme Court established the constitutional right to privacy. This permits the separation of the sexes in all places involving sleeping, disrobing and all other private functions."

Annie and I had found that such opinion masquerading as unalloyed fact on this—as on many other ERA issues—prevailed in the press. And pamphlets by organizations such as Common Cause and the League of Women Voters were distributed all over the country declaring the bathroom issue to be absolutely invalid because of "the constitutionally guaranteed right of privacy."

On NBC-TV, Jane Wells, the national campaign manager of the official lobby ERAmerica, dismissed the issue out of hand: "The Unisex bathrooms!" she declared. "There are more jokes made about that. Practically nobody takes it seriously. Sometimes I don't even think the opposition takes it seriously. I think they do it for the news value."

These were the casual means, Annie and I discovered through our researches, by which information on this issue and many others has been served up by the press, the ERA lobbyists and other advocates of the amendment. We had been aware for some time that this conventional wisdom wasn't backed by any reliable body of legal precedent. Students of the history of the privacy concept know that its relevance to ERA not only is unestablished, but actually uncertain. Annie and I realized this from our reading, yet we couldn't find any really definitive, official reference we could cite that would establish the point with real authority.

There had been testimony by constitutional scholars during the congressional debates of ERA. Professor Paul Freund of the Harvard Law School testified in 1970 that ERA "would require that there be no segregation of the sexes in prisons, reform schools, public restrooms, and other public facilities." And Professor Philip Kurland, editor of the *Supreme Court Review* and professor of law at the University of Chicago Law School, made these responses when Senator Sam Ervin asserted: " . . . the law which exists in North Carolina

302

and in virtually every other state of the Union which requires separate restrooms for boys and girls in public schools would be nullified, would it not?"

> PROFESSOR KURLAND: That is right, unless the separate but equal doctrine is revived.
>
> SENATOR ERVIN: And the laws of the states and the regulations of the Federal Government which require separate restrooms for men and women in public buildings would also be nullified, would it not?
>
> PROFESSOR KURLAND: My answer would be the same.

After a while, Annie and I thought of the Congressional Research Service, which researches and prepares official reports for members of Congress. What, we speculated, if we could persuade a member of the U.S. Congress to request a new study by the American Law Division of the Congressional Research Service aimed at clarifying the implications of ERA for the so-called right of individual privacy? We were confident that such a report from the Library of Congress would again show that the ERA publicists were deplorably overstating their case.

We thus began our campaign to convince some member of Congress that it would be very useful to the on-going debate over ratification of the ERA to have such a report prepared. We soon found that not everybody on Capitol Hill considered the "potty issue" to be as significant as we did. In fact, most people just thought it was a joke, and not a few, I'm sure, just thought we were nuts! We persisted, however, and at last, with the help of a well-connected friend in Virginia, we succeeded in enlisting the assistance of a U.S. senator.

When the nine-page report issued by the Congressional Research Service on May 10, 1976, arrived—several months after our campaign began—it was exactly what we had anticipated. It traced the evolution of the idea of privacy in constitutional law and concluded:

> Because the U.S. Supreme Court has failed to define the right of privacy in clear-cut terms and because the trend has been to apply the right narrowly, confining it specifically to fact situations relating to marriage, procreation, family relationships, and child rearing and education, it is difficult to ascertain exactly what the relationship between the proposed equal rights amendment and the right of privacy will be. . . . It is a matter of interpretation as to whether or not those cases are relevant to an analysis of the meaning of the right of privacy under the proposed equal rights amendment.

In other words, Supreme Court decisions have not extended the "right of privacy" to any situations even resembling those of such public accommodations as restrooms. There is no proof courts won't be forced to require sexually integrated toilets in the world of ERA. (If this is a ludicrous prospect, it's no more so than the idea of forced busing would have seemed to many at the time of the civil rights debates of the early 1960s.)

The press has persistently portrayed such issues as unisex toilets and the prospect of sending women into combat as "emotional" and "scare tactics," instead of investigating the issues in depth. This has been true of the question of women being drafted, even though most ERA proponents say this is what they want and even pro-ERA legal scholars declare that this is what the amendment will bring.

For instance, as an explanation of the defeat of state

304

ERAs in New York and New Jersey in 1975, *Boston Globe* columnist Ellen Goodman wrote: "There were more scare tactics used against the ERA than were ever mustered against fluoride. The 'antis' raised the old specter of the unisex toilet and the coed army. . . ." Yet, if the question of unisex toilets is uncertain, there's no doubt at all that increasing the participation of women in all phases of the military is exactly what the promoters of ERA expect.

The League of Women Voters in its "Brief in Support of Ratification" has stated: "Under the Equal Rights Amendment, women will definitely be subject to military obligation—as well as exemptions and deferments —as are men, and they will be entitled to military benefits on the same basis as men."

Feminist attorney Susan Ross of the American Civil Liberties Union has declared: "If there is a draft, the ERA means that women would have the same responsibilities as men. Of course, it also means you can enact sex-neutral exemptions, so that if Congress wanted to exempt parents of young children, for example, it could as long as the exemption applied to men as well as women. Women who met the physical standards could also be assigned to combat. What it does is force women to think more seriously about their responsibilities as citizens, where they stand on any war, whether they're going to work for or against that war, and I personally think that's a good thing. It has to be faced head-on that this is one of the results of the ERA, and that we no longer will be second-class citizens to be shoved around because we haven't served in the army."

A law review article, endorsed by the prime congressional sponsors of ERA, that appeared in the *Yale Law Journal* in 1971 states: "The Equal Rights Amendment will result in substantial changes in our military institutions. The number of women serving, and the positions they occupy, will be far greater than at present. Women will be subject to the draft, and the requirements for enlistment will be the same for both sexes. In-service and veterans' benefits will be identical. Women will serve in all kinds of units, and they will be eligible for combat duty. The double standard for treatment of sexual activity of men and women will be prohibited." This article, which Senator Bayh inserted in the *Congressional Record,* has been cited by the Citizens' Advisory Council on the Status of Women as one of the most significant interpretations of the meaning of ERA that is likely to influence the courts.

The council also states: "The legislative history of the Equal Rights Amendment is unusually comprehensive and clear. Both houses of the Congress passed the same version, and there was a remarkable unanimity among the chief proponents, expressed fully in the majority report of the Senate Judiciary Committee. . . ." And the report of the Senate committee declares: "It seems clear that the Equal Rights Amendment will require that women be allowed to volunteer for military service on the same basis as men. . . . It seems likely as well that the ERA will require Congress to treat men and women equally with respect to the draft. This means that, if there is a draft at all, both men and women who meet the physical and other requirements, and who are not exempt or deferred by law, will be subject to conscription. Once in the service, women, like men, would be assigned to various duties by their commanders, depending on their qualifications and the services' needs."

The authors of the *New York Times*–CBS report *Rebirth of Feminism* wrote: "Proponents of the ERA agree . . . that passage of the Equal Rights Amendment would subject women to the draft as well as men. . . .

306

Some argue that the idea of drafting women is a good idea in its own right, ERA notwithstanding. They feel that all young people should serve their country in some way, either in the armed forces or some other kind of national service. . . ."

The ERA was quickly ratified by 21 states in the first six months after it was approved by Congress in 1972. Like Annie and me, a lot of people accepted ERA naively before they really gave much thought to what the amendment would mean. Since then, opposition in many states has grown, despite efforts of a national network of supporters whose lobbying activities were primed with hundreds of thousands of dollars of public money through the various state and federal Status of Women groups.

Impetus and federal funding for this campaign was increased on January 9, 1975, when President Ford issued Executive Order No. 11832, setting up the National Commission on International Women's Year and appointing pro-ERA members. The commission promptly made ERA ratification its "top priority issue" and resolved to use federal funds, facilities and personnel thus placed at its disposal to spearhead a comprehensive national ERA campaign.

This was done through ERAmerica, which the IWY Commission soon established and charged with the task of mobilizing and coordinating as many national organizations as possible in an all-out drive to get the amendment ratified. These professionals—now with up to $5 million appropriated by Congress for their activities—weren't fussy about the means they used. One organization playing a key role, for instance, was the Los Angeles advertising agency Ogilvy & Mather Inc., whose executives approached ratification of the constitutional amendment as a "marketing problem," conducting a half-million-dollar media campaign to "sell"

307

the measure to women in four key states targeted in 1976.

Actress Jean Stapleton, an avid ERA supporter, lent her portrayal of Edith Bunker to ads in the Ogilvy & Mather campaign, which was based on a distorted and misleading version of the position of women in American society. One magazine ad, for instance, pictured the TV actress over headlines declaring: "As Edith Bunker, I don't have equal rights. As Jean Stapleton, I don't either."

Phyllis Schlafly analyzed this ad in one of her Eagle Forum newsletters, saying:

> *The pro-ERAers obviously have no good arguments* for ERA—else they would not have to resort to such obvious lies.
>
> (a) Mrs. Bunker says: "My Social Security benefits are lower." That is false. Mrs. Bunker will be able to draw Social Security benefits based on Archie's earnings—even though Mrs. Bunker never held a paying job in her life! Social Security gives benefits to the homemaker even though she never pays into the system. If ERA is ratified, Mrs. Bunker will *lose* her Social Security benefits—because she would have to be "equal" with men, and men don't get benefits unless they have a job and pay into the system.
>
> (b) Mrs. Bunker says: "My life insurance rates are higher." That is false. Call any life insurance agent and check. Women pay *lower* life insurance rates than men of the same age because *women* live longer.
>
> (c) Mrs. Bunker says: "As a widow, I'd have to pay a big inheritance tax on my very own home." That is false. If her home is her "very own," she does not have to pay any inheritance tax at all.
>
> (d) Mrs. Bunker says: "There are hundreds of jobs that pay one salary to men, a lower one to a woman." This is illegal under the Equal Employ-

ment Opportunity Act of 1972. If Mrs. Bunker
knows of any such jobs that pay less to a woman,
she should report it to the government—not run
ads. THE LESSON OF ALL THIS IS: Don't get
your legal advice from Mrs. Archie Bunker!

Will homemakers really lose their Social Security
benefits, as Mrs. Schlafly suggests? There can be no
doubt that feminists are seeking a situation in which
the protected status of the housewife would no longer
be recognized, and there are indications that officials at
the Social Security Administration are already looking
to this prospect as one means of easing the tremendous
burden on the Social Security system, which was
strained even further when the Supreme Court applied
the unisex principle and extended the same death benefits to widowers as it provides to widows.

Dr. Arvonne S. Fraser, president of the feminist
Women's Equity Action League, says the Social Security system would have to be revised under ERA:

> Women are increasingly aware of, and vocal
> about, the fact that the U.S. Social Security system
> does not treat them as individual beneficiaries of
> the system, even though they are required to pay
> equal contributions of taxes when working under
> "covered" occupations (those covered by the So-
> cial Security Act as amended, originally passed in
> 1935).
>
> The system presumes that the married woman,
> whether she works inside or outside the home, is
> the economic dependent of her husband.
>
> The system provides that a male worker, on re-
> tirement, receives a benefit and a "dependent"
> wife's benefit. A married woman who has worked
> in covered employment may draw a benefit based
> either on her own earnings or the "dependent"
> wife's benefit which is based on her husband's

309

earnings—whichever is larger. As a result, a
woman working in covered employment can pay
into the system throughout her work life and receive a benefit no larger or only slightly larger
than she would have received had she never
worked outside the home.

It's difficult to view this criticism (which is a frequent complaint from feminists) as anything but an attack on the family system. This is an example of the
feminist drive to remove every vestige of support of the
traditional family roles, to make it official government
policy to explicitly deny that men are, and ordinarily
should be, the primary breadwinners, and that women
are and should be the homemakers in our society. It's
a peculiar sort of devotion shown by feminists (who
belittle the homemaker because she doesn't get an official paycheck) to try to take away from housewives the
one claim to protection in old age that the government
provides to citizens. The irony is complete when you
consider that it's being done under the banner of
"equal opportunity" for women.

ERA advocates perennially say that to determine
how the amendment will be interpreted, we should
look to the intentions of the legislators as expressed in
the legislative history. But if you study this material
you find that what it actually contains is massive evidence that the purpose of ERA is indeed to bring about
a thoroughly unisex society.

What this legislative history consists of has been defined by the Citizens' Advisory Council on the Status
of Women (a strong promoter of ERA) in these words:

The Federal courts will be interpreting the
Amendment in those cases where citizens believe
that the Congress or the States have not amended

310

their laws or official practices to conform. The courts in interpreting amendments to the Constitution traditionally give great weight to the intent and purpose of the Congress and the State legislatures in ratifying the amendments. In this connection the great importance of the "legislative history" is often not understood.

In addition to the Senate Judiciary Committee report and the debate in both houses of the Congress, the courts will have available a very thoroughly researched and clear law review article endorsed by Congresswoman Martha Griffiths, chief sponsor in the House of Representatives, distributed by her to all members of the House, and inserted in the Congressional Record by Senator Birch Bayh, chief proponent in the Senate. One of the co-authors was Professor Thomas Emerson, whose testimony before both Judiciary Committees had been very influential and whose views had been incorporated in the views of the proponents on both committees. The importance of this article is underscored by Senator Ervin's statement in his minority views in the Senate Judiciary Report, calling it "one of the best guides to a general interpretation of the Equal Rights Amendment." For these reasons, this article "The Equal Rights Amendment: A Constitutional Basis for Equal Rights for Women" (80 *Yale L.J.* 871) will carry more weight with the courts than a law review article ordinarily would.

The council's report also calls the legislative history of ERA "unusually comprehensive and clear," and for the most part I have to agree. What the council doesn't say is that the intentions expressed in the history are feminist and unisex all the way, and *that* we are about to see.

Although the *Yale Law Journal* article of April 1971 is most often linked to the name of the distinguished professor Thomas I. Emerson, he was in fact but a co-

311

author, the burden of the work having been done by three law students, Barbara A. Brown, Gail Falk, and Ann E. Freedman (all of whom were members of the Class of 1971, the same year their article appeared, and all of whom were "active in the women's movement," according to the article). If you read the piece, you are indeed left with little doubt that it was written by avid feminists. It is a feminist tract, and it begins:

> American society has always confined women to a different and, by most standards, inferior status. The discrimination has been deep and pervasive. Yet in the past the subordinate position of more than half the population has been widely accepted as natural or necessary or divinely ordained. The women's rights movement of the late nineteenth and early twentieth centuries concentrated on obtaining the vote for women; only the most radical of the suffragists called into question the assumption that woman's place was in the home and under the protection of man. Now there has come a reawakening and a widespread demand for change. This time the advocates of women's rights are insisting upon a broad reexamination and redefinition of "woman's place."

Just how broad are the changes intended by the Yale feminists is indicated a few lines later, where they say, "Our legal structure will continue to support and command an inferior status for women so long as it permits *any* differentiation in legal treatment on the basis of sex. . . ." Still further on, they declare: "The transformation of our legal system to one which establishes equal rights for women under the law is long overdue. Our present dual system of legal rights has resulted, and can only result, in relegating half of the population to second-class status in our society. What was begun in the Nineteenth Amendment, extending to women the right of franchise, should now be completed by guaranteeing equal treatment to women in all areas of legal rights and responsibilities."

The Yale law students (spearheaded of course by Professor Emerson) go on in their conclusion to say:

> The call for this constitutional revision is taking place in the midst of other significant developments in the movement for women's liberation in this country. The movement as a whole is in a stage of ferment and growth, seeking a new political analysis based upon greater understanding of women's subordination and of the need for new directions. The resulting political discussion has brought forth many possibilities, including changes in work patterns, new family structures, alternative forms of political organization, and redistribution of occupations between the sexes. A number of feminists have argued for increased separation of women from men in some spheres of activity or stages of life. Dialogue and experimentation with many forms of social, political and economic organization will undoubtedly go on as long as the women's movement continues to grow.
>
> Underlying this wide-ranging debate, however, there is a broad consensus in the women's movement that, within the sphere of governmental power, change must involve equal treatment of women with men. Moreover, the increasing nationwide pressure for passage of an Equal Rights Amendment, among women both in and out of the active women's movement, makes it clear that most women do not believe their interests are served by sexual differentiation before the law. Legal distinctions based upon sex have become politically and morally unacceptable.
>
> In this context the Equal Rights Amendment provides a necessary and a particularly valuable political change. It will establish complete legal

313

equality without compelling conformity to any one
pattern within private relationships. Persons will
remain free to structure their private activity and
association without governmental interference. Yet
within the sphere of state activity, the Amendment
will establish fully, emphatically, and unambig-
uously the proposition that before the law women
and men are to be treated without difference.

I think we have to view this kind of "history" as part
educated guesswork, part ideological aspiration, and
part pure fiction. For instance, the suggestion that a
wide segment of American women support ERA and
that "most women do not believe their interests are
served by sexual differentiation before the law" was
not borne out by the opinion polls available in 1971.
And even by 1975 Market Opinion Research was finding that 47 percent of American women were unaware
of ERA, and 74 percent of those who were aware of it
didn't feel they knew enough about the amendment to
form an opinion. Nonetheless, recognizing the limitations of this legislative history as prophecy, let's take a
look at some high points of what the Yale feminists say
the results of ERA would probably be:

(1) "The Equal Rights Amendment will result in substantial changes in our military institutions. The number of women serving, and the positions they occupy,
will be far greater than at present. Women will be subject to the draft, and the requirements for enlistment
will be the same for both sexes. In-service and veterans' benefits will be identical. Women will serve in
all kinds of units, and they will be eligible for combat
duty. The double standard for treatment of sexual activity of men and women will be prohibited. . . . The
drafting of women into the military will expose them to
tasks and experiences from which many of them have

until now been sheltered. The requirement of serving will be as unattractive and painful for them as it now is for many men. On the other hand, their participation will cure one of the great inequities of the current system. As long as anyone has to perform military functions, all members of the community should be susceptible to call. When women take part in the military system, they more truly become full participants in the rights and obligations of citizenship."

(2) Concerning homosexuality: "Following the rule of narrow construction of criminal statutes, courts will most likely invalidate sodomy or adultery laws that contain sex discriminatory provisions, instead of solving the constitutional problems by extending them to cover men and women alike."

(3) Likewise prostitution: "Just as the Equal Rights Amendment would invalidate prostitution laws which apply to women only, so it would require invalidation of laws specially designed to protect women from being forced into prostitution. . . . Here, as with other criminal laws, a court would probably resolve doubts about congressional intent by striking down the law."

(4) "Sex differentiation and sex discrimination pervade laws about overt sexual behavior and behavior with sexual overtones, reflecting the confluence of social stereotypes about gender and sexuality. Many of the laws, such as seduction laws, statutory rape laws, and laws prohibiting obscene language in the presence of women, embody a stereotype of women as frail and weak-willed in relation to sexual activity. Others, such as the prostitution and 'manifest danger' laws, display a contradictory social stereotype: women who engage in certain kinds of sexual activity are considered more evil and depraved than men who engage in the same conduct. The Equal Rights Amendment would not permit such laws, which base their sex discriminatory clas-

315

sification on social stereotypes. Courts would generally strike down these laws rather than extend them to men. . . ."

(5) "The present legal structure of domestic relations represents the incorporation into law of social and religious views of the proper roles for men and women with respect to family life. Changing social attitudes and economic experiences are already breaking down these rigid stereotypes. The Equal Rights Amendment, continuing this trend, would prohibit dictating different roles for men and women within the family on the basis of their sex. Most of the legal changes required by the Amendment would leave couples free to allocate privileges and responsibilities between themselves according to their own individual preferences and capacities."

(6) Under the amendment, courts would probably "do away with the rule that refusal to accompany or follow a husband to a new domicile amounts to desertion or abandonment," and a husband "would no longer have grounds for divorce in a wife's unjustifiable refusal to follow him to a new home, unless the state also permitted the wife to sue for divorce if her husband unjustifiably refused to accompany her in a move."

(7) "With respect to children, the traditional rule is that the domicile of legitimate children is the same as their father's. Even those states which permit a married woman to have a separate domicile from her husband appear to retain this rule with respect to the child's domicile. The Equal Rights Amendment would not permit this result."

(8) "The Equal Rights Amendment would not permit a legal requirement, or even a legal presumption, that a woman takes her husband's name at the time of marriage. . . ."

(9) And about the husband's duty to support his wife and children: "Criminal nonsupport laws are the legal system's most heavy-handed technique for enforcing the husband's current duty of support. Nonsupport was not an indictable offense at common law. But criminal statutes in all but three states now penalize a man's desertion or nonsupport of his wife, and all American jurisdictions set criminal penalties for nonsupport of young children. While these laws typically penalize either parent who fails to provide support for a minor child, the duty of interspousal support is placed solely on the man.

"The child-support sections of the criminal nonsupport laws would continue to be valid under the Equal Rights Amendment in any jurisdiction where they apply equally to mothers and fathers. However, the sections of the laws dealing with interspousal duty of support could not be sustained where only the male is liable for support. Applying rules of narrow construction of criminal laws, courts would have to strike down nonsupport laws which impose the duty of support on men only. . . . With regard to civil enforcement of support laws, courts could take a more flexible approach. The Equal Rights Amendment would bar a state from imposing greater liability for support on a husband than on a wife merely because of his sex. However, a court could equalize the civil law by extending the duty of support to women. . . . Like the duty of support during marriage and the obligation to pay alimony in the case of separation or divorce, nonsupport would have to be eliminated as a ground for divorce against husbands only, or else extended to the wife where the husband was without resources and the wife had the financial capacity to support him."

(10) Concerning child custody: "The Equal Rights Amendment would prohibit both statutory and com-

mon law presumptions about which parent was the proper guardian based on the sex of the parent. Given present social realities and subconscious values of judges, mothers would undoubtedly continue to be awarded custody in the preponderance of situations, but the black letter law would no longer weight the balance in this direction."

One of the most significant parts of the legislative history of ERA is the record of the congressional debates of nine amendments to ERA introduced by former Senator Sam Ervin of North Carolina. "These Amendments take on more than mere historical interest in several ways," declares a report of the Congressional Research Service. "First, excerpts from the debate on the proposed amendments to the ERA provide an excellent summary of the objections to, and support of, the equal rights amendment. By defining his objections in the form of individual amendments, Senator Ervin made it possible to easily identify pro and con summaries of the various issues. . . . Further, the *Congressional Record* debate on the amendments to the ERA, with the final vote tallies, may be used as evidence of legislative intent. Legislative intent is also indicated by the majority and minority reports of the Senate Committee on the Judiciary. . . ."

Specifically, the amendments proposed by Senator Ervin would have:

(1) Exempted women from service in combat.

(2) Exempted women from compulsory military service.

(3) Preserved laws which protect women in the work force.

(4) Preserved traditional legal protections of wives, mothers and widows.

(5) Held fathers responsible for support of their children.

(6) Preserved laws which secure privacy to men or women, boys or girls on the basis of sex.

(7) Preserved laws which make sexual offenses punishable as crimes.

(8) Substituted these words for the present ERA: "Neither the United States nor any State shall make any legal distinction between the rights and responsibilities of male and female persons unless such distinction is based on physiological or functional differences between them."

(9) Offered the states an alternative law along with the present ERA which would have been worded: "Equality of rights under the law shall not be denied or abridged by the United States or by any State on account of sex. The provisions of this article shall not impair the validity, however, of any laws of the United States or any State which exempt women from compulsory military service, or from service in combat units of the Armed Forces; or extend protections or exemptions to wives, mothers, or widows; or impose upon fathers responsibility for the support of children; or secure privacy to men or women, or boys or girls; or make punishable as crimes rape, seduction, or other sexual offenses."

This last amendment was defeated in the Senate 82 to 9, and each of the other Ervin amendments (with the exception of one that was withdrawn) fell by a similarly wide margin, providing powerful testimony that whatever the intentions of Congress were, the Senate at least was not anxious to avoid doing away with laws requiring husbands to support their wives, exempting females from military combat, retaining separate restrooms, outlawing sexual offenses, or preserving traditional protections for wives, mothers, widows and women in the labor force. As a matter of fact, the part of the legislative history most often cited in defense of

ERA, Senator Bayh's Judiciary Committee majority report, is just about the only ambiguous note among these various documents. Although this brief wrap-up by the Judiciary Committee pretends to tie together the many confusing loose ends of this legislation for the guidance and enlightenment of the courts of tomorrow, it actually contradicts parts of the review article in the *Yale Law Journal* and ignores entirely the views of numerous constitutional scholars whose testimonies are also part of the legislative history. In short, there is every reason to suppose that future courts have all the material they need to throw our legal system into confusion for years to come. The one thing that every document in the history supports, however, is that under ERA there must be no distinction made between males and females before the law.

The following episode from the record of the Congressional debates serves, almost comically, to illustrate the depth and quality of the intellectual consideration given to ERA before it was presented to the 50 states for ratification. As we look in on the U.S. Senate, Senator Ervin has just introduced his amendment No. 1058, which the clerk is reading to the senators:

"This article shall not apply to any law prohibiting sexual activity between persons of the same sex or the marriage of persons of the same sex."

SENATOR ERVIN: Mr. President, the *Wall Street Journal* for August 13, 1970, published an editorial entitled "The Ladies and the Constitution." I read that editorial:

"That Constitutional Amendment liberating women broke on the public consciousness so quickly no one's quite sure what its real effect would be.

"'Equality of rights under the law shall not be denied or abridged by the United States or by any

State on account of sex' is what it says. Sounds fine, at least until the lawyers and courts get at it, but it's been languishing in Congress since 1923. Lately Congressman Celler, who's against it, has kept it bottled up without even committee hearings. But when Congresswoman Griffiths strongarmed it out on the floor with a discharge petition, it whizzed through the House by 346 to 15.

"The upshot is that it was passed with only an hour of debate, which wasn't exactly time enough to clear up all the little hazy areas. Everyone seems to think it would finally implement that unassailable principle that women ought to get the same pay as men for the same work, but someone ought to take time to notice the words do not mention private employers. We were assured that it wouldn't affect such things as maternity benefits or rape laws, somehow. And what with a volunteer army almost here we don't need to worry about its implications for the draft.

"Well, we're all for the ladies, but even so, before we write some new words into the Constitution it'd be nice to know what they really do mean."

Frankly, Mr. President, I do not know what the ERA means in one aspect. Therefore, I have offered [this amendment to the ERA].

Now, Mr. President, the idea that this law would legalize sexual activities between persons of the same sex or the marriage of persons of the same sex did not originate with me. I do not know what effect the amendment will have on laws which make homosexuality a crime or on laws which restrict the right of a man to marry another man or the right of a woman to marry a woman or which restricts the right of a woman to marry a man. But there are some very knowledgeable persons in the field of constitutional law, such as Prof. Paul Freund of Harvard Law School, Prof. James White of the Michigan Law School, and Prof. Thomas Emerson of Yale Law School, who take the position that if the equal rights amendment becomes

321

law, it will invalidate laws prohibiting homosexuality and laws which permit marriages [only] between men and women.

The constitutional amendment which the Senator from Indiana is proposing states that: "Equality of rights under the law shall not be denied or abridged by the United States or by any State on account of sex."

Professor Freund of the Harvard Law School and Professor White of the University of Michigan Law School have reasoned that the ERA will mean that activities which are permitted between members of different sexes cannot be the basis of criminal prosecution against members of the same sex. Thus, State criminal laws relating to sexual conduct between members of the same sex will be unconstitutional under the ERA because it denies them equality of rights because of their sex. Marriage laws, in the same way under the ERA, could not be restricted to members of different sexes. In other words, the professors reason that laws and activities which are allowed to members of different sexes will have to be extended to members of the same sex or they will be denied their "equality of rights" . . . on account of their sex, as the ERA states.

In the hearings before the Senate Judiciary Committee last year, Prof. James White of the Michigan Law School mentioned these bizarre results which would flow from passage of the ERA. Prof. White said: "With the exception of Illinois and perhaps a few other states, there are laws on the books which make it a crime to engage in certain kinds of homosexual activity. First of all, I suppose the amendment would bring in question all that law. . . . I think the question is, is this the way we should do away with it or should we allow the states to control this themselves?"

Prof. Paul Freund of the Harvard Law School also testified during the Judiciary Committee hearings that: "Indeed, if the law must be as undiscriminating concerning sex as it is toward race, it

322

would follow that laws outlawing wedlock between members of the same sex would be as
invalid as laws forbidding miscegenation. Whether
the proponents of the amendment shrink from
these implications is not clear."

Prof. Thomas Emerson of the Yale Law School
mentioned in an article in the *Yale Law Journal*
that: "Courts will most likely invalidate sodomy or
adultery laws that contain sex discrimination provisions, instead of solving the constitutional problems by extending them to cover men and women
alike."

I do not agree with these results and frankly I do
not feel the Members of the Senate intend the results which Prof. Freund of the Harvard Law
School, Prof. White of the Michigan Law School,
and Prof. Emerson of the Yale Law School say will
flow from the passage of the ERA regarding homosexual activity.

SENATOR BAYH: Mr. President, will the Senator
from North Carolina yield to me for a question,
please?

SENATOR ERVIN: I will be glad to yield to the
Senator from Indiana for a question.

SENATOR BAYH: That is exactly what I wanted to
ask the Senator, and I appreciate his courtesy.
I have not had a chance to give a great deal of
lengthy study to homosexuality, but I would ask
the Senator, is homosexuality limited to men
or to women?

SENATOR ERVIN: Some forms of it are and some
are not. But if there is a problem here, as these
legal scholars say, perhaps the Senator's Constitutional Amendments Subcommittee should study
the subject before we pass a constitutional amendment which legal scholars say could affect this area
of the law.

SENATOR BAYH: Is homosexuality limited to
men or to women? In other words, if a State legislature says it is against the law—

SENATOR ERVIN: They make a distinction. Unlike this amendment, the phraseology relating to

323

that matter does make a distinction between men and women, as a rule. It applies the term "homosexuality" to abnormal sexual activities between men—

SENATOR BAYH: But is this—

SENATOR ERVIN (continuing): And sometimes to abnormal sexual activities between women.

SENATOR BAYH: How is this term defined by the statutes which concern the Senator from North Carolina? I ask this question not to get involved in anything that might be embarrassing, but we do have to be specific here.

SENATOR ERVIN: The Senator from Indiana is asking a question, but the Senator from North Carolina would not have the time, if he had the learning, to explain to the Senator from Indiana what the laws of the 50 States have to say on the subject. But I will tell the Senator what some very smart constitutional lawyers, including Prof. Paul Freund of Harvard, Prof. James White of Michigan Law School, and Prof. Thomas Emerson of Yale Law School, have had to say about the effect of this amendment in the general field of sexual activity and marriage relations.

SENATOR BAYH: The Senator has been kind to permit me to ask the question which he has not yet answered.

SENATOR ERVIN: I profess my inability to educate the distinguished Senator from Indiana on the phraseology of all the laws of the 50 States which make homosexuality a crime, but they are multitudinous, and perhaps there should be a subcommittee study of them before the Senate acts.

SENATOR BAYH: The Senator from Indiana would—

SENATOR ERVIN: If the Senator will remember his Bible, he will recollect that sodomy was practiced in Nineveh and that was the reason Nineveh was wiped from the face of the earth.

SENATOR BAYH: Let me suggest that the argument the Senator proposes at this point might have been relevant at the time of Nineveh, but it does not seem relevant today. I refer to the original question the Senator was considerate enough to accept from the Senator from Indiana. That, I do not think, has been answered. I think it is possible to make a real distinction between the sexuality of a man or woman and various acts they practice. There are, of course, very real physical differences between men and women.

SENATOR ERVIN: But the act says that there are not.

SENATOR BAYH: Mr. President, I asked the Senator—

SENATOR ERVIN: The Senator is not now propounding a question.

SENATOR BAYH: Yes I am. I am now trying to redefine it so that the Senator might finally answer it. He has not yet answered. I asked the question whether the word "homosexuality," or act of homosexuality, or statutes prohibiting homosexuality are confined to men or women.

SENATOR ERVIN: It depends on the phraseology of the statute.

SENATOR BAYH: I wish the Senator would describe a homosexual act.

SENATOR ERVIN: I am not going to describe homosexual acts on the floor of the Senate.

SENATOR BAYH: The Senator from Indiana did not want to embarrass anyone. However, I am trying to get at the different definitions of homosexuality. The Senator described various capacities that men or women have.

SENATOR ERVIN: The *Yale Law Review* article by a great student of constitutional law, Thomas Emerson, who Senator Bayh has deemed a great legal scholar, says that this constitutional amendment would invalidate every statute which makes homosexuality or lesbian activity dependent on the sex of the participant.

SENATOR BAYH: Would it be possible for a State legislature, after the passage of this amendment, to enact a statute saying that it shall be unlawful under the laws and statutes of State X to participate in

325

any type of homosexuality whatsoever, p-e-r-i-o-d?

SENATOR ERVIN: If the Senator had studied a little anatomy as well as a little law, he would find that there are some offenses which go under the general term of homosexuality which only men can commit. And that is true with respect to discrimination against sex being wiped out. This act of sexuality would be made lawful instead of unlawful under the amendment and I am against this result.

SENATOR BAYH: Mr. President, we have time, and I would like to get the Senator's opinion. If he does not want to give it, that's all right. However, he has significant constitutional expertise. We might differ as to the wording of different statutes. However, the question I propound is whether it would be possible for such a State statute to be enacted. The Senator from Indiana is not an expert on anatomy. However, he is an expert on his own anatomy.

SENATOR ERVIN: That ought to be enough to apprise the Senator from Indiana with the fact that there are certain acts of homosexuality that only men can commit.

SENATOR BAYH: I have read about it. However, I have not had any expertise in that area.

SENATOR ERVIN: I am not implying that the Senator had and neither have I.

THE PRESIDING OFFICER: The Senators will suspend until the galleries come to order. There will be no demonstrations in the gallery with reference to what is taking place on the floor.

SENATOR ERVIN: This is on my time, and I prefer to speak on my time. Let the Senator from Indiana speak on his time.

SENATOR BAYH: Mr. President, may I yield myself two minutes?

SENATOR ERVIN: No. I have the floor. The Senator from Indiana can have the floor after I have had a chance to speak. I do not mind questions, but I do mind being heckled.

SENATOR BAYH: Was the Senator from North Carolina being heckled?

SENATOR ERVIN: Yes. The Senator from Indiana is heckling the Senator from North Carolina and trying to impede the Senator from North Carolina in his effort to explain the thoughts of Prof. Freund of Harvard, Prof. White of Michigan Law School and Prof. Emerson of the Yale Law School who say that laws dealing with homosexual activity will be unconstitutional after passage of this amendment.

SENATOR BAYH: Would the Senator from North Carolina permit me to strike my questions from the Record?

THE PRESIDING OFFICER: Will the Senator from North Carolina yield to the Senator from Indiana? The Senator from North Carolina has the floor.

SENATOR ERVIN: No, I do not yield.

SENATOR BAYH: May I ask unanimous consent?

SENATOR ERVIN: I do not yield for that purpose.

THE PRESIDING OFFICER: The Senator from North Carolina has declined to yield, and the Senator from North Carolina has the floor.

SENATOR BAYH: May I propound a parliamentary inquiry?

THE PRESIDING OFFICER: Will the Senator from North Carolina yield for a parliamentary inquiry?

SENATOR BAYH: Is not a parliamentary inquiry appropriate at any time? I merely want to find a way to remove whatever remarks I made that might cause my good friend to think that I was heckling him.

THE PRESIDING OFFICER: The Chair has ruled that the Senator from North Carolina has the floor. No parliamentary inquiry may be made without the permission of the Senator from North Carolina.

SENATOR BAYH: Will the Senator from North Carolina permit me to make a parliamentary inquiry?

SENATOR ERVIN: I do not know why the Senator from Indiana wants to heckle the Senator from North Carolina and prevent the Senator from North Carolina from telling the Senate what these legal scholars think.

SENATOR BAYH: The Senator knows that is not the intention of the Senator from Indiana.

327

SENATOR ERVIN: The Senator from Indiana will not permit the Senator from North Carolina—and I hate to say it, but the truth compels me to say so— to proceed for a minute without an interruption. And when the Senator from North Carolina yields for a question, the Senator from Indiana makes a speech on the time of the Senator from North Carolina.

If the Senator from Indiana thinks that the Senator from North Carolina ought not to be permitted to express his views on this matter uninterruptedly, the Senator from Indiana can continue to engage in this heckling. But the Senator from North Carolina, in order that he not be impeded too much and in order that he may be privileged to resume this discussion at a time when the Senator from Indiana and the Senator from North Carolina will have had an opportunity to read the statutes of some of the States, the Senator from North Carolina will temporarily withdraw the amendment.

THE PRESIDING OFFICER: The amendment is withdrawn.

Neither the Congress nor the press have ever given much attention to the fact that many scholarly minds see in ERA's terse, absolute wording the potential for serious and widespread legal and social disruption. In 1923 the late Justice Felix Frankfurter wrote: "Only those who are ignorant of the nature of law and of its enforcement and regardless of the intricacies of American constitutional law, or indifferent to the exacting aspects of woman's industrial life, will have the naiveté or the recklessness to sum up woman's whole position in a meaningless and mischievous phrase about 'equal rights.' "

Harvard's Professor Freund has said, "Not every legal differentiation between boys and girls, men and women, husbands and wives, is of an obnoxious charac-

328

ter, and . . . to compress all these relationships into one tight little formula is to invite confusion, anomaly, and dismay."

Perhaps the most prophetic and profound words ever written on this subject were these by Dr. Jonathan H. Pincus, professor of neurology at the Yale Medical School, who, in a letter to the *New York Times*, wrote:

> If family stability plays an important role in the well-being of our nation, it is hard to envision the Equal Rights amendment just passed by the House of Representatives as a constructive act. The bill seems not to have been discussed adequately or maturely but rather shouted through under pressure from a relatively small band of zealots. It seems to me that the removal of legal responsibility from a man for supporting a family, giving the family a name and protecting his daughters from the sort of influences the U.S. Army might have in store for them before marriage is likely to have some effect on the manner in which men relate to their wives and children and vice versa; those traditional ties will be weakened.
>
> One must agree with women's liberation groups that the liberating effect of Equal Rights will apply to men as well as to women. What they are both being liberated from is nothing less than the restrictions of traditional roles in a family structure. One has the right, indeed the duty, to ask, "Is this good?" Marriage has received some rather bad publicity of late; it is considered a breeding ground of neurosis, a prelude to divorce in more than 30 of 100 cases and a burden to the free spirit seeking self-fulfillment. Day care, communal living arrangements and release of women and men from domestic duties are the modern vogue.
>
> Despite this, and supported by my observations as a physician, I am convinced that solid, happy family life is the foundation of mental health and happiness. Basic to a healthy family is the concept

329

of role: husband and father, wife and mother, son or daughter. With the restrictions and discipline which stem from these roles, allowing for individual variations, one has the cement which binds a family for life.

Perhaps I am unduly cynical about the ability of people liberated from their responsibilities to make wise choices concerning the path to happiness and contentment; but I would predict that the Equal Rights amendment and many of the other goals of its proponents will bring social disruption, unhappiness and increasing rates of divorce and desertion. Weakening of family ties may also lead to increased rates of alcoholism, suicide and, possibly, sexual deviation. Conceivably this is merely a theoretical parade of horribles. There are genuine questions which should be asked and discussed before our Constitution is amended for the purpose of producing social change. There is no evidence that such deliberations have been made or planned. Is the Equal Rights amendment to be the Tonkin Gulf Resolution of the American social structure?

Since 1971, when Dr. Pincus wrote this letter, we have seen his "theoretical parade of horribles" become more real each day as the ideas of women's "liberation" have been popularized. And by the summer of 1976 we saw the first shock wave of feminism-in-action rock many of those who have been willing to believe that libbers don't really mean what they say, that a feminist society won't *really* be very different, only equal, and just, and, well, *better*. So when HEW's Office of Civil Rights ruled that events in public schools such as mother-daughter teas and father-son banquets constituted illegal sex discrimination under Title IX of the 1972 Education Amendments, it stirred a hornet's nest across the country. Many people acted as though it

330

were just some terrible mistake. President Ford bounded up from his morning newspaper to call HEW Secretary David Mathews to order him to suspend the ruling immediately. The *Washington Star* called the ban "a nonsensical intrusion." The *New York Times* said it was "ridiculous." The *Washington Post* cited it as "rulemania" and "a real lulu," attributing the decision to HEW's "nutty rule-making machine." One columnist called the author of the letter announcing the HEW ruling a "dingle-brain bureaucrat." A *Post* editorial, headlined "Civil Rights Madness," declared:

> The father-son/mother-daughter fracas, after all, is not the first of these weird episodes, and it is unlikely to be the last. There are enough laws and enough rules and regulations and enough civil ser-

vants to see to that. In fact, in our judgment it
almost doesn't matter, except in terms of getting
the present ruling unruled, whether the fault is to
be found in the relevant statute itself or in some
government official's interpretation of it. For the
great gluepot of government is filled with a mixture of both, and it has been our observation in
recent years that when these senseless dicta are
put forth they can almost invariably be traced back
to that no-fault gluey condition in which no single
law or civil servant can be said to be responsible
for making the thing happen.

You might know that an organization that has promoted the Equal Rights Amendment and the sex-role
revolution as much as the *Post* has would attribute such
occurrences when they surface to a general, nebulous,
gluey condition, wherein no exact cause can quite be
traced. Even columnist George Will, whom we would
have expected to know better, blamed the episode on
vague laws and misguided bureaucrats.

The reality, of course, is that the father-son ruling
was no fluke of the bureaucracy at all. It was just the
feminist ideology put into practice. From the very beginning, the feminists who instigated Title IX and the
ERA have fully intended to ban all school activities
that aren't thoroughly unisexual. The HEW equal opportunities specialist who wrote the letter announcing
the ruling, Ms Helen Walsh, said, "It was very routine.
I thought the decision was very rational. The letter
pointed out that having parents' night, instead of fathers' or mothers' night, would allow fatherless boys
and motherless girls to be included."

The feminists at NOW were outraged by the president's interference with what they regarded simply as
reasonable enforcement of the law. A spokeswoman for
NOW said such father-son social gatherings should be
outlawed because they perpetuate harmful sexual ster-

eotypes. She said this was just one more example of how the Civil Rights Act is "being nickled and dimed to death."

Feminist columnist Jane O'Reilly declared that politicians and the press were mistaken in treating the issue as trivial. "No one whom I have read or heard has stopped to ask *why* HEW made its decision," she said. "Everyone has assumed that one-parent exclusive school events are good things, and HEW wrong and stupid. The assumption indicates how lightly people skim over the implications of equality for women." Far from being an inappropriate intrusion, Ms O'Reilly asserted, "Title IX of the Civil Rights Act of 1972 is designed to interfere with those traditional systems and structures of discrimination. Eventually, equal sports budgets will mean equal awards and equal public interest. Equal access to courses and colleges will mean equal intellectual efforts. Fathers will have a future too. And mothers will have a present. Women and men will be selling insurance. Men and women will be serving coffee. Eventually, women may even get equal pay. No wonder they are trying to make a bureaucratic joke out of it. But she who laughs last laughs best."

If President Ford and all the others whose comprehension of the battle over sex roles was just peripheral in 1976 were still able to view the father-son flap as merely a bureaucratic blunder, more knowledgeable observers on both sides of feminist issues knew it was a precursor of serious conflicts to come.

Columnist Patrick J. Buchanan prophesied that if ERA should become law of the land, the father-son ruling would be back again.

The next time it will not be issued by some regional bureaucrat who can be collared by his boss. It will come down from the bench of a federal

333

judge, and the nation will have nowhere to look for rescue from this arbitrary Diktat excepting only the United States Supreme Court.... Within a fortnight after the ERA is nailed to the Constitution, NOW will be in the courtroom of a sympathetic U.S. judge who will, as HEW did, outlaw such events as sexist and discriminatory.

If a majority of the U.S. Supreme Court can find forced busing inside the 14th Amendment, it takes no stretch of the imagination to interpret ERA as outlawing father-son and mother-daughter nights, fraternities which refuse female members, and boys clubs, and the sexist 82nd Airborne Division.

And Phyllis Schlafly declared,

This flap clearly shows what is wrong with a simple-sounding law that flatly bars all "sex discrimination." Rational people don't see anything wrong about discriminating against men by having a Mother-Daughter Breakfast, etc.

This proves the radical, extreme goals for a *gender-free society*. You will be forbidden by law to separate men and women or treat them differently any time, for any purpose, no matter how worthy, or how much desired by the majority. This is the goal of NOW and the women's lib movement, and under the new HEW Regulation, they intend to pursue this goal by *Federal* enforcement.

In this instance, President Ford was able to order HEW to rescind its ruling. If the lawyers decide that, under the law, HEW is correct and Ford is wrong, then Congress can remedy the problem by an amendment to the Education Amendments of 1972—exactly as they solved the problem when HEW ordered the sex-integration of fraternities and sororities.

BUT, IF ERA IS IN THE CONSTITUTION, no phone call by the President, and *no* amendment

passed by Congress, can do *anything* to prevent
the absolute nonsense that will be required. Why?
Because the U.S. Constitution is "the supreme law
of the land," and it supersedes any other law or
ruling.

In a letter to the editor of the *Washington Star,* a
reader wrote: "Congratulations to HEW on its recent
tour de force with Title IX. Never have I encountered
such finely reasoned arguments that so effectively cut
through this treacherous legal thicket. Only HEW, in
its collective wisdom, could have seen through to the
underlying perniciousness of these separate father-
son/mother-daughter gatherings in our high schools
and root them out before they become a real threat to
our society. A capital performance! It's a continuing
source of comfort to know that we have such savants in
government so readily available to guide us where we
so obviously are not competent to guide ourselves."

Three weeks after the uproar over father-son events,
the whole thing erupted again when it was discovered
that HEW's Office of Civil Rights had declared that a
boys' choir for fifth and sixth graders in Wethersfield,
Connecticut, violated Title IX. The press still regarded
it as a case of bureaucratic blundering. Said a *Washington Star* editorial: "Perhaps a review of every ruling
made . . . under the sex discrimination statute would be
in order. Who knows what other bureaucratic absurdities have issued from the office in the name of eliminating sex discrimination?"

Said my Annie: "They still don't understand the situation, do they? But they'll catch on—eventually."

Sexism–That New Word in Webster's

Thumbing through a new *Webster's Dictionary* a while back, I was surprised to see a new word nestled neatly right between *sex hormone* and *sex kitten*. There is now, the G. & C. Merriam Company was informing me, a word known as *sexism*. If I was puzzled as to why the Merriam-Webster people wanted to dignify such an atrocity by putting it in their dictionary, I was also baffled by their definition. *Sexism* and *sexist*, they would lead us to believe, refer to "prejudice or discrimination based on sex, esp. discrimination against women."

I was so disconcerted by this discovery that I wrote the folks at G. & C. Merriam a letter inquiring what on earth had prompted them to botch the matter so badly. My query was answered by James G. Lowe, who told me that the company's editorial staff first noticed these words in 1970 in several underground newspapers. Since then, he said, "both words have gained widespread acceptance as evidenced by their use by major

337

journalists in a variety of publications." The Merriam-Webster files, he told me, contained examples of the usage of these words culled from 27 different publications.

Mr. Lowe's letter didn't shed much light on the question that really bothered me, however—namely, how they had decided on such a *phony* definition of the feminist words. Everyone must know that the idea of "sexism" goes far beyond matters of prejudice. *Sexism* denotes a special political orientation and view of the world, like *pacifism, heathenism* or *ultramontanism.* It is only remotely linked to anything we usually consider to be discrimination. Why didn't the definition in the dictionary reflect this?

Sexist is most often used to refer to traditional sex roles. While it's true that feminists believe our sex roles involve intrinsic patterns of discrimination against women, this is after all an insurgent interpretation, laboriously established only by those steeped in lib ideology. *Sexism* actually refers to whatever is perceived by feminists as having anything to do with the ordinary sex roles of society. This is the prevalent meaning applied throughout the mass media. In a newspaper story on "sexist toys," we read: "One game on the market illustrates vividly that sexism is not entirely dead. It's the 'Miss America Pageant Game,' a Parker Brothers product. 'Swimsuit' is part of the competition, just like [*sic*] in Atlantic City." Who but an advocate of the feminist ideology would think of the Miss America Pageant as an example of "prejudice or discrimination"?

Similar examples of this meaning can be plucked from dozens of pages of the book *Unlearning the Lie—Sexism in School.* One passage, for example, states: "... the feminists said they wanted access to classrooms and curriculum. They wanted sexist books removed from the library." ("Sexist" books are those that

338

reflect the reality of society's sex roles. The only books that feminists consider "nonsexist" are those which herald the utopian unisex culture.) Another passage in *Unlearning the Lie* reads: ". . . I feel the same way about boys and guns. If you insist that they can't play with them, the guns become objects of fierce desire. I feel the child's needs have to be taken into consideration. If you derogate a sexist television program that they're watching and enjoying, they feel that you're putting *them* down. . . ." (Like sexist books, a "sexist television program" is the kind that does not reflect unisex values.)

Feminists in our community, not long ago, objected to a book for elementary school kids called *Mommies Are for Loving*, because it contains phrases like "Mommies are for saying No . . . and drying tears and scrubs in tubs. . . . Mommies are for lots of things but best of all Mommies are for loving." (We must by all means protect children from such dangerous sexist ideas!)

And a writer in the *Christian Science Monitor*, concerned about sexism in children's literature, declares: "Sex-role stereotyping! What does this mean for the children's department of a public library? . . . It should be remembered that a book must meet many requirements when being considered for library collection. Projecting a non-sexist image is not enough to warrant purchase. . . . Perhaps for an interval it may be necessary to accept books that deliberately show Jane can be a lawyer, an astronaut, or a plumber."

Sexism and *sexist* are also used often to refer to the attitudes of anyone who takes account of the differences between the sexes. According to feminist belief, there are no significant differences and anyone who suggests that there are is a sexist. A sexist is also any man who does not take pains to suppress the fact that he is aware, or aroused, or interested in a woman's

339

body. A key axiom of feminist belief is that a woman shouldn't be regarded unduly as a sex object, and that any sign or indication that a man is interested in her bosom or bottom rather than in her mind is prima facie evidence of his blatant sexism. This usage is especially popular among the lip-service libbers. The unisex principle is also expressed in the attitude of feminism that dictates absolute sameness in the experiences and accoutrements of males and females in childhood. According to this ideological requirement, even a Jack-in-the-box is considered irretrievably sexist until its marketing includes a Jill-in-the-box too. Clearly, the Webster people have overlooked the greater part of the meanings these words are most often used to express.

But there is more involved here than Webster's neglect of a word. What I see happening as a result of the lib assault on our language is a frightening acceleration of the recent trend away from rational discourse in our society. The fact is that the new language of liberation the feminists have introduced (for example, *liberated woman, male chauvinist pig, consciousness raising, male supremacy, female oppression, up front* and *sexist*) has not been a means of better describing reality or of giving information, but *a means of expressing and controlling attitudes.* The feminists claim to abhor stereotypes, but the litany they have introduced has as its main function the establishing and enforcing of rigid stereotypic attitudes toward the relations of the sexes.

No new terms would have been needed to describe the ideas of the feminists. The purpose of words such as *consciousness raising* and *male chauvinist* is to replace critical thought with easy labels that exalt or condemn and that even the least articulate among us can employ to instantly define any pertinent situation. This is what the famous scholar of language Joseph Church has called "word magic." He wrote:

340

Apart from its frankly primitive manifestations, as in incantations and spells, word magic takes such everyday forms as talking away unpleasant facts, taking refuge in fantasy, making grandiose promises and then feeling so virtuous that any further action becomes superfluous, inventing evidence to win an argument, and, in general, reshaping reality verbally to suit our own desires.... There comes a time when the individual is so solidly oriented to an orderly, predictable concrete reality that he can dismiss as "nonsense" or "hot air" verbal formulations that contradict his knowledge. His knowledge, of course, may be erroneous, but that is not the issue.

Feminist thought and expression, which was never as deep or as profound as the true believers imagined, has very quickly hardened into an orthodoxy far more rigid and constraining than the sex roles it was intended to replace. Unhappily, the litany of lib has taken hold at a time in our history when self-indulgence is at its height and critical thought and intellectual honesty are at an all-time low. The result, I am saddened to report, is an ocean of distorted information and half-baked ideas relieved only rarely by anything even resembling serious critical comment.

"The word *sexism*," according to the *Guidelines for Equal Treatment of the Sexes in McGraw-Hill Book Company Publications*, "was coined, by analogy to *racism*, to denote discrimination based on gender. In its original sense, *sexism* referred to prejudice against the female sex. In a broader sense, the term now indicates any arbitrary stereotyping of males and females on the basis of their gender."

Feminists insist on this analogy to racism, even though most people see little similarity between the relations between the sexes and the history of abuses

341

against black people (which actually *did* include slavery). The idea that women have been slaves of men is ludicrous to most people. Many would argue, I think, that the sexes are mutually enslaved to each other, or else mutually liberated, depending on the particular people and their relationships.

No, it takes a special view of the world and the relations of the sexes to embrace the idea of sexism. It's definitely a political concept, part of the feminist ideology. Sexism is *not* a fact. It is one way of interpreting certain facts, sometimes of distorting them. Moreover, the push to root out expression and behaviors identified by feminists as "sexist" isn't a normal result of democratic action or of sober social planning. As we'll see in such documents as the McGraw-Hill guidelines, it is more of a mass media crusade by feminist true believers. And as is usual in crusades, there is less sense than nonsense, less concern with the real values and needs of real people than with smiting the enemies (sexism, male chauvinists, "nonachieving" women at home, et cetera) and implanting the banner of the holy cause.

Feminists are not interested in encouraging a kind of society in which people can strive for what they want, as they suggest, so much as in molding everyone's desires to their particular vision. They are trying, for instance, to shape our experiences by changing the laws in ways that, more and more, impose the unisex values on our daily lives (as by outlawing father-son and mother-daughter events in schools). Likewise, they are trying to mold our lives by altering the language and images we experience in everyday life. Everyone has heard by now of the grave hazards sex-role stereotyping is said to hold for young minds.

And so we find ourselves assailed by such absurdities as the McGraw-Hill guidelines and other feminist guides that are being used by many publishers and school boards all over the country to purge books and other materials of the dread sexism. This is how McGraw-Hill explains it:

> We are endeavoring through these guidelines to eliminate sexist assumptions from McGraw-Hill Book Company publications and to encourage a greater freedom for all individuals to pursue their interests and realize their potentials. Specifically, these guidelines are designed to make McGraw-Hill staff members and ... authors aware of the ways in which males and females have been stereotyped in publications; to show the role language has played in reinforcing inequality; and to indicate positive approaches toward providing fair, accurate, and balanced treatment of both sexes in our publications.

Not long after the McGraw-Hill guidelines appeared with 16 pages of do's and don'ts, the Macmillan Publishing Company came out with a 96-page production "to help authors, artists, and editors cope with problems inherent in adapting to newly-raised consciousness. ..." Macmillan's guidelines made it clear that this publisher doesn't approve of stereotypes of *any* kind. "We must be sensitive," the reader is told, "to all text and art that generalizes about people on the basis of irrelevant characteristics, such as physical appearance, monetary status, age, or special abilities. Some objectionable examples are: dumb athletes, stupid beautiful women, skinny intellectuals wearing glasses, fat social misfits, old ladies with twenty cats, or emphasis on the upper classes alone to portray the 'typical' lifestyle in history."

I couldn't help wondering if the Macmillan proscriptions included not writing about officious publishers who insist on shackling authors with their own sterile notions about what the real world is like. Columnist Nicholas von Hoffman said of the Macmillan directive: "It might be more in keeping with ideals of education in a nontotalitarian society to understand stereotypes instead of abolishing them. Many athletes seem dumb for the very good reason they spend their time cultivating their bodies; the same reasoning can be applied to dumb blondes and bookworms. TV is crowded with health spa ads offering hope to fat social misfits, and if you don't know a poor, lonely old lady who has nobody but her cats to talk to, you are probably a Radcliffe student." (The president of Radcliffe College had written a glowing endorsement in the preface of the Macmillan guidelines.)

Let's take a look at these guidebooks for the nation's writers and artists and consider their significance for our literature, our culture and our lives. The McGraw-Hill booklet opens with a little lecture on the feminist view of traditional sex roles:

> Men and women should be treated primarily as people, and not primarily as members of opposite sexes. Their shared humanity and common attributes should be stressed—not their gender difference. Neither sex should be stereotyped or arbitrarily assigned to a leading or secondary role.... Though many women will continue to choose traditional occupations such as homemaker or secretary, women should not be type-cast in these roles but shown in a wide variety of professions and trades: as doctors and dentists, not always as nurses; as principals and professors, not always as teachers; as lawyers and judges, not always as social workers; as bank presidents, not always as tellers; as members of Congress, not always as members of the League of Women Voters.

344

The guide does not say so, but I gather it is better to show men as the members of the League of Women Voters. In any case, we are told that "men should not be shown as constantly subject to the 'masculine mystique' in their interests, attitudes, or careers. They should not be made to feel that their self-worth depends entirely upon their income level or the status of their jobs. They should not be conditioned to believe that a man ought to earn more than a woman or that he ought to be the sole support of a family."

The book goes on and on with McGraw-Hill Book Company's (that is to say, the feminist) vision of how we should all be indoctrinated to think:

> An attempt should be made to break job stereotypes for both women and men. No job should be considered sex-typed, and it should never be implied that certain jobs are incompatible with a woman's "femininity" or a man's "masculinity. . . ." [The quotes around those words tell us that there really are no such things as femininity and masculinity, in case we thought there were.] Teaching materials should not assume or imply that most women are wives who are also full-time mothers, but should instead emphasize the fact that women have choices about their marital status. . . . Materials should never imply that all women have a "mother instinct" or that the emotional life of a family suffers because a woman works. Instead they might state that when both parents work outside the home there is usually either greater sharing of the child-rearing activities or reliance on day-care centers. . . . Men and women should be shown engaged in home maintenance activities, ranging from cooking and house-cleaning to washing the car and making household repairs. Sometimes the man should be shown preparing the meals, doing the laundry, or diapering the baby, while the woman builds bookcases or takes out the trash. . . .

Girls should be shown as having the same abilities, interests, and ambitions as men and boys. . . . Sometimes men should be shown as quiet and passive, or fearful and indecisive, or illogical and immature. Similarly, women should sometimes be shown as tough, aggressive, and insensitive. . . . The smarter, braver, or more successful person should be a woman or girl as often as a man or boy. . . . The taller, heavier, stronger, or more active person should not always be male, especially when children are portrayed.

Both the McGraw-Hill and the Macmillan guidelines press the unisex ideal from beginning to end. For example, Macmillan lists stereotyped images to be avoided alongside their suggested alternatives. *Don't* show females wearing aprons, we are instructed; show "males and/or females in aprons when appropriate to the story." *Don't* show "Mother sewing while Dad reads"; instead show "Mother working at her desk while Dad reads or clears the dining room table." *Don't* show "Mother bringing sandwiches to Dad as he fixes the roof"; rather show "Mother fixing the roof, building a cabinet." *Don't* use "pink for girl babies, blue for boys"; the trick is either to avoid these colors altogether or "use both together in nurseries, on cribs, baby carriages, clothing, etc." *Don't* show "girls surrounded by dolls, baby carriages, kitchen equipment." *Do* show "girls and boys amid varied objects: basement workroom, tools, chemistry sets, nature collections, books, fishing rods, musical instruments—and dolls." McGraw-Hill advises: "Women and girls should be portrayed as active participants in the same proportion as men and boys in stories, examples, problems, illustrations, discussion questions, test items, and exercises, regardless of subject matter. Women should not be stereotyped in examples by being spoken of only in connection with cooking, sewing, shopping, and similar activities."

The effects of feminist revisionism are apparent in many of the schoolbooks put out in recent years. Holt, Rinehart and Winston, for instance, changed an illustration in a sixth grade social studies book in 1976, reversing sex roles. Where the picture in the 1972 edition shows father and son carrying vegetables into the kitchen and the mother and daughter preparing them, the new version has the females lugging, and the father —in an apron—and son preparing the food.

I get an eerie feeling of 1984 to realize that such guidelines have emerged from countless meetings and seminars held by professional planners such as those we heard from earlier at MIT. These feminist true believers are not only determined that we are all going to have a unisex world, whether we want it or not—they are trying to bring it about by misrepresenting reality

I get an eerie feeling of 1984 . . .

to the nation's school children. As far as I'm aware, this is a new departure for us as a society. In the past, we may have withheld knowledge of certain realities from children, and wisely I think, on the theory that they had no need to deal with every kind of problem at tender ages. But I believe this is the first time we have planned so systematically and on so massive a scale to deliberately provide our youth with misinformation.

The truth, of course, is that males and females are significantly different, and their roles in our society remain noticeably distinct. Pictures or descriptions that show similar numbers of males and females as secretaries, nurses, homemakers, accountants, engineers, construction workers or physicians are false representations of what exists in the world around us. (It's a curious fact that many of the same "progressive" people who have insisted in recent years on exposing young children to books revealing every sordid and vicious aspect of life, from violent sexual assaults to drug culture, now are determined to revise the literature of our schools to hide the realities of the sexual division of labor that characterizes our society.)

Feminists teach that women have been ignored and disdained in our culture. Yet our cultural centers are filled with statuary ennobling the image of woman, from the Statue of Liberty to the Madonna of the Trail. Throughout our capital city—from President's Park, Memorial Bridge, the great libraries, museums and archives to the statuary of the Capitol and Supreme Court —the proud and stately figure of woman is immortalized. We even refer to our most powerful aircraft and ships, to our most devastating storms, to liberty, wisdom, peace and justice, to nature, to the moon and planets, to our country, to the earth itself, as "she."

Beyond the classrooms, the unisex revisionists are attempting to modify the way all of us think and speak about things. We are supposed to stop saying *house-wife* and say *homemaker* instead, because one person who takes care of the home out of 20,000 might be a man. Don't say "Housewives are feeling the pinch of higher prices," instructs McGraw-Hill; say "Consumers (customers or shoppers) are feeling the pinch of higher prices." We shouldn't speak of secretaries as "she," they say, even though more than 99 percent of them are female. Don't say anything that might give a youngster the idea that our society has sex roles, even though it does, and even though the vast majority of us don't see a thing in the world wrong with keeping things that way.

To the McGraw-Hill suggestion that we replace such forms as *fireman* and *aviatrix* with *fire fighter* and *aviator* columnist George Will responded: "The word 'fireman' efficiently reflects reality: virtually all firefighters have been men. If women want to fight fires, banning the word 'fireman' won't help and its continued existence will be no hindrance. And I, for one, do not mind if my airline pilot is female, but I don't want to be taken 38,000 feet up by a pilot who feels insecure in the presence of the word 'aviatrix.'"

William F. Buckley, Jr., responded in similar style to a bulletin of the National Council of Teachers of English urging writers to use "sex-neutral terms." He said: "Unhappily, there is no way in the English of Shakespeare, Milton, Pope, and Faulkner, to get rid of the synecdoche, 'man,' which, as in 'mankind,' means man and woman. Clifton Fadiman wrote years ago that the English language is wonderfully resourceful, but that 'there are some things you *just can't do with it.*' One of them is to replace 'man' in some of the situations in which it is indispensable."

The columnist also presents us with an analysis of

one suggestion by the council, which advises us not to write: "The average student is worried about his grades," but instead to say: "The average student is worried about grades."

"There again," says William Buckley, "you will note a difficulty. The two sentences do not mean exactly the same thing. In the first, the student is worried about his (or her) grades. In the second, the student is worried about grades as a generic concern. Perhaps he is worried about, say, the role that grades play or do not play in getting into graduate school. Anyway, there is a residual indistinction, and English teachers shouldn't be teaching people how to write imprecisely."

As a writer, and occasional instructor and public speaker, I have been especially annoyed by the totally unnecessary, redundant and distracting feminist practice of trying to employ both masculine *and* feminine pronouns instead of relying on the standard form *he* (which according to every dictionary I have ever seen refers to a person of either sex, or one whose sex is unknown or immaterial). This habit has become distressingly widespread in recent years, thanks equally, I expect, to those who don't know any better and to those whose deliberate intention is to encourage a greater awareness of the unisex idea and to spread the self-conscious use of the language of lib as widely as possible.

To give an impression of how ridiculous the "he or she" form really is when used consistently, I once rewrote a paragraph from the 1968 edition of Dr. Spock's *Baby and Child Care*, in which Dr. Spock told readers, "I want to apologize to the mother and father who have a girl and are frustrated by having the child called *him* all through this book. It's clumsy to say *him or her* every time, and I need *her* to refer to the mother." Imagine the tedium if instead of being reasonable Dr. Spock had written his entire book like this:

Think of the baby's first year this way: He or she wakes up because he or she's hungry, cries because he or she wants to be fed. He or she is so eager when the nipple goes into his or her mouth that he or she almost shudders. When he or she nurses, you can see that it is an intense experience. Perhaps he or she breaks into perspiration. If you stop him or her in the middle of a nursing, he or she may cry furiously. When he or she has had as much as he or she wants, he or she is groggy with satisfaction and falls asleep. Even when he or she is asleep, it sometimes looks as if he or she were dreaming of nursing. His or her mouth makes sucking motions, and his or her whole expression looks blissful. This all adds up to the fact that feeding is his or her great joy. He or she gets his or her early ideas about life from the way feeding goes. He or she gets his or her first ideas about the world from the person who feeds him or her.

I'm often amused to note that even practiced feminists become confused by the awkwardness of this form when the pronouns occur more than once close together in a talk. In written passages, it's common for writers to unconsciously abandon the form altogether in favor of a simple *he* after the first few references, often picking up the double references again farther on, totally unaware of the lapse.

According to the antisexists, if you really want to see the ultimate outrages of sexism before your own eyes, just turn on a TV set. For several years, feminists had made loud and aggressive complaints to the advertising industry and broadcasters about what they considered to be blatantly "sexist" programming and advertising. So in March 1975, the National Advertising Review Board issued its "Report on Advertising Portraying or Directed to Women" which formalized the perspectives of the feminists into a critique of advertising on TV. The report stated:

Advertising considered sexist is resented by a growing number of men and women in various walks of life. New points of view toward women and toward women-related advertising are gaining acceptance in colleges, high schools, and in labor, church, and social groups in all parts of the nation through many new publications, through wide exposure in the mass media, and even through the direct-action machinery of "consciousness-raising" sessions.

This statement, it seems to me, is a candid admission of the organized crusade that was under way in 1975 among all of these institutions to spread the "new points of view," of which the advertising report was a typical part. It wasn't an intelligent or critical report, but merely presented the lib litany right down the line. It was the same ideological attack against existing sex roles that we saw in the McGraw-Hill and Macmillan guidelines. The report was critical of TV commercials for three basic reasons: (1) because women were not portrayed as often as men as being high achievers in the professional world, (2) because women are often portrayed as sex objects, and (3) because women are frequently portrayed as housewives who use cleaning products. Like the publishers' guidelines, the National Advertising Review Board report contained numerous pages of checklists and instructions for creating ads that do not offend the unisex dream.

And, as usual, the report ignored completely the key point that the so-called sexist ads just happen to reflect reality. Far fewer women are "lawyers, doctors, business executives, scientists, engineers, athletes, professors, or judges" (to borrow the list from the report) than are men. Perhaps that has something to do with why they are seen less often in these roles on the TV screen.

As for the portrayal of women as sex objects, the bodies and faces of attractive women hold tremendous fascination for both women and men. The dullest, least talented woman in the world can bring excitement and pleasure to millions of people through TV just by standing on a stage or leaning back on a mattress, boat, or automobile. This pleases the viewer, helps the advertiser sell his goods, and provides income for the model —everybody is delighted with the arrangement except the unisex fanatics who want to make all of us pretend we perceive both sexes in exactly the same way.

As for the ad review board's complaint about the portrayal of housewives, this reflects the snobbery of professional-class savants with nothing better to do with their time than trying to impose their own values on the rest of us. Here are some excerpts from the report:

> The advertising of household products poses special problems. Housework is an emotionally charged subject. Feminist literature is replete with complaints that housework has been women's special burden. Books of fact and fiction have stressed the lonely, repetitive drudgery of housework as a waste of women's talents. The fact that housekeeping has been made easier by efficient appliances, convenience foods, and other modern practices that advertising has helped bring into common use, does little to alter critical perceptions of the job itself.... An endless procession of commercials on the same theme, however, all showing women using household products in the home, raises very strong implications that women have no other interests except laundry, dishes, waxing floors, and fighting dirt in any form. Seeing a great many such advertisements in succession reinforces the traditional stereotype that a "woman's place is *only* in the home...." The advertising of household products often involves psychologically unflattering por-

trayals of women. In some instances, they are depicted as being obsessed with cleanliness, as being
embarrassed or feeling inadequate or guilty because of various forms of household dirt. Other advertisements show women being mean or catty to
each other, or being envious or boastful about cooking or cleaning accomplishments in the home. In
summary, the image of the housewife in advertising appears frequently to be not only a circum-
scribed one, but also that of a person with a
warped sense of values.

I'll bet a lot of housewives would say the same thing
about the feminist planners who inhabit media review
boards. The reality of life is that cleaning has to be
done, and many women with perfectly healthy values
take pride and even pleasure in accomplishing this
work. It is the *feminists* who have tried to stigmatize
women who do housework as menial and worthless,
not advertisers of household goods. The image of
women portrayed in ads for cleaning products is basically that of constructive, hard-working, dedicated
wives anxious to do their work as efficiently and cheer-
fully as possible so they can go on to other activities.
Since the reality is that most women's primary responsibility is to the home, objective observers must see that
most of these TV ads provide useful role models which
encourage people to take pride in this important work.

As for sexism in TV dramas and movies, we have
long heard feminist complaints that women are belit-
tled, made to look helpless or stupid, and that most of
the time the stories show women incompetently getting into trouble, and the men demonstrating their brav-
ery and strength in saving them. It is certainly true that
there is inherent drama in situations where vulnerable
women are struggled over by strong men. We love to
see such adventures and romances over and over, pre-

cisely because they reflect the differences between the sexes and the play of sexuality that we experience in life. Men *do* assault, dominate, struggle over and protect women. Men *do* dominate the arenas of business, science, sports and vice in the real world. Women *are* attracted to strong, aggressive men. If such expressions of reality disqualify a drama for the feminist film festival award, they still qualify programs on TV for a reasonable share of viewer popularity, as they have throughout literary history.

For the past couple of years, Annie and I have been studying the matter of how women and men have been depicted in films and in TV dramas over the years. I guess we've watched as many old movies and situation comedies as anybody, and it's been difficult for us to see that one sex has been shown in any better light, all in all, than the other. Productions since the 1920s have consistently presented images of aggressive career women, courageous heroines and gutsy female villains in numbers comparable to reality. And nobody who grew up watching the likes of the Marx Brothers, Abbott and Costello, Jerry Lewis, Don Knotts and Woody Allen or following the weekly foibles of Henry Aldrich, Chester A. Riley, Dagwood Bumstead, Ralph Kramden, Ed Norton, Maxwell Smart or Archie Bunker could think that men can't be just as stupid as women can be any day of the week. Contrary to feminist interpretations of the cinema, movies of the past 50 years have shown us about as many daredevil females and screwball men as the other way around. The truth is that feminist writers have distorted their accounts of the diverse ways the sexes have been presented in the visual media, and no one without the feminist bias has been interested enough to explore the subject. It is thanks to the fact that TV programming is still determined by *popular* appeal, and not by liberal orthodoxy, that we have even the semblance of real life on our screens. It is only because advertisers are still motivated to appeal to large audiences of ordinary people, rather than to the feminist elite, that unisex programs have not become important on TV.

Except for this link with the real world provided to people by TV, the unisex campaigners would be much further along toward the feminist goal of indoctrinating the nation. As it happens, writers and producers haven't been able to figure out how to produce popular TV shows and commercials based on the dull and regimenting orthodoxy of unisex. For most people, a few minutes of unisex goes a long, long way. But elsewhere in the mass media, the unisex principles prevail and distortion is so routine that you virtually cannot believe any report you hear today about the condition or relative status of women.

For instance, during 1976 it was widely reported in the press that "women's earning power and income stability make them as good a risk as men when it comes to buying a home, according to a government-sponsored study. . . ." When Annie obtained the report of the study called "Women in the Mortgage Market" from the U.S. Department of Housing and Urban Development, it turned out that the newspaper stories reflected the interpretation of the folks who wrote the report, but little about the real income differences between men and women.

The feminist report, in typical fashion, highlighted claims that were not supported by the information of the text. In the first place, the sample population chosen for the study was 5,083 women 30 to 44 years of age, thus eliminating from consideration women in their prime childbearing years. Even if the results of a study of such a selective sample showed women to be as good a risk for loans as men (which this one did not),

356

it still would be useless as a basis for inferences about women in general. No matter. Even this select group of women did not compare well to men.

One of the main questions the study sought to answer was how reliable are family incomes in which the wife is a major contributor compared to those in which the husband is the sole breadwinner. Lenders of mortgage loans have traditionally discounted the wife's earnings based on the prudent assumption that such earnings are less stable than the husband's and therefore pose a greater risk that the family will default on a higher mortgage.

Feminists have challenged this assumption, and this report was publicized as disproving its validity. Yet, if you read the *details* of the report, you find that to the contrary, the assumption is *supported*. "The data show," states the government report, "that marital disruptions are twice as likely in two-income families than [*sic*] in the traditional 'husband is the breadwinner' structure. Marital disruptions occurred between 1966 and 1970 in 3.5 percent of the sample families classified in 1966 as 'wife not working'; the disruption rate for the 'wife working' portion of the sample was approximately 7 percent. This observation tends to confirm lenders' fears about marital problems, especially if one income is not sufficient to sustain the joint mortgage loan." In fact, the report states that "a one thousand dollar increase in the wife's earnings is associated with a one percentage point increase in marital separation rates."

Besides marital disruptions that interfere with a borrower's ability to repay, lenders must also be concerned about the likelihood of substantial decline in the family's income when deciding to which applicants to grant a mortgage. "The probability of this precarious financial situation occurring during one or more of the

357

critical years of a mortgage," states the report, "is, on the average, 12 percent for families in which the wife does not work and 16 percent for two-earner families. . . ." This means that from the lenders' point of view, the loan that depends on the income of a wife is subject to a 25 percent greater risk than one that depends only on the income of a male breadwinner!

When the writers of this amazing document reached the section dealing with single women and women who are the heads of families, they revealed an approach to the problem that must bring a laugh to even the most sober reader. Feminists have complained because single women and female family heads are not considered as good a risk for loans as married men. (Married men are the standard, because the fact is that they are overwhelmingly more reliable as borrowers than any other classification of people.)

The authors of this report attempt to demonstrate that single women are as good a risk as men by comparing the women's "projected income growth," that is, the degree to which their income is likely to increase in the years ahead, to that of married men. And on page 28 of the report there is indeed a chart purporting to show that the income of single women, while lagging behind for the first two years, will then take off and eventually even *surpass* that of the married males! We discover the reason for this unexpected surge a couple of pages later, where the authors state: "The probability that a single woman or woman head of household will marry (or remarry) is implicit in these family income growth and income projections. If a woman who is not married in 1966 marries (or remarries) during the longitudinal study period, her adjusted stable family income includes the earnings and other stable income of her new husband. . . ." Well, well, well, isn't that cute? It turns out upon careful investigation that the

358

reason a lender should consider a single woman just as good a risk as a married man is because in a couple of years she will probably get married and her husband will be able to help pay off the mortgage!

As far as the dependability of women who are heads of families is concerned, forget it. The report says that they are up to 150 percent more likely to experience a significant decline in income than are married men! It

It turns out that a single woman is "just as good a credit risk" as a married man because she will probably get married and her husband will pay off the mortgage!

is impossible to find justification in this report for the claim that women are in general just as good a credit risk as men, yet that is what the authors suggested in their introduction and summary, and that is the theme played up in newspaper stories from coast to coast.

We have seen numerous reports which purport to show that professional women in various fields with the same number of years of experience earn less money than their male counterparts. These studies appear to be valid until you realize that their authors don't compare salaries of men and women according to the number of years they have actually worked in their profession, but rather according to the number of years since they received their professional degrees. This kind of comparison ignores completely the fact that a large percentage of the female professionals have dropped out of their field for a number of years to raise families. Yet, such studies are reported far and wide as proof of sexist discrimination against women.

Unpopular as the position may be these days, there are people who deny that there has been any discrimination against women at all. Harvard sociologist Nathan Glazer spoke to a group not long ago about the relation of women to academic institutions in decades past. "I do not think," he said, "in all honesty, that there was a situation of a great number of women—say in 1967 before the rise of the women's liberation—who thought they were unjustly treated. I did not see that. I did not experience it. They were not unjustly treated in terms of admissions to graduate programs. They were not unjustly treated in terms of grants and loans and fellowships. They were not unjustly treated in being considered for entry jobs and they were not unjustly treated in promotions. There were other factors involved. Many women can now report on what is now a change of taste in insensitive remarks, like: 'Go and get married and have babies.' Well, the fact is that the dropout rate for women in graduate programs happened to be twice that of men; it was not an illegitimate remark to make."

In 1975, when a team of statisticians and social scientists at the University of California studied patterns of admission to the Graduate Division at Berkeley, they found that in contrast to common belief, "the evidence for campus-wide bias in favor of men is extremely weak; on the contrary, there is evidence of bias in favor of women."

When the results of this highly sophisticated and thoroughgoing study were published in *Science,* the investigators stated:

> We would conclude from this examination that the campus as a whole did not engage in discrimination against women applicants. This conclusion is strengthened by similarly examining the data for the entire campus for the years 1969 through 1973. In 1969 the number of women admitted exceeded the expected frequency. . . . These data suggest that there is little evidence of bias of any kind until 1973, when it would seem significant evidence of bias appears, in favor of women. This conclusion is supported by all the other measures we have examined. . . . In most of the cases involving favored status for women it appears that the admissions committees were seeking to overcome long-established shortages of women in their fields. Overall, however, it seems that the admissions procedure has been quite evenhanded. Where there are divergences from the expected frequencies they are usually small in magnitude . . . and they more frequently favor women than discriminate against them.

Author and scholar Thomas Sowell, writing in the *New York Times Magazine* recently, reported findings

361

in his research similar to what Annie and I have discovered in our readings:

Despite a tendency to consider women as a "minority," both the history and the present situation of women are quite different. Contrary to a fictitious history about having come a long way, baby, women today have less representation in many high-level positions than 30 or 40 years ago. In earlier times, women made up a higher proportion of doctors, academics, people in *Who's Who*, and in professional, technical and managerial positions generally. If you plot on a graph the proportion of women in high-level jobs over the past several decades, and on a parallel graph the number of babies per woman, you will see almost an exact mirror image. That is, as women got married earlier and earlier and had more and more babies, their careers declined. In recent times, as the "baby boom" passed and both marriage rates and childbearing declined, women have started moving back up the occupational ladder relative to men— though in many cases not yet achieving the relative position they held in the 1930's. This upturn was apparent before "affirmative action" quotas.

If you go beyond the sweeping comparisons of "men and women" that are so popular, it is clear that marriage and childbearing have more to do with women's career prospects than employer discrimination. In 1970—before mandatory "goals and timetables"—single women in their 30's who had worked continuously since high school averaged higher earnings than single men in their 30's who had worked continuously since high school. In the academic world, single women with Ph.D.'s achieved the rank of full professor more often than single men who received their Ph.D.'s at the same time—and this again, before quotas.

In those days, according to Professor Glazer, "it was not the case that women were out there hollering that

362

they had been discriminated against. It was women who weren't being discriminated against who hollered that other women had been discriminated against. At which point the women who didn't have very good jobs or who weren't thinking about academic careers, or were personally happy nursing a Ph.D. at home with husband and children decided that it wasn't a bad idea and said they had been discriminated against and went out to get some easy money."

Whether you like Professor Glazer's stark analysis or not, you will probably agree that things might be getting a little out of hand. We now have homosexuals lobbying for passage of a National Gay Civil Rights Bill, first introduced into Congress by Congresswoman Bella Abzug, to "prohibit discrimination in employment, housing, education and other areas on the basis of affectional or sexual preference." What does such a bid for legitimization of behaviors forbidden by society imply? Does it mean that all we have to do to legitimize behaviors that have traditionally been considered wrong is to invent a new name for the offenders and cast society's disapproval in terms of persecution and discrimination? Let's see, we could start with cheaters. During the West Point cheating scandal of 1976, wasn't the defense's position that it was all right to cheat, because nearly everybody was doing it? Well, then, let's not call them "cheaters" anymore. We could call them "helpmates," and get them all together to push for legislation to make it illegal for anyone to turn away a helpmate because of his preference for unorthodox methods of passing the tests society imposes. After we've protected the rights of cheaters, we could go on to perjurers—shall we call them "spoofers"? Next, we might salvage the rights of drinking drivers. Let's call them "jovials." There are thousands of jovials arrested or harassed every year who haven't hurt anyone—yet. And then, we could do prostitutes, exhibitionists, drug-push-ers. And what about pedophiles? They have a *terrible* image. (I have learned, however, that the new drugstore pornography magazine *Hustler* is already working on this one through a regular feature called "Chester the Molester," the adventures of a cartoon character who molests children.)

The backlog of discrimination cases at the Equal Employment Opportunity Commission in Washington climbs every year, recently topping 130,000. Even though the commission processes more grievances each year than it did the last, it is perpetually overwhelmed by ever increasing numbers of complainants. Can you imagine what the situation would be like if the government watchdogs were to outlaw *all* kinds of discrimination?

For many months, Annie and I have kept a file of references in the press to groups, other than the usual blacks and women, which someone claims are serious victims of discrimination. Here is our list: Short people, fat people, homely people, people with poor personalities, old people, stutterers, people with only one eye, blind people, diabetics, epileptics, dyslexic children, alcoholics, drug addicts, Indians, Italian Americans, Latin Americans, Polish Americans, Jews, deaf people, crippled people, emotionally disturbed people, people with cancer, gifted children, teenagers, young adults, pregnant women, Baptists, Catholics, Mormons, bald people, migrant workers, bachelors, smokers, non-smokers, people who talk too much, shy people, teetotalers, Orientals, police officers, male secretaries, gypsies, men with high voices, "only" children, people with negative attitudes, people who rent their homes, homosexuals, ex-convicts, muscle men, men who don't like sports, single people, people with accents, pushy people, people with dimples, people who can't remember names, and folks with small pupils.

There is scientific evidence for the belief that the

size of the pupils of your eyes, believe it or not, might be *the* most important factor determining how well people like and accept you. The study of "pupillometry" has shown that people with large pupils, especially if their eyes are blue so that the pupils are easily seen, are perceived as much more attractive, trustworthy and acceptable. President Jimmy Carter is a sensational example of how far and how fast such eyes can take a person who nourishes their promise. It may turn out, contrary to the current wisdom, that the people most deserving of affirmative action programs are those who are unconsciously discriminated against because of their pinpoint pupils.

Author Peter Wyden, writing of middle-class American children in the early 1960s (the young adults of today), commented: "To these children, it seems to me, life is a popularity contest where the 'square,' the 'odd,' the 'retard,' the non-team player, and, heaven help us, the 'unpopular' person will find the going discouraging rather early in the game." This sort of discrimination (which I suspect is the most prevalent kind among today's Pepsi Generation) isn't the kind one can get up a march about, even if it is just as disheartening as the more popular varieties.

I personally haven't got the slightest doubt that an individual's personality, size, speech and basic appearance are far more significant to his fortunes in this world than his race or sex. If you are tall and attractive, blessed with a charming personality, and equipped with reasonable intelligence and energy, there is little that will prove a barrier to your success—poor health or bad habits, maybe, but certainly not your race or sex.

Another way the word *sexism* has been used refers to the fact that men pursue women sexually. The new breed of "liberated" women often seem surprised that this male inclination doesn't stop during business hours. "For years," states an article in the *New York Times*, "many women accepted it as a job hazard. Now, with raised consciousness and increased self-assurance, they are speaking out against the indignities of work-related sexual advances and intimidation, both verbal and physical."

Lin Farley, the director of the women's section of the Human Affairs Program at Cornell University, testified in 1975 before the Commission on Human Rights of New York City: "Sexual harassment of women in their place of employment is extremely widespread. It is literally epidemic." Some of the forms of such sexist harassment mentioned by Miss Farley were "constant leering and ogling of a woman's body . . . continually brushing against a woman's body . . . forcing a woman to submit to squeezing or pinching . . . catching a woman alone for forced sexual intimacies . . . outright sexual propositions, backed by threat of losing a job . . . [and] forced sexual relations."

If these are the hazards of working with sexists on the job, feminists have considered just as sexist the husband who prefers that his wife stay home and be spared all of the torment. And I've often heard liberated types belittle the wife who would be happier if

366

her husband didn't accompany female colleagues on trips. "Would they worry that hubby would have homosexual relations if he were going on the trip with another man?" one woman jibed.

And yet, if you consider the statistics on such matters, the old-fashioned spouses would seem to have legitimate concerns. Whereas homosexual relations among business colleagues are thought to be quite rare, heterosexual affairs are common. In fact, statistics reported by *Redbook* from its survey of more than 100,000 women in 1975 indicate that the incidence of adultery is 43 percent greater among working women than among full-time homemakers. And a 1976 *Redbook* survey indicates that sexual harassment of women on the job "is not epidemic; it is pandemic—an everyday, everywhere occurrence," which according to the magazine affects "nearly 9 out of 10" working women. This suggests that husbands may have good reason for concern when their wives go out to work.

Another problem with the sexism concept is that it doesn't take into account the advantages women have that are basically unavailable to men. Many women who are outstanding successes in the business world readily admit that they have used their feminine wiles to good advantage, and pulled off coups where men had failed. According to sociological studies, women are far more successful in improving their social status through marriage than men are. In fact, more than eight times as many women are able to rise to a higher social class by "marrying up" than are males.

Even feminist contempt for the fascination that breasts hold for males becomes unseemly when you realize that it is due to this universal masculine propensity that most breast cancers are discovered at an early stage (husbands, it turns out, uncover more lumps in their fumblings than women and doctors put together).

The most notable advantage women have that men don't, of course, is the option to be full-time homemakers if they wish. In its *Women in America* survey of 1976, the Gallup Poll found that when asked what the ideal life for them would be, half of American women choose to marry and make their primary contribution in the home. There is little question that these women see a tremendous advantage to the sex-role system that allows them to live the kind of life they prefer. To them, there are values at home to be pursued, benefits to their men and to children, and peace of mind that comes from discovering their own ways to spend time and effort. And these values too must be accounted for.

The pop feminists usually base their bids to move women out of the home on the promise of "fulfillment in a career." Mike McGrady, the writer who stayed at home for a year to write *The Kitchen Sink Papers—My Life as a Househusband,* urged housewives into the labor market with these words: "Go ahead. There is a world out here, a whole planet of possibilities. The real danger is that you won't do it. If Gutenberg had been a housewife, I might be writing these words with a quill pen. If Edison had been a housewife, you might be reading them by oil lamp. . . . The life you save will surely be your own."

But most of us, male or female, are not Gutenbergs or Edisons, and some of us, sad to relate, may not even be able to land one of those swell jobs as lawyers, architects or journalists for a nifty women's magazine. What are the less than brilliant women to do?

"After discussing women as physicians," wrote one women's liberation enthusiast, "it is only fair to discuss women as streetcleaners. The Soviet Union is always held up as a horrible example of what happens when women's liberation is tried; we have all seen the pictures of the elderly women, scarves tied around their heads, sweeping the streets in the Moscow winter. These pictures and their captions are supposed to make us feel sorry for those women in a way we would not feel sorry for male streetcleaners. But I don't think we should shrink from the notion of streetcleaning as an occupation appropriate to the physically fit of both sexes. Streetcleaning is probably healthier and more interesting than clerical work, and when these jobs are well paid they are much sought after." (The female source of this enthusiastic paragraph is a Ph.D. who works, as it happens, not in the streets, but as a professor of economics at the University of Maryland.)

Perhaps, Ms Edison and Ms Gutenberg, we ought to give this matter a bit more thought. . .

Let's All Live at the Bazaar

The young woman in the brand-new baby blue pants suit had just finished telling the employment counselor the vital details of her circumstances: she had a wonderful, loving husband who made a very good living for their family ... she had three small children at home that she loved caring for ... and before she was married she had spent five years in the business world and had hated every minute of it.

"But, my dear woman," said the agent in a puzzled voice, "why then are you looking for a job?"

"Because," she replied, "I can't stand being the only unliberated woman on my block!"

If many women today are not in *exactly* the same state of mental ambivalence as the lady in this apocryphal story, they're not far from it. We've already observed the contempt feminists express for the role of the housewife, and the determination of feminists in the media and elsewhere to pressure the homemaker out of the home and into a job. If you read the articles in newspapers and magazines today, and listen to the voices on TV talk shows, you get the impression that the values of the marketplace are all that matter anymore, and that the highest purpose any of us can have is to earn money and to perform tasks designated by a company, the government or some other organization as having official meaning and value. The idea that individuals may have their *own* values, goals and purposes, quite aside from those of organizations, or committees, or the state, seems to have temporarily dropped from our cultural awareness. We are attaining equality of aspiration along with equal opportunity.

If the opportunity of America is a good thing, many seem to have decided, then *equal* opportunity is even better. The trouble is that "equal" has come to mean that everybody gets the same, *not* the same opportunity to achieve, but the *same*—the same values, the same purposes, the same pleasures, goals, perspectives and rewards. The highest ideal of a lot of people with great opportunity to influence our lives today is to make us all as alike as possible. This has actually been the trend for a long time. In 1956, the psychologist Eric Fromm wrote in a book that has been a favorite of mine, *The Art of Loving:*

> In contemporary capitalistic society the meaning of equality has been transformed. By equality one refers to the equality of automatons; of men who have lost their individuality. *Equality today means "sameness," rather than "oneness."* It is the sameness of abstractions, of the men who work in the same jobs, who have the same amusements, who read the same newspapers, who have the same feelings and the same ideas. In this respect one must also look with some skepticism at some achievements which are usually praised as signs of our progress, such as the equality of women. Needless

to say I am not speaking against the equality of women; but the positive aspects of this tendency for equality must not deceive one. It is part of the trend toward the elimination of differences. Equality is bought at this very price: women are equal because they are not different any more. The proposition of Enlightenment philosophy, *l'ame n'a pas de sexe*, the soul has no sex, has become the general practice. The polarity of the sexes is disappearing, and with it erotic love, which is based on this polarity. Men and women become the *same*, not *equals* as opposite poles. Contemporary society preaches this ideal of unindividualized equality because it needs human atoms, each one the same, to make them function in a mass aggregation, smoothly, without friction; all obeying the same commands, yet everybody being convinced that he is following his own desires. Just as modern mass production requires the standardization of man, and this standardization is called "equality."

A little reflection on the social purposes behind this long-range trend to standardization reveals a pervasive and disturbing preoccupation on the part of social planners with how we spend our time. The imperatives of the factory and the executive suite, the insistent need to get things done, reach out and try to dominate every aspect of our lives. You might think that as a society becomes more and more affluent, as ours has done, we could afford to enjoy more leisure time. Instead, we seem to race faster and faster through our days. Leisure has once again become a social offense. The most severe indictment laid against the housewife has been that, according to some lights, she wastes valuable time that could be spent productively earning a paycheck.

McCall's recently told its readers: "Opinion makers now define the ideal woman as one who is 'fulfilling

373

herself through meaningful work'—outside her home. Her husband shares in the housework and her children go to day-care centers. . . ." And Susan Brownmiller, puffed with pride in 1976 over her publishing success, said in an interview in *Mademoiselle:* "Women feel they have no excuse any longer for not going out and getting a job and they are right. A lot of housewives are angry at us feminists. For years they thought they were being the proper women and now even the news magazines keep saying that they are not, we are. It is hard to admit that you've been wrong for twenty-five years. And it is even harder to take that first step to get out of the house. Where are you going to go? What are you going to do? File clerk? Secretary? But they were wrong. And they should be more concerned that their daughters don't make the same mistake."

In the face of this feminist imperative to earn money at any cost and the economic fact of a long-range slump in the job market, some women have even turned to vice. But that doesn't daunt the enthusiasm of the dedicated libber. In the midst of the Washington sex scandals of 1976, feminist Ann Lewis, an administrative assistant to U.S. Congressman Stanley Lundine (D-N.Y.), declared: "Look, as long as we have a society that pays a woman more for selling her ass than for using her brain, this is going to go on. If a woman can make $20,000 a year as a call girl, more power to her. It beats standing on her feet selling girdles all week for $98. I wish they'd all give ten percent to the women's movement."

But the values of the marketplace are imposed upon our personal lives at a cost. In the first place, as our pace of life becomes more hectic, our efficiency is reduced and our productivity reaches a point of diminishing returns. We rush from task to task, yet actually produce less that is of value than we might on a more leisurely schedule. What's worse, we place increasing stress on our organisms and greatly increase our vulnerability to diseases of overstrain, poor diet and aggravated living. We lose sight of the purposes of our labors in our all-out dedication to the work of producing goods and services. Forcing the homemaker out of the home seems to me to be the final phase of this absurd rush to turn over every aspect of our lives to the cold commandments of the marketplace.

As we approach the condition, reflected throughout the Soviet period in Russia, in which the great majority of women work outside the home, we are falling into the same pattern that they have, one of conflict between the social manipulators and the personal interests of ordinary citizens. In *The Family in Soviet Russia* we read: "It has long been official policy to state directly or to hint that all able-bodied Soviet citizens, including women with young children, should be at work building communism. Moreover, work for women is said to bring about sex equality and is also seen as conducive to the desired communist upbringing of children in state-sponsored child-care institutions. Opportunities in the educational system are plentiful; equal pay and treatment plus generous provisions for rest leave, medical care, and the nursing connected with maternity are accorded on the job; the national need for labor power has always been great; and the daily pressure of agitation and propaganda is very strong."

We learn further on that "a markedly negative image is often generated of those Soviet women who do not work, especially if there are no children or only one child. The most scathing tone is reserved for those who receive a higher education or technical education at state expense but lose all interest in work as soon as they marry. When such bad examples are pilloried in the daily press, some pains are usually taken to show that the woman in question is irresponsible and parasitic in general. . . . The intent of such portraits is to convey strongly the idea that work is a prime social duty, that women who could but do not perform are shirkers, and that they are likely to be morally corrupt in other ways as well. . . ."

On the other hand, we also learn that "many Soviet men, and women too, still share the sentiment expressed by the old saying: 'A house without a housewife is an orphan. . . .' Thus, some at least in the population draw a conclusion contrary to that proposed by the classical Marxist view that social production for women is a progressive step. In such families, when the wife does work, both men and women are very conscious of making a sacrifice in the way of comfort, domestic order, and above all by their inability to give a proper upbringing to their children. . . ."

Leona Schecter wrote in *An American Family in Moscow* not long ago, after having spent two years in the Soviet capital:

> All the women I knew had begun to question the socialist myth of the liberated mother free to pursue her professional goals while the state takes care of her children. The women found minimal satisfaction both in this part-time motherhood and in often-humdrum jobs. There was a growing attitude among educated women that they could fulfill a more important function by raising their own children than by working. . . . Among Soviet women in their late forties and fifties, there was an assumption that going to work was natural. . . . But among this generation of women in their twenties and thirties, the trend was away from the post–World War II spirit, toward a desire for domesticity once they became mothers. Many young women expressed dissatisfaction with public child care, and longed to be liberated from the necessity of bringing home a paycheck.

376

Author Scott Burns in *Home, Inc.* says we will shortly realize that we have grossly erred in not recognizing the true significance of the household economy:

> How large would this invisible economy be if it could be measured in dollars? *Very* large. According to one study, the total value of all the goods and services produced by the household economy in 1965 was about $300 *billion*. This was about equal to the gross national product of the Soviet Union at that time. If all the work done within the household by men and women were monetized, the total would be equal to the entire amount paid out in wages and salaries by every corporation in the United States. Similarly, the assets commanded by households, worth more than a trillion dollars, produce an annual return in goods and services almost equal to the net profits of every corporation in the United States. Very, very little of this appears in conventional accountings for the gross national product.

And according to Burns, the household economy is not getting any smaller. Rather "it is growing. Its rising relative importance has radical and positive implications for how we perceive both the present and the future." Furthermore, he says, "a major implication . . . is that *women are abandoning the household at precisely the wrong time;* they are, in effect, transferring from lifeboat to sinking ship. This new pleasure of rising above steerage is likely to be short-lived. The painful irony is that various studies have shown that the average woman at home is worth as much as (or even more than) she is in the paid, market economy."

Arlene Rossen Cardozo, founder and director of the "Woman at Home" workshops in Minneapolis, Minnesota, interviewed hundreds of women before writing her book, *Woman at Home*, describing how millions of women use the freedom provided by conventional homelife creatively and intelligently to satisfy their own needs as well as those of their families: "There is a vast discrepancy between feminist theory and the realities faced by working mothers. The discrepancy results from the great paradox of the women's movement —the fact that most women's liberation leaders are women without first-hand experience in making happy family lives—women who have been divorced, or who are unmarried—while many of their followers are women with husbands and children. Nonetheless, feminist theorists have maintained to their followers that a woman can combine a stimulating full-time career and a fulfilling family life; that she can have it both ways."

Arlene Cardozo further says: "Superwoman has become a prototype for all women, including those with husbands and children. Theoretically, Superwoman has a challenging creative career, through which she contributes to society; and in addition, she spends 'quality' time at home with her family. Without the benefit of pep pills to infuse her with artificial energy, or tranquilizers to calm her nerves and ulcers, she runs a beautifully managed ship. She's with the family until the sitter comes, the children are dropped off at day-care, or leave for school; then she's out the door herself for a full and creative day away from home."

If that's not enough, "Superwoman has unique employment opportunities. She has a 'man's job' at a 'man's pay,' but unlike most men with 'stimulating,' 'creative,' 'fulfilling' jobs like hers, she is not expected to bring work home with her. She leaves her work and decision-making responsibilities at the office, shuts off her worldly mind at 5:00 P.M., races through traffic, and is relaxed when she arrives home at 5:30 (the children have either let themselves in with keys earlier, been with a sitter, or been picked up from day-care). Superwoman converses with them, serves dinner, has a pleasant evening with the family at home, or attends a concert or movie with her husband. Superwoman doesn't let herself go to pieces or to pot; she manages to get in some exercise, read the latest books, and have a hobby or two."

What is more, "Superwoman is free weekends to catch up on household management, grocery shopping, and cooking. (The theorists say that Superwoman's husband should help with these things, otherwise he's a masculine oppressor.) Thus, Superwoman and her family spend the weekend doing chores, which supposedly brings them closer together."

Contrary to this computerized image of woman, however, says Mrs. Cardozo, a real family woman is concerned with nurturing interpersonal relationships that are more than something tacked onto life after a day at the office. Too many women who try to merge career and family find, instead of fulfillment, new problems, tensions and frustrations. "The most frequent complaints of the woman who combines working outside home with raising a family are generalized feelings of overcommitment and dual loyalties; alienation from her family, boredom with her job, lack of time for personal self-development, and feeling that what she's gaining from her job is not creative fulfillment, but money."

"I've come to grips with the fact that working neither enhances my relationships with my family nor gives me a feeling of personal fulfillment," admits one of Mrs. Cardozo's interviewees, a librarian. "I am working for the money. Even with child-care costs, my salary raises us from the $15,000 a year my husband earns to over $20,000. My job pays for the extras—the furniture, clothes, trips, that we otherwise couldn't have."

Another woman, an attorney in a large law firm, told

379

her: "My profession has taken more out of me, and out of our family life, than it's been worth. I feel that by working I've sacrificed a closeness I might have shared with my three children, had I not been divided in my loyalties all these years."

You don't have to conjure images of apple pies cooling in the kitchen window and mom kissing skinned elbows and bringing pipe and slippers to dad in order to recognize that many important things go undone when every member of the family is trying to compete in the workaday world. What has happened to our appreciation of the quiet pleasures and comforts represented by a happy home? Houses have never cost more, but the quality of the homelife inside of them has never seemed so expendable as it does today. There simply is no substitute for the happy combination of reliable breadwinner husband and devoted wife and mother when it comes to raising a family in an atmosphere that does not resemble changing shifts at a McDonald's hamburger shop. There is no feasible alternative to the housewife as a way to keep husbands smiling and productive, children aspiring and loved, and houses clean and full of the joys and pleasures of living. All of these things need doing, and there is just no other way, realistically, for them to get done. What is more, when homemakers are treated with the respect they deserve, as they were until recently, most of the women love their role. It has only been since feminists succeeded in degrading the work—because it involves scrubbing and cleaning, devotion to family and feminine interests—that the pride of women at home has been hurt. This is another example of the transfer of one of the more destructive prejudices of the intellectual, professional and social elites—looking down on those who use their hands—to the sanctuary of the home.

Dr. Lorand wrote in *Love, Sex and the Teenager:* "Berating girls for wanting large families, or for being unenthusiastic about intellectual subjects is not going to help the situation at all. There is no reason for women to work after marriage if they don't care to, nor does it make sense for college graduates to feel guilty if they do not go on to graduate school after marriage. A woman should be allowed the freedom of enjoying her fundamentally sex-assigned job of being a housewife and a mother—a 'nest-builder,' as one Smith College graduate recently described herself, expressing joy in her children and home."

When mothers try to combine caring for a small child with full-time work or school, "the child is always short-changed," says Dr. Lorand. "Responsibility for his well-being must be left entirely to others, and this is a serious deprivation. The child who is first in his mother's heart and interests knows it, and it makes a great deal of difference in the way he feels about her and about himself. There is no substitute for the deep sense of joy and loving pride the healthy mother feels and communicates to the child as she cares for him and observes his progress. This favorable 'atmosphere,' this warm 'climate' which the mother effortlessly creates for the baby day after day by the way she feels about it, cannot be duplicated by someone else, unless of course it is someone who has assumed the permanent role of mother, as in adoption. Whenever the normal feminine desire to nurture the young is interfered with, both mother and child are losers."

This same conviction was expressed to me recently by my sister-in-law, Donna, who said, "I don't understand how mothers of small children can go out to work and leave them. I tried it and my baby became very insecure. For one thing, he started waking up at night. I'm sure it was because he missed being with me and

381

wanted my attention. He had almost quit nursing altogether before I went back to work, but afterward, he wanted to nurse all the time. His whole disposition changed. He became whiny and cranky, and for the first time, he started hitting people. I came to really feel bad about leaving him to go to work, and finally I decided that it wasn't worth it. I know I wouldn't leave a child again like that. I'm sure this happens to the children of many working mothers. The closeness between mother and child is something very special that both of them need. I don't care what anybody says, children need their mothers."

Dr. Lorand is outraged by feminists who want to push women out of the home. "Innumerable women have no career ambitions, and there is no reason why they should," she says. "A girl is not wasting her education if she does not go on to graduate work or enter a profession. It is a great pity when girls are made to feel that their brains and talents are wasted if, after completing their basic formal education, they prefer to channel their knowledge and talents into homemaking and motherhood. This desire should be respected, not deplored. It is the expression of an important normal difference between the psychology of men and the psychology of women."

Contrary to the notions of feminists, says Dr. Lorand, "it does not mean a return to the errors of the past when girls were regarded as incapable of serious intellectual interests and therefore as inferior beings. It means acquiring an appreciation of women as females, which precludes the error of encouraging them to behave as if they were men. Such an attitude implies that the development of feminine qualities and the achievement of basically feminine goals are not as valuable as duplicating the achievements of men. This was the inevitable feminist error: an overcorrection of the past."

382

Men are mentally more penetrating, more creative, but this is only part of the story, according to Dr. Lorand. "The masculine gift of major creative thinking is considered by many to be a limited compensation for the gift of bodily creativity which nature has bestowed on women . . . ," she says. "With regard to the sexes nature has with her usual wisdom divided the gifts and tasks equally between them. But from time to time there is a rebellious attempt to deny that such a division exists. Woman's greatest creativity and genius is of the body and the emotions, man's is of the mind. Woman plays the major role in replenishing the earth and nurturing the inhabitants thereof, man in enriching the earth, discovering its secrets and bringing them under his control. Each sex has areas of superiority, and they defy comparison."

"The principle of classical ballet is woman," declares George Balanchine, the celebrated choreographer of the New York City Ballet. "The woman is queen. Maybe women come to watch men dance, but I'm a man. I know. The man is prince consort. It's like Elizabeth and What's His Name, or the Dutch one. If the women were less important, it would not be ballet."

"The woman's body is more flexible, there is more technique," states Balanchine. Asked why, he says, "Why is Venus the goddess of love, not a man? That's the way it is. Woman is like that. They don't have to fight, go to war. Men can be generals if they want, or doctors, or whatever. But the woman's function is to fascinate men, to make them work. Men write poetry to dedicate it to woman. Otherwise, there would be no poetry, because who would it be dedicated to?"

I think feminists just don't appreciate the value of the contributions of most women. I've never understood how, on the one hand, feminists can bemoan the "slavery" of the woman who has to do housework and, on the other, maintain that housekeeping requires so little time, energy and thought that any self-respecting woman ought to be able to get it all done by 10 o'clock in the morning, and have the rest of the day free for any number of other, more important, things.

It seems people's houses are being cleaned much less since the denigration of the housewife began. I came across an item in the newspaper not long ago which reported "a proliferation of lice, fleas and cockroaches in Belgian homes," which the Ministry of Health in Brussels attributed directly to women's lib there. Dr. Georges Claus, director of social services for the ministry, said: "Man and wife now more often go to work together in the morning and are often too tired to start cleaning up the house when they get back in the evening. They watch TV and then go to bed. In many cases cleaning up is limited to dusting on Saturday morning if the car does not come first." I know of plenty of people who do the same thing in this country these days. I don't know whether they have lice or not.

I do know that the quality of life is diminished when home values are eclipsed by those of the shop. I've often asked my students to discuss this question in class, and I have been impressed with the frequency that I hear plaintive references to the "hectic pace," the "narrow routine," or the "rat race" that life for most of us has become.

"It's a grind," said a mother of two who works for an insurance company. "Theoretically we're way ahead by me working, but by the time I pay for clothes and transportation, and all the other things, I wonder. With worry about the kids, and trying to get the housework done—and it never *does* get done—I really wonder if it's worth it."

"I think we have lost a lot of fun," another working mother commented. "We used to have more time for

384

light-heartedness and play that doesn't seem to happen anymore. The whole house is on a schedule."

A husband put it like this: "My wife wanted to go to work, and I guess it is making her happy, but life around our house sure ain't what it used to be. I guess I'm old-fashioned."

I find there are lots of "old-fashioned" people of all ages who deeply regret our fading domesticity.

On the other hand, there is a breed of homemaker, such as my wife Annie, who is college educated, politically aware, health-conscious and fully occupied creating a meaningful and supportive homelife. Let her speak for herself:

> I can't imagine any occupation that is more creative and satisfying than being a housewife for a husband you love and have freely chosen to marry. For instance, I love to cook, but, more than that, I'm determined to fix the most nutritious diet possible for my family. It takes a lot of time to buy the right foods, and plan and prepare meals that aren't only economical and tasty, but that don't lead your husband closer to the risk of heart disease or stroke. I make almost all of our food—even apple sauce, cereal and salad dressings—from scratch. It also takes care and effort to educate Jim and myself to stay aware of the importance of things like diet and exercise. I exercise every day, and it makes all the difference in how I feel, and think, and act. And I know that if it weren't for me and my example, and encouragement, Jim would seldom exercise at *all*. That's just the way he is. But he does exercise regularly, eats right, and gets enough sleep, because that's the kind of routine I nag him into following—and he loves it.
>
> One of the biggest problems in the world today seems to be that people are so busy *doing* things that they don't have time to think, or to read. I recall a comment that Mrs. Jimmy Carter made dur-

385

ing the Democratic primaries of 1976. She said that she had been campaigning full-time for her husband for a year or more, traveling all around giving speeches, and didn't have time to read anything except position papers. She said that the last book she had read was a 30-year-old novel. I think it's too bad when a person's life is so hectic. Unfortunately, it's all too common. I believe you need time to reflect. I read quite a lot every day, and take on voluntary projects as they appeal to me, and I can tell you that I have more interesting things to talk about than what my husband usually encounters in his life at the office (at least from what Jim has told me). I know from my own experience in the working world that most "career" women spend far

more time in gossip about clothes, men and problems of mundane life than on subjects likely to stir one's intellectual interest. There is no place that a person has more opportunity and freedom to pursue an intellectual life than at home, if that is really what one wants to do, because the life of the mind requires a flexible schedule, periods of quiet, and time to indulge in contemplation. I arrange for Jim and me both to have these at home.

As far as housework is concerned, I do it all myself, and I'm proud of it, because it is personal, necessary work for my home that must be done. I get great satisfaction from housework, and I was interested to learn, not long ago, that most housewives agree with me. Researchers at Cornell conducted the most extensive investigation of homemakers' attitudes, interviewing 1,300 women, and they found that 72 percent expressed high satisfaction with their work.

What my husband does is most important in terms of pay. What I do is most important in terms of the substance of our lives. But both of us are *equally* important as people. So I don't think of being a housewife as an occupation. When you put it that way, you taint tasks that are basic and personal with the oppressiveness of the paid job. That has been an awful disservice to women. I don't want a paid job, and I don't want a paycheck for what I do. My home and marriage, and the contents of my day, are beyond the calculations of the labor market, and as far as I'm concerned, the work that I do is invaluable, and I know my husband feels the same way.

I feel a quiet personal satisfaction in comparing my wife's attitude toward the value of her time and energies with those of people such as were described by a young woman who worked for the Congress on Capitol Hill not long ago. She told an interviewer: "Some people's full-time job was to keep up with the gossip. I

387

couldn't believe it. It's the Capitol Hill Syndrome. They come in the office, get a cup of coffee, read the newspaper and talk to friends. Then they go to the Plastic Palace [a cafeteria in the Russell Senate Office Building] to say Hi to everybody. They spend the whole day gossiping. Their work piles up and the A.A.s [administrative assistants] feel sorry for them because they're basically good people. They aren't fired. Instead, their work is given to everybody else."

Arlene Cardozo suggests that such women who go out to work may just be fooling themselves: "The option of non-structure is open to the woman at home raising her family, but is out of the range of experience of most men and women working away from home. The chance to think, to read a book, take a walk, visit with an old friend, or make a new one, are among many non-structured activities which are unavailable to most persons except on weekends or vacations. Yet a woman at home, raising a family, has these opportunities on a daily basis."

Whatever her stage of life, Mrs. Cardozo suggests, a woman can take advantage of the unique situation being at home provides. "The woman who is motivated by her own interests, rather than pressure from outside forces, to engage in structured activities," she declares, " . . . can do so without leaving home to fill a niche in the workaday world. . . . The success ethic assumes that the way to develop the self lies outside the self. Thus, the woman who desires to pursue other interests in addition to raising her family frequently goes out to an office where she fits herself into an already defined category, complete with a label, believing that in saying to herself and the world, 'I'm a fashion co-ordinator,' 'I'm a secretary,' or 'I'm a lawyer' she somehow establishes her identity. Such a woman hasn't found a new identity, she's found a new mask."

388

I know many people feel strongly that it is terribly destructive to place homelife on the economic bargaining block. After Annie's article criticizing the effects of women's lib appeared in the *National Observer,* she received scores of letters from women all over the country, and later corresponded and spoke with lots of others. Many of these women expressed the feeling that their views are little reflected in today's media, despite the fact that they are far more numerous than the feminist true believers who set the trend. I wish there were space to print all of the thoughts these women expressed, but instead we've excerpted passages and random comments which seem to Annie to express something important about what the majority of women feel to be the value of their lives and labors.

This is part of what Mrs. Mary Greene of Mount Sinai, New York, wrote:

> There is no such animal as "just a housewife."
> Managing a household successfully and happily is
> a task that takes all sorts of talents and a large dose
> of patience and stamina. But it is so much more
> demanding and rewarding than a routine job, even
> though much of it can be tedious. It depends on
> one's attitude. . . . Every mother who denigrates
> her profession, for whatever reason, fails to appre-
> ciate that she is not simply spawning another hu-
> man infant, but is responsible through genetic in-
> put, of course, but also through love, attention,
> instruction, discipline, and teaching values, for the
> development of an adult human being. And upon
> the quality of her commitment depends in a real
> sense the future of mankind. She is responsible for
> her small fraction of the next generation, and this
> act of creation should be something of which she
> feels proud. . . . Unless a paid job is necessary, it
> seems to me other activities are more valuable. . . .
> The man is stimulated to achieve and exert his

professional skill more if his wife is not competing. . . . Child care by government . . . is a particularly pernicious concept . . . e.g., children need a family structure, mothering and fathering, for security and the possibility of being individuals, not complacent little dittos, as they are apt to become when raised communally.

Mrs. Lynne Larson, writing from Burley, Idaho, says:

I graduated as an English major from Brigham Young University in 1970 and worked as a full-time promotions editor and writer for two years before my marriage. During this time I wrote many articles, ads, features, and stories which were published nationally. I had what might be considered a "rewarding profession." The point is, I had a choice—career or marriage. I have only to feel my husband's embrace or see my little girl's smile to know I made the right decision. Of course, I still enjoy intellectual pursuits, and I resent the "loud minority" picturing me as inherently stupid because I love my husband and appreciate him for going to work every day so I can stay home with the baby I also love.

Sure, there's a lot of boredom to housework. There are times when I miss the intellectual stimulation offered by college and career, but, good grief, not every aspect of my husband's job is scintillating either. Whose is? Yet he fulfills his responsibility every day as provider. Who am I to demand to be relieved of mine or to complain to him because I have to do the ironing?

As for men and women being alike, I say BUNK! Don't these people realize that much of the beauty of the world, of human experience, of life, comes about because men and women are different—the poems, the songs, the legends, the attitudes, the aspirations. Why destroy it all under the guise of "equality"?

Another mother comments:

> As for women being abused or unfulfilled by the
> homemaking role, it seems to me that any woman
> who can't find anything more creative in raising a
> child than changing diapers is unlikely to find
> much satisfaction in any other kind of work she
> may do either. A more varied, challenging, impor-
> tant and rewarding job is hard to imagine. . . .

Mrs. Joyce Carroll, a mother of two grade-school children in Harrisburg, Pennsylvania, writes:

> The most important function in my life is to
> create the kind of atmosphere at home that gives
> my husband the haven he needs to escape from the
> pressures of the everyday world. I did *not* say to
> enable him to escape from reality! What I mean is,
> to make his home the kind of place he is anxious to
> return to. I want my husband to think of his home
> as a pleasant change from his daily routine. I
> would be utterly crushed if he preferred the com-
> pany of his friends at the local tavern over coming
> home to his wife and children. I consider it my
> duty to create the kind of atmosphere at home that
> he craves and needs—any extra effort on my part is
> well rewarded.

And another Pennsylvania mother says:

> The values of homelife are so much more impor-
> tant than working outside the home. I can't see
> why any woman with little children would want to
> leave them for a job unless they just need the
> money so badly. There are so many things that
> need to be done as well as those that keep a
> woman involved and interested. The most impor-

391

tant thing to me is making my family happy. I have tried to show my children how to live, so they will be kind, fair and considerate of others. A job could never make up for the fun my children and I have shared together. We played sports and games, and even though they are older now, we still enjoy each other.

A letter from Mrs. Ruth Rizzo of White Bear Lake, Minnesota, describes her view of life and marriage:

I think my most important function in life— which was God's plan for me—is and has always been to be a devoted and loving wife and mother. I have found that my rewards have been a thousand-fold (if we are looking for rewards) in every effort I have made to make life pleasant and enjoyable for my family. I truly believe that a woman's greatest fulfillment comes through her family's achievements. . . .

I do not in any way envy the life of any other woman or man, especially the so-called career woman. In fact, they have my sympathy rather than envy. If any homemaker thinks a career outside the home can be more fulfilling or rewarding than providing for the needs of a family, she is sadly mistaken. There is no job on earth—whatever it is— that doesn't have a certain drudgery in it and the only way husbands can cope with the monotony of everyday work is their satisfaction in the knowledge that they are providing for their families and it is to the family that husbands can escape from the working world. I think the so-called glamor of being a career woman has been over-rated and over-romanticized. Most women can be very satisfied reflecting in the success of their husbands— they don't need their own career to be happy. When a wife is an inspiration to her husband, she knows it—and more important, he knows it—and any recognition gained by the husband can be mutually shared by both.

A neighbor of ours, the mother of two youngsters, agrees, but she says it's not always easy to endure the pressures people put on women (even mothers of small children) to get out of the home. She comments:

Women I know are always asking me what I do. When I tell them I'm busy with my children, they say: "But that's nothing. What do you do with all your time?" They think I should have a job or be involved in the Junior League—something to help society, they say. I just tell them that when I have any time left over I like to enjoy myself and they think that's terrible. I don't care if they want to belong to clubs. They enjoy that. They have luncheons and parties and social events, but I just don't like that sort of thing. Why should they try to make me feel guilty because I don't want to do what they like to do?

Lucille Michie of Santa Rosa, California, writes:

These women who claim that there is nothing challenging in homemaking and raising children are denying their femininity and creativity. They are looking over the fence to the other side thinking the grass is greener over there. I have seen my husband come home dog-tired after a day's work in the office, put on his work clothes and work many more hours on our fifteen-acre fruit ranch. I'm sure that he would rather come home, put his feet up and rest. I also helped in the harvest, but it never entered my mind that I was wasting my time and talents in seeing that he had a clean home, good food and pleasant surroundings when he was home.

I do not see my role in life as being too different from that of my husband. We complement each other. But I wouldn't be a man for all the tea in China. We worked together to create a home and

393

security for ourselves and our family and enjoyed all the phases of rearing our family. But he had the hardest job. I was not driven by time as he was, even though when the children were young, I worked ten to twelve hours a day. I had the pleasure of bearing the children (yes, I mean that), and was able to watch their development more closely and enjoy them more than he was.

Of course there have been areas where I felt pressured to do things that I didn't want to do, jobs that were not exactly to my liking. But who ever got the idea that life was not full of tasks that were unlovely? That unwanted work has to be done as part of the daily drudgery of providing for oneself and family. These tasks can be done with pride, and I'm sure that they are not confined to the female's lot. Those gals who think they can avoid this by trying to compete with men in a competitive job are just fooling themselves. There are frustrations wherever one finds himself. . . .

I think the thing that bothers me most is the militant actions of a minority of determined women trying to change the roles of the sexes. What is lost sight of is the fact that unless science develops another means of procreation, it is still the woman who bears the child. Children are the hope of the generations to come and cannot be left to a haphazard upbringing. This is best accomplished in a two-parent home. I would hate to see the home broken up by some of the militant ideas of women's lib. In their efforts to bring about "liberation," they are literally "throwing out the baby with the bath water." Unfortunately they are well-organized and do not hesitate to take on anyone who disagrees with them. Some men try to give them everything they are shouting for in the attempt to appease them. Some of our lawmakers are cowed by their rhetoric, and by going along with them may destroy our very culture.

And the following words came from Carol Rutte of Veneta, Oregon:

My relationship with my husband is very important to me, and grows as we grow as individuals. Many of my capacities have been realized because of this relationship, and an important part of this is the function I have of helping his personal growth. Much of this has come because of our sharing and communication. Another important function of my life is the development of our two young children, opening up their world, giving a richness of experience to them so that their innate abilities may grow and develop.

I have used knowledge, creativity and intelligence in being a wife. I have been able to be a sounding board, an equal in discussions with my husband as he has achieved a Master's Degree and now as he is on his way to a Doctorate. He has shared a lot of his reading, classes, etc., with me and we talk about this, sharing experiences and ideas. I have also helped him some on term papers.

As I see it, the development of our boys is the greatest catalyst to my knowledge, intelligence, and creativity. It is a continuing challenge to meet their needs, emotional, intellectual, social and physical. Running a household well is no small use of these gifts either, especially shopping well for food, clothing, toys, books, keeping repairs up, raising a garden, keeping an environment healthful for children.

Yes, my role is different from that of men. Presently, my career is nurturing children, keeping a smooth-running home, as well as keeping abreast of things myself. I taught school for almost ten years before I was married, but I would rather have the kind of life I have now. Teaching is interesting and challenging, but it is also a drag at times. There is more independence, creativity and meaning in what I am doing now.

The values I find at home that are not experienced in the world of work are the warmth, love and meaning in what I do. The world of work is usually impersonal, distant, superficial, expedient. What I'm doing at home has a lot of meaning since it is for those I love most, and it has lasting effects. . . . I think women have definite feminine gifts of sympathy, understanding, warmth, softness and love that they can contribute. Men are physically more powerful, achievers, aggressive. The sexes should be equal in rights, pay, opportunities, etc., but women are now taking on the masculine roles and qualities instead of bringing feminine qualities to their work—a loss to the world of the unique gifts of woman. . . .

My life is successful and meaningful, because I see myself as important to the development and growth of the people I live with, my husband and children. I see my work now as the growth of these relationships. I see the pre-school years of my boys as the most critical of their lives. I want to give them a warm, loving home where they are secure and intellectually challenged. No one can do a better job of this than I can. . . . Having children calls on a person's deepest abilities at times. It takes an adult to deal with them.

Evelyn Kerrigan, a grandmother of four in Miami, Florida, says she feels very strongly about the duties of motherhood:

A mother's foremost ambition should be to train her children in a way that will benefit mankind. She has the best opportunity to influence and mold their lives as she spends the most time with them —hopefully. It is true that young ones imitate and mimic their elders, so it is of utmost importance that mothers be an example to their children. Most of the ills of our society today stem from the poor home life many people have had. It is a mother's responsibility to love, nurture, and admonish her offspring when necessary. To shift this responsibility to another person is to shirk her primary duty. If a person elects to have children, it is her responsibility to see that they are taught to be constructive, contributing members of society. The mother's role needs to be strengthened in today's society.

In this decade it has become increasingly unpopular to stay home with children and be a homemaker. Instead, more and more emphasis is being placed on material things, expensive homes, new automobiles, private schools, etc. So it becomes necessary to have two salaries to keep up. For a mother to be concerned about her children, to want to know where they are, to know the activities they are engaged in, and who their friends are is rare today, and such mothers are accused of being overprotective. Many parents are content to let society take over their roles, and educators today complain bitterly that their time is spent teaching children the basics which should have been taught in the home. Unless our society is strengthened by more responsive parents—parents who care deeply for their children, parents who are willing to sacrifice, to deny themselves some of the luxuries of life—our quality of life will only deteriorate. . . .

Mrs. Helen McKinnie of Colorado Springs, Colorado, says that to her mind there are values more important than getting more material goods:

> I often pressure myself to try to do more than is possible, but since I stopped my part-time job, there is more time to do what is important to me (such as keeping the laundry current, mending, baking bread, attending classes). I personally feel I'm more able to cope with the pressure, or challenge, of making the household expense part of our income go around than I am of going to work to make more money. Even though I was able to pay dental bills, buy nicer eyeglasses, buy more at Christmas, etc., with the extra I earned—there were always *many* more things we'd like than there was money for. I think our appetites (just because we're human) are insatiable, so fitting into a budget is more satisfying than trying to make "enough" money. Besides, what a thrill it is for Chuck to surprise me with earrings or to give me unexpected money for a treat for myself or the kids. . . . I think contentment is much more important than "things."

As Arianna Stassinopoulos has pointed out in her book *The Female Woman*, "The housewife, far from being a captive of her work, has far more freedom in it than most men. She does not have to work at the speed of the conveyor belt or the dictates of the foreman. She is free from the discipline of stopwatch and dial, clocking in and clocking out, rule book and bureaucrat. Her world is large enough to be challenging, small enough to be meaningful. . . ."

One letter Annie received seemed to express this freedom and meaning most beautifully. It was from Mrs. Ann Cepollina of Annandale, Virginia. She was widowed when she was 20 years old and three-and-a-half months pregnant, and she wrote Annie a long letter about the values in her life today:

I am not a "women's libber," although I like to think of myself as being a progressive person, moving with the times. In my own marriage I am able to move about and grow freely, and my husband and I have a good relationship. He is a very devoted Christian, husband, father and friend.

I have always, all my life, wanted to be a wife and mother, and confidence in your position comes from first-hand experience. At 20, you may be apprehensive about a lot of things, and by 30, you may be doing those things in half the time, with time to spend on your own interests too.

I am an organized person, maintain a schedule for doing my chores, and spend a few hours every day getting these chores done. I put a limit to how much I will do, for you could work all day if you allowed yourself to, and all night, too, on housework! I plan and make preparations for the evening meal early in the day, and our children have their chores to do every morning—make their beds, dress, brush their teeth, comb their hair, feed our dog, empty the trashcans, set the fireplace for the evening fire, and practice their piano lessons. We try to put the chores behind us first, which leaves time for homework, games and outings later in the day after school. I have a very good friend and we get together as many mornings of the week as we can for a mid-morning coffee break. This helps you to realize that the things you go through in everyday life are really very normal. I usually take a short nap in the afternoon, because my husband requires less sleep than I do and a nap insures him a smile when he walks through the door, and our children a more patient mother. . . .

I have many things in life that I enjoy doing—sewing, crocheting, needlepoint, knitting, shopping, writing letters to friends and family . . . getting together with friends. . . . As a family, our best time is when we are all together, either helping the children with their homework, or on a family outing to the movies, ice capades, or hiking in the mountains, or just watching a special at home in front of the fireplace. . . . I love to cook and enjoy new recipes and cookbooks. . . .

With the Girl Scout troop I have, we use creativity constantly. . . . It is especially rewarding to work with our own children and see them master a skill that we have taught them. My daughters are learning needlepoint, embroidery and crocheting now, and they could already nearly run the house if anything happened to me. . . .

I consider that my husband's life is public relations at the office and my life is public relations at home. And, while on this train of thought, I would like to say that a few years ago, I flew to another state for a funeral. I rented a car on this very rainy day, drove an hour to the funeral, returned afterwards and turned the car in, took the bus to the airport, and caught a flight home. This trip erased any pangs of jealousy I may have had that these business trips are all fun. They are necessary and frequent in today's world, but not all fun to be sure! My husband travels often, and I just busy myself with a project around the house, or do volunteer work for our school or church. . . .

There are a lot of things I do every day that I don't particularly enjoy doing, but I love a clean home, which means better health for all of us, and which teaches our children to take pride in their home and keep their things nice too. You have to make yourself do things every day, and this is a very real part of the self-discipline that we all face. . . . My husband and I may disagree occasionally, but we always work out our differences amicably with give and take in both directions. We have long-range and short-range goals . . . and this is especially important, because when a crisis arises and affects our short-range goals, we may have to take a slightly different path than we started on, but we still have our long-range goals to work toward. . . .

I regard every minute of my life as precious and everything I do as important—from the most menial task to the greatest pleasure I may have in life. My truly greatest gift is that I have my husband and children, and that we all love each other and have good health. . . .

May Kordell of Kensington, Maryland, wrote:

In most jobs the average woman does, anyone with comparable training or experience could do the job. But in the home and with the family, this is not true. No one can take the place of a mother with her children. A maid can greet the children when they come home from school, and give them a snack, but it is not the same as the real mother being there to greet them and to share their day with its troubles and joys.

I think that if everything were just alike for men and women, then the world would be a very dull place to live. There would be no excitement. I have never been able to understand why some women object to a difference of jobs for men and women. . . . Why does everything have to be the same?

Ordinary people with family values. If they're oppressed, they haven't found out about it yet. The homemaker's role is also valued by many women who have had interesting and exciting careers, from executives to film stars, and have found their greatest satisfactions in staying home and taking care of a family when the time came. Not long ago, in Pamplona, Spain, actress Audrey Hepburn discussed her reasons for leaving her fabulous career to be a housewife.

"My parents were divorced when I was very young," she told Clarke Taylor, a writer for *Pageant*. "I lived with my mother and grandmother during a war which was something else, which tore us all apart. And my brothers were taken prisoner by the Germans. Maybe all of this added up to my caring so much about the family and wanting us to be together. And as the world becomes a more difficult place for us to live in, day by day, the home is the last refuge. It's the only thing we've really got. Crossing the street is a hazard. We don't know what tomorrow will bring. Life has become hazardous and worrying, and the only thing we can really be sure of is each other, at home. It's one's only sort of protection and the only way you have of strengthening yourself to face every day and the future. I believe it's important for the children as well. If they've had this kind of influence for some years, they'll have more stamina for whatever future they're going to have. They in turn have to create a home and they'll need something steady. How can they create it if they haven't had it?"

Audrey Hepburn said she could not find any way to be a wife and mother and an actress at the same time. "There is nothing wrong with being called a housewife!" she insists, and says her family comes home for lunch every day. "It's not that they need me. I need them and I miss them. You know, a lot goes on in the life of a little boy in the time it takes to make a movie. He comes home from school in the afternoon, doesn't find you there, and goes off to do his homework with no one around. And he should have a mother to wake up to, and who can take him out and be with him. It's true at any age. My boy of 15 is in boarding school most of the time, but when he does come home—most weekends—he shouldn't come home to an empty house. And a husband shouldn't come home at night to a tired wife who has already gone to bed to learn her lines before going to sleep."

Another actress who can afford to live any way she wants, Joanne Woodward, has made similar statements. She told an interviewer:

> You just can't leave a child to a housekeeper or the nanny, as a lot of women do. Otherwise you shouldn't have children. I do not believe, being a prime example of one, in being a working mother. If you're going to work, *work*. If you're going to be a mother, that is an exciting career, if you feel equipped to do it. If not, you shouldn't have children.
>
> If I had it to do all over again, I would make a decision one way or the other. My career has suffered because of the children and my children have suffered because of my career. And that's not fair. I've been torn and haven't been able to function fully in either arena. I don't know one person who does both successfully, and I know a lot of working mothers.

I think the intuitive feeling of all of these women affirms the insights of Erich Fromm's *Art of Loving,* in which—I always remember—he defines real love as care, respect, responsibility and knowledge. He says:

> Motherly love . . . is unconditional affirmation of the child's life and his needs. . . . Affirmation of the child's life has two aspects; one is the care and responsibility absolutely necessary for the preservation of the child's life and his growth. The other aspect goes further than mere preservation. It is the attitude which instills in the child a love for

403

living, which gives him the feeling: it is good to be on this earth! These two aspects of motherly love are expressed very succinctly in the Biblical story of creation. God creates the world, and man. This corresponds to the simple care and affirmation of existence. But God goes beyond this minimum requirement. On each day after nature—and man—is created, God says: "It is good." Motherly love, in this second step, makes the child feel: it is good to have been born; it instills in the child the *love for life*, and not only the wish to remain alive. The same idea may be taken to be expressed in another Biblical symbolism.

The promised land (land is always a mother symbol) is described as "flowing with milk and honey." Milk is the symbol of the first aspect of love, that of care and affirmation. Honey symbolizes the sweetness of life, the love for it and the happiness in being alive. Most mothers are capable of giving "milk," but only a minority of giving "honey" too. In order to be able to give honey, a mother must not only be a "good mother," but a happy person—and this aim is not achieved by many. The effect on the child can hardly be exaggerated. Mother's love for life is as infectious as her anxiety is. Both attitudes have a deep effect on the child's whole personality; one can distinguish indeed, among children—and adults—those who got only "milk" and those who got "milk and honey."

Similar thoughts were expressed not too long ago by a pediatrician, Dr. Sally E. Shaywitz, in an article in the *New York Times Magazine* entitled "Career and Motherhood: Can They Mix?" Dr. Shaywitz says that research today is demonstrating how crucial is the presence of the mother to the child's early development. And when her own baby came, she says, "I learned that while it is true, as I had assured myself earlier, that the quality rather than the quantity of mothering is of paramount importance, nevertheless a mother must be there all the time in order to be there at those unpredictable times when the quality of her mothering will really count. No matter how hard a working mother may try, she cannot schedule the critical moments of her child's day to fall between the time she gets home and the time her child falls asleep. A child cannot program triumphs, injuries or worries to coincide with mother's free time."

Dr. Shaywitz regrets the pressures that are being put on women today to leave their children and go back to the marketplace. "As a mother and a pediatrician, I have witnessed the devastating effect of this downgrading of motherhood. A great wrong is being done many competent young women who desire to mother their children. They should be made aware that there *are* women who enjoy the traditional roles of wife and mother—not because they are incapable of other roles, but because these are what give them the most satisfaction. Indeed, vast numbers of educated and intelligent women have 'made it' in the world of work and still find motherhood to be a more rewarding calling."

I believe this whole idea of judging people solely according to the standards of competition and achievement in the marketplace is ruining our ability to appreciate the values of the home. Many people today are foolishly assuming that they will be happiest married to a person with vocational achievement similar to their own. In reality, the opposite is often true. Many men appreciate their wives most because they are a comforting *relief* from the aggressive, contentious, self-absorbed personalities who inhabit much of the world of work. But I think the reason many people make this error today is that murky thinking is so prevalent, and it is easier to conceive of things that are similar belonging together than to appreciate the value of relations that are complementary. Appreciation of the value of complementary sex roles is much more subtle than the simple idea of "equality," or "sameness," but I think those who understand it and use it are happier and more successful.

Not long ago, the press was full of comments and guffaws over the Total Woman ideas of Marabel Morgan. Articles appeared with comments from everybody from Barbara Walters to Mort Sahl concerning their opinions of the new "antilib" movement. As Annie and I studied this evolving social commentary (which few writers took very seriously) we concluded that despite all the hoopla that the media made over Marabel and her ideas, nearly everyone missed the central, very important point. The core of the Total Woman philosophy, popularized by Marabel's book, is the recognition of the complementary nature of sex roles and the validity of the housewife's role as a valuable, socially productive and personally rewarding vocational choice. The first priority of the Total Woman is to create a happy and productive home. This means, first of all, becoming a full and constructive person herself, then arranging to inspire satisfying and fulfilling ways in her husband, and then in her children. The reason the Total Woman was mostly ridiculed (and actually denounced) by the writers in the press is that the concept depends on recognizing the differences between the sexes and capitalizing on them to promote harmonious and complementary sexual relations. All of these are ideas the mass media have been hard at work to suppress. The Total Woman also tries to give both her husband and children "milk and honey"—ingredients the cynical press is likely to dilute in gin.

The values of the marketplace have temporarily eclipsed traditional awareness of the fundamental importance of wholesome homelife, because the latest fad of the press is the image of the liberated woman, dedicated only to herself. Every celebrity followed by the media must have been asked by now what it means to be liberated. I think the majority of American women might be pleased by these thoughts from Gladys Hunt's delightful little book *Ms. Means Myself,* in which she tells what she thinks "liberation" ought to mean to a woman:

> She may take her pen in hand to protest; she may deliver speeches about the principles she believes important in women's rights, but she will not let a bitter spirit ferment within her.
>
> As a married woman with children she is certain enough of her goals to be unmoved by the excesses of radical feminists whose definition of fulfillment automatically requires finding a job.
>
> She may even be among the mothers who actually like having their kids around them, giving them lunch, reading them stories, talking, and knowing them as people. She enjoys being a mother and a wife. When she said "yes," she knew there would be diapers as well as roses. The crusaders didn't ask her before declaring that "all women suffer from economic exploitation, from psychological deprivation, and from exploitative sexuality." She would have cast a negative vote.
>
> Or she may even be so liberated that she can enjoy leisure, a rare commodity in our day, and use it to good advantage. Imagine the privilege of ordering your own day and filling it with pleasures and duties you count worthwhile!
>
> The most significant of all evidences of true liberation is the ability to love and enhance another's personhood. The angry feminist has not learned nor experienced this freedom. She does not know the awesome, expanding creativity of love....

Care, respect, responsibility and knowledge do not spring from the commotion and conflict of the marketplace. They may survive there and lend civility to the proceedings, but they seem to be generated by the deeper commitments between men and women, parents and children, that grow at home. We hear a lot today about the reluctance of young men and women to commit themselves to one another. But commitment is just the beginning of a complete relationship (I didn't say a "meaningful" relationship). The pledge of marriage only begins what is supposed to be seen as an ascension of the couple through trials, achievements, disappointments and rededication, as an aspiring, supportive team. From such devotion between millions of men and women, and passed on through their young, comes that civilizing power that, it seems to me, gives worth and meaning to the strife and strivings at the bazaar.

And then there are those with other ideas . . .

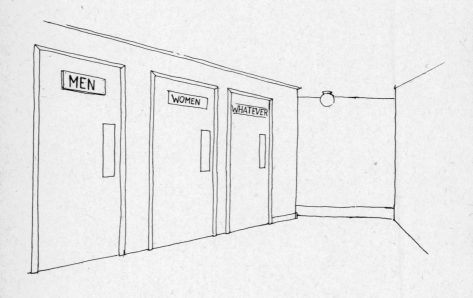

Repeat:
They Do Know What
Is Best for Me . . .
They Do Know . . .

SHE: Who cares if we have unisex bathrooms? It doesn't bother me.

HE: My wife doesn't like the idea.

SHE: Oh, she's just feeling threatened. Hasn't she ever ridden on an airplane?

HE: Yeah, but come to think of it, I'm not too crazy about the idea either. There would be a lot of standing in line, wouldn't there? . . . Do you mean to say that all of the restaurants, airports, theaters—things like that— will have to convert their restrooms into rows of little bathrooms?

SHE: I don't know. As far as I'm concerned, everybody can just use the ones we already have. I don't care what sex the person is next to me. What difference does it make?

HE: Maybe they could have a men's, a women's, and a third one anybody could use. But don't you think a lot of women would be reluctant to go into restrooms where men could hang around—you know, rapists, peeping Toms, things like that?

SHE: I hadn't thought of that. There would be a certain danger there . . . but I guess, even so, it would be worth it.

HE: How so?

SHE: Well, we have to be equal. If that's the way it has to be, well . . .

HE: But I don't think most people want to have unisex toilets. I can't believe very many women feel the way you do about it.

SHE (laughing): Oh, they'll get used to it.

I've had some variation of this conversation with several people in recent years. It usually ends with the person telling me how unenlightened I am and why she knows what is good for me better than I do. If you talk a little longer, she usually ends up telling you how the women's movement is really just about giving more options to women. Feminist Nora Ephron is the only lib-believer I've found who perceives (or admits) this inconsistency. She wrote:

> Every so often, I turn on the television and see one of the movement leaders being asked some idiot question like, "Isn't the women's movement in favor of all women abandoning their children and going off to work?" (I can hear David Susskind asking it now.) The leader usually replies that the movement isn't in favor of all women doing anything; what the movement is about, she says, is options. She is right, of course. At its best, that is exactly what the movement is about. But it just doesn't work out that way. Because the hardest thing for us to accept is the right to those options. I hear myself saying those words: *What this movement is about is options.* I say it to friends who are frustrated, or housebound, or guilty, or child-laden, and what I am really thinking is, If you really got it together, the option you would choose is mine.

No one can deny that if you are encouraging women to leave the job they are doing and to consider doing something else, you *are* pointing to other options. And politically, this is a good talking point, an effective catchword. But, as we have seen, women in this century have not lacked options. The real force of women's lib is not merely to open new opportunities so much as to goad women out of their traditional family roles in the home and into unisex roles in the labor force. If you study the words of the army of writers, professors, politicians and miscellaneous functionaries who are propelling this drive, you see that this is unquestionably the case.

"No one can sensibly advise a woman to become a homemaker today," declared Catherine East, the executive secretary of the Citizens' Advisory Council on the Status of Women, at a meeting to discuss possible changes in marriage laws that was held in Falls Church, Virginia, in 1975.

Around that same time, we heard economist and lib advocate Eliot Janeway say on Dinah Shore's television talk show: "There is no family in America today with only one source of income that can make it [financially]." He urged that tax deductions for child care be established, and said that getting women out into jobs is "the greatest single source of growth in this country."

In an interview featured in *U.S. News & World Report* in 1976, career consultant Margaret Higginson was asked if she thought there is anything wrong with a woman not wanting to work outside the home. She replied, "I'd say it's bad in the sense that she needs to develop skills that will enable her to go out and earn a living if she has to. Her husband may leave her, divorce her, die of a heart attack, or become handicapped so that he can't work. She no longer can take it for

413

granted that she's going to be cared for all her life. . . . And it's often better for the husbands, too. Why should men have to assume responsibility for women all their lives? That role is no longer appropriate in our society."

In another *U.S. News & World Report* interview a few months later, sociology professor Joan Huber declared, "You see, with both men and women working, a couple can have a really smashing life if they don't take mamma out of the labor market to rear the kids."

Cornell law professor Judith Younger, writing in the *New Republic,* presents the lib ideal this way:

> The movement takes the position that both spouses should share *all* the family's work, subject only to obvious biological limitations (men can't bear children), and sees family life as a partnership of equals. Far from destroying family life, the movement shores up well-founded families; they grow stronger as their members grow in independence, self-reliance and self-esteem. Spouses who have these qualities live together because they believe in each other and in their joint undertakings, not because laws or mores require it or because they are afraid of fending for themselves.
>
> What is the real explanation for the increasing rate of family dissolution? It is the simple but distressing fact that most families are not well-founded.

But the simplicity such lib-believers see may have more to do with the fact that they view the world through the lens of their closed system than with a simple reality. First they decide what they think is important in marriage and family life, attempt to spread these values through consciousness-changing activities, and then say the reason so many people are getting

414

divorced is because the marriages were no good in the first place. Another candid admission from Nora Ephron sheds light on this circular process, as she describes her own experience with consciousness-raising:

> What finally happened with my group ... was that it became an encounter group. . . . One of the women in the group was told by three members that her marriage sounded lousy. And I don't want to pretend that I had nothing to do with that—I was one of the three women who told her. As time went on, we all fell into the pattern. We felt free to give advice—and not friendly, gentle advice, the kind that is packed with options; this was more your I-think-you're-crazy-to-stand-for-a-minute-more-of-that kind of advice. What was especially interesting about it—and I gather this is fairly common in encounter groups—is that in spite of all this advice, none of us really wanted any one of us to get better. There was one woman in the group whose sex life was so awful that it made us all feel lucky; I think we would have been quite disturbed if she had shown up, one Monday, having straightened the whole thing out. . . .

It should be obvious to anyone who investigates women's lib that its essential function is to spread the doctrine. Although we frequently hear the words "true believer" tossed about, it's useful to remind ourselves of the nature of the kind of people Eric Hoffer described in his book two decades ago. He says, "A man is likely to mind his own business when it is worth minding. When it is not, he takes his mind off his own meaningless affairs by minding other people's business ... [which] expresses itself in gossip, snooping and meddling, and also in feverish interest in communal, national and racial affairs. In running away from ourselves we either fall on our neighbor's shoulder or fly at his throat." (This is what Betty Friedan refers to as the proper preoccupation of "self-actualizing people" who have "a sense of mission in life that makes them live in a very large human world, a frame of reference beyond privatism and preoccupation with the petty details of daily life.")

Here is what Sally Quinn wrote in the *Washington Post* about the career of feminist Susan Brownmiller:

> She did everything. She got involved in civil rights, and went to Mississippi. She flirted with the Communist Party, fought against the Vietnam war, picketed and went to meetings, wrote passionate articles and generally identified herself with every radical movement there was. She even lived for a time with lawyer-activist Mark Lane. She seemed almost to be looking for the perfect cause.
>
> Later she went to Philadelphia and worked as a street reporter for CBS, and then moved to New York to become a network news reporter for ABC hoping to get on camera. She didn't. . . . So she quit and began freelancing. . . .

"So there I was," said Ms Brownmiller, "holding my own, freelancing, when the women's movement started. I threw myself into consciousness-raising groups." The true believer had found her cause. She helped found the New York Radical Feminists in 1968, and in 1970 she led the feminist invasion of the offices of the *Ladies' Home Journal*.

It is remarkable to me that the writings of so many feminists contain detailed admissions that they themselves have not discovered how to live even vaguely satisfying lives, accompanied by equally fervent assertions that they know how all the rest of us should live

416

and how to solve the social problems of the whole world.

"The attitude of rising mass movements toward the family is of considerable interest," says Hoffer. "Almost all our contemporary movements showed in their early stages a hostile attitude toward the family, and did all they could to discredit and disrupt it. They did it by undermining the authority of the parents; by facilitating divorce; by taking over the responsibility for feeding, educating and entertaining the children; and by encouraging illegitimacy. . . . As one would expect, a disruption of the family, whatever its causes, fosters automatically a collective spirit and creates a responsiveness to the appeal of mass movements."

We have already seen how the feminist network is working through all of our major institutions, spending hundreds of thousands of dollars of public funds to spread the lib beliefs. All across the U.S. they have conducted conferences for homemakers at which panels of feminist sociologists, lawyers and economists raise questions of the risks of life housewives face: *What will happen to you if your husband loses his job, or has an accident, or a heart attack? What if he runs off with a younger woman? If you are suddenly divorced, will you be able to take care of yourself? Do you know that you are not entitled to benefits from your husband's Social Security coverage until you have been married 20 years, and that if you go to work your own Social Security payments are like money thrown away? And why should they reduce your Social Security benefits 15 percent if your husband dies? Do you think it is fair that housewives are not paid a salary? Don't you think you should be given paid vacations, regular time off and weekends free like other workers?*

After the women are sufficiently full of doubts and

417

insecurities, the experts on the panel and in the workshop sessions explain the mysteries of how these problems might be overcome. What are needed to alleviate the awful risks housewives face are jobs, disability insurance, medical insurance, pension plans, greater access to education, scholarships, loans, day-care centers, restructuring of the family and of the job market . . . perhaps a guaranteed income from the government . . . yes, marriage is much too risky . . . society should guarantee you security . . . you'll need help to change the family structure. . . . And finally the women go home, with anxieties they had never even thought of before.

These conferences to mobilize women into the lib forces have been sponsored piecemeal by state Status of Women councils, but in 1976 the U.S. Congress appropriated $5 million so the feminists in charge of the International Women's Year Commission could conduct their own in every one of the 50 states, followed by a national conference. In addition, plans were initiated to make these efforts a permanent function of the federal government by establishing a National Center for Women as an independent agency in the executive branch, empowered, among other things, to:

> (1) review, monitor, coordinate, and evaluate all Federal agency programs which have an impact on women;
> (2) establish and maintain a clearinghouse on information of Federal, State, and local public agency programs which are of interest to women;
> (3) make available and publish information on research relevant to women conducted by any Federal agency including making available the results of evaluations conducted by the Center and current statistics relevant to the status of women gathered by any agency of the Federal Government together with an analysis of such statistics made by the Center;

(4) conduct educational projects and research including holding conferences to improve the condition of women;

(5) cooperate with Federal, State, and local public agencies, including State and local commissions on the status of women, in coordinating programs and activities on behalf of women;

(6) refer complaints on sex discrimination received by the Center to the appropriate Federal agency;

(7) make recommendations to the President and to other Federal agencies relating to improving the administration of programs affecting women;

(8) make recommendations to appropriate Federal agencies to assure that the United States participation in international organizations entail the full participation of women;

(9) receive and review reports issued by Federal agencies having sex discrimination enforcement and investigative powers;

(10) make recommendations to the President and to the Congress for legislation to enhance the status of women and the integration of women in the administration of Federal programs; and

(11) report annually to the President and to the Congress on the progress of Federal agencies in advancing the status of women.

While proponents justify these governmental undertakings on grounds that the efforts will represent and serve the viewpoints of all women in America, in the past this has not been shown to be true. In 1976, for instance, a federal court was obliged to issue an injunction prohibiting the International Women's Year Commission from lobbying for the ERA or otherwise promoting the amendment or any other legislation at the state and national conferences paid for with its $5 million in federal funds.

A list of organizational functions, such as those listed

above for the proposed National Center for Women, seem innocent enough unless you have had adequate exposure to the extensive mischief such powers allow. This is true more than ever these days when so many people engaged in journalism and the social sciences have abandoned all pretense of striving for objectivity and indulge themselves in outright advocacy.

You can get a feel for the potential abuses of, say, items 3, 4 and 7 in the above list of powers by considering the results of an interesting little research project that Annie and I did on one eminent sociologist qua feminist whom the federal government brought to Washington in recent years to serve as "scholar-in-residence" at the U.S. Commission on Civil Rights.

Dr. Jessie Bernard, professor emerita of sociology at our alma mater, Penn State University, has been lecturing and writing at the taxpayers' expense in favor of the dissolution of traditional family roles. A superstar of the national feminist network, she is a "scholar" who has rejected the traditional marriage, sex roles, the idea of having a private family household, and our normal conception of parenthood. She lays out these opinions, thinly disguised as scholarship, in several books, of which her recent *Future of Marriage* is an arresting example. (It's interesting to note that the American Association of University Women gave Dr. Bernard its 1976 Achievement Award for "stimulating public awareness of the changes in the social fabric of marriage and the family" and for her work as a creative scholar in sociology. That she is *creative* I readily agree and will demonstrate below.)

She reveals her attitude toward scholarship in this book when she states:

> Radical young sociologists are now forcing us to recognize that a value judgment is implicit in the choice of any research topic, and young women

420

sociologists are applying this tenet to research on marriage. The most painstaking report on the status quo is not value-free. "Social scientists," Arlie Hochschild reminds us, "write about what interests them. But these interests are socially conditioned, among other things by sex." Even the research done by women has been from a male perspective. Why had we cared so little about what this research was telling us about the marriages of wives? Why were we so complacent about what it showed? Why did the pathology—*pathology* is really not too strong a word—of the situation not move us? . . . Researchers in the academic tradition are not paid for their opinions. Indeed, they are rebuked for them by their professional colleagues. Opinions imply or constitute judgments, evaluation, and, worse still, feeling. The proper academic feels uncomfortable when pressed for an opinion on his findings, for statements not about their "statistical significance"—which in any event are mandatory for researchers—but for statements about their human meaning. The young woman in the consciousness-raising group [which Dr. Bernard had attended] who felt threatened by my objectivity sensed quite clearly that such objectivity was itself a value judgment. . . . The message of the radical young woman had reached me. . . . All that one could possibly hope to do is help turn attention to the "structured strains" built into the wife's marriage. I hope that this [book] can do at least that much.

In other words, Dr. Bernard had gone to a consciousness-raising group (which she discusses earlier in the book), and while sitting on the floor with a group of young radical women, she had been convinced that "my academic objectivity, my lack of involvement, my impersonality, was giving off bad vibrations. This incident gave me something to think about, including my stance vis-à-vis research and also my discipline."

The Future of Marriage is a study in what happens

when someone who is supposedly an academic scholar abandons the aspiration to scientific discipline and objectivity to promote ideological opinions. It's also an example of the kinds of ideas we can expect to be promoted at the proposed National Center for Women. Dr. Bernard is not satisfied to divide marriage into roles of husbands and wives; she says marriage can constructively be conceptualized as separate marriages experienced by each partner. This idea suits the lib orientation very well, since the whole idea of lib is to *divide* the parties to marriage, to separate and conquer. From here it is just a step for Dr. Bernard to oppose conventional marriage, because "to be happy in a relationship which imposes so many impediments on her, as traditional marriage does," she says, "a woman must be slightly ill mentally."

She therefore considers the third chapter of this book —"The Wife's Marriage"—to be the most important one. Here she discusses various studies which, she says, show that "more wives than husbands report marital frustration and dissatisfaction; more report negative feelings; more wives than husbands report marital problems; more wives than husbands consider their marriages unhappy, have considered separation or divorce, have regretted their marriages; and fewer report positive companionship. . . ."

While taking great pains to give the *impression* of discussing both the pros and cons of her subject, Dr. Bernard dismisses out of hand the points of view she opposes. When she confronts the studies, for example, which show that most women marry and that married women are happier than the unmarried, she says it is because "women have internalized the norms prescribing marriage so completely that the role of wife seems the only acceptable one. And since marriage is set up as the summum bonum of life for women, they

422

interpret their achievement of marriage as happiness, no matter how unhappy the marriage itself may be. They have been told that their happiness depends on marriage, so, even if they are miserable, they *are* married, aren't they? They *must* therefore be happy." This shows the typical professional-class arrogance of the would-be social engineers—of the "experts"—who think they know better than people themselves what is good for them and what will make them happy.

It is interesting to observe the twisting and turning of lib advocates like Dr. Bernard as they circumnavigate to try to squeeze the facts of social research into their preconceived ideology. For instance, she insists on the absolute determinism of rigid sex-role conditioning in childhood upon the aspiration, abilities and expectations of adults. Yet she doesn't even attempt to explain the contradiction when she reports that "only about a third of the girls among high school graduates showed interest in the domestic arts a generation ago, and even fewer—less than a fifth—among college women. The figures would be less today. . . ." One would think that if it's true that females are so easily fooled into imagining they like what they are told they are supposed to like, and if it's true that girls are subjected from the cradle to conditioning which teaches them to believe that they have only one acceptable occupation in life— that of homemaker—by the time of high school and college they would be not only interested in the domestic arts, but *absorbed* in their mastery. I think the reason this is not the case is that socialization of girls toward homemaking is nothing like the broad determinative force that libbers pretend. Girls grow up much as do boys with an awareness of multiple options for possible careers in adult life.

Let me just discuss briefly one example of the "scholarship" of Jessie Bernard, this honored feminist aca-

423

demic, to show how she handles the statistical evidence that underlies the basic argument of her book. In fact, it's the data she calls "the truly spectacular evidence for the destructive effects of the occupation of housewife on the mental and emotional health of married women. . . ."

Her prize exhibit—which is supposed to establish the dire, oppressed condition known as the "housewife syndrome"—turns out to be a table which she has abstracted from a government report (Series 11, Number 37) called *Selected Symptoms of Psychological Distress* (you can write for this to the National Center for Health Statistics in Rockville, Maryland).

This table (which she calls Table 27) shows that among samples of women interviewed as part of the National Health Survey between 1960 and 1962, women who said they were "usually keeping house" reported slightly higher incidences than expected in most of 12 symptoms of psychological distress (heart palpitations, dizziness, headaches, fainting, perspiring hands, nightmares, trembling hands, insomnia, inertia, nervousness, nervous breakdown and the feeling of impending nervous breakdown). The women

Table 27
Selected Symptoms of Psychological Distress
among White Housewives and Working Women.

Symptom	Housewives	Working Women
Nervous breakdown	+1.16	−2.02
Felt impending nervous breakdown	− .12	+ .81
Nervousness	+1.74	−2.29
Inertia	+2.35	−3.15
Insomnia	+1.27	−2.00
Trembling hands	+ .74	−1.25
Nightmares	+ .68	−1.18
Perspiring hands	+1.28	−2.55
Fainting	+ .82	−2.69
Headaches	+ .84	− .87
Dizziness	+1.41	−1.85
Heart palpitations	+1.38	−1.56

who said they were "usually working" reported some-what lower incidences than expected in most of these categories.

Dr. Bernard presented *only* the information provided by her Table 27, with this comment:

> If this chapter were a musical composition, Table 27 would be accompanied by a loud clash of symbols [*sic*]. And a long silence would ensue to give a chance for its emotional impact to be fully experienced. For Table 27 provides one of the most cogent critiques yet made of marriage as it is structured today.
>
> Dismissing the housewife syndrome, as some unsympathetic observers do, is like telling a man dying of malnutrition that he's lucky he isn't dying of cancer. Perhaps he is. But this is no reason to dismiss malnutrition because it is slower and less dramatic. The conditions producing both are worthy of attack as epidemiological challenges. In terms of the number of people involved, the housewife syndrome might well be viewed as Public Health Problem Number One.

I can only imagine the impact of Table 27 upon people who read statistical tables with the emotional avidity of concert-goers, but for anyone who looks at this table to try to make some sense of it, serious questions arise. Dr. Bernard abstracted these figures from Table 18 of the National Health Survey report, but she left out the information provided in the original report which is necessary for one to interpret these values. As any student of statistics would immediately observe, Dr. Bernard failed to tell her readers which of these figures are high enough to be considered as beyond the range of mere statistical error. In other words, from the information that she provided in her book, it's impossible to tell what the figures in Table 27 mean.

For that reason, Annie and I decided to send for the original report, and what we finally discovered was that Dr. Bernard had no basis at all for making inferences from these data about the psychological condition of housewives. In the first place, the original report states: "The statistical level of significance used to indicate a significant variation in a given symptom rate for the four groups compared [i.e., men and women, White and Negro] with what could be expected with age-adjusted rates within each sex-race group was set at 1.96 standard errors (p=.05 level) of the deviation of the actual from the age-adjusted expected rate, with a minimum of 20 cases in the sample for the given aspect of the demographic variable."

In plain language, this tells us that the only values in Table 27 that have *any significance whatsoever* as being either higher or lower than what the researchers expected are those figures greater than 1.96. As you can see, in the column under Housewives, the only number this high is the value for inertia, which is +2.35. In other words, despite the great emphasis given to this table by Dr. Bernard—as a major underpinning for the entire thesis of her book—the housewives in this study differed from what was normal only in that *they reported a slightly higher level of inactivity than the investigators had expected.* This is hardly a basis for declaring housewives "pathological," and as the researchers explain in the introduction to the report (which Dr. Bernard failed to mention as well):

> Proper interpretation of the data presented herein necessitates the statement of a few caveats. The fact that an examinee responds in an affirmative manner to an item on a symptom checklist cannot in itself be taken as reliable evidence of mental distress, and no attempt was made to clas-

sify individuals as well or impaired on the basis of these self-reported complaints. The emphasis in this report was on comparative findings rather than on absolute figures of impairment in the population.

Further, because the data were gathered by means of a self-report technique, they must be viewed as a reflection of what individuals are willing to state about themselves in the setting of a medical clinic, and as such may be affected by a social desirability bias, i.e., a cultural difference in the willingness to admit certain symptoms or weakness about one's self. . . .

As Table 27 shows, the working women were significantly lower than average in six of 12 symptoms, but this does not reveal anything about the psychological status of housewives, and as the author of the report suggests, we must consider the possibility that even this small difference may tell us more about the comparative willingness of working women and housewives to reveal their complaints than about any actual psychological advantage women in the labor force may have as compared to others.

To make sure my judgment was right, I decided to write a letter to the person at the National Center for Health Statistics who drafted the report in the first place, Dr. Harold J. Dupuy. This is what Dr. Dupuy replied:

Since in my evaluation I consider that reporting of five or more symptoms would be necessary to indicate severe or serious mental distress, the mean or average number of symptoms reported for any group is not high enough to warrant characterizing any group, as a whole, as being severely distressed.

427

Later, I chatted with Dr. Dupuy over the phone, still trying to make sure that I understood him correctly. "Listen," he said, "the mean for married and housekeeping women doesn't even reach a difference of one full symptom. A group or individual would have to have a mean of more than five symptoms for *me* to consider them severely distressed." In other words, the amount of distress found in these patients would have to have been more than twice as great as it was before the author of the study would say he had found evidence that housewives suffer serious psychological distress.

Dr. Dupuy laughed out loud when I told him that Jessie Bernard had called the psychological problems of housewives Public Health Problem Number One. He said that he wouldn't make any inferences about the mental health of housewives on the basis of these data, and that he isn't sure that housewives actually have any more psychological problems than single or working women. "They may just be more involved in their work, having committed themselves to greater personal responsibilities," he told me.

I spoke to Dr. Dupuy again some time later, after he had obtained a copy of Jessie Bernard's book and read her extravagant interpretations of his work for himself. What did he think of it, I asked.

"Poetic license," he said with a chuckle.

Despite impressions conveyed by elaborate footnoting and referencing in books—so that works such as Dr. Bernard's are given the appearance of scholarship and importance—distortions such as this by ideologists and other enthusiasts are common today. In fact, they constitute a veritable sea of misinformation. It's hard to guess the total impact of this when the press spreads these ideas far and wide and the government and so many other institutions promote such ideas all across the land.

The far-reaching and dire effects of this pattern were driven home in an article in the *Washington Star* on November 9, 1975, by Biloine W. Young and Grace B. Bress. "Since World War II," they declare, "governmental bodies have grown increasingly dependent on experts, especially social scientists, to provide scholarly background for policy decisions on complex social problems. Judges, politicians, bureaucrats, and legislative bodies have come to rely heavily on social science writings and testimony as to the likely outcome of proposed educational or social interventions. The influence of social scientists has affected the lives of millions of Americans. . . . Yet dependency on experts for 'the truth,' like all dependency, exacts its price. It renders lay audiences vulnerable to manipulation in the direction the expert wishes."

The article points to the tragedy that has resulted from the influence of social science advocates who have allied themselves with the goals of the civil rights movement in recent years. "So strong have been both the sense of white guilt and the desire to correct the wrongs of the past," the authors say, "that some social scientists have published exaggerated claims for their research; in some cases data have been distorted to serve predetermined political goals." They present a deeply disturbing account of circumstances surrounding the decisions of courts over the past decade to demand the imposition of racial quotas upon school systems of cities across the U.S. on the basis of evidence they say was misrepresented by sociologist James S. Coleman and others involved in the creation and promotion of a report on the educational effects of segregated schools.

The Coleman Report apparently contained little real evidence to support the idea that integration of the schools would improve the academic achievement of black students. What it did show strongly, however,

429

was that the most important factor underlying achievement in school is the family background of the students. The report was authorized by the Civil Rights Act of 1964 to provide evidence "concerning the lack of availability of equal educational opportunities for individuals by reason of race, color, religion or national origin." What the investigators found to their surprise was that the schools and related facilities for blacks and whites were not very different, and that the differences that did exist were statistically unrelated to the academic achievement of students.

Despite this, say Young and Bress, the "Coleman Report's most widely publicized assertion, though not its best-documented finding, was that integration will improve the academic achievement of black students. This assertion became the 'scientific' rationale for court-mandated plans to impose racial quotas in Northern schools. Based on an inadequate and largely theoretical body of research evidence, the 'integration hypothesis' assumed that school integration would raise black academic performance to match white norms and would improve race relations among students through 'equal status contact.' "

As we now know, the forced busing to achieve racial balance in schools in many cases accomplished the opposite of what its promoters intended, increasing segregation instead of diminishing it, heightening racial conflict rather than lessening it. In 1975, while others wondered what went wrong, James Coleman, after years of supporting the policy of mandatory racial balance, publicly disassociated himself from the legal and political decisions related to forced integration, and asserted that his report had been misused by the courts. He denied that it had ever represented a scientific rationale for reorganizing school systems to improve educational opportunities for blacks, declaring that recent

430

research had brought him to the conclusion that forced integration, together with the flight of middle-class people from the cities, has actually reinforced the racial segregation it was meant to overcome.

Young and Bress conclude that

> with many other social scientists, James S. Coleman fell victim to this conflict between neutral, "value-free" scholarship (concerned with finding "the truth") and commitment to what he perceived as desirable social policy (promoting "the good"). His example is important, because he was probably the most influential social scientist–advocate of the 1960s, a scholar whose research and recommendations were translated into political, social and educational interventions on a national scale. In the last decade Coleman has testified . . . in many of the most important congressional hearings and desegregation cases. His testimony, writings, interviews and public statements have carried enormous weight with fellow experts, the education establishment, judges, politicians and the press. . . . It is a paradox of history, one more in the long list of tragedies for black Americans, that the good intentions and noble goal of equal educational opportunity have become distorted into the futile and largely counterproductive symbolic gesture of imposing racial quotas to "prove" an absence of discrimination. Americans in the 1970s will inevitably become more aware of the uncertainties surrounding social intervention.

There is, however, serious question whether such an awareness will spread enough to head off the push by the federal government, the feminist movement and the education establishment to launch a national program of early education already intended, I have no doubt, to reach every child in the U.S. Despite the facts that public demand for such a program is less than compelling, and evidence of the efficacy of day care as a substitute for home care is lacking, the drive to create positions for welfare recipients, displaced teachers and miscellaneous other disadvantaged persons while moving mothers into jobs as clerks, cabbies and cashiers proceeds apace. Senator (now Vice President) Walter Mondale, the principal Senate supporter of the multi-billion dollar program outlined in his Child and Family Services Bill, declared in a committee hearing:

> The Bureau of Child Care, which is set forth in this measure, establishes a new federal office which does not exist and permits it to run day-care centers anywhere in the country, in any fashion it wishes, with no involvement of state and local government. The bureau can completely disregard state departments of welfare and probably will. It ignores the present system and sets up an entirely new delivery system.

A *Wall Street Journal* editorial asked wryly, "The family will be aided by turning child care over to strangers so more mothers can go out and work, and by levying taxes to support the service on families who care for their own children?" (It was instructive to note in the *New York Times* a short while later that an audit had disclosed that New York City's day-care program has been wasting more than $37 million annually.)

And Phyllis Schlafly, reporting on this burgeoning new movement that would establish a new office of Child and Family Services within the Department of Health, Education and Welfare, remarked: "If you think that HEW is already interfering too much in local education, just wait until it gets its hands on this new office with extra billions to spend to engineer the edu-

432

cational, mental, emotional, physical, and behavioral needs of children from birth through graduation."

Our public awareness will have to become a virtual explosion if it is to catch up with the social interventions being hatched for us in the next few years. Such an awakening is doubly important when you realize that more and more the nation has fallen away from reliance on democratic processes of decision-making and into a pattern of letting "progressive" result-oriented judges rule. Advocates and their committees of experts, impatient or dissatisfied with the popular will, have been frightfully successful in recent years in persuading judges sympathetic to their ideology to decree far-reaching changes in the social landscape. Who will be the experts upon whom the federal government and the judges will rely to carry out the assault on the sexes in the years ahead? What will the social interventions they conceive for us mean to our lives?

Well, Harvard economist John Kenneth Galbraith is *one* such expert the federal government has relied on in the past. His book *Economics and the Public Purpose* has been influential in university courses (which is where I came upon it). I understand that it has also been an influence upon government policies in the country just north of us. In this book, Professor Galbraith declares that socialism is "imperative" in America, and like Lenin, whom he quotes, he links this imperative to women's lib. He wrote:

> The reasonable goal of an economic system is one that allows all individuals to pursue socially benign personal goals regardless of sex. There should be no required or conditioned subordination of one sex to another. This, with the techniques by which such rights are presently denied to women, requires a substantial change in the way

decisions on consumption are made within the household. These, at a minimum, ought to be appraised for their administrative cost to the participants. This means that the woman, as the administrator, should have the decisive voice on the style of life, for she shoulders the main burden. Or, if decisions are made jointly, the tasks of administration—cleaning, maintenance and repair of dwelling, artifacts, vehicles or planning and management of social manifestations—should also be equally shared. Either convention could, if adopted, bring a drastic change in present consumption patterns.

Galbraith's language, among all of the feminist writers, conveys most trenchantly the quality our personal lives will attain if the feminist revolution should succeed. The most mundane matters will be determined, not by individuals (with their awful conditioning), but by committees. He continues:

However, the more plausible solution involves an attack on a more fundamental cause. That, at the deepest level, involves the concept of the family in which one partner provides the income and the other supervises the details of its use. . . . With industrialization and urbanization men and women no longer share in tasks of production in accordance with strength and adaptability. The man disappears to the factory or office, the woman concentrates exclusively on managing consumption. This is a conventional arrangement, not an efficiently necessary division of labor; at a simple level of consumption it is perfectly possible for one person to do both. Without denying that the family retains other purposes, including those of love, sex and child-rearing, it is no longer an economic necessity. . . . It follows that, with economic development, women should be expected and encouraged to regard marriage not as a necessity but as a traditional subordination of personality, one that is sustained by custom and the needs of the planning system. It should be the choice of many to reject the conventional family in return for other arrangements of life better suited to individual personality.

This means also, as a practical matter, that women, if they are to be truly independent, must have access to income of their own. This is obviously necessary for survival outside the traditional family. And it makes possible an independent existence—for shorter or longer periods—within the context of the family.

Professor Galbraith goes on to make the same recommendations pushed by other feminists—more jobs for women, "professional" care for all children, flexible working hours as the norm in industry, quotas for women at all salary levels of the work force, and educational institutions that "discriminate affirmatively in favor of women."

In the final pages of his chapter telling us what's in store for us in "The Equitable Household and Beyond," Professor Galbraith reveals admirably the dimensions of change intended by many of those who have told us lib is just about "equal pay" and "options." He states:

The consequence of the emancipation of women —and the rationalization of the household—will be a substantial change in patterns of life. Thus suburban life—as a wealth of commonplace comment affirms—is demanding in the administrative requirements of its consumption. Vehicle maintenance, upkeep of dwellings, movement of offspring, extirpation of crabgrass, therapy of pets, the heavy demands of social intercourse involving competitive display of housewifely competence are among the innumerable cases in point. . . . There will be more professionally prepared food. There will be less home cooking, the quality of which, though often dubious, is ardently celebrated in the convenient social virtue. Similarly there will be increased reliance on external services rather than home-installed machinery—on laundries, professional housecleaning and public transport instead of wife-operated and -maintained washing machines, housecleaning apparatus and automobiles. Professional entertainment will replace the social intercourse associated with exhibition of womanly talent in food preparation, home decoration, gardening and the dispensation of alcohol. Plausibly there will be an increased resort to the arts. The arts, unlike, for example, competitive display of social craftsmanship, are relatively undemanding in administration, and they involve tasks which are themselves interesting and preoccupying.

Another voice at Harvard for engineering this socialist equality is Christopher Jencks, who said in his book *Inequality*,

We need to establish the idea that the Federal government is responsible not only for the total amount of national income but for its distribution. If we want substantial redistribution, we will not only have to politicize the question of income equality but alter people's basic assumptions about the extent to which they are responsible for the neighbors and their neighbors for them. As long as egalitarians assume that public policy cannot contribute to economic equality directly but must proceed by ingenious manipulations of marginal institutions like the schools, progress will be glacial. If we want to move beyond this tradition, we will have to establish political control over the economic institutions that shape our society. This is what other countries usually call socialism. Anything less will end in the same disappointment as the reforms of the 1960's.

What would life be like for women if the engineers should be successful? Consider these words of one of the most revered feminist thinkers, Simone de Beauvoir, to Betty Friedan in 1975:

> No woman should be authorized to stay at home to raise her children. Women should not have that choice, precisely because if there is such a choice, too many women will make that one. It is a way of forcing women in a certain direction. . . . We see it

IN HONOR OF THE
GREAT COMMITTEE
ON THE FULFILLMENT
OF PERSONKIND

as part of a global reform of society which would
not accept that old segregation between man and
woman, the home and the outside world. We think
that every individual, woman as well as man,
should work outside and have the possibility,
either by communal living, collectives, or another
way of organizing the family, of solving the
problem of child care. Something along these lines
is being tried in China. For example, on a certain
day everyone in the community—men, women,
and children, as far as they are capable—come together to do all the washing or darning of socks. It
wouldn't be your husband's socks; it would be all
the socks, and the husbands would darn them, too.
Encouraging women to stay at home will not
change society. . . . In my opinion, as long as the
family and the myth of the family and the myth of
maternity and the maternal instinct are not destroyed, women will still be oppressed.

When Simone de Beauvoir speaks of feminist revolution on a global basis, she is speaking of a prospect that
lib believers in many parts of the world are working to
make a reality. Although it became apparent at the International Women's Year Conference in Mexico City
in 1975 that the women of the world are far from united
in their views, the unisex idea is fashionable now in
many of the Western industrialized countries. Recent
reports indicate that there is a trend toward state-fi-
nanced day care for children in European countries
such as Belgium, Holland, France and Italy, and that a
long-range commitment to state-supported nursery
schools has been made in Great Britain. These ideas
are most advanced in the socialist countries.

The ideas of feminism, of course, are far from new to
Soviet Russia. They were tried there with disastrous
effects in the 1920s and early 1930s. Just as the lib
believers in the United States today are pushing for

open marriage, easy divorce, sexual license, easy abortion, devaluation of the family, abolition of sex roles, group living, sharing of housework, and universal child care by the state, the early Soviet Communists tried to incorporate these same ideas (every one of them). The results of their experiment with complete sexual equality 50 years ago are described in this passage from Amaury de Riencourt's *Sex and Power in History:*

> In a few short years the great experiment began to fall apart. Men, stripped of their former paternal power and responsibilities, became neglectful toward their families and left the burden of the upbringing of the younger generation to the women—wives and mothers, usually assisted by the irreplaceable *babushkas*, older female relatives, who substituted for the planned but usually nonexistent collective day-care centers. The collapse of family solidarity resulted in the mushrooming of juvenile delinquency on a staggering scale, and far from raising the status of woman, the revolution proved to be utterly demoralizing. Rather than freeing woman, it had freed *man* from sexual restraints and domestic responsibility, the two great gifts of stable marriage to woman. . . . In fact, the new Soviet female was sexually oppressed as she had never been before. . . .

And, de Riencourt declares,

> In exchange for a few formal rights, Soviet women have been among the most exploited human groups in our century. A startling statistic given out in the Moscow *Kommunist* of November 1963 reveals that at the turn of the century, the average lifespan of a Russian woman was two years less than that of the average man, and that in the early 1960s, it was *eight years less.* The author of

439

the article places the responsibility for this relative reduction of Soviet woman's life expectancy squarely on multiple abortions and "the traumas of living conditions and working conditions."

These events resulted when the same basic demands of women's lib today, formulated by Friedrich Engels in 1884 in his *Origin of the Family, Private Property and the State,* were put into practice in the chaotic period following the Russian Revolution. Engels' uni-sex principles for liberating women into every part of the labor force, abolishing the traditional family, became the doctrine of the left socialist labor movement and the eventual Communist parties and socialist governments. In her book *Does Socialism Liberate Women?* Hilda Scott wrote that Engels' work "provided a program for the socialist women's movement which has remained virtually unmodified down to the present. First the complete equality of man and woman before the law; then woman's economic independence through employment outside the home, this to be made possible through the assumption of household duties by society. For all of these things the abolition of capitalism was a necessity. . . ." Next Hilda Scott quotes Engels himself:

> "The peculiar character of man's domination over woman in the modern family, and the necessity, as well as the manner, of establishing real social equality between the two, will be brought out in sharp relief only when both are completely equal before the law. It will then become evident that the first premise for the emancipation of women is the reintroduction of the entire female sex into public industry; and that this again demands that the specific feature of the individual family of being the economic unit of society be abolished."

440

Only those who look no further than the here and now could imagine that women's lib has no other implications than those feminists in the U.S. generally discuss. The idea of the equalization of men and women was from the beginning a key concern in the Marxist indictment of capitalist society. If you look at those countries that have already tried the unisex ideas, such as Russia, Communist China, Israel and Sweden, you find that men in those places still prevail in the higher jobs of government and the professions. Most women fill jobs—*oh yes!*—but they work primarily in labor, in service jobs the regimes want done to boost the national productivity.

"Whatever equality between the sexes is achieved in Marxist lands," declares de Riencourt, "is due merely to the fact that their relatively inefficient regimes cannot afford the supreme capitalist luxury: a large idle female population. . . ." All of these countries habitually promote the theme of female equality because they need the women's backs on the production line. In years past, it has been considered a sign of our great productivity and strength as a nation that we didn't find it necessary to force wives and mothers—contented homemakers—out into the labor force.

Perhaps Sweden is a likely model of where the values of the sexual revolution could lead our own society in the years ahead. Unlike ourselves, the Swedes seem to take naturally to social engineering, and under the Social Democratic Party formed the most advanced welfare state in the world around the values of amorality, materialism, hedonism and complete sexual liberation. The freedom of the individual was sacrificed to the interests of the total state, which in exchange removed all traditional morality from its laws and encouraged all of the conditions that seem to be emerging as progressive wisdom in the U.S., such as contractual

441

marriage, easy divorce, easy abortion, unmarried cohabitation, illegitimacy (which in Sweden is now legitimate), sex education, pornography, and universal daycare services. In addition, the state sided with the children against their elders in order to mold them to the official values. The mass media became organs of advocacy, working to help form the opinions desirable to the regime. The attitudes of the people were molded by squads of "experts." All trends we recognize as ascendant in our own society today.

Roland Huntford has written in *The New Totalitarians:* "It is an acknowledged aim of Social Democratic ideologists (and others) in Sweden to break up the traditional family, because it fosters individuality and because it perpetuates class distinction and social disability."

Amaury de Riencourt calls this approach to social control the Spartan model, because it is "modeled on that of the most successful and durable totalitarian state of antiquity, Sparta." He wrote:

> In the Spartan model, man the citizen becomes a slave of the state, and so do woman and child. A rough equality of sorts is established between them, not because her status rises up to his, but because his sinks down to hers; they are both equal in their total subordination to the state. This is amply illustrated by the fate of woman in the Spartan regimes established by the twentieth century's great revolutions.

Whether you look at the outcomes of the "liberation of women" in Nazi Germany, the Soviet Union, Red China or the Israeli *kibbutz*—and de Riencourt examines them all—you do not find women on the whole rising to the professional or political status of men. While a few may reach such status, the history of uni-

442

sex revolution teaches that in the long run women are freed from homes and children largely to do low-paying manual work dictated by the state.

When I think of this I can't help but think of a paperback book that Annie and I came across in a book store at one of America's great universities. It was published in Red China. The writing and printing were of such a quality that it could have been produced by American writers on Madison Avenue. It cost only fifty cents, less than any other book in the store, and was entitled *New Women in New China*. This is how it began:

> In China, men and women are equal. The broad masses of working women are politically emancipated and economically independent. There is scarcely a field of work from which women are barred, the only exceptions being those that might injure their health. There are women machine-tool operators, geological prospectors, pilots, navigators, spray-painters, engineers and scientific researchers. Women are playing increasingly important roles in China's socialist revolution and socialist construction.
>
> Women also take direct part in managing state affairs. Communist Party and revolutionary committees at all levels, from the people's commune to the provincial and national bodies, all have women members. Women are elected to the National People's Congress and to membership on the Central Committee of the Chinese Communist Party. . . .
>
> None of this would have been conceivable before China's liberation in 1949. . . . Women's emancipation entered a new historical stage in China during the Great Leap Forward of 1958, when the country's agricultural production rose to new heights. Tens of millions of housewives stepped out of their homes to join in socialist construction. The forming of rural people's communes with a diversified economy, extensive irrigation projects and industry opened to women much wider fields

of work. Women were trained to operate modern farm tools, machines and tractors, and served as technicians in water conservancy, forestry, fishing and meteorology.

In the cities, housewives set up and worked in small factories that were mushrooming everywhere. This was followed by the establishment of public dining-rooms, nurseries, kindergartens and other services by the factories and enterprises or neighborhood committees to relieve working women of household chores. Children can stay in the nurseries or kindergartens by the day, or live there throughout the weekend with their parents. Many neighborhood committees run service centers where laundry, tailoring, mending and many other jobs are done for working women.

Engels said: "The emancipation of women and their equality with men are impossible and must remain so as long as women are excluded from socially productive work and restricted to housework, which is private. The emancipation of women becomes possible only when women are enabled to take part in production on a large social scale, and when domestic duties require their attention only to a minor degree." The experience of Chinese women in 1958 began their understanding of how to emancipate themselves completely.

Chinese women now work, study, rest and take part in political and cultural activities along with the men. Many women have emerged as socialist-minded and professionally expert cadres. . . . Chairman Mao says: "Times have changed, and today men and women are equal. Whatever men comrades can accomplish, women comrades can too."

But in contrast to these all too familiar phrases sent to us for fifty cents from Peking, de Riencourt says,

All in all, except for some wives of powerful men, few women play any important part in Red China. Only a small fraction of the leadership, at

444

any level, is female, and the closer one gets to the hard core of power, the less direct influence women possess; females occupy the lower rungs of the revolutionary ladder. What is traditionally known as "big mannism" prevails in Red China as it does in Soviet Russia, and there are no real signs that it is waning. Womanpower was successfully used as a battering ram against the old Confucian fortress; now that the fortress has collapsed, it is used as productive economic power. As for the rest of it, regardless of pious wishes and forecasts, the "socialist liberation" of Red Chinese womanhood, one can only quote a familiar Chinese expression: "a light breeze that leaves no traces at all."

Many breezes are blowing in America today. And the experts, the politicians, the journalists, so many of those who say they know what is right and good, tell us to be equal—man and woman—and thoughtfully we reply: Equal to what?

In Conclusion: A Few Concerned Words from an Unseasonably Happy Housewife

When Jim and I first began our studies of the conflict over sex roles a few years ago, I could not have conceived of the web of social realities we would eventually uncover. I almost blush to admit that in those days my thoughts about what was real and significant in the politics of social change were formed to a distressing extent by what I read in the *Washington Post* and heard on the evening news. I guess the most important thing I've learned through our researches for this book is the absolutely astounding degree to which the mass media direct the points of view of their audiences without necessarily resorting to conspicuous editorial comment. By choosing to report certain facts and events, but not others, by adopting a certain slant, writers and editors are the creators of much of what we generally accept as real. When the goal of scrupulous objectivity is dropped in favor of outright advocacy, the values of the journalists become identical with the illusions they create in the media and the democratic pro-

447

cess is seriously threatened. I believe this is the situation today.

The effects of this threat are extended through habitual tricks of the trade, such as failing *utterly* to challenge assumptions and premises of favored groups and causes. Another one is using special tag-words for certain people or groups. And then there are those lovely little catchwords (remember the Equal Rights Amendment *for women, sexism* and *male chauvinist?*). Wasn't it Oliver Wendell Holmes who said that a good catchword can obscure the truth for fifty years?

The press has promoted the issue of the place of women in our society to the point of making it a national obsession. The ideological involvement of the press in popularizing the ideas and language of lib is exposed in its easy acceptance of the feminist slant. A female who takes her sex too seriously is always called a *feminist*, never a *female chauvinist*. On the other hand, there are no *masculinists* (who might be considered to be the men who take just a *healthy* degree of pride in the characteristics of their sex). No, when such men are mentioned in reports of the drama of the unisex assault, they are male chauvinists all.

If you read the popular press, you get the impression that feminists are merely crusaders after simple justice, defenders of all that is just and good. Yet, anyone who takes a closer look knows it isn't so. In 1976, when the *Washington Post* and Harvard University questioned 2,469 organizational leaders, including representatives of the news media, business, politics, the arts and sciences, on a wide range of social issues, a major conclusion drawn in the final report of the survey was:

> The one group that appears most radical, on this measure [redistribution of income] and many others throughout the study, is composed of leaders of the feminist movement. Some 40 percent of

448

the feminists interviewed were members of the National Organization for Women. Others came from Federally Employed Women, the Coalition of Labor Union Women, the National Women's Political Caucus, the Commission on the Status of Women and the Women's Equity Action League. . . . Of all groups in the leadership study, the feminist leaders emerge as the most radical in every measure of social, cultural and economic attitudes and goals.

The *Post*-Harvard report further characterized the feminists with these words:

Despite their obvious commitment to what they see as bettering the lot of women everywhere, and despite their apparent success in heightening sensitivity to the problems of women, the feminist leaders are looked on with what might best be termed scorn, when they are looked on at all by other leadership groups and society at large.

Feminists are discerned by other leadership groups as having virtually no influence at all—a position they deserve, according to the other leaders. By ratios of 5 to 2 among those in the general population expressing an opinion, the majority of American women are said to disagree on most matters with leaders of the feminist movement. Sentiment is much the same among most of the leadership groups. . . .

The feminists, leaders in the fight to bring women liberation in terms of careers and jobs, are more dissatisfied with the careers and jobs they themselves have than any other group, including blacks, in the study. They complain the most about lack of creative opportunities, about pay, about chance for advancement. . . . They rank near the bottom of all groups in amount of time they spend with their families, and at the very bottom in terms of satisfaction they say they draw from family life. Many of them appear to have given up on family life as most Americans understand it.

Of course feminists are radicals who are antagonistic toward the values of most people in our society, but you would never know it from the images portrayed in most newspapers and magazines in recent years.

Pages and pages of enthusiastic, applauding space are given to coverage of a Janet Guthrie who tries to race with the boys in the Indianapolis 500, but when reporters cover the U.S. Open chess tournament, the thought never crosses their minds to ask the winner of the women's championship why she thinks it is that gals can't compete with the men. When the time comes to cover chess tournaments, the reporters act as though they'd never even heard of women's lib. The greatest revelation to me has been the sheer volume of unchallenged, undetected and widely repeated misinformation that is spread. The marketplace of ideas, I've found, is littered with distortions, deceptions, misrepresentations and fraud waiting to be uncovered. Some of it is accidental (none of us is perfect), and some of it is not.

The word *myth* has been employed like a malicious rumor to cast doubt and suspicion on every value and belief that doesn't fit into the unisex scheme. Anything that doesn't suit the latest editorial fashions in prejudice is dubbed a "myth," while the lib-line writers create new myths such as the one that says girls have been routinely raised to be passive, or reared to be housewives. (Girls in the neighborhood where *I* grew up played many sports right along with the boys, and I had never really cooked or cleaned in my life until my husband taught me how.) In this media environment, so-called scholars can build careers by publicly impugning the mental health of housewives without much fear of being criticized in the press. At the same time, high school guidance counselors across the country can be pressured by feminist groups to encourage young women to be physicians instead of homemakers. And no voice is very likely to raise a question—such as *why*, if unisex is so smart, are the female doctors committing suicide four times as often as the men? (Even as I write this, I can hear the orthodox answer coming back: "They've been conditioned to do it. It's all due to conditioning." The supreme *non*answer of our times.) We have become a people unable to ask the right questions and face facts, because we have all of the advantages of a mass media marvelously contrived to obscure them.

Some time ago, a woman who had read an article in which I was critical of women's lib wrote to ask, "Don't you think you should show appreciation for the benefits that feminists have gained for women?" My answer to that question was that I am all in favor of anything that truly benefits women, or men for that matter, just as long as it isn't accomplished by misrepresenting the realities of human nature, maligning the character of housewives, creating tension between the sexes, devaluing marriage and family, or confusing the sexual identities of children.

The press has long promoted the lib line encouraging the belief that wives have become almost as important as breadwinners as their husbands, despite the fact that working wives typically boost their families' incomes only 15 percent above those of families with wives who stay at home. Feminists like to publicize the fact that women who work full-time earn on the average only 60 percent as much as males. But how often do they point out that seven times as many men as women are heads of families, that the average man spends twice as many years on the job, works three times as much overtime, and contributes nearly three times as much money to support his family as does the working woman?

When the truth is told, you find that five times as

many men as women are the sole supporters of their families. Men are more than twice as likely to be holding two or more jobs, and the average man keeps his job 40 percent longer than the average woman. No, the much-publicized difference in pay that is supposed to demonstrate our oppression doesn't mean that at all. It simply means that the vast majority of us are *not* career women. Our roles are different from men's. And the reason men earn 40 percent more than women is *because they are working so long and hard for the women they are bringing all that money home to.*

I recall the issue of *Time* featuring the "Women of the Year" of 1976 on the cover. The article inside said, "More than 40% of all employed women work in the traditional female ghettos, as salesclerks, secretaries, bookkeepers, receptionists, telephone operators. . . ."

I thought what a terribly destructive thing for anyone to say—especially writers on a national news magazine —to put down people who work in lower-level but *very important* jobs in this way. Sure, you could call the jobs of janitor, refuse collector, sales clerk, cab driver and unskilled laborer the traditional *male* ghettos, but what justification can there be for insulting the pride of any person who does honest work? I think a lot of our social problems stem from just this sort of professional-class mentality, which shows contempt for those who serve in lower-paid, but nonetheless essential jobs. I think we should honor the pride and self-esteem of everyone who obeys the law and who labors—whether in the home for the benefit of her family or in even the most menial of positions in the labor force.

Over and over again we're told that it's "too risky" to be a housewife today. Isn't *that* an inspirational point of view? What a *brilliant* approach to human motivation and achievement the feminists have brought us. Let me see . . . shall our next campaign—after we've

452

completely done in the housewife—be to persuade the police officers that their job is too risky? What about firemen, or construction workers, or small businessmen? Shall we eventually give recruits in basic training for the military services orientation lectures about how soldiering and sailoring are much too risky, and so they would all be much better off if they went home and studied medicine or architecture, or became scholars-in-residence?

When did we become a nation of people whose first concern in life is to avoid all possible risk? If this had been the spirit of our ancestors, they would never have risked taking the boat trip to the new world, never mind taming the wildernesses of a virgin continent. Those who try to demoralize housewives by raising fears and probing for insecurities are busybodies whom any healthy person—whether wife, husband or gate-keeper of the mass media—*ought* to send packing to find some worthwhile activity of their own to perform. As for women with empty nests, or in any other phase of life, for heaven's sake leave us to do what *we* choose. If we want to get a job (and if we will take the time and trouble to develop marketable skills), we can do it. If we desire education, there are already more than enough educational facilities available to meet the demand. If we have leisure and wish to spend it playing golf or tennis or bridge, shopping, or just watching TV —that shouldn't concern Betty Friedan or Gloria Steinem or Susan Brownmiller, or anyone else but us. Women are adult citizens who can be trusted to do whatever attracts their interests, stimulates their aspirations, or fulfills their needs. *We don't need feminist busybodies or government functionaries to guide our lives.*

Women should be aware of opportunities to build security for their later years. Wives should make certain that their husbands have taken advantage of pension, savings and insurance plans that will protect them both in later life. Couples ought to plan together to develop investments if they can, and to make sensible wills. There are many books available to guide the woman who may not have given enough thought to these important personal matters. And every woman, and man, *should* give them serious thought. But there is a limit to how much anyone should worry about catastrophes that *might* happen someday. "A coward dies a thousand deaths, a brave man only one" is still a good thing to remember, whether you want to be a successful man *or* woman. I also like to recall advice my father-in-law is fond of giving: "Live for today, and plan for tomorrow." There is, however, more to life than economic security. I believe it's much more important to a healthy personality to be able to risk yourself in an aspiring marital relationship, giving fully your love, devotion and courage, than to have all the protections the social manipulators could ever provide.

The feminists focus on the dingiest, least mature aspects of our social existence. They dwell on images of men leaving their wives for younger women after having watched too many TV commercials flaunting the curvaceous charms of young models. They would rather call the cup half empty than half full, ignoring the fact that most men *don't* desert their wives, but typically show a high degree of dedication not only to wives, but to daughters, mothers, aunts, sisters and grandmothers. It's a sign of social decline that we no longer extol the best behavior, but revel in overemphasizing the worst, foolishly encouraging the breakdown of standards.

Contrary to feminist notions, *housewife* is an ancient and honorable word. It's been part of the English language at least since the Middle Ages, and it refers to any married woman in charge of a household—specifically, *Webster's* tells us, one "who occupies herself with the domestic affairs of her household and who engages in no employment for pay or profit." She may be rich or poor, and she might or might not do her own cleaning or ironing, but if her fundamental concern is management of a household, she should be proud to be known as a "housewife."

Our studies of the unisex assault don't suggest that the drive to destroy the credibility of the housewife's role is due simply to the arrogant and insistent snobbery of the many professional women (mostly feminist journalists) who disdain anyone who uses a broom or dishcloth (unless, of course, it happens to be a man). There is plenty of that kind of snobbery among feminists, and even lip-service libbers, no doubt, but I'm sure there is far more to it than that.

The inescapable fact about housework and child care is that after all the clever magazine articles have been written and after everyone has agreed that these are generally unglamorous tasks around which to organize one's day (and, yes, even after all the corners have been cut), these duties still must be done by *somebody*. The real issue, after all, isn't whether such work needs to be done—it's who will do it. There is absolutely no sign that very many men are ever going to do half of the housework, except perhaps in those households where *half* means *hardly any*. The notion of the "househusband" remains a perennial ritual fantasy apparently enjoyed exclusively by feminists and the press.

If you read the literature of feminism and take the women at their word (which most writers in the news media have never been *quite* willing to do), you find that the feminist answer to the question of who will take over the responsibilities of the housewife is plain. The government will do it. In the most ambitious feminist vision, housewives—whom they regard as unpaid household labor—will be liberated to the labor force, while subsidized cleaning crews go from house to house and children go from house to day-care center. This is what the real issues of feminism boil down to: will we ultimately entrust our lives and the futures of our children to the traditional ministrations of independent families, or will we turn over responsibility for even the most personal aspects of our lives to the central government? The bottom line of the assault on the sexes is really whether we prefer the Total Woman or the Total State.

I would consider myself, perhaps, to be a Modified Total Woman. I don't wear Saran Wrap to meet my husband at the door, but I *do* try to meet him there, and I firmly believe that the smartest women still put finding a good man and keeping him happy FIRST. I think that in the years just ahead, many people are going to have reasons to regret a lot of the half-cocked decisions some young women are making these days, especially those who have swallowed all of that business about women being just the same as men. To begin to see what's ahead, you need only to compare the pie-in-the-sky notions of feminists, who urge all young women to seek a career, with the bleak forecasts of the availability of such jobs. In *The Feminine Mystique*, Betty Friedan began the ludicrous feminist tradition of pretending that the world is loaded with fulfilling, entertaining jobs. She wrote: "Women, as well as men, can only find their identity in work that uses their full capacities. A woman cannot find her identity through others—her husband, her children. She cannot find it in the dull routine of housework. . . . The feminine mystique has succeeded in burying millions of American women alive. There is no way for these women to break out of their comfortable concentration camps except by finally putting forth an effort—that human effort which reaches beyond biology, beyond the narrow walls of home, to help shape the future. . . ."

Beyond the routine destructiveness of calling people's occupations "concentration camps" and "ghettos," this kind of twaddle—which is all too characteristic of the feminist movement—is completely out of touch with reality. It's exactly the "dull routine" of housework and office work and of *most* work that is unfortunately essential to keep society running. (There are, of course, drawbacks to every job.) The idea that the libbers can give all of us the fulfillment and joy that they obviously have not been able to obtain for themselves is a joke. And when you consider the probable consequences of choices made by women whom the feminists have influenced that tend to weaken the institutions of marriage, home and family, it's a *grim* joke indeed.

While the language of lib emphasizes "equality" and "freedom," what is actually occurring at the psychological and social levels is the breakdown of the sense of commitment and duty that husbands and wives, parents and children, feel for one another. This begins with feminists who try to destroy the confidence of women in the protections of marriage and the security and value of their wifely status in the home. Once the wife is persuaded to shift the focus of her life away from home, husband and children, the sense of mutual commitment between family members tends to evaporate as they come to spend little time together and the home becomes less significant as a primary focus of concern and sustenance. As the wife withdraws her confidence in the husband as breadwinner and protector, he in turn often feels less called upon to perform traditional duties, and gradually the sense of living with a group of independent agents affects everyone. This has become a common pattern.

The very same feminists who will tell you that

457

women's lib has nothing to do with the breakdown of family life can be heard encouraging wives to publicly disagree with their husbands as a sign of their liberation—just as though it weren't also the first indication that the couple is no longer functioning as a team.

The campaign to shift loyalties and responsibilities away from the family is also aided by a widespread contempt among the secular press, and humanists such as Betty Friedan, for the beliefs and values of people who hold a traditional belief in God. I have been so impressed that among the many women who have written to me from all across the country, those who seem to express the greatest joy and satisfaction in life, who truly seem to be living the richest lives, are almost invariably the ones who mention the central place that religion plays in their lives. I find it incredible that so many writers in the media appear to dismiss religion and spiritual values as unimportant (even as a sign of ignorance), when in truth nobody *knows* that there is not a God. I can understand the agnostic, who admits this, and can't bring himself to believe. But I can't understand the attitude of those who arrogantly and, I think, irrationally disparage viewpoints of people who believe in God, especially when so much practical evidence indicates that such believers tend to fare better than others in nearly every way. Study after study in recent years suggests that people with strong religious beliefs are happier, healthier, enjoy more satisfying marriages and sex lives, and in general experience much more enthusiasm and purpose in life than other people. Scientists may not be able to explain exactly why religious folks seem to have such an edge in dealing with the troubles and stresses of living, but I think anyone who routinely looks down on the religious life is only fooling himself.

I haven't the tiniest doubt that the deterioration of

family life is the key factor in the massive problems of juvenile alienation we are experiencing in our society. But I believe it goes much deeper than this. The popular wisdom in recent years has been that it is old-fashioned and stodgy for people to think in terms of making lifelong commitments in marriage or to carry any special sense of obligation to children, or to the old or infirm. A fundamental principle of feminist liberation is that whatever you do as a woman, you must not sacrifice your independence in favor of misplaced confidence in a man. What if he leaves you? What if you are divorced? What if he dies? These are the fears they put before housewives. I would like to ask another sort of question—what if *we* have a stroke, or are crippled, or lose our sight? People are stricken every day and forced to live out their lives with physical affliction or disfigurement. These are constant risks of living. Now that duty and commitment have come to mean so little, shall we expect that if physical disaster strikes us, our spouses will be justified in throwing us on the scrap heap like so much damaged goods? Where does it stop once you accept the principle that marriage, or parenthood, or being a son or a daughter, is just a temporary arrangement without compelling burdens of mutual obligation? I don't understand this principle of limited trust and responsibility with which family members are supposed to invest themselves today—the "I'm committed as long as it's easy" kind of thinking. But I *do* understand where it leads.

It doesn't take a prophet to notice that we're heading exactly where the feminist theorists have told us in their literature that they want us. When we have an "equal rights" amendment that removes the special obligation of the husband to support his family, and relieves the wife of all responsibility to live with her husband or to provide care for him or their children . . .

459

when we have congressional legislation facing us that
would institutionalize feminist principles in the
schools (Title IX), establish a feminist agency in the
federal bureaucracy (National Center for Women Act),
and establish government day-care programs across the
nation (Child and Family Services Act) . . . and when
the full force of feminist pressure in recent years has
been directed at pushing women out of the home—
then it's not too difficult to draw the conclusion that the
current game plan for the sexes is to transfer the traditional responsibilities of family life out of their care
and into the hands of the federal bureaucracy.

All of these activities are defended as offering
women new freedoms and benefits, a new equality, but
they really presage social changes that conflict with
liberty.

What is actually occurring is a kind of semantic siege
by the social engineers, who in order to have clients
must first define ever-expanding groups of people as
sick, oppressed, disadvantaged, discriminated-against
or enslaved. This process, which has been focused on
the young, the old, the ineffectual and the female in
recent years, is now being directed toward the family,
which could be its ultimate victim. The kinds of "help"
the government can offer the family are the very invita-
tions to dependency that spell its decline as a vital and
elemental institution.

The kind of "equality" gained through massive government power is really an idiot equality which de-
stroys all prospects that people will be treated more
equitably in the society. It's a movement to level
everyone to the lowest common denominator, sapping
out the variety, individuality, strength and spiritual dimensions of our lives in favor of mechanical guidelines
for everything, set and sealed for us all in Washington,

460

stifling the urge of a diverse people to fashion their lives according to their own distinctive tastes, aspirations, abilities and creative impulses.

Who but a true believer would *want* to make everyone live the same kind of life? Who would worry about whether or not everyone else is adequately fulfilling himself or has an interesting enough life? Could a person who is genuinely trying to pursue his own life, liberty and happiness be so concerned with the petty details of everyone else's? Or is it, exactly as Eric Hoffer says, that people who can't live their own lives with any sense of achievement and satisfaction feel compelled to turn their interests to meddling with the lives of others. I think so. I think that people who feel empty, bored and inadequate in their own affairs are often driven to try to demonstrate that, really, they possess the great *secret* of successful living and are even qualified to instruct the rest of us. Betty Friedan says that she and other writers of the early 1960s set out to change the image of the American woman and the family togetherness theme in women's magazines because they had grown *bored* with it. Not long ago she wrote: "For fear of being alone, I almost lost my own self-respect trying to hold on to a marriage that was based no longer on love but on dependent hate. It was easier for me to start the women's movement which was needed to change society than to change my own personal life."

Of course inequities do exist. People are often discriminated against for one reason or another, and we should try to encourage as much equality of opportunity as possible. We certainly must stand firm as a society for equality before the law. But this need not mean that we must be led into the idiot equality of a sterile unisex society planned by people no one has

461

voted for, implementing vast changes the majority of Americans don't want and wouldn't approve in an honest referendum.

Alexis de Tocqueville wrote: "When inequality of conditions is the common law of society, the most marked inequalities do not strike the eye. When everything is nearly on the same level, the slightest are marked enough to hurt it. Hence the desire for equality always becomes more insatiable in proportion as equality is more complete." This captures the real problem of the feminists, who would engineer a new society to make us all live out their own vision—not because women are confronted with burdensome or frustrating inequalities or lack of opportunity, but precisely because some women cannot find satisfactions through the exercise of the many options open to them. Midge Decter is exactly right when she observes that the feminists suffer not from too little freedom, but from the fact that they don't know what to do with all the freedom they already have. Those who choose to sacrifice, or neglect, home and family for a career, or more likely a job, are never quite confident that they've made the right choice. And so, they want to eliminate the need to make a choice altogether by insisting that every woman must work. This is the real psychology behind the feminist drive for universal day care and a new social norm that forbids women to stay at home.

I grew up in a free country that has provided us with the highest standard of living in the world, a country now faced with serious problems and choices. We who have been the consumers of almost a third of the world's raw materials are now faced with the prospect of scarcity. The cheap energy is gone, and environmental hazards pose dire challenges to our ingenuity. We face grave problems of overpopulation, crime, world food crisis and ravaging disease. We have real enemies in the world against whom we must maintain a powerful and vigilant defense. On every hand are burgeoning social dilemmas we must solve if we are to survive as a people. If we are to preserve our free enterprise system, our way of government and our freedom, we simply can't afford the weakening of moral, intellectual and physical standards we've endured over the past decade and more. A healthy society must keep up the vitality to assert its morality and standards, and to prescribe necessary roles, without apology or hesitation.

We know that nothing in life is really guaranteed, which is why the Declaration of Independence doesn't promise life, liberty and *happiness*—just the "pursuit of happiness." Each person, I believe, has to figure out what happiness means to him, and until you do that—really get to know what will be satisfying for you—then you aren't likely to find it. America is the place where it has at least been possible to try. The very qualities that are necessary for success in the search for happiness in freedom—self-awareness, creative thinking, imagination, decisiveness, initiative and perseverance—are exactly the qualities that are crippled by the mentality that encourages people to turn to the government for their benefits and opportunities.

The unisex assault is part of the encompassing trend that seeks to involve the government ever more intimately in our lives through affirmative action programs, quotas, government child-care programs, regulation of the schools, and schemes for sex-role engineering. But the more the government seeks to control the details of our lives, the more the pathology of the ghetto seems to spread into the middle classes, bringing deterioration of family, rising illegitimacy, illiteracy, violent crime, addiction, and venereal disease. The drive to provide equal benefits to groups—neatly legislated and "free" in a gift-wrapped box—promises to defeat the kind of liberty that encourages the hope, initiative and struggle of people who prize both civilization and the opportunity to shape the destinies of their own lives.

When the historian and philosopher Will Durant was interviewed in 1975 on the occasion of his ninetieth birthday, he lamented the decline of marriage and family in our culture. "That is unfortunate," he said, "because they are two marvelous forms of order that can be pillars of strength in the flux of modern life. If you get rid of the state, the family can maintain order. But get rid of the family and you have nothing."

The values and the commitments between people that hold society together have been greatly weakened by the secular relativism that has so permeated our colleges and schools. The anything-goes philosophy prevails. Children are no longer learning the traditional virtues of honesty, self-restraint, patriotism, ambition and discipline—or respect for life, knowledge, truth and property. We are at a crisis in the continuity of the American character. Surely we must recognize that we can't make up for the lack of personal character and commitment in ourselves as a people by shifting responsibility for our personal lives into the hands of government functionaries. It is imperative that we acknowledge the importance of providing strong examples of good moral character—creating real cultural heroes again—presenting our youth with symbols of leadership and inspiration they can look up to. This is possible only if we have the courage to stand up for the institutions and values upon which our way of life depends. We must get away from the influence of the hordes of whiners and finger-pointers who cripple creative endeavor by dwelling on the shortcomings of some, and refusing to support any standard or principle that places a premium on character, performance, perseverance or skill. We must stand up strongly for our basic institutions, for marriage and family, the sanctity

464

of the marital bond and of fidelity, the integrity of our laws, and the principle of binding our economic policies to the realities of the marketplace. We have to reverse the current tendency toward weakened public and personal principle and lack of commitment to long-range national interest, and discredit the growing dependency of public and private enterprises on subsidies, guarantees and privileges from the federal government.

We ought to remember and heed well the words of Caspar W. Weinberger in his last speech upon retiring in 1975 from the office of secretary of Health, Education and Welfare:

> Our country was built by people of energy, daring and ingenuity—the Edisons, the Wright Brothers, the Helen Kellers, the Fultons, the Carnegies, the great musicians and artists and countless others brimming with dreams and filled with the courage to reach out and realize those dreams whatever the odds.
>
> Their kind of daring was nurtured in a social climate that rewarded risk-takers and practical visionaries. If we now proceed mindlessly to change that climate to one favoring a faceless gray egalitarianism, we will have lost all that has made America great and enabled us to help so much of the world.
>
> The real social agenda of America, still unfinished, is to discover and reward excellence wherever we find it—under a black skin, a white skin, in a female or male, in a Catholic, a Jew, a Protestant or an agnostic. That is the real purpose of equal opportunity.
>
> If we fail to see this as our real agenda, we risk delivering our destinies over to the cold and lifeless grip of a distant egalitarian government whose sole purpose is to ensure an equally mediocre existence for everyone, achieved at the cost of personal liberty.

The real agenda of the leaders of the feminist assault is exactly to deliver the foundations of our democratic society as we have known it into that cold and lifeless grip. It is an insidious threat against which most people have been too unsuspecting and preoccupied to guard, but which they should recognize and resist.

If the hazard of the recent past has been that most people misperceived the true nature of the unisex assault, underestimating the significance of its effects on our laws and social life, the danger now is that they may be gulled into believing that the threat has passed. By 1975 we were hearing reports of the women's lib movement splitting into factions and falling into disarray. In early 1976, Betty Friedan was bemoaning feminism's "period of crisis," and by Halloween we were reading Veronica Geng's "Requiem for the Women's Movement" in *Harper's*. But on November 2, with the election of the new "progressive" administration, hope for lib was miraculously born again. The determined women of the feminist network in Washington, with the nod of the president-elect, were already pouring names and qualifications of the faithful into a new computerized personnel index, dubbed TalentBank 77, a sophisticated system especially conceived to expedite the installation of liberationist sisters into new positions of federal influence.

By the time the new administration had completed its appointments, more feminists had been moved into subcabinet positions than ever before. This was of course far from enough to satisfy the ambitions of the lib power-seekers, who had hoped to force installation of several of their sisters into the cabinet of the man who as a candidate had told them he wanted to be remembered as "the president who did for women what Lyndon Johnson did for blacks." As it turned out, President Carter resisted the efforts of the lib network to a considerable extent, appointing two women to his cabinet but rejecting most of the feminist candidates as lacking sufficient administrative or political experience to serve in the top posts. Meanwhile, he assured the lib lobby that he would "build a base" of female assistant secretaries and deputy secretaries from which future cabinet members could be drawn. And Mrs. Jimmy Carter, recipient of NOW's ERA Medallion award for her work to get the amendment ratified, redoubled her efforts to push the feminist law to victory. At last the libbers saw hope that the movement might actually achieve all of the political momentum and leverage necessary to accomplish their whole unisex program.

Whatever the lib pundits and pop feminists of the media may tell us as the coming events unfold, you can be sure that the crusade of the real feminists, the dedicated true believers, presses on. Despite the inauspicious showing of feminist candidates around the country in the popular elections of 1976, the political initiatives of the drive to unisex are now more threatening than ever before. This assault on the traditional dynamic of life that is sparked between the sexes is being carried out relentlessly on hundreds of fronts, not merely through words, slogans and protests, but by the diligent acquisition of administrative power and the methodical changing of regulations and laws. And I shudder to realize that long before the last law has been altered, it may already be too late.

Selected Bibliography

Andelin, Helen B. *Fascinating Womanhood*. New York: Bantam Books, 1975.

Beard, Mary R. *On Understanding Women*. New York: Greenwood Press, 1968.

Beard, Mary R. *Woman as Force in History*. New York: Macmillan, 1946; New York: Collier Books, 1973.

Beard, Mary R. *Woman's Work in Municipalities*. New York: Appleton, 1915.

Beauvoir, Simone de. *The Second Sex*. New York: Knopf, 1953.

Berger, Peter L. *Invitation to Sociology*. New York: Anchor Books, 1963.

Bernard, Jessie. *The Future of Marriage*. New York: World, 1972.

Bernard, Jessie. *The Future of Motherhood*. New York: Dial, 1974.

Bickel, P.J. *et al.* "Sex Bias in Graduate Admissions: Data from Berkeley." *Science*, February 7, 1975.

Blake, Judith. "The Changing Status of Women in Developed Countries." *Scientific American*, September 1974.

Bronfenbrenner, Urie. "The Origins of Alienation." *Scientific American*, August 1974.

Bullough, Vern L. *The Subordinate Sex: A History of Attitudes Toward Women*. Chicago: University of Illinois Press, 1973.

Burns, Scott. *Home, Inc.* New York: Doubleday, 1975.

Burton, Gabrielle. *I'm Running Away from Home, But I'm Not Allowed to Cross the Street.* New York: Avon, 1975.

Carden, Maren Lockwood. *The New Feminist Movement.* New York: Russell Sage Foundation, 1974.

Cardozo, Arlene Rossen. *Woman At Home.* New York: Doubleday, 1976.

Chafe, William H. *The American Woman.* New York: Oxford University Press, 1972.

Church, Joseph. *Language and the Discovery of Reality.* New York: Random House, 1961; Vintage Books, 1961.

Dalton, Katharina. *The Menstrual Cycle.* New York, Pantheon, 1969.

Davidson, Julian M. "Hormones and Sexual Behavior in the Male." *Hospital Practice,* September 1975.

DeBenedictis, Daniel J. *Legal Rights of Married Women.* New York: Cornerstone Library, 1969.

DeCrow, Karen. *Sexist Justice.* New York: Random House, 1974.

DeCrow, Karen. *The Young Woman's Guide to Liberation.* Indianapolis: Pegasus, 1971.

Decter, Midge. *Liberal Parents, Radical Children.* New York: Coward, McCann & Geoghegan, 1975.

Decter, Midge. *The New Chastity and Other Arguments Against Women's Liberation.* New York: Coward, McCann & Geoghegan, 1972.

Durant, Will and Ariel. *The Lessons of History.* New York: Simon and Schuster, 1968.

Ephron, Nora. *Crazy Salad: Some Things About Women.* New York: Knopf, 1975.

Fasteau, Marc Feigen. *The Male Machine.* New York: McGraw-Hill, 1974.

Filene, Peter Gabriel. *Him/Her/Self: Sex Roles in Modern America.* New York: Harcourt Brace Jovanovich, 1974.

Firestone, Shulamuth. *The Dialectic of Sex: The Case for Feminist Revolution.* New York: Morrow, 1970.

Flexner, Eleanor. *Century of Struggle: The Women's Rights Movement in the United States.* New York: Atheneum, 1973.

Freeman, Jo. *The Politics of Women's Liberation.* New York: McKay, 1975.

Friedan, Betty. *The Feminine Mystique.* New York: Norton, 1963.

Friedan, Betty. *It Changed My Life: Writings on the Women's Movement.* New York: Random House, 1976.

Fromm, Erich. *The Art of Loving.* New York: Harper & Brothers, 1956.

470

Gager, Nancy, ed. *Women's Rights Almanac 1974*. Bethesda, Md.: Elizabeth Cady Stanton, 1974.

Galbraith, John Kenneth. *Economics and the Public Purpose*. Boston: Houghton Mifflin, 1973.

Geiger, H. Kent. *The Family in Soviet Russia*. Cambridge: Harvard University Press, 1968.

Geng, Veronica. "Requiem for the Women's Movement." *Harper's*, November 1976.

Gilder, George F. *Naked Nomads*. New York: Quadrangle, 1974.

Gilder, George F. *Sexual Suicide*. New York: Quadrangle, 1973.

Ginzberg, Ely *et al. Life Styles of Educated Women*. New York: Columbia University Press, 1966.

Goffman, Erving. *The Presentation of Self in Everyday Life*. New York: Anchor Books, 1959.

Greer, Germaine. *The Female Eunuch*. New York: McGraw-Hill, 1971.

Gunn, John. *Violence*. New York: Praeger, 1973.

Hark, Ann. "Jills of All Trades." *Ladies' Home Journal*, February 1929.

Harrison, Barbara Grizzuti. *Unlearning the Lie: Sexism in School*. New York: Liveright, 1973.

Hendin, Herbert. *The Age of Sensation*. New York: Norton, 1975.

Hoffer, Eric. *The True Believer*. New York: Time Incorporated, 1963.

Hole, Judith, and Ellen Levine. *Rebirth of Feminism*. New York: Quadrangle, 1971.

Huber, Joan, ed. *Changing Women in a Changing World*. Chicago: University of Chicago Press, 1973.

Hunt, Morton. *Sexual Behavior in the 1970s*. Chicago: Playboy Press, 1974.

Huntford, Roland. *The New Totalitarians*. New York: Stein and Day, 1971.

Imperato-McGinley, Julianne *et al.* "Steroid 5a-Reductase Deficiency in Man: An Inherited Form of Male Pseudohermaphroditism." *Science*, December 27, 1974.

Janeway, Elizabeth. *Man's World, Woman's Place: A Study in Social Mythology*. New York: Morrow, 1971.

Johnston, Jill. *Lesbian Nation: the Feminist Solution*. New York: Simon and Schuster, 1973.

Klagsbrun, Francine. *The First Ms. Reader*. New York: Warner, 1973.

Koedt, Anne, ed. *Radical Feminism*. New York: Quadrangle, 1973.

Lenin, V.I. *The Emancipation of Women.* New York: International Publishers, 1972.

Levin, Robert J. "The Redbook Report on Premarital and Extramarital Sex: The End of the Double Standard?" *Redbook,* October 1975.

Lichtenstein, Grace. "Kill, Hate—Mutilate!" *The New York Times Magazine,* September 5, 1976.

Lifton, Robert Jay, ed. *The Woman in America.* Boston: Beacon Press, 1971.

Linder, Staffan Burenstam. *The Harried Leisure Class.* New York: Columbia University Press, 1970.

Lopata, Helena Znaniecki. *Occupation: Housewife.* New York: Oxford University Press, 1971.

Lorand, Rhoda L. *Love, Sex and the Teenager.* London: Macmillan, 1969.

Maccoby, Eleanor Emmons, and Carol Nagy Jacklin. *The Psychology of Sex Differences.* Stanford, Cal.: Stanford University Press, 1974.

Mead, Margaret. *Sex and Temperament in Three Primitive Societies.* New York: Morrow, 1935; New York: Dell, 1968.

Millett, Kate. *Sexual Politics.* New York: Doubleday, 1970.

Money, John, and Patricia Tucker. *Sexual Signatures: On Being A Man or A Woman.* Boston: Little, Brown, 1975.

Morgan, Marabel. *Total Woman.* Old Tappan, N.J.: Fleming H. Revell, 1973.

Morgan, Robin, ed. *Sisterhood Is Powerful: An Anthology of Writings from the Women's Liberation Movement.* New York: Random House, 1970.

New Women in New China. Peking: Foreign Languages Press, 1972.

O'Neill, George and Nena. *Open Marriage: A New Life Style for Couples.* New York: Evans, 1972.

O'Neill, William. *Everyone Was Brave.* Chicago: Quadrangle, 1969.

Peale, Ruth Stafford. *The Adventure of Being A Wife.* Englewood Cliffs, N.J.: Prentice-Hall, 1971.

Pearsall, Ronald. *Edwardian Life & Leisure.* New York: St. Martin's Press, 1973.

Riegel, Robert E. *American Feminists.* Lawrence: University Press of Kansas, 1963.

Riencourt, Amaury de. *Sex and Power in History.* New York: McKay, 1974.

Rosaldo, Michelle Zimbalist, and Louise Lamphere. *Woman, Culture & Society.* Stanford, Cal.: Stanford University Press, 1974.

Roshco, Bernard. *Newsmaking.* Chicago: The University of Chicago Press, 1975.

Rossi, Alice S., ed. *The Feminist Papers: From Adams to de Beauvoir.* New York: Columbia University Press, 1973.

Ruina, Edith, ed. *Women in Science and Technology.* Cambridge: MIT Press, 1973.

Ryder, Norman B. "The Family in Developed Countries." *Scientific American,* September 1974.

Safran, Claire. "What Men Do to Women on the Job." *Redbook,* November 1976.

Schecter, Leona *et al. An American Family in Moscow.* Boston: Little, Brown, 1975.

Scott, Hilda. *Does Socialism Liberate Women?* Boston: Beacon Press, 1974.

Sexton, Patricia Cayo. *The Feminized Male.* New York: Random House, 1969.

Shaywitz, Sally E. "Catch 22 for Mothers." *New York Times Magazine,* March 4, 1973.

Smith, Page. *Daughters of the Promised Land.* Boston: Little, Brown, 1970.

Socarides, Charles W. *Beyond Sexual Freedom.* New York: Quadrangle, 1971.

Sochen, June. *The New Woman: Feminism in Greenwich Village, 1910–1920.* New York: Quadrangle, 1972.

Sowell, Thomas. "A Black 'Conservative' Dissents." *New York Times Magazine,* August 8, 1976.

Sprung, Barbara. *Non-Sexist Education for Young Children.* New York: Citation Press, 1975.

Stassinopoulos, Arianna. *The Female Woman.* New York: Random House, 1974.

Stimpson, Catharine, ed. *Women and the "Equal Rights" Amendment: Senate Subcommittee Hearings on the Constitutional Amendment, 91st Congress.* New York: Bowker, 1972.

Sussman, Barry. "Elites in America: A Washington Post-Harvard Survey." Five-part series in *The Washington Post,* September 26–30, 1976.

Thompson, Mary Lou. *Voices of the New Feminism.* Boston: Beacon Press, 1970.

Tiger, Lionel. *Men in Groups.* New York: Random House, 1969.

473

Tocqueville, Alexis de. *Democracy in America.* 2 volumes. New York: Knopf, 1951.

Tripp, Maggie, ed. *Woman In the Year 2000.* New York: Arbor House, 1974.

Weiss, Paul. *Sport: A Philosophic Inquiry.* Carbondale, Ill.: Southern Illinois University Press, 1969.

Williams, Duncan. *Trousered Apes.* New York: Churchill Press Limited, 1971; Dell, 1973.

The Woman Question: Selections from the Writings of Karl Marx, Frederick Engels, V.I. Lenin, Joseph Stalin. New York: International Publishers, 1970.

Index

Aaron, Betsy, 154–55
Abortion, 20, 49, 56, 84, 101, 270, 439, 442
Abzug, Bella, 50, 363
Ackerly, William, 244
Adams, Annette, 22
Adams, Harriet Chalmers, 25
Addams, Jane, 24
Advertising: and the sex-role revolution, 36–37, 48, 148–49, 351–54
Alda, Alan, 50, 293–95
Alice Doesn't Day, 157–60
Allred, Gloria R., 299
American Association of University Women, 420
American Civil Liberties Union, 305
American Home, 133–35
Andelin, Helen B. (Fascinating Womanhood), 164–65
Asimov, Isaac, 152; The Human Body, 215
AT&T, 35–37, 43, 224–25
Athearn, Forden (How to Divorce Your Wife), 243
Atkinson, Ti-Grace, 11–12, 47, 102

Balanchine, George, 383
Balukas, Jean, 216
Banker, Stephen, 211–12
Bayh, Birch, 50, 292–93, 311, 323–28
Beard, Mary, 20; Woman as Force in History, 16–17
Beauty contests, 11, 26
Beauvoir, Simone de, 113, 437–38
Bell, Terrel H., 87–88
Benedict, Ruth, 25
Berger, Peter L. (Invitation to Sociology), 256, 262
Bernard, Jessie (The Future of Marriage), 420–28
Better Homes and Gardens, 166–67, 301
Birth control, 74–75, 79, 84, 232
Blake, Judith, 168–71
Boston Marathon, 211, 216
Bress, Grace B., 429–31
Bridge, female performance in, 223–24
Bronfenbrenner, Urie, 280–82
Brothers, Joyce, 79
Brown, Barbara A., 312–13
Brownmiller, Susan, 453; Against Our Will: Men, Women and Rape, 220–21, 275
Buchanan, Patrick J., 333–34
Buckley, William F., Jr., 349–50

Burns, Scott (Home, Inc.), 377
Burton, Gabrielle (I'm Running Away from Home, But I'm Not Allowed to Cross the Street), 32, 107–08, 196, 219–20
Business and Professional Women's Clubs, 117

Cameron, Paul, 202
Campbell, Bernard (Human Evolution), 264–65
Camp Fire Girls, 53, 160
"Captain Kangaroo," 42
Carbine, Pat, 50
Carden, Maren Lockwood (The New Feminist Movement), 111, 118
Cardozo, Arlene Rossen (Women At Home), 377–80, 388
Carnegie Corporation, 60
Carter, James Earl (Jimmy), 365, 466–67
Carter, John Mack, 44
Carter, Rosalynn (Mrs. Jimmy), 385–86, 467
Castle, Irene, 24
CBS (television and radio network), 44–46
Celler, Emanuel, 321
Census Bureau, 25, 155
Center for Disease Control, 77–78
Chess, female performance in, 222–24, 450
Child neglect, 89–92
Child-rearing, attitudes toward, 101–2, 108, 111–13, 142–44, 152, 162–64, 170–74, 249, 251–56, 266, 270, 375–408 passim
Christian Science Monitor, 301
Church, Joseph, 340–41
Civil Service Commission, 51
Coalition of Labor Union Women, 449
Cohabitation, 65–71, 73–85, 141, 442
Coleman, James S., 429–31
Common Cause, 302
Congress, U.S., 230, 235, 291, 302–28 passim, 363, 387–88, 418–20; and the National Commission on International Women's Year, 50, 307, 418–19; and Title IX, 49, 52–53, 330–35; and unisex legislation, 54–55; and the Vocational Education Act, 54–55
Conlan, John B., 71–72
Consciousness changing, 12–13, 37, 58–62, 108–11, 118, 271, 414–15
Corman, Avery, 251–52

Cosmopolitan, 123, 166, 169
Council on Interracial Books for
    Children, 60
Crawford, Claire, 295–96
Credit Union National Association, 26
Cronkite, Walter, 297
Crutcher, Anne, 145
Curie, Marie, 24
Curtis, Charlotte, 135

Dalton, Katherina *(The Menstrual
    Cycle)*, 183
Davidson, Julian M., 187
Day care, 29, 31, 46, 49, 52, 101–2, 113,
    162, 270, 280–81, 329, 375, 431–35,
    438–39, 444, 456, 460, 463
"Dear Abby," 79, 301
DeCrow, Karen, 47
Decter, Midge, 74, 462; *The New
    Chastity and Other Arguments
    Against Women's Liberation*, 203–4
Defense Department, 235
Democratic Women's Alliance, 54
DeMott, Benjamin, 81
Discrimination, 337–38, 341, 363–66,
    461–62, 465; denial of, 16–27, 162–64,
    169–72, 177, 272–79, 342, 348, 352–56,
    360–68, 382–83, 385–95, 398–401,
    450–54
Divorce, 20, 56, 87, 243, 330, 439, 442
Dixon, Marlene, 99, 114
Douglas, Kathy (Mrs. William O.), 295
Douglas, William O., 145–46
Dow, Peter B., 71–72
Dreifus, Claudia *(Woman's Fate)*,
    109–11
Dunbar, Roxanne *(Sisterhood Is
    Powerful)*, 112
Duncan, Isadora, 24
Dupuy, Harold J., 427–28
Durant, Will, 464
Durbin, Karen, 142–43
Dushoff, Ira M., 215

Earhart, Amelia, 24
East, Catherine, 100, 103, 413
Eastwood, Mary, 100
Ederle, Gertrude, 24
Education Amendments (Title IX),
    52–53, 59–60, 330–35, 460
Education: and problems of youth,
    73–74, 87–88, 94; and the sex-role
    revolution, 33–43, 49–62,
    70–73, 99–102, 111, 201, 255, 260–61,
    330–35, 338–39, 342–50
Emerson, Thomas I., 311, 313, 321, 323,
    325, 327
Engels, Friedrich, 444; *Origin of the
    Family, Private Property and the
    State*, 440
Ephron, Nora *(Crazy Salad)*, 412, 415

Equal Employment Opportunity
    Commission, 52, 364
Equality: and assault on sex roles, 32,
    34–35, 37–38, 49, 98, 103–5, 111–12,
    117–18, 166, 207, 243, 265–70, 279–80,
    309–20, 329–35, 338–49, 372–73, 390,
    406, 411–12, 435–45, 448, 457–59,
    461–62, 467; and sex differences,
    204–5, 211–20, 224–41, 255–56,
    263–65, 267–68, 275–80; support for,
    29, 118, 177, 396, 465
Equal Rights Amendment (ERA), 16, 46,
    55, 101, 105, 117, 213, 235–36, 448–59,
    467; Ervin amendments to, 318–28;
    and the federal government, 293, 298,
    302–4, 307–10; and feminism, 296–98,
    312–14; issues of, 288–96, 299–310,
    314–35; and the law, 288–91, 302–35;
    legislative history of, 310–30; and
    NOW, 49, 467; and public debate,
    287–302; and status of women groups,
    51–52, 298–99, 302, 306–8, 310–11,
    419; and unisex bathrooms, 299–305,
    319; and women in the military,
    304–7, 314–15, 318–19
ERAmerica, 295, 302, 307–8
Ervin, Sam, 287, 302–3, 311, 318–28

Falk, Gail, 312–13
Family Circle, 168
Family disintegration, and problems of
    youth, 87–92
*Family in Search of a Future: Alternate
    Models for Moderns, The*, 70–71
*Family in Transition: Rethinking
    Marriage, The*, 70–71
Farley, Lin, 366
FBI, 225
Federally Employed Women, 51, 449
Feminists: hardcore, 175–76, 467;
    network of, 48–52, 99–105, 117–18,
    157, 161, 175–76, 291–93, 417–22,
    466–67
Fleming, Pat, 202
Flexed-arm hang: and chin-ups, 208–10
Ford, Betty (Mrs. Gerald R.), 295
Ford, Gerald R., 50, 293, 307, 331,
    333–34
Forrester, Jay W., 33
Forum, 180
Frankfurter, Felix, 328
Fraser, Arvonne S., 309–10
Frederick, Calvin J., 245–46
Freedman, Ann E., 312–13
Freeman, Jo *(The Politics of Women's
    Liberation)*, 100, 102–5, 117
Freund, Paul, 302, 321–23, 327–29
Friedan, Betty, 47, 97, 107, 113–14, 138,
    252–53, 437, 453, 458, 461, 466; *The
    Feminine Mystique*, 105–6, 111–12,
    121–32, 456–57

476

Fromm, Eric (*The Art of Loving*), 372–73, 403–4
Frost, David, 11, 15

Gagnon, John Y., 79–81
Galbraith, John Kenneth (*Economics and the Public Purpose*), 433–36
Gallup Opinion Poll, 159–60, 368
Geiger, H. Kent (*The Family in Soviet Russia*), 375–76
General Accounting Office, 235–40
General Electric Co. (GE), 42–43
Gilder, George, 81, 150–51; *Sexual Suicide*, 92–94, 203, 265
Ginsberg, Ruth Bader, 292
Girl Talk, 298
Glamour, 157, 166, 169
Glazer, Nathan, 362–63
Goldstein, Jane, 217
Good Housekeeping, 163
Goodman, Ellen, 305
Goolagong, Evonne, 211
Gould, Shane, 180
Graham, Katharine, 290
Graham, Martha, 24
Greer, Germaine (*The Female Eunuch*), 114–15
Griffiths, Martha, 50, 287, 311, 321
Guidelines for Equal Treatment of the Sexes in McGraw-Hill Book Company Publications, 341–49, 352
Gunn, John (*Violence*), 191
Guthrie, Janet, 145, 450

Hamburg, David A., 194
Hanson, Bob, 228–29
Hark, Ann, 22–23
Harrison, Barbara Grizzuti (*Unlearning the Lie: Sexism in School*), 60–61, 338–39
Health, of Americans, 85–86
Heide, Wilma Scott, 47
Heller, Naomi, 68
Henderson, Ralph H., 78
Hendin, Herbert (*The Age of Sensation*), 66, 246–47
Hepburn, Audrey, 401–3
HEW, 51–53, 59–60, 330–35
Hicks, Nancy, 54
Higgenson, Margaret, 413–14
Hills, Carla, 135–36
Hoffer, Eric (*The True Believer*), 415–17, 461
Hoffman, Nicholas von, 344
Holt, Rinehart and Winston, 347
Homicide, 87
Homosexuality, 29, 44, 49, 53, 56, 65–67, 71, 79, 92–93, 101, 108, 111, 114–16, 118, 157, 160, 174–76, 315, 320–28, 363–64, 367

Housewife role: attitudes toward, 13–15, 105–7, 113–15, 122, 125, 133–35, 141–45, 163–65, 168–74, 176, 266, 270–77, 280, 308–10, 339, 342, 349, 352–54, 368, 371–408 *passim*, 413–14, 421–28, 437–38, 441, 443–44, 455–57; value of, 272–77, 354, 366, 368, 385–406, 454–55
Huber, Joan, 414
Huntford, Roland, (*The New Totalitarians*), 442
Hunt, Gladys (*Ms. Means Myself*), 407
Hustler, 364

Imperato-McGinley, Julianne, 187
Institute of Life Insurance, 249–50
Israel: and sexual equality, 255–56, 441–42
"Issues and Answers," 293–94

Jacklin, Carol Nagy (*The Psychology of Sex Differences*), 184–85
Jacobson, Aileen, 255
Janeway, Eliot, 413
Jencks, Christopher (*Inequality*), 436–37
Johnson, Haynes, 33–54
Johnston, Jill (*Lesbian Nation*), 114
Jong, Erica, 82
Judge, Mary, 21
Justice Department, 52, 100

Kane, Al. Philip, 91–92
Keller, Helen, 24
King, Billie Jean, 117-18, 168
Kingsbury, John, 35–36
Kump, Magdaline, 21–22
Kurland, Philip, 302–3
Kuscsik, Nina, 211

Labor Department, 48–49, 146–47; Women's Bureau of, 51, 102–3, 267
Ladies' Home Journal, 44, 45, 115, 130–31, 167, 416
Landers, Ann, 79
Lawrence, D. H. (*Lady Chatterley's Lover*), 66
League of Women Voters, 55, 176, 302, 305
Lesbian Feminist Liberation, 175
Lesbian Mothers National Defense Fund, 53
Library of Congress, 20, 303–4, 318
Life, 130–31
Lindh, Pat, 47, 50
Lip-service libbers, 175–77, 340
Lofton, John, 116
Look, 130–31

477

Lorand, Rhoda L., 260–61; *Love, Sex and the Teenager*, 201, 221–22, 381–83
Luce, Clare Booth, 127–28
LuKacs, John, 20

McCall's, 123, 125–31, 163–64, 179, 301, 373–74
Maccoby, Eleanor Emmons (*The Psychology of Sex Differences*), 184–85
McGrady, Mike (*The Kitchen Sink Papers*), 368
McKnight, Dorothy, 218
MacLaine, Shirley, 116, 202
MacLean, Paul D., 196–97
Macmillan Publishing Company, 343–44, 346, 352
MACOS (Man, A Course of Study), 71–73
Mademoiselle, 123, 129–30, 142–43, 166, 297
Males: and female competition, 180, 207–27
Manpower Administration, 25–26
Marriage, 19–20, 56–58, 81, 85, 271–77, 288, 316–19, 329–30; alternatives to, 70–71, 173, 248–49, 434–35; attitudes toward, 89, 101, 114–16, 142–44, 151–52, 163–65, 172–74, 385–87, 389–402, 405–08, 413–15, 417, 421–28, 433–39, 442, 457–59; deterioration of, 68, 91–95, 457–59
Marshall, Karol, 245
Masculinization of the brain, 188–90
Mass media: analyzing women, 15, 276; and ERA, 290–302, 304–5, 328, 330–35; and feminist activists, 44–49, 52–53, 55–56, 98, 102, 105, 115, 117–18, 261, 448–50; and sex-role engineering, 28, 34, 36–37, 42–43, 138–53, 157, 171, 173, 179–81, 251–52, 254–55, 258–60, 266, 273, 337–56 *passim*, 442, 450–53; and trends, 68, 79, 83, 89, 121–42, 173, 240–41, 337–38, 356, 360, 447–48, 450
Mead, Margaret (*Coming of Age in Samoa*), 25
Menstruation, effects of, 183–84
Mesta, Perle, 24–25
Millard, Charles, 82–85
Millet, Kate, 32, 112–13
MIT, 33–43
Mizerak, Steve, 216
Modern Romances, 300–301
Mondale, Walter, 54, 432
Money, John, 69, 189
Moral relativism, 67–70, 174, 464
MORE, 208
Morgan, Marabel, 201–2, 406; *Total Woman*, 165

Mothers, working, 86–87, 90–92, 170, 279–80, 371–76, 378–82, 384–85, 401–5
Ms., 54, 113, 132, 165–68, 290
Muggeridge, Malcolm, 94–95
Mushroom Effect, The, 103–4
Myerson, Bess, 301

Nastase, Ilie, 211
National Advertising Review Board, 351–54
National Assessment of Educational Progress, 87–88
National Center for Women, 418–20, 460
National Council of Teachers of English, 349–50
National Fertility Study, 170
National Health Survey, 424–28
National Observer, 145, 298, 389
National Science Foundation, 71–72
National Secretaries Association, 162–63
National Women's Agenda, 53–54, 160–61
National Women's Political Caucus, 115, 155, 160, 175, 449
Nature vs. nurture, 197, 451
NBC Television, 145–46, 149–52
Newsweek, 45, 135–36
New Woman, 132, 143–45, 168, 190, 266
New Women in New China, 443–44
New York Times, 44–46
Norton, Mary Therese, 24
NOW (National Organization for Women), 11–12, 98, 102–3, 449, 467; and homosexuality, 44, 49, 157; and the mass media, 44, 46–49; platform of, 49; and schools, 49, 53, 332–33; speaking for women, 47–49, 161, 175–76

Ocko, Felix, 244–45
Ogilvy & Mather, Inc., 307–8
O'Keeffe, Georgia, 24
Oppenheimer, Valerie Kincade, 36
O'Reilly, Jane, 48, 112, 333

Parade, 45, 141, 180, 190, 301
Patrick, L. M., 216
Paul, Alice, 287
Petit, Tom, 145–46
Pincus, Jonathan H., 329–30
Playboy Foundation, 55
Pogrebin, Letty, 115–16
Polansky, Norman A., 89–90
Polikoff, Nancy, 47
Polymorphous perverse sexuality, 282–83
Pop feminism, 105, 176, 368, 467

Professional class, influence of, 157, 160–61, 176, 368–69, 420, 428–31, 442, 450, 452–53, 460
Pupillometry, 364–65

Quinn, Sally, 416
Quotas, 34–35, 37–38, 226–27, 235, 275, 362, 429–31, 435

Ramey, Estelle, 255
Rape, 220–21, 275, 315, 319
Raspberry, William, 94
Reader's Digest, 251, 301
Rebirth of Feminism (New York Times–CBS report), 45–46, 100–2, 296, 306–7
Redbook, 167, 251, 301, 367
Reich, Wilhelm, 220
Religion, 55, 111, 113–14, 458
Richards, Renee, 215
Reincourt, Amaury de (Sex and Power in History), 272, 439–42, 444–45
Rimmer, Robert, 70
Roche, Josephine, 22
Rockefeller Foundation, 55
Roosevelt, Eleanor, 127–28
Roshko, Bernard, 140
Ross, Susan Deller, 305
Ruckelshaus, Jill, 47, 50, 293–95, 298
Ruina, Edith, 37–41

Safer, Morley, 240–41
St. Denis, Ruth, 24
Saline, Carol, 143
Salk, Lee, 251
San Francisco Chronicle, 44
Saturday Evening Post, 130–31
Schecter, Leona (An American Family in Moscow), 376
Schlafly, Phyllis, 287, 294–95, 308–09, 334–35, 432–33
Schlossberg, Harvey, 228
Schroeder, Patricia, 135
Scott, Hilda (Does Socialism Liberate Women?), 440
Seib, Charles, 290–91
Self-actualization, 69, 90, 416
Seventeen, 258–59
Sex differences, 382–83; in animal behavior, 191–95; emotional, 226, 228, 232–34, 271–72; and hormones, 183–90, 196; in human behavior, 183–93, 196–205; mental, 221–24, 271–72; obscured by feminists, 182, 201, 260–61, 339–40; obscured by mass media, 179–181, 189–90,195, 205, 207–08, 209–11, 241; physical, 179–83, 208–21, 231–33, 236–40,

267–68, 275, 277–80; in sexuality, 92–94, 180, 195–205, 274–75
Sex, promiscuous, 19–20, 29, 65–71, 73–85, 92–94, 141, 174, 245, 282–84, 439, 441–42; restraint of, 81–85
Sex-role engineering: and federal government, 27, 34–35, 37, 43, 48–55, 234–40, 267, 330–35, 418–20, 459–60, 463, 466–67; by organizational forces, 33–43, 53–60, 247–51, 337–60; and roles, 246–84, 310, 338–56
Sex roles: attitudes toward, 28–29, 34–43, 90–95, 163–74, 413–14, 420–28, 433–45; in the 1920s, 19–20; significance of, 253–84, 394–97, 401–08; and social structures, 262–71, 273–75, 282–84
Sexually transmitted diseases, 75–84 passim
Shaness, Natalie, 84
Shanahan, Eileen, 297
Shaywitz, Sally E., 404–5
Shelley, Martha (Sisterhood Is Powerful), 115
Sheridan, James, 224
Simon, William A., 79–81
Smith, Hilda, 100
Smith, Page (Daughters of the Promised Land), 18–19, 268–69
Snyder, Tom, 149–52
Socarides, Charles W. (Beyond Sexual Freedom), 282–84
Social engineering, 33–43, 417–45
Social Security, 308–10
Society, decline of, 86–95, 273–74
Sowell, Thomas, 361–62
Sparmblack, Donna, 381–82
Spock, Benjamin (Baby and Child Care), 350–51
Stapleton, Jean, 295, 308–09
Stassinopoulos, Arianna (The Female Woman), 308
Status of Women groups, 48, 50–52, 55, 100, 103–4, 157, 298–99, 302, 306–08, 310–11, 513, 417–19, 438, 449
Steinem, Gloria, 32, 50, 54, 97–98, 163, 295, 453
Stein, Gertrude, 24
Stevens, John Paul, 145–46
Stoller, Robert J. (Sex and Gender), 187–88
Students for a Democratic Society, 116–17
Suicide, 87, 244–45, 330
Supreme Court, U.S., 46, 145–46, 288–89, 301–2, 304, 309, 334
Switzer, Kathrine, 216

Thatcher, Margaret, 145
Tiger, Lionel, 47–48
Time, 45, 146–47, 452

Tocqueville, Alexis de, 462
Today's Health, 79, 141–42, 251
Toner, Frank J., 42-43, 48
Toomey, Kathryn, 56–57
True believers, 175–76, 415–17, 467
Tyler, Leona, 36

United Methodist Church, Women's
    Division of, 160
United Nations, 48
United States Air Force, 232–38
United States Army, 234–35, 239
United States Marine Corps, 208, 235,
    238–39
United States Military Academy, 208,
    231–32, 363
United States Naval Academy, 208–10,
    230–31
United States Navy, 235, 239–40
U.S News & World Report, 45, 136, 190,
    297, 413–14

Virginia Slims American Women's
    Opinion Poll, 156, 171–73
Viva, 198–99
Vocational Education Act, 54–55

Wall Street Journal, 320–21, 432
Walters, Barbara, 50, 150–53
Washington Journalism Center, 47
Washington Post, 45, 51, 139–40, 208,
    287–92 *passim*, 331–32, 448–49
Washington Star, 48, 195, 331, 335
Watkins, Kenneth W., 90–92
Webster's Dictionary, 337–38, 340
Weinberger, Caspar, W., 465–66
Weiss, Paul *(Sport: A Philosophic
    Inquiry)*, 181–82
Wells, Jane, 295–96, 302
White, James, 321–23, 327
Wightman, Hazel, 24
Willebrandt, Mabel, 22
Will, George F., 332, 349
Williams, Duncan *(Trousered Apes)*,
    69–70
Woman's Day, 46, 142, 166–67
Women: athletes, 24, 180, 208–20;
    attitudes of, 28, 156, 158–65, 168–77,
314; and careers, 122–29, 135–36,
    139–47, 152, 156, 169–74, 256, 266–67,
    276, 368–69, 378–82, 390, 392, 404–5,
    441–45, 456–57; in colonial America,
    18; and credit, 356–60; in men's jobs,
    22–23, 30, 133, 136–38, 141, 224–41,
    267–69, 275; in the 19th century,
    18–19; in the 1920s, 19–25; and World
    War I, 19, 21
Women's Action Alliance, 53
Women's Equity Action League, 103,
    309, 449
Women's liberation: activism of, 25–27,
    49, 53, 55–56; 58–62, 111–14, 117–18,
    155, 157–61, 291–93, 338–39, 363,
    415–22; attitudes toward, 27–29, 33,
    90–94, 97–98, 156–65 *passim*, 174–77,
    195, 246–47, 298, 376–94 *passim*, 405,
    407, 448–51; and collectivism, 108–09,
    111–17, 375–76, 415–20, 432–45,
    456–57, 459–66; and crime, 88; and
    family disintegration, 88–95, 112–16,
    243–44, 269–71, 280–82, 329–30, 376,
    457–59; goals of, 32–33, 98–105,
    108–18, 175–76, 201, 252–54, 260–61,
    296, 309–20, 338–43 *passim*, 413–67
    passim; and problems of youth, 89–92,
    244–45, 247, 261, 280–82; in socialist
    countries, 255–56, 375–76, 437–45
Women's magazines: contents of,
    122–34, 165–68, 266
Women Sports, 168
Woodward, Joanne, 403
Work: attitudes toward, 92–94, 156,
    162–64, 168–74, 263–74, 276, 371–80,
    384–408, 413–14 453; and
    motherhood, 170–74, 279–81, 375–76,
    378–82, 384, 390–97, 401–5; and
    sexual harassment, 228–30, 366–67
Working wives, glorification of, 133–36,
    141–45, 371–76, 378–79, 451
Working Woman, 143
Worthington, Robert, 41–42

Yale Law Journal, 305–6, 311–18, 320,
    323, 325
Young, Biloine W., 429–31
Younger, Judith, 414
YWCA, 43, 55–56, 176